5/68

Latin American Women Writers

Latin American Women Writers

A Resource Guide to Titles in English

Kathy S. Leonard

The Scarecrow Press, Inc.
Lanham, Maryland • Toronto • Plymouth, UK
2007

SCARECROW PRESS, INC.

Published in the United States of America
by Scarecrow Press, Inc.
A wholly owned subsidiary of
The Rowman & Littlefield Publishing Group, Inc.
4501 Forbes Boulevard, Suite 200, Lanham, Maryland 20706
www.scarecrowpress.com

Estover Road
Plymouth PL6 7PY
United Kingdom

British Library Cataloguing in Publication Information Available

Library of Congress Cataloging-in-Publication Data
Leonard, Kathy S.
  Latin American women writers : a resource guide to titles in English / Kathy S. Leonard.
    p. cm.
  Includes bibliographical references and indexes.
  ISBN-13: 978-0-8108-6015-5 (hardcover : alk. paper)
  ISBN-10: 0-8108-6015-5 (hardcover : alk. paper)
  1. Latin American fiction–Women authors–Translations into English–Bibliographies.
  I. Title.
  Z1609.F4L47 2007
  [PQ7085]
  016.863008'09287–dc22   2007022464

∞™ The paper used in this publication meets the minimum requirements of
American National Standard for Information Sciences—Permanence of
Paper for Printed Library Materials, ANSI/NISO Z39.48-1992.
Manufactured in the United States of America.

Contents

Acknowledgments

I would like to gratefully acknowledge Iowa State University for awarding me a Faculty Professional Development Assignment for 2006-2007, which allowed me uninterrupted time to prepare this book. As always, I also thank Michael Porter for reviewing portions of the manuscript. Tosca and Cedar deserve a special mention for the joy they bring to my life and their unending moral support.

Preface

Introduction
There is a wealth of published literature in English by Latin American women writers, but it can be difficult to locate due to the lack of bibliographic resources available that make easy access possible. In 1997, I published a bibliographic guide titled *Index to Translated Short Fiction by Latin American Women in English Language Anthologies*, and, although the guide was useful and timely, it was somewhat limited in scope. Due to the abundance of other types of narrative that have been published in the last ten to fifteen years by Latin American women writers, I felt the need to create a new guide which better reflects this increase in literary production.

Purpose
The purpose of this volume is to allow scholars, researchers, instructors, and students access to a comprehensive listing of narrative pieces by Latin American women writers in English. It is my hope that these works will be incorporated into the curriculum of courses dealing with Latin American literature, ethnic studies, women's studies, and other courses where matters of Latin America are of interest.

Organization
This volume contains seven indices: Authors by Country of Origin; Authors/Titles of Work; Titles of Work/Authors; Autobiographies/Biographies and Other Narrative; Anthologies; Novels and Novellas in Alphabetical Order by Author; and Novels and Novellas by Authors' Country of Origin. Each entry in the indices is accompanied by an alpha-numeric code which is used for cross-referencing in the other indices. There is a great deal of repetition and overlap among the indices, which is intentional. As a researcher, I found many of the bibliographies I consulted difficult to work with due to the constant necessity to flip from one index to another. This guide is organized for ease of use, and each index provides a variety of information that should eliminate the need to refer to the others. If a reader is searching for a particular author name, it may be found listed in alphabetical order in the

Authors/Titles of Work index, which then guides the reader by code number to the other indices where that author's work appears. For example, if a work is an auto-biography, the reader will see the code "AB" followed by the first letter of the author's last name and a number. Readers can then turn to the Autobiographies/ Biographies and Other Narrative index and easily find the entry by the proper code number where the work is annotated. If the reader is searching for a particular title, it may be found in the Titles of Work/Authors index. This index contains all individual literary pieces included in the book, listed in alphabetical order according to title, followed by the author's name and the code number where the work is identified by type of narrative and the location in this guide. A reader interested in locating all works by a particular author can find them in the Authors/Titles of Work index where entries are organized by author name in alphabetical order followed by all her narrative pieces.

Author names are alphabetized according to English-language conventions. There are, however, a few oddities. There are a number of surnames which begin with "de" or "de la," as found in Rima de Vallbona and Teresa de la Parra. When alphabetizing such names, the convention in Hispanic countries is to list them as follows: Vallbona, Rima de, and Parra, Teresa de la. I have chosen to list these names under "D" considering the "de" as the first element in the last name. This approach is taken due to the nature of this volume, which most likely will be consulted by many readers who are not speakers of Spanish and may not be familiar with the conventions of alphabetization of Spanish surnames. Alphabetization of titles in the Titles of Work/Authors index follows conventional English language norms. However, for words containing the "ñ," which does not exist in the English alphabet, it can be found following the letter "n" as is the Spanish language convention.

Variations will be seen in the spelling of a few authors' names. For example, Carmen Lira/Lyra and Liliana Heker/Hecker. These variations are indicated and recorded as found in the source work. There are also a number of literary pieces that have been translated more than once with titles that vary. For example, Luisa Valenzuela's story "El custodio blancanieves" has been translated as "The Snow White Guard" and "The Snow White Watchman." Cristina Peri Rossi's story "El museo de esfuerzos inútiles" has been translated as "The Museum of Futile Endeavors," "The Museum of Useless Efforts," and "The Museum of Vain Endeavours." These titles are all listed in alphabetical order in the corresponding indices.

Scope

The indices in this volume include all forms of narrative: short story, autobiography/biography, novel, novel excerpt, novella, and other types of narrative written by Latin American women dating from 1898 to 2007. Approximately 3,060 individual titles are included by more than 500 authors; this includes 193 anthologies, 110 autobiographies/biographies or other narrative, and 242 novels written by 123 authors from 16 different countries. There has been no attempt to group the works included here by theme, although some of the anthologies themselves are organized in such a manner. Work that is *not* found in this guide includes narrative pieces published in periodicals or literary journals, with the exception of several journals which are special issues published as anthologies. One such journal is *The American Voice: New Voices from Latin America and Spain*, with guest editor Marjorie Agosín. Although many interesting dissertations have appeared in the last few years dealing with Latin American women's narrative and autobiography, these are not included in this volume. I have chosen to exclude children's literature (geared toward readers under 12 years of age) but have included adolescent literature (for readers 12 years of age and above). Although not technically within the scope of this volume, I have included some stories in Spanish when they occur in bilingual anthologies or other bilingual works. Included at the end of the volume is a bibliography of other useful resources dealing with Latin American women's literature.

Latin American or Latina Authors

The act of labeling an author as Latin American or Latina can be rather tricky and even more so when attempting to classify writers whose backgrounds and experiences may be similar, yet dissimilar enough to warrant the use of various terms to identify them. A number of the anthologies listed in this volume do not adequately identify the authors as either Latina, Chicana, Hispanic, Mexican-American, or Latin American. In such cases, I drew from my knowledge and experience to determine if the author was an appropriate candidate for inclusion in this volume. However, for the most part, this guide includes authors who were born in Latin America and either continue to live there or have immigrated to the United States. In most cases, without consulting directly with an author, it would be impossible to know how or if she prefers to be categorized. Rather than attempting to second guess an author's desires, I prefer to err on the side of inclusion rather than exclusion.

Language of Publication

My original intent was to include in this volume only works that had been originally written in Spanish or Portuguese and translated into English. However, I found that by doing so I would be excluding many Latin American women authors who write in English. While some authors are monolingual and publish in their native Spanish or Portuguese and rely on translators for the publication of their work in English, others are completely bilingual and publish in both languages. Rosario Ferré from Puerto Rico often writes in Spanish and translates her own work into English. Other writers, although bilingual, choose to write in English, such as Esmeralda Santiago, whose work is then often translated into other languages, including Spanish, by professional translators without the author's input. To better reflect the linguistic diversity of narrative currently being published, I have chosen to list the title of pieces originally written in either Spanish or Portuguese and include the phrase "originally written in English" if this is the case.

Conclusion

It is now quite common to find works by Latin American women writers in English included in anthologies published in the United States. One might expect this work to be published in "specialized" anthologies, and by this I refer to those including the term "Latin America" somewhere in the title. However, we now find Latin American women authors included in anthologies with titles such as *You've Got to Read This: Contemporary American Writers Introduce Stories That Held Them in Awe*; *American Fiction: States of the Art*; and *World Literature: An Anthology of Great Short Stories, Drama, and Poetry*. These titles are quite telling. Latin American women authors such as Luisa Valenzuela, Isabel Allende, and Julia Alvarez are now not only considered part of the North American literary scene where their names regularly appear alongside the most revered and popular U.S. authors, but they are increasingly being included in anthologies of the best world literature as well. This is a welcome trend that is sure to continue, thus exposing new generations of readers to the highly creative and diverse literature being produced by Latin American women writers.

Authors by Country of Origin

This index lists all authors included in the book organized by their country of origin. To find work by each author and its location within the book, turn to the index titled Authors/Titles of Work.

Partnoy, Raquel
Pizarnik, Alejandra
Plager, Silvia
Poletti, Syria
Roffé, Mercedes
Roffé, Reina
Safranchik, Graciela
Shua, Ana María
Solá, Marcela
Steimberg, Alicia
Strejilevich, Nora
Toledo, Mirta
Traba, Marta
Ulla, Noemí
Valenzuela, Luisa
Varsavsky, Paula
Vásquez, María Esther
Verolín, Irma

BOLIVIA

Adriázola, Claudia
Arnal Franck, Ximena
Ayllón Soria, Virginia
Barrios de Chungará, Domitila
Bedregal, Yolanda
Bruzonic, Erika
Calvimontes, Velia
de Quiroga, Giancarla
Dorado de Revilla Valenzuela, Elsa
Estenssoro, María Virginia
González, Nelly S.
Gutiérrez, Marcela
Kuramoto, Beatriz
Limpias Chávez, Viviana
Loayza Millán, Beatriz
Maldonado, Clara Isabel
O'Hara, Maricarmen
Paz, Blanca Elena
Quiroga, María Soledad
Reyes, Sandra
Rivero Santa Cruz, Giovanna
Santos, Rosario
Vallejo, Gaby

BRAZIL

Albues, Tereza
Alves, Miriam
Benedetti, Lúcia
Bins, Patricia
Bojunga-Nunes, Lygia
Bulhões Carvalho da Fonseca, Emi
Colasanti, Marina
Correia Dutra, Lia
Coutinho, Sonia
Cunha, Helena Parente
de Jesús, Carolina María
de Queiroz, Rachel
Denser, Márcia
Dolores, Carmen
Dupré, Leandro Sra.
Fagundes Telles, Lygia
Fanaro, Silvia
Felinto, Marilene
Fernándes de Oliveira, Cicera
França, Aline
Galvão, Patricia (Pagu)
Grossman, Judith
Hilst, Hilda
Jamardo Faillace, Tania
Jorge, Lidia
Kosminsky, Ethel
Lispector, Clarice
Lispector, Elisa
Lopes de Almeida, Júlia
Luft, Lya Fett
Machado, Ana María
Melo, Patricia
Miranda, Ana
Moncorva Bandeira de Mello,
    Emilia
Nery, Adalgisa
Pallotini, Renata
Pereira, Teresinka
Piñón, Nélida
Rheda, Regina
Ribeiro, Stella Car
São Paulo Penna e Costa, Marília
Silveira de Queiroz, Dinah

Szoka, Elzbieta
Van Steen, Edla
Verissimo, Bruna

CHILE
Agosín, Marjorie
Aguirre, Margarita
Aldunate, Elena
Allende, Isabel
Aninat, María Flor
Artigas, Gloria
Balcells, Jacqueline
Barros, Pía
Basáñez, Carmen
Basualto, Alejandra
Blanco, Marta
Bombal, María Luisa
Brunet, Marta
Casanova, Cecilia
Castedo, Elena
da Fonseca, Cristina
de Fokes, María Asunción
del Río, Ana María
del Valle, Rosamel
Díaz-Diocaretz, Miriam
Diez Fierro, Silvia
Eltit, Diamela
Farias, Alejandra
García Huidobro, Beatriz
Gligo, Agata
González Valdenegro, Sonia
Guerra Cunningham, Lucía
Güiraldes, Ana María
Guralnik, Sonia
Jara, Marta
Larraín, Luz
Liberman, Gloria
Lobo, Tatiana
Lorca de Tagle, Lillian
Lorenzini, María Eugenia
Mallet, Marilú
Maturana, Andrea
Mistral, Gabriela
Montecinos, Sonia

Mujica, Barbara Louise
Niemeyer, Margarita
Orfanoz, Luz
Petit, Magdalena
Pizarro, Ana
Quevedo, Violeta
Rendic, Amalia
Romo-Carmona, Mariana
Saris, Lake
Sepúlveda-Pulvirenti, Emma
Serrano, Marcela
Silva Ossa, María
Subercaseaux, Elizabeth
Valdivieso, Mercedes
Vásquez, Ana
Vidal, Virginia
Yáñez, María Flora

COLOMBIA
Acosta de Samper, Soledad
Angel, Albalucía
Araujo, Helena
Buitrago, Fanny B.
Chávez-Vásquez, Gloria
Chehade Durán, Nayla
de Castillo, Francisca Josefa
Restrepo, Laura
Torres, Anabel
Zapata Pérez, Edelma

COSTA RICA
Campbell, Shirley
Collado, Delfina
de Vallbona, Rima
González, Luisa
Kalina, Rosalina
Kalina de Piszk, Rosita
Lira (Lyra), Carmen
Macaya, Emilia
Naranjo, Carmen
Odio, Eunice
Oreamuno, Yolanda
Pinto, Julieta
Urbano, Victoria

CUBA

Agüero, Omega
Alonso, Dora
Alonso, Nancy
Alzola, Concepción T.
Bahr, Aída
Behar, Ruth
Beltrán, María de la Merced
Bevin, Teresa
Bobes, Marilyn
Boudet, Rosa Lleana
Boza, María del Carmen
Bravo Utrera, Sonia
Cabrera, Lydia
Campos, Julieta
Casal, Lourdes
Chaviano, Diana
Cossío y Cisneros, Evangelina
Cruz, Celia
Cruz, Soledad
Cruz Varela, María Elena
de Anhalt, Nedda G.
de Aragón, Uva
de Diego, Josefina
Díaz Llanillo, Esther
Engle, Margarita
Fernández, Alina
Fernández de Juan, Adelaida
Fernández Pintado, Mylene
García, Cristina
García, María Cristina
García Caizada, Ana Luz
Gómez de Avellaneda y Arteaga,
    Gertrudis
Herranz Brooks, Jacqueline
Hospital, Carolina
Lamazares, Ivonne
Levis Levine, Ester
Lima, Chely
Llano, María Elena
López Gonzáles, Pilar
López Kónina, Verónica
Marrero, Teresa
Martín, Rita

Medina, C. C.
Menéndez, Ana
Montero, Mayra
Morejón, Nancy
Novas, Himilce
Objeas, Achy
O'Reilly Herrera, Andrea
Perrera, Hilda
Ponte Landa, Miguelina
Portela, Ena Lucía
Puig Zaldívar, Raquel
Remba Nurko, Natania
Reyna, Bessy
Ríos, Soleida
Rivera, Beatriz
Rivera Valdés, Sonia
Ro, Mirta
Robles, Mireya
Rodríguez, Aleida
Rojas, Marta
Rosel, Sara
Sánchez, Magaly
Sánchez-Bello, Bertha
Saralegui, Cristina
Shapiro Rok, Ester Rebeca
Simo, Ana María
Suárez, Karla
Tamayo, Evora
Valdés, Zoe
Valdés-Rodríguez, Alisa
Veciana-Suárez, Ana
Vega Sorova, Ana Lidia
Veiga, Marisella
Yáñez, Mirta

DOMINICAN REPUBLIC

Alvarez, Julia
Cartagena Portalatín, Aída
Contreras, Hilma
Hernández, Angela
Perez, Loida Maritza
Santos-Febres, Mayra
Strauss de Milz, Ivonne
Vicioso, Sherezada (Chiqui)

ECUADOR
Andrade, Carolina
Bravo, Mónica
Buenaño, Aminta
Chiriboga, Luz Argentina
Fierro, Fanny
Garcés, María del Carmen
Holst, Gilda
Manzano, Sonia
Martínez, Nela
Miraglia, Liliana
Ortiz Salas, Mónica
Rumazo, Lupe
Solís de King, Fabiola
Viteri, Eugenia
Yánez Cossío, Alicia

EL SALVADOR
Alegría, Claribel
Escudos, Jacinta
Tula, María Teresa

EQUATORIAL GUINEA
Nsue Angüe, María

GUATEMALA
Lubitch Domecq, Alcina
Menchú, Rigoberta

HONDURAS
Díaz Lozano, Argentina

MEXICO
Alcalá, Kathleen
Alves Pereira, Teresina
Amor, Guadalupe
Ardó, Araceli
Arredondo, Inés
Baez, Carmen
Barrera, Luz Mercedes
Beltrán, Rosa
Benítez, Sandra
Bermín, Sabina
Bermúdez, María Elvira

Bernal, Acela
Bornstein, Miriam
Borton de Treviño, Elizabeth
Boullosa, Carmen
Calderón, Sara Levi
Campobello, Nellie
Campos, Julieta
Cárdenas, Magolo
Castellanos, Rosario
Castillejos Peral, Silvia
Cerda, Marta
Clavel, Ana
Cohen, Regina
Conde Zambada, Hilda Rosina
Dávila, Amparo
de Anhalt, Nedda G.
de la Cruz, Sor Juana Inés
Domecq, Brianda
Dueñas, Guadalupe
Durán, Gloria
Escalante, Beatriz
Esquibel Tywoniak, Frances
Esquivel, Laura
Estrada, Josefina
Galeana, Benita
Garro, Elena
Glantz, Margo
Gómez Rul, Ana María
Guijosa, Marcela
Guillermoprieto, Alma
Gutiérrez Richaud, Cristina
Hernández, Luisa Josefina
Hiriart, Berta
Hoffman, Kitzia
Ibarra, Cristina
Jacobs, Bárbara
Krauze, Ethel
Laurent Kullick, Patricia
Lavín, Mónica
Loaeza, Guadalupe
Mansour, Mónica
Mastretta, Angeles
Mayo, C. M.
Medina, Eufelia

Mendoza, María Luisa
Molina, Silvia
Mondragón Aguirre, Magdalena
Mujica, Barbara Louise
Muñiz-Huberman, Angelina
Nissan, Rosa
Pacheco, Cristina
Poniatowska, Elena
Puga, María Luisa
Ríos, Mi-Chelle L.
Roffiel, Rosamaría
Ruíz de Burton, Amparo
Seligson, Esther
Solís, Bernarda
Swain, Regina
Torres, Olga Beatriz
Valencia, Tita
Velázquez, Gloria
Vicens, Josefina
Villegas de Magnón, Leonor
Viramontes, Helena María

NICARAGUA
Aguilar, Rosario
Belli, Gioconda

PANAMA
Algandona, Lilia
Benedetti, Giovanna
Britton, Rosa María
de Crespo, Elda L. C.
López, Griselda
Peralta, Bertalicia
Reyna, Bessy
Rojas Sucre, Graciela
Tejeira, Isis

PARAGUAY
Pla, Josefina

PERU
Arana, Marie
Cabello de Carbonera, Mercedes
Calvo-Roth, Fortuna

Cevasco, Gaby
de Ferrari, Gabriella
del Barco, Mandalit
Dughi, Pilar
Fort, María Rosa
Fox, Lucía
González de Fanning, Teresa
Gorriti, Carmen Luz
Gorriti, Juana Manuela
Guevara, Bethzabé
Lohman, Catalina
Matto de Turner, Clorinda
Mellet, Viviana
Pollarolo, Giovanna
Riesco, Laura
Rossel Huicí, Gladys
Ruiz Rosas, Teresa
Sala, Mariella
Solari, María Teresa

PUERTO RICO
Ambert, Alba
Braschi, Giannina
Cadilla de Martínez, María
Delgado, Ana María
Ferré, Rosario
García Ramis, Magali
Levins Morales, Aurora
Lugo Filippi, Carmen
Mohr, Nicholasa
Morales, Rosario
Nolla, Olga
Ortiz Cofer, Judith
Pantoja, Antonia
Ponce, Mary Helen
Santiago, Esmeralda
Sapia, Yvonne V.
Torres, Lidia
Umpierre, Luz María
Valle, Carmen
Vega, Ana Lydia
Zavala, Iris

UNITED STATES
de la Cuesta, Barbara

URUGUAY
Blanqué, Andrea
Cabral, Cristina
Di Giorgio, Marosa
Lago, Sylvia
Peri Rossi, Cristina
Porzecanski, Teresa
Posadas, Carmen
Rodríguez-Cabral, Cristina
Santos, Beatriz
Schroeder, Agustina
Somers, Armonía
Valdés, Ana

VENEZUELA
Antillano, Laura
Aizenberg, Edna
Daviú, Matilde
de la Parra, Teresa
Freilich de Segal, Alicia
Friedman, Joan E.
Lerner, Elisa
Palacios, Antonia
Stolk, Gloria
Velásquez, Edith

Authors/Titles of Work

This index lists all authors in alphabetical order followed by titles of their work in alphabetical order. Alpha-numeric codes refer to the type of work and in which index it may be found. "A" refers to the Anthologies index where authors and editors are listed alphabetically and where authors whose works are included in those anthologies may also be found. "N" indicates the Novel and Novellas in Order by Author index, and "AB" indicates the Autobiographies/Biographies and Other Narrative index. Authors and editors of anthologies are not listed in this index unless they are also Latin American women writers. However, they are listed in the Titles of Work/Authors index.

Absatz, Cecilia (Argentina)
Ballet Dancers, A G3
A Ballet for Girls, A L6
Feiguele, A G3

Acosta de Samper, Soledad (Colombia)
Dolores/Dolores, A S8
Trabajo para la mujer/Work for Women, A S8

Adriázola, Claudia (Bolivia)
Buttons, A S5.1

Agosín, Marjorie (Chile)
Adelina, A M16
Afternoon Tea, A A1
The Alphabet, A A1.9
The Alphabet in My Hands: A Writing Life, A A1, AB A2
Alfama, A A1.9
Allison, A A1.9
Always from Somewhere Else (excerpt), A A1.4
Always from Somewhere Else: A Memoir of My Chilean Jewish Father, AB A2.1
America and My Mother, A A1

A Foreigner's Nights, A A1
Forests, A A1.3
Frida and Moises, A A1
Frida, Friduca, Mami, A S3.1
Gabriela, A A1
A Gabriela Mistral Reader, A A1.2
Gabriela Mistral: The Audacious Traveler, AB A2.4
Gardens, A A1
The Georgia House, A A1
Georgian Soil, A A1
A Glorious Body, A A1
The Godmothers, A A1
God's Place, A A1
The Gold Bracelet, A A1.3
Goodbye, Pablo Neruda, A A1
The Goyim, A A1
Grandmother's Shoes, A A1
The Gringos, A A1
Guardian Angels, A A1
Guest, A A1
Guillermina Aguilar, A A1.9
Gypsy Woman, A A1
Gypsy Women, A A1.3
Halloween, A A1
Happiness, A A1, A A1.3
Happiness: Stories by Marjorie Agosín, A A1.3
Hebrew, A A1
The Hebrew Institute, A A1
Helena of Vienna, A A1
The Hen, A A1.3
High Treason, A A1
Homecoming, A A1
The House, A A1
House of Lights, A A1.9
The House of Memory: Stories by Jewish Women Writers of Latin America, A A1.4
Houses by the Sea, A A1.3
A Huge Black Umbrella, A C6
I Tell Them We Are from Here, A A1
Identities, A A1
An Immense Black Umbrella, A A1.3
The Immigrant Girls, A A1
An Invitation to Travel, A A1
Ireland, A A1.9
Isla Negra, A A1, A S12
The Island of Swallows, A A1

My Accent, A A1
My Apron, A A1
My Aunts, A A1
My Birthday, A A1
My Childhood, A A1
My Cousin Rafael, A A1
My Desk, A A1
My Grandfather, A A1
My History Teacher, A A1
My House, A A1
Naked, A A1.3
Names, A A1
Nana, A A1, A A1.3
Nape, A A1
A Necklace of Words: Stories by Mexican Women, A A2
Neighbors and Friends, A A1
New Year's by the Sea, A A1
New Year's Day 1997, A A1
Night, A A1
North, A A1.3
Ocean Retreats, A A1.9
Of Parties and Other Audacities, A A1
Old Age, A A1
Olga, A A1.9
Omama Helena, A A1
Orphanages, A A1.3
Osorno (excerpt), A B10
The Other Women, A A1
Pablo Neruda, A A1
Passover, A A1
Photographs, A A1.3
Photographs I, A A1
Photographs II, A A1
Photographs III, A A1
The Piano, A A1
Pine Trees, A A1.9
Pisagua, A A1.3
The Place I Want to Die, A A1.9
A Place of Memories, A A1
Poetry, A A1
The Pools, A A1
Pork Sausages, A A1.3
Postcards, A A1.9
Prairies, A A1.3
Protection, A A1

The Texture of Fear, A A1
They Say, A A1
Thinking about Oblivion, A A1
This Love, A A1.9
Tickle of Love, A A1.9
Tidal Pools, A A1
To Be a Stranger, A A1
To Breathe, A A1
To Know the Night, A A1
To Mend the World: Women Reflect on 9/11, AB A2.6
To Set Foot in America, A A1
The Tower, A A1.9
Train Station, A A1
Travelers, A A1
Traveling the Length of My Country, A A1
United States, A V5
Violeta, A A1
The Wanderer, A A1.9
Wanderings, A A1
Warnings, A A1.9
Water, A A1.3
Wax Candles, A A1.3
Weddings, A A1.9
Wellesley College, A A1
What Is Secret: Stories by Chilean Women, A A1.8
White, A A1
Why Do I Write?, A A1
Widowhood, A A1.9
The Wind, A A1
Wine, A A1.9
Wisdom, A A1
Witches, A A1.9
With My Children, A A1
With the Nanas, A A1
Women in Disguise, A A1.9
Women in Disguise: Stories by Marjorie Agosín, A A1.9
Women Friends/Comadres, A A1
Words, A A1
You'll Learn It Tomorrow, A A1

Agüero, Omega (Cuba)
A Man, a Woman (excerpt from *El muro de medio metro*), A B1, A M19

Aguilar, Rosario (Nicaragua)
Doña Ana, A A5
Doña Beatriz, A A5

Doña Isabel, A A5
Doña Leonor, A A5
Doña Luisa, A A5
Doña María, A A5
Epilogue, A A5
First Interlude, A A5
Fourth Interlude, A A5
The Lost Chronicles of Terra Firma, A A5, N A1
The Lost Chronicles of Terra Firma (excerpt), A O6
Second Interlude, A A5
Third Interlude, A A5

Aguirre, Margarita (Chile)
The Black Sheep, A R17
Cleaning the Closet, A A1.8

Aizenberg, Edna (Argentina/Venezuela)
Latin American Jewishness, A Game with Shifting Identities, A A1.7

Albues, Tereza (Brazil)
Pedra Canga, N A2

Alcalá, Kathleen (Mexico)
Altar, A J6
Cities of Gold, A L8
Flora's Complaint, A S20
The Flower in the Skull, N A3
Spirits of the Ordinary: A Tale of Casas Grandes, N A3.1
Treasures in Heaven, N A3.2

Aldunate, Elena (Chile)
Butterfly Man, A A1.8

Alegría, Claribel (El Salvador)
The Ancestor Room, A A8.1
Appointment in Zinica, A A8.1
Ashes of Izalco (with Darwin J. Flakoll), N A5
Aunt Elsa and Cuis, A A8.1
Aunt Filiberta and Her Cretonnes, A A8.1
The Awakening, A R17
The Blue Theatre, A A8.1
Boardinghouse, A S5
Carmen Bomba, A A8.1
Cipitio, A A8.1
The Day of the Cross, A A8.1
The Deaf Mutes of Ca'n Blau, A A8.1

The Talisman (novella), A A8, N A4
Tamales from Cambray (excerpt from the novel *Izalco Ashes*), A Y1
They Won't Take Me Alive: Salvadoran Women Struggle for National Liberation,
    AB A4
The Versailles Tenement, A A8.1
Village of God and the Devil (novella), A A8
Wilf (1), A A8.1
Wilf (2), A A8.1
Wilf (3), A A8.1
The Writer's Commitment, A A1.6

Algandona, Lilia (Panama)
Nightmare at Deep River, A J4

Allende, Isabel (Chile)
An Act of Vengeance, A C27, A S13
And of Clay Are We Created, A A9, A C13, A S14
Aphrodite: A Memoir of the Senses, N A6.1
Aphrodite: A Memoir of the Senses (excerpt), A S9
Aphrodite: The Love of Food and the Food of Love, N A6
City of the Beasts, N A6.2
Clarisa, A A9, A S17
Conversations with Isabel Allende, AB R3
Daughter of Fortune, N A6.3
A Discreet Miracle, A A9
Ester Lucero, A A9
Eva Luna, N A6.4
Eva Luna (excerpt), A B1
Forest of the Pygmies, N A6.5
Gift for a Sweetheart, A A9, A B4
The Gold of Tomás Vargas, A A9
Guggenheim Lovers, A D3
The Hour of Truth, A A1.6
The House of the Spirits, N A6.6
The House of the Spirits (excerpt), A B1, A F3, A L1
If You Touched My Heart, A A9, A B3
Inés of My Soul, N A6.7
The Infinite Plan (excerpt), A B13
The Infinite Plan: A Novel, N A6.8
Interminable Life, A A9
The Judge's Wife, A A9, A C2.1, A E3
Kingdom of the Golden Dragon, N A6.9
The Language of Flowers, A H6
Letters of Betrayed Love, A A9
The Little Heidelberg, A A9
My Invented Country: A Nostalgic Journey through Chile, AB A6

Of Love and Shadows, N A6.10
Our Secret, A A9, A C19, A C29, A J8
Paula, N A6.11
Paula (excerpt), A R7
Phantom, A G4
Phantom Palace, A A9
Portrait in Sepia, N A6.12
The Proper Respect, A A9
Revenge, A A9
The Road North, A A9
Rosa the Beautiful (excerpt from *The House of the Spirits*), A P7
The Schoolteacher's Guest, A A9
Simple María, A A9
The Stories of Eva Luna, A A9
Toad's Mouth, A A9, A C25
Tosca, A A9, A R17
Two Words, A A3, A A9, A F5, A M8.1, A M12.1, A T4
Wicked Girl, A A9, A M8.4
Walimai, A A9, A K7
Zorro: A Novel, N A6.13

Alonso, Dora (Cuba)
Cage Number One, A A1.5, A O6
Cotton Candy, A E4
The Rat, A C7
Sophie and the Angel, A C27
Times Gone By, A K5

Alonso, Nancy (Cuba)
Seventh Thunderbolt, A B9
Thou Shalt Not Deviate, A B9
A Tooth for a Tooth, A Y2

Álvarez, Julia (Dominican Republic)
Anteojos, A W1
Before We Were Free, N A7
The Blood of Conquistadores, A C25.1
A Cafecito Story, N A7.1
Consuelo's Letter, A A12
Customs, A P10
Daughter of Invention, A A17, A R1
El Doctor, A F7
How the Garcia Girls Lost Their Accents, N A7.2
How the Garcia Girls Lost Their Accents (excerpt), A A13, A K1
How Tia Lola Came to Visit/Stay, N A7.3
I Came to Help, A B22

In the Name of Salomé (excerpt), A B13
In the Name of Salomé: A Novel, N A7.4
In the Time of the Butterflies, N A7.5
Joe, A N4
The Kiss, A M16
New World, A C22
Our Father, A M20
Latina Self-Portraits: Interviews with Contemporary Women Writers, AB H1
Planting Sticks and Grinding Yucca: On Being a Translated Writer, A D2
Resistance Writ Small, A B22
Saving the World, N A7.6
The Secret Footprints, N A7.7
Something to Declare, AB A7
Snow (from *How the García Girls Lost Their Accents*), A V5
The Summer of the Future, A C20
The Summer of the Future/El verano del futuro, A C21
Switching to Santicló, A S3
Ten Hispanic Authors, AB H2
Yo!, N A7.8

Alves, Miriam (Brazil)
Finally Us...: Contemporary Black Brazilian Women Writers, A A11
Words, A A11

Alzola, Concepción T. (Cuba)
Don Pascual Was Buried Alone, A S7.1

Ambert, Alba (Puerto Rico)
Losses, A F7
A Perfect Silence, A D6
Persephone's Quest at Waterloo: A Daughter's Tale, A S3.1
Rage Is a Fallen Angel, A C18

Amor, Guadalupe (Mexico)
The Small Drawing Room, A C30

Andrade, Carolina (Ecuador)
The Death of Fausto, A R9

Angel, Albalucía (Colombia)
Down the Tropical Path, A R17
The Guerrillero, A M8.6
Monguí, A M15
The Spotted Bird Perched High Above Upon the Tall Green Lemon Tree (excerpt),
    A F3

Aninat, María Flor (Chile)
The Department Store, A A1.8

Antillano, Laura (Venezuela)
The Moon's Not a Piece of Cake (La luna no es pan de horno), A P8

Arana, Marie (Peru)
American Chica: Two Worlds, One Childhood, AB A8
Cellophane, N A8

Araujo, Helena (Colombia)
Asthmatic, A C27
The Open Letter, A A1.5

Ardó, Araceli (Mexico)
It Is Nothing of Mine, A M10

Arnal Franck, Ximena (Bolivia)
The Pianist, A S5.1

Arredondo, Inés (Mexico)
The Brothers, A A15
Mariana, A A15
The Mirrors, A A15
New Year's Eve, A A15
The Nocturnal Butterflies, A A15
On Love, A A15
Orphanhood, A A15
Puzzles, A B18
Shadow in the Shadows, A A15
The Shunammite, A A15, A M8.6
The Sign, A A15
The Silent Words, A A15, A M10
Subterranean River, A F10
The True Story of a Princess, A A2
Underground River, A A15
Underground River and Other Stories, A A15

Artigas, Gloria (Chile)
Corners of Smoke, A L3

Ayllón Soria, Virginia (Bolivia)
Prayer to the Goddesses, A B8

Baez, Carmen (Mexico)
The Cylinder, A J7

Bahr, Aída (Cuba)
Absences, A B9
Little Heart, A B9
The Scent of Limes, A Y2

Balcells, Jacqueline (Chile)
The Boy Swept Away in a Tree, A B2
The Boy Who Took Off in a Tree, A A1.8
The Buried Giant, A B2
The Enchanted Raisin, A B2
The Enchanted Raisin, A A1.5, A B2
How Forgetfulness Began, A B2
The Mermaids' Elixir, A B2
The Princess and the Green Dwarf, A B2
The Thirsty Little Fish, A B2

Barrios de Chamorro, Violeta (Nicaragua)
Dreams of the Heart: The Autobiography of President Violeta Barrios de Chamorro,
   AB B1

Barrios de Chungará, Domitila (Bolivia)
Let Me Speak (excerpt), A B1
Let Me Speak! Testimony of Domitila. A Woman of the Bolivian Mines, AB B2

Barros, Pía (Chile)
Abelardo, A B5
Appraisals, A B5
The Baby's Afternoon, A B5
Coup, A B5
Estanvito, A B5
Foreshadowing of a Trace, A F3
Horses Are a Gringo Invention, A B5
The Inheritor of Wisdom, A B5
Looking at Manet, A B5
Messages, A B5
No Circles, A B5
Núñez from Over Here, A B5
Portal, A B5
Routine Inspection, A B5
Scents of Wood and Silence, A A1.8, A R17
Shoes, A B5
Short-Lived Summers, A B5
A Smell of Wood and of Silence, A F3
Story for a Window, A B5
Transitory Fears, A B5
Waiting Game, A B5

When the Patagonians Hunted Stars, A B5
Windows, A B5

Basáñez, Carmen (Chile)
Not without Her Glasses, A A1.8

Basualto, Alejandra (Chile)
A Requiem for Hands, A A1.8

Bedregal, Yolanda (Bolivia)
"Good Evening, Agatha," A A1.5
How Milinco Escaped from School, A L3
The Morgue (excerpt from the novel *Bajo el oscuro sol*), A L3
The Traveler, A B8

Behar, Ruth (Cuba)
Bridges to Cuba. Puentes a Cuba, A B6
Everything I Kept: Reflections on an "Anthropoeta," A B22
In the Absence of Love, A A1.4
The Jewish Cemetery in Guanabacoa, A S18.2
Translated Woman: Crossing the Border with Esperanza's Story, AB B3

Belli, Gioconda (Nicaragua)
A Christmas Like No Other, A S3
The Country under My Skin: A Memoir of Love and War, AB B4
The Inhabited Woman, N B1
Just a Woman, A S3.1

Beltrán, María de la Merced (Cuba/France)
Travels through Cuba, A A4

Benedetti, Giovanna (Panama)
The Rain on the Fire, A J4
The Scent of Violets, A J4

Benedetti, Lúcia (Brazil)
My Uncle Ricardo, A S1

Benítez, Sandra (Mexico)
Bitter Grounds, N B2
El Pajarero, A F7
Night of the Radishes, N B2.1
A Place Where the Sea Remembers, N B2.2
Sleeping with One Eye Open: Women Writers and the Art of Survival, AB K1
The Weight of All Things, N B2.3

Bermín, Sabina (Mexico)
Bubbeh, N B3

Bermúdez, María Elvira (Mexico)
The Puzzle of the Broken Watch, A Y3

Bernal, Acela (Mexico)
The Taste of Good Fortune, A J3

Bevin, Teresa (Cuba)
Havana Split, N B4

Bins, Patricia (Brazil)
Destination, A A1.5

Blanco, Marta (Chile)
Maternity, A A1.8, A O6
Sweet Companion, A R5.1

Blanqué, Andrea (Uruguay)
Immensely Eunice, A H13

Bobes, Marilyn (Cuba)
Ask the Good Lord, A B25
In Florence Ten Years Later, A H13, A R10
It's a Good Thing, A B9
Somebody Has to Cry, A Y2
This Time Listen to What I Say, A B9

Bojunga-Nunes, Lygia (Brazil)
The Companions, A B15, N N2
Fast Friends, A B15
My Friend the Painter, A B15.1, N N2.1
Summer, A B15
A Time of Trouble, A B15

Bombal, María Luisa (Chile)
Braids, A A14, A B16
The Final Mist, A B16
House of Mist, N B5, N B5.1
The Last Mist (excerpt), A F3
New Islands, A B16, A I1, A Y4
New Islands and Other Stories, A B16
The Secret, A A1.8
The Shrouded Woman, N B5.1, N B5.2

Sky, Sea and Earth, A A1.5, A A1.9, A C19
The Story of María Griselda, A A3
The Tree, A B16, A C27, A G10, A H12.1, A M7, A M12, A M14, A R16, A T5
The Unknown, A B16

Borinsky, Alicia (Argentina)
All Night Movie, N B6
Dreams of the Abandoned Seducer, N B6.1
Mean Woman, N B6.2

Bornstein, Miriam (Mexico)
On the Border: Essential Stories, A A1.4

Bortnik, Aída (Argentina)
Celeste's Heart, A S18.1

Borton de Treviño, Elizabeth (Mexico)
My Heart Lies South: The Story of My Mexican Marriage, AB B5

Bosco, María Angélica (Argentina)
Letter from Ana Karenina to Nora, A L6
Letter from Nora to Ana Karenina, A L6

Boudet, Rosa Lleana (Cuba)
Potosí II: Address Unknown, A Y2

Boullosa, Carmen (Mexico)
Cleopatra Dismounts, N B7
Impossible Story, A H13
Leaving Tabasco, N B7.1
Mary, Why Don't You? (Impossible Dialogue in One Act), A D4
The Miracle-Worker, N B7.2
Seeing Is Believing, A D12
So Disappear, A P9
Storms of Torment, A G5
They're Cows, We're Pigs, N B7.3
III, A D4

Boza, María del Carmen (Cuba)
Scattering the Ashes: A Memoir, AB B6

Braschi, Giannina (Puerto Rico)
The Adventures of Mariquita Samper, N B8
The Adventures of Mariquita Samper, A B20
Assault on Time, A B20

Blow Up, A S16
Book of Clowns and Buffoons, A B20
The Building of the Waves of the Sea, A B20
Empire of Dreams, A B20, N B8
Empire of Dreams (excerpt), A B4
Epilogue, A B20
Gossip, A B20
I Don't Have It, and I Wanted It (excerpt from *Empire of Dreams*), A R19
The Life and Works of Berta Singerman, A B20
Manifesto on Poetic Eggs, A B20
Mariquita Sampe's Childhood, A B20
Pastoral, or, The Inquisition of Memories, A B20
Poems of the World, or, The Book of Wisdom, A B20
Portrait of Giannina Braschi, A B20
The Queen of Beauty, Charm, and Coquetry, A B20
The Raise, A B20
Requiem for Solitude, A B20
Song of Nothingness, A B20
The Things that Happen to Men in New York!, A B20
Yo-Yo Boing!, N B8.1

Bravo, Mónica (Ecuador)
Wings for Dominga, A B8

Bravo Utrera, Sonia (Cuba)
Decision, A B9

Britton, Rosa María (Panama)
Death Lies on the Cots, A P9
Love Is Spelled with a "G," A J5
The Wreck of the Enid Rose, A J4

Brunet, Marta (Chile)
Black Bird, A S12
Down River, A A1.8
Francina, A J9.1
Solitude of Blood, A A1.5, A O6, A Y5

Bruzonic, Erika (Bolivia)
Inheritance, A B8

Buenaño, Aminta (Ecuador)
The Strange Invasion that Rose from the Sea, A B8

Buitrago, Fanny (Colombia)
Caribbean Siren, A B21
The Sea from the Window, A H13
Señora Honeycomb, N B9

Bulhões Carvalho da Fonseca, Emi (Brazil)
In the Silence of the Big House, A S1

Bullrich, Silvina (Argentina)
The Bridge, A F9
The Divorce, A M15
The Lover, A L6
Self Denial, A L6
Tomorrow I'll Say Enough, N B10

Cabello de Carbonera, Mercedes (Peru)
La hija del mashorquero/The Executioner's Daughter, A S8

Cabral, Cristina (Uruguay)
25 August, 1988

Cabrera, Lydia (Cuba)
Daddy Turtle and Daddy Tiger, A B25
The Hill Called Mambiala, A I1, A M15
The Hill of Mambiala, A B21
How the Monkey Lost the Fruit of His Labor, A H10, A M8.6
The Mire of Almendares, A P7
Obbara Lies But Doesn't Lie, A M15
The Prize of Freedom, A C28, A E3
Susundamba Does Not Show Herself by Day, A R17
Tatabisako, A P7
Turtle's Horse, A H12
Walo-Wila, A A14, A H12

Cadilla de Martínez, María (Puerto Rico)
Indigenous Profile, A C28

Calderón, Sara Levi (Mexico)
The Two Mujeres, N C1

Calny, Eugenia (Argentina)
Drifting Balloons, A G3
In the Hero's Shadow, A G3
Siesta, A L6

Calvimontes, Velia (Bolivia)
Coati 1950, A L3

Calvo-Roth, Fortuna (Peru)
Growing up Sephardi in Peru, A A1.7

Campbell, Shirley (Costa Rica)
Closing the Circle that Began in Africa, A D5

Campobello, Nellie (Mexico)
Cartridge: Tales of the Struggle in Northern Mexico (excerpt), A A14
Cartucho and My Mother's Hands, A C3
Cartucho: Men of the North, A C3
The Dumb One, A C3
The Executed (from *Cartucho*), A C3
Far Away Where She Lived a Life Shattered by Rifles' Ravages, A C3
Fill Your Heart with My Respect, A C3
General Rueda, A A2
Her God, A C3
Her Love, A C3
Her Skirt, A C3
Jacinto's Deal, A C3
A Letter for You, A C3
The Men Left Their Mutilated Bodies Awaiting the Succor of These Simple Flowers,
    A C3
Men of the North (excerpt from *Cartucho*), A C3
The Men of the Troop, A C3
My Mother's Hands, A C3
Once I Sought Her, A C3
Our Love, A C3
Plaza of the Lilacs, A C3
Reader, Fill Your Heart with My Respect, A C3
She and Her Machine, A C3
She Is Here, A C3
She Was, A C3
Tales of the Struggle in Northern Mexico (excerpt from *Cartridge*), A A14
Under Fire (from *Cartucho*), A C3
A Villa Man Like So Many Others, A C3
When We Came to a Capital City, A C3
You and He, A C3

Campos, Julieta (Cuba/Mexico)
All the Roses, A P7, A C4
Allegories, A P9
The Baptism, A C4

Celina or the Cats, A C4
Celina or the Cats, A C4
The City, A C4
The Fear of Losing Eurydice: A Novel, N C2
The House, A C4, A R17
On Cats and Other Worlds, A C4
A Redhead Named Sabina (excerpts), A P7
She Has Reddish Hair and Her Name is Sabina, A M10
She Has Reddish Hair and Her Name is Sabina, N C2.1

Campra, Rosalba, (Argentina)
Dream Tiger, A C11

Cárdenas, Magolo (Mexico)
But What If I Liked the Panchos, Not the Beatles, A L9

Cartagena Portalatín, Aída (Dominican Republic)
Colita, A L9
Donna Summer, A E3
The Path to the Ministry, A F3.1
They Called Her Aurora (A Passion for Donna Summer), A E4
Wasted Effort, A D5

Casal, Lourdes (Cuba)
The Founders: Alfonso, A B25, A D5, A G2.1
A Love Story According to Cyrano Prufrock, A R10

Casanova, Cecilia (Chile)
The Unmarriage, A R5.1

Castedo, Elena (Chile)
Ice Cream, A P9
Paradise, N C3
Paradise (excerpt), A F2
The White Bedspread, A A1.8, A P10

Castellanos, Rosario (Mexico)
Aceite guapo, A C8
Another Way to Be: Selected Works of Rosario Castellanos, A A10
Arthur Smith Finds Salvation, A C8
Balún Canán, A A2
The Book of Lamentations, N C4
The Book of Lamentations (excerpt), A G2
City of Kings, A C8
Coming of the Eagle, A C8

Cooking Lesson, A A6, A A10, A G10, A I1, A M15
Culinary Lesson, A C27
The Cycle of Hunger, A A10
Death of the Tiger, A C8, A G4, A M8.6
The Eagle, A A6
Fleeting Friendships, A A6
The Fourth Vigil, A C8
The Gift, Refused, A C8
Indian Mother, A A1.6
The Luck of Teodoro Méndez Acúbal, A A10, A C8
Modesta Gómez, A C8
The Nine Guardians, N C4.1
The Nine Guardians (excerpt from *Balún Canán*), A A10
Office of Tenebrae (excerpt), A F9
A Rosario Castellanos Reader, A A6
Tenebrae Service (excerpt from *Oficio de tinieblas*), A A10, A M10
Three Knots in the Net, A A6, A A10
The Truce, A C8
The Wheel of Hunger, A C8
The Widower Román (novella), A A6

Castillejos Peral, Silvia (Mexico)
Tomorrow the World Ends, A J3

Cerda, Marta (Mexico)
After Canaries, A C12
Amanda's Motives, A C12
And the Crows Cawed, A C12
At the Baptismal Font, A C12
The Best Night, A C12
Between the Lines, A C12
Blame It on Hormones, A C12
Blue in the Family, A C12
City of Children, A C12
The Congregation in the Park, A C12
Epilogue, A C12
The First Time, A C12
Geography Lesson, A C12
German Dollars, A C12
Good Habits, A C12
A Happy Family, A C12
Heard in Passing, A C12
Hide-and-Seek, A C12
In the Dream Clock, A C12
It's Their Fault, A C12

Last Night at Night, A C12
Last Night, Mariana, A C12
Mirror of a Man, A B18
Multiverse, A C12
Office Machine, A C12
No-Man's-Land, A C12
No One Knows for Whom One Works, A C12
Office Machine, A C12
Right Place, Wrong Time, A C12
The Same Stock, A C12
Señora Rodríguez and Other Worlds, A C11, NC5
A Time of Mourning, A B18, A C12, A P9
With Respect to the Sky, A C12
Without Knowing That It Is You, A C12

Cevasco, Gaby (Peru)
Between Clouds and Lizards, A B8

Chávez-Vásquez, Gloria (Colombia)
AKUM: La magia de los sueños/The Magic of Dreams. A Bilingual Novel, N C6
The American Legend of the Creation of the Brain (La leyenda americana de la
    creación del cerebro), A C15
A Broken Vase (Un búcaro roto), A C15
A Consulate's Tale (Un cuento de consulado), A C15
The Firefly and the Mirror (La luciérnaga y el espejo), A C15
From La Alameda to New York (De La Alameda a Nueva York), A C15
The Human Virus (El virus humano), A C15
The Lookout (El Mirador), A C15
Opus Americanus: Short Stories, A C15
The Origins of Bureaucracy (Orígenes de la burocracia), A C15
Sincronio, the Bird of Wonder (Sincronio, el ave fénix), A C15
Sister Orfelina (Sor Orfelina), A C15
The Subwaynauts (Diario de un subwaynauta), A C15
The Termites (Las termitas), A C15

Chaviano, Diana (Cuba)
The Annunciation, A B7

Chehade Durán, Nayla (Colombia)
The Vigil, A L3
The Visit, A L3

Chichotky, Graciela (Argentina)
An Essential Tool, A A 1.7

Chiriboga, Luz Argentina (Ecuador)
Drums under My Skin (excerpt), A D5
Under the Skin of the Drums (excerpt from *Bajo la piel de los tambores*), A B12,
    A B19

Clavel, Ana (Mexico)
Dark Tears of a Mere Sleeper, A J3

Clucella, María Isabel (Argentina)
Tango and Feathers, A C11

Cohen, Regina (Mexico)
Jazzbluesing, A J3

Colasanti, Marina (Brazil)
Little Girl in Red, on Her Way to the Moon, A S1

Collado, Delfina (Costa Rica)
Garabito the Indomitable, A J4
The Indian Mummy, A J4

Conde Zambada, Hilda Rosina (Mexico)
Sonatina, A J3

Contreras, Hilma (Dominican Republic)
Between Two Silences, A C26
The Burial of Marisol, A C26
The Fire, A C26
Hair, A C26, A E4
Hey Mama, A C26
Mambrú Did Not Go to War, A F3.1
The Man Who Died Facing the Sea, A C26
Now We Will Be Happy, A C26
Stalker, A C26
A Visit, A C26
The Wait, A C26
The Window, A C26, A M19

Correia Dutra, Lia (Brazil)
A Perfect World, A S1

Cossío y Cisneros, Evangelina (Cuba)
To Free Cuba, A C28

Coutinho, Sonia (Brazil)
Every Lana Turner Has Her Johnny Stompanato, A S1
Those May Afternoons, A V2.1

Cruz, Celia (Cuba)
Celia: My Life: An Autobiography, AB C5

Cruz, Soledad (Cuba)
Fritters and Moons, A F3.1

Cruz Varela, María Elena (Cuba)
The Exterminating Angel, A G2.1
Love Song for Difficult Times, A G2.1

Cuero, Delfina (Mexican-American)
*Delfina Cuero: Her Autobiography, an Account of Her Last Years, and Her
    Ethnobotanic Contributions*, AB C6

Cunha, Helena Parente (Brazil)
Woman between Mirrors, N C7

da Fonseca, Cristina (Chile)
Endless Flight, A A1.8
Memories of Clay, A A1.8

Dávila, Amparo (Mexico)
Behind Bars, A M15
Haute Cuisine, A M8.6
In Heaven, A C27
Shoes for the Rest of My Life, A C27
Welcome to the Chelsea, A M8.8

Daviú, Matilde (Venezuela)
Ofelia's Transfiguration, A L9
The Woman Who Tore Up the World, A F3

de Anhalt, Nedda G. (Cuba/Mexico)
A Concealing Nakedness, A A2
Shared Memories, A A1.7

de Aragón, Uva (Cuba)
I Just Can't Take It, A Y2
Round Trip, A B25

de Castillo, Francisca Josefa (Colombia)
Su vida/Her Life, A S8

de Crespo, Elda L. C. (Panama)
Maruja, A M18
Seña Paula, A M18
Village Fiesta, A M18

de Diego, Josefina (Cuba)
Internal Monologue on a Corner in Havana, A Y2

de Ferrari, Gabriella (Peru)
Gringa Latina: Woman of Two Worlds, AB D2

de Fokes, María Asunción (Chile)
Vanessa and Victor, A A1.8

de Jesús, Carolina María (Brazil)
Beyond all Pity (excerpt), A B24
Child of the Dark (excerpt), A A14
Child of the Dark: The Diary of Carolina María de Jesús, AB D3
Childhood, A G7
Diary: 1955 (excerpt from *Beyond All Pity*), A B24

de la Cruz, Sor Juana Inés (Mexico)
Carta al R. P. M. Antonio Núñez / Letter to the R. P. M. Antonio Núñez, A S8
Poesía/ Poetry, A S8
A Woman of Genius/La respuesta a Sor Filotea: The Intellectual Autobiography of Sor Juana Inés de la Cruz, AB D4

de la Cuesta, Barbara (United States)
The Gold Mine, N D1
If There Weren't So Many of Them You Might Say They Were Beautiful, N D1.1

de la Parra, Teresa (Venezuela)
Iphigenia: The Diary of a Young Lady Who Wrote Because She Was Bored, N D2
Mama Blanca, A R18
Mama Blanca's Memoirs: The Classic Novel of a Venezuelan Girlhood, N D2.1
No More Mill (excerpt from *Mama Blanca's Souvenirs*), A A14
The Story of Señorita Dust Grain, Ballerina of the Sun (Historia de la Señorita Grano de Polvo, bailarina del sol), A P8

de Queiroz, Rachel (Brazil)
Dora, Doralina, N D3
Metonymy, or the Husband's Revenge, A G13, A J1, A M8.2, A M8.6

del Valle, Rosamel (Chile)
Eva, the Fugitive, N D6

Delgado, Ana María (Puerto Rico)
The Room In-between, N D7

Denser, Márcia (Brazil)
The Vampire of Whitehouse Lane, A S1

Di Giorgio, Marosa (Uruguay)
The Wild Papers (excerpt), A A3

Diaconú, Alina (Argentina)
Blue Lagoon, A C11
The Storm, A A3
Welcome to Albany, A A3
The Widower, A A3

Díaz-Diocaretz, Miriam (Chile)
Juani en tres tiempos, A G7

Díaz Lozano, Argentina (Honduras)
And We Have to Live, N D8
Henriqueta and I, N D8.1
Mayapan, N D8.2

Díaz Llanillo, Esther (Cuba)
My Aunt, A Y2

Diez Fierro, Silvia (Chile)
The Sailor's Wife, A L3
We Must Keep Fanning the Master, A L3

Dolores, Carmen (Brazil)
Aunt Zézé's Tears, A G6, A J1
A Drama in the Countryside, A S1

Domecq, Brianda (Mexico)
The Astonishing Story of the Saint of Cabora, N D9
Balzac, A D4
Eleven Days, N D9.1
Galatea, A D4
In Memoriam, A D4
The Turtle, A A2

Dorado de Revilla Valenzuela, Elsa (Bolivia)
The Parrot, A B8

Dos Santos, Estela (Argentina)
Celeste Goes Dancing, A D10

Dueñas, Guadalupe (Mexico)
A Clinical Case, A C30
The Guardian Angel, A A2
Mariquita and Me, A B18
The Moribund, A T5

Dughi, Pilar (Peru)
The Days and Hours, A B8

Dujovne Ortiz, Alicia (Argentina)
Courage or Cowardice?, A P2.1
Eva Perón, AB D5

Dupré, Leandro Sra. (Brazil)
We Were Six (excerpt from the novel *Éramos seis*), A S1

Durán, Gloria (Mexico)
Malinche: Slave Princess of Cortez, AB D6
María de Estrada: Gypsy Conquistadora, ND10

Durán Trujillo, Marie Oralia (Mexico)
Autumn Memories: My New Mexican Roots and Traditions, AB D7

Eltit, Diamela (Chile)
Custody of the Eyes, N E1
E. Luminata, N E1.1
Even if I Bathed in the Purest Waters, A P9
The Fourth World, N1.2
Luminated (excerpt from the novel *Lumpérica*), A C10
Sacred Cow, N 1.3

Engle, Margarita (Cuba)
On the Morning of His Arrest..., A P10.1
Singing to Cuba, N E2
Skywriting: A Novel of Cuba, N E2.1
Uncle Teo's Shorthand Cookbook, A M16

Escalante, Beatriz (Mexico)
Magdalena, a Fable of Immortality, N E3

Escudos, Jacinta (El Salvador)
Look at Lislique, See How Pretty It Is, A S5

Esquibel Tywoniak, Frances (Mexico)
Migrant Daughter: Coming of Age as a Mexican-American Woman, AB E2

Esquivel, Laura (Mexico)
Between Two Fires: Intimate Writings on Life, Love, Food and Flavor, AB E3
Blessed Reality, A C25.1
The Law of Love, N E4
Like Water for Chocolate (excerpt), A B4, A B13, A L1
Like Water for Chocolate: A Novel in Monthly Installments, with Recipes, Romances, and Home Remedies, N E4.1
Malinche, AB E3.1
Swift as Desire, A M10
Swift as Desire, N E4.2

Estenssoro, María Virginia (Bolivia)
The Child that Never Was, A C27

Estrada, Josefina (Mexico)
June Gave Him the Voice, A L2
Women in Captivity, A J3

Fagundes Telles, Lygia (Brazil)
The Ants, A C19, A F1
The Consultation, A F1
The Corset, A C25
Crescent Moon in Amsterdam, A F1
The Day to Say "No!," A S21
Dear Editor, A F1
Fourteen Female Voices from Brazil: Interviews and Works, AB S6
The Girl in the Photograph, N F1
Happiness, A C23
Herbarium, A F1
The Hunt, A E3
Just a Saxophone, A J1, A S1
The Key, A A1.5
Lovelorn Dove (A Story of Romance), A F1
The Marble Dance, N F1.1
The Presence, A F1
Rat Seminar, A F1
The Sauna, A C10, A F1
The Structure of the Soap Bubble, A R17
Tigrela, A F1, A M8.6

Tigrela and Other Stories, A F1
The Touch on the Shoulder, A F1
Turtledove or a Love Story, A V2.1
WM, A F1
The X in the Problem, A F1
Yellow Nocturne, A F1

Fanaro, Silvia (Brazil)
The Day I Met Miss America, A R8

Farias, Alejandra (Chile)
The Fish Tank, A A1.8

Felinto, Marilene (Brazil)
The Women of Tijucopapo, N F2

Fernándes de Oliveira, Cicera (Brazil)
We Women Suffer More than Men, A G7

Fernández, Alina (Cuba)
(Fidel) Castro's Daughter: An Exile's Memoir of Cuba, AB F1

Fernández de Juan, Adelaida (Cuba)
The Egyptians, A Y2
Journey to Pepe, A B9
Oh Life, A B9

Fernández Moreno, Inés (Argentina)
A Mother to Be Assembled, A L3

Fernández Pintado, Mylene (Cuba)
Anhedonia (A Story in Two Women), A Y2

Ferré, Rosario (Puerto Rico)
Amalia, A F4.1, A J, A P9
The Battle of the Virgins, A C9
Bella durmiente, A R14
The Bitches Colloquy, A R19
Boffil and Rivas de Santillana, A A12
Captain Candelario's Heroic Last Stand, A F4
The Dreamer's Portrait, A C16, A F4.1
The Dust Garden, A F4.1
Eccentric Neighborhoods, N F3
Eccentric Neighborhoods (excerpt), A A12, A B13
Flight of the Swan, A M20

Flight of the Swan, N F3.1
Fording Río Loco, A A12
The Fox Fur Coat, A F4.1
The Gift, A C25, A D6, A F4
The Glass Box, A F4.1, A M16
The House on the Lagoon, N F3.2
The House that Vanished, A F4.1
How I Wrote "When Women Love Men" (essay), A F4.1
Isolda's Mirror, A F4
Latina Self-Portraits: Interviews with Contemporary Women Writers, AB H1
Marina and the Lion, A F4.1
Mercedes Benz 220 SL, A E3, A F4.1, A F6, A G4
On Destiny, Language, and Translation, or, Ophelia Adrift in the C & O Canal (essay),
    A F4.1
The Other Side of Paradise, A F4.1
Pico Rico, Mandorico, A V4
The Poisoned Story, A E4, A F4.1
The Poisoned Tale, A C27
Rice and Milk, A F3
The Seed Necklace, A F4.1
Sleeping Beauty, A F4.1, A I1, A V4
Sweet Diamond Dust (novel), A F4
Sweet Diamond Dust: A Novel and Three Stories of Life in Puerto Rico, A F4,
    N F3.3
This Noise Was Different, A F3.1
When Women Love Men, A B23, A F4.1, A G10, A M15
The Youngest Doll, A F4.1
The Youngest Doll, A A14, A B11, A C19, A F4.1, A K1, A M19, A P4, A V4
The Youngest Doll (excerpt), A A14

Fierro, Fanny (Ecuador)
Hidden Pleasure, A B1

Fort, María Rosa (Peru)
Tarma, A C6

Fox, Lucía (Peru)
The Wedding, A E3

França, Aline (Brazil)
A Mulher de Aleduma (excerpt), A B24

Freilich de Segal, Alicia (Venezuela)
Cláper, N F4
Cláper (excerpt), A A1.4

Friedman, Joan E. (Venezuela)
El Azar-Fate Put the Novel *Cláper* in My Hands, A A1.7

Futoransky, Luisa (Argentina)
The Melancholy of Black Panthers, A A1.4
*Son cuentos chinos (*excerpt from the novel), A K2.1

Galeana, Benita (Mexico)
Benita, AB G1

Gallardo, Sara (Argentina)
The Blue Stone Emperor's Thirty Wives, A A3
The Man in the Araucaria, A A3, A O6

Galvão, Patricia "Pagu" (Brazil)
Industrial Park: A Proletarian Novel, N G1

Gambaro, Griselda (Argentina)
The Impenetrable Madam X, N G2

Garcés, María del Carmen (Ecuador)
The Blue Handkerchief, A B8

García, Cristina (Cuba)
The Agüero Sisters, N G3
The Agüero Sisters (excerpt), A B13
Basket of Water (excerpt from *Dreaming in Cuban*), A G9
*Bordering Fires: The Vintage Book of Contemporary Mexican and Chicana and
    Chicano Literature*, A G2
Cars of Cuba, AB G2
Cubanísimo: The Vintage Book of Contemporary Cuban Literature, A G2.1
Dreaming in Cuban, N G3.1
Dreaming in Cuban (excerpt), A A16, A K1
A Handbook to Luck, N G3.2
Inés in the Kitchen, A K4, A P10.1
Latina Self-Portraits: Interviews with Contemporary Women Writers, AB H1
The Leatherback, A A12
Monkey Hunting, N G3.3
A Natural History (excerpt), A A12
The Nature of Parasites, A A12
Tito's Goodbye, A C18, A P10
Tree Ducks, A A12

García, María Cristina (Cuba)
Havana USA: Cuban Exiles and Cuban Americans in South-Florida, 1959-1994, AB G3

García Caizada, Ana Luz (Cuba)
Disremembering a Smell, A Y2

García Huidobro, Beatriz (Chile)
Until She Go No More, A S12

García Ramis, Magali (Puerto Rico)
Cocuyo Flower, A E4
Corinne, Amiable Girl, A F3.1, A R19
Every Sunday, A M19, A R19
Happy Days, Uncle Sergio, A K1, N G4
Happy Days, Uncle Sergio (excerpt), A O6
A Script for Every House, A A1.3, A P9
The Sign of Winter, A B21

Garro, Elena (Mexico)
Before the Trojan War, A C10
Blame the Tlaxcaltecs, A C27
The Day We Were Dogs, A I1, A M15
First Love and Look for My Obituary: Two Novellas, N G5
It's the Fault of the Tlaxcaltecas, A M8.6
Perfecto Luna, A E3
Recollections of Things to Come, A A2, N G5.1
A Secure Home, A B17
The Tree, A P7

Glantz, Margo (Mexico)
Coatlicue Swept, A A2
English Love, A H13
The Family Tree (excerpt), A A1.4
The Family Tree: An Illustrated Novel, N G6
Genealogies, A A1.5, A S18.1
Genealogies (excerpt), A L9
Shoes, A A1.4
The Wake, N G6.1

Glickman, Nora (Argentina)
A Day in New York, A F2
Dios salve a América, A T6
El último de los colonos, A T6
The Jewish White Slave Trade and the Untold Story of Raquel Liberman, AB G4

The Last Emigrant, A B10, A C27
Tag-sale, A T6

Gligo, Agata (Chile)
The Bicycles, A A1.8

Gómez de Avellaneda y Arteaga, Gertrudis (Cuba)
Cuauhtemoc: The Last Aztec Emperor, an Historical Novel, N G7
Sab: An Autobiography, N G7.1

Gómez Rul, Ana María (Mexico)
Lol-Há: A Maya Tale, N G8

González, Luisa (Costa Rica)
At the Bottom: A Woman's Life in Central America, AB G5

González, Nelly S. (Bolivia)
Bolivian Studies Journal: Issue Dedicated to Alcides Arguedas, A G8

González de Fanning, Teresa (Peru)
Estudio comparativo de la inteligencia y la belleza en la mujer/A Comparative Study
  on Intelligence and Beauty in Women, A S8

González Valdenegro, Sonia (Chile)
A Matter of Distance, A A1.8

Gorodischer, Angélica (Argentina)
Camera Obscura, A A1.4, A R17
Kalpa Imperial: The Greatest Empire That Never Was, N G9
Letters from an English Lady, A A3
Man's Dwelling Place, A M8.6
The Perfect Married Woman, A A3
The Resurrection of the Flesh, A A3
Under the Flowering Juleps, A A3
Under the Yubayas in Bloom, A E3

Gorriti, Carmen Luz (Peru)
The Legacy (A Story from Huancayo), A B8

Gorriti, Juana Manuela (Argentina)
The Black Glove, A G11
Carta a Antonio Romero Ortiz/ Letter to Antonio Romero Ortiz, A S8
Cartas a Ignacio de Cepeda/ Letters to Ignacio de Cepeda, A S8

Confidence of a Confidence, A G10
The Deadman's Fiancee, A G11, A M9
Dreams and Realities: Selected Fiction of Juana Manuela Gorriti, A G11
Gubi Amaya, A G11
If You Do Wrong Expect No Good, A G11
The Mazoquero's Daughter, A G11
The Quena, A G11
To His Regret, A G10
Travels through Argentina, Peru, and Bolivia, A A4
Treasure of the Incas, A G11
A Year in California, A G11

Grossman, Judith (Brazil)
On the Way to Eternity, A V2.1

Guerra (Cunningham), Lucía (Chile)
Encounter on the Margins, A A1.8
Más allá de la máscaras. (Beyond the Masks), N G10
The Street of Night, N G10.1
The Street of Night (excerpt), A B13
The Virgin's Passion, A C27

Guevara, Bethzabé (Peru)
The Señorita Didn't Teach Me, A B8

Guido, Beatriz (Argentina)
End of a Day, N G11
The House of the Angel, N G11.1
The House of the Angel (excerpt), A F3
Takeover, A L6
Ten Times around the Block, A L6
The Usurper, A M8.6

Guijosa, Marcela (Mexico)
Regarding My Mestiza Self, A A2

Guillermoprieto, Alma (Cuba)
Dancing with Cuba: A Memoir of the Revolution, AB G7
Samba, AB G8

Güiraldes, Ana María (Chile)
The Family Album, A A1.8, A O6
Up to the Clouds, A A1.8

Guralnik, Sonia (Chile)
Sailing Down the Rhine, A A1.4, A A1.8

Gutiérrez, Marcela (Bolivia)
The Feathered Serpent, A B8

Gutiérrez Richaud, Cristina (Mexico)
Woman with Short Hair and Great Legs, N G12

Heker (Hecker), Liliana (Argentina)
Bishop Berkeley or Mariana of the Universe, A C27, A H4
Early Beginnings or Ars Poetica, A H4, AM8.8
Family Life, A H4
Georgina Requeni or the Chosen One, A H4
Jocasta, A H4, A M8.3, A M8.4
The Letter to Ricardo, A D10
Spick and Span, A H13
The Stolen Party, A H4, A M8.5, A M8.6
The Stolen Party and Other Stories, A H4
When Everything Shines, A A3, A O6

Hernández, Angela (Dominican Republic)
How to Gather the Shadows of the Flowers, A E4, A F3, A O6
Silvia, A F3.1
Teresa Irene, A P9

Hernández, Luisa Josefina (Mexico)
Florinda and Don Gonzalo, A A14

Herranz Brooks, Jacqueline (Cuba)
An Unexpected Interlude between Two Characters, A R10

Herrera, Matilde (Argentina)
Eduardito Doesn't Like the Police, A R17

Hilst, Hilda (Brazil)
Agda, A J1, A S1, A V2.1
An Avid One in Extremis, A A1.5
Natural Theology, A A1.5

Hinojosa, María (Mexican-American)
Raising Raúl: Adventures Raising Myself and My Son, AB H3

Hiriart, Berta (Mexico)
Maestra Arellano, A R8

Hoffman, Kitzia (Mexico)
Old Adelina, A F9

Holst, Gilda (Ecuador)
The Competition, A L3
Reunión, A R9

Hospital, Carolina (Cuba)
A Century of Cuban Writers in Florida: Selected Prose and Poetry, A H10
Cuban American Writers: Los atrevidos, A H9
My Cuban Body, A S18.2

Ibarra, Cristina (Mexico)
The Little Eastern Star, A J3

Ingenieros, Delia (Argentina)
Odin, A B17, A K6

Iparraguierre, Sylvia (Argentina)
Tierra del fuego, N I1
Alongside the Track, A D10.1

Irupé Sanabria, Ruth (Argentina)
Las Aeious, A B22

Jacobs, Barbara (Mexico)
Aunt Luisita, A P9
The Dead Leaves, N J1
The Time I Got Drunk, A G5

Jamardo Faillace, Tania (Brazil)
Dorceli, A S1

Jamilis, Amalia (Argentina)
Department Store, A L6
Night Shift, A L6

Jara, Marta (Chile)
The Dress, A A1.8
The Englishwoman, A A1.8, A O6

Jorge, Lidia (Brazil)
The Painter of Birds, N J2
The Murmuring Coast, N J2.1

Jurado, Alicia (Argentina)
Saying Goodbye through Twenty-five Centuries, A C11

Kalina, Rosalina (Costa Rica)
Golem, A A1.4

Kalina de Piszk, Rosita (Costa Rica)
A Costa Rican Journey, A A1.7

Kazumi Stahl, Anna (Argentina)
Natural Disasters, A D25.1

Kociancich, Vlady (Argentina)
An Englishman in Mojacár, A D10.1
False Limits, A S7.2, A T7
A Family Man, A P9
Knight, Death, and the Devil, A C27, A M8.6
The Last Days of William Shakespeare, N K1

Kosminsky, Ethel (Brazil)
Memories of Comings and Goings, A A1.7

Kozameh, Alicia (Argentina)
Steps under Water, N K2
Two Hundred Fifty-nine Leaps, the Last Immortal, N K2.1

Krauze, Ethel (Mexico)
Isaiah VII, 14, A L2
Where Things Fly, A A2

Kuramoto, Beatriz (Bolivia)
The Agreement, A B8

Lago, Sylvia (Uruguay)
Golden Days of a Queen of Diamonds, A H13
Homelife, A E3

Lamazares, Ivonne (Cuba)
Cousin Sarita, A H10

The Sugar Island, N L1

Lange, Norah (Argentina)
Childhood Copybooks (excerpt from *Cuadernos de infancia*), A C10

Larraín, Luz (Chile)
The Bone Spoon, A A1.8

Laurent Kullick, Patricia (Mexico)
Crazy Cuts, A J3

Laurini, Myriam (Argentina)
Lost Dreams, A P1

Lavín, Mónica (Mexico)
Day and Night, A M10
The Lizard, A G5
Nicolasa and the Lacework, A A2
Nicolasa's Lace, A J3
Points of Departure: New Stories from Mexico, A L2
Why Come Back?, A L2

Lerner, Elisa (Venezuela)
Papa's Friends, A S18.1

Levins Morales, Aurora (Puerto Rico)
African Creation, A R19
And, A L4
California, A L4
Child of the Americas, A S18.2
A Child's Christmas in Puerto Rico, A T8
Distress Signals, A L4
Doña Carmelita, A L4
Dulce de naranjo, A S3
El bacalao viene de más lejos y se come aquí, A G7, A Y5
The Flute, A L4
Gardens, A L4
Getting Home Alive, A L4
Heart of My Heart, Bone of My Bone, A L4
If I Forget Thee, A L4
Immigrants, A D6, A L4, A T8, A V5
In My Grandmother's House, A L4
Kitchens, A G9, A L4, A T8

Letter to a Compañero, A L4
1930, A L4, A T8
Oh Jerusalem, A L4
Old Countries, A L4, A T8
The Other Heritage, A T8
Puertoricanness, A D1, A G9, A L4, A T8
A Remedy for Heartburn, A F2
Revision, A B22
South, A L4, A T8
A Story, A L4
Storytelling, A L4
Tito, A L4

Levinson, Luisa Mercedes (Argentina)
The Angel, A L5
Beyond the Grand Canyon, A L5
The Boy, A L5
The Boy Who Saw God's Tears, A A3
The Castle, A L5
The Clearing A G10, A L6, A Y5
Cobweb of Moons, A L5
The Cove, A C27, A L5
The Dream that Was Violated, A C1
Fearful of Valparaíso, A L5
The Girl with the Grey Woolen Gloves, A L5
In the Shadow of the Owl, N L2
The Islet, A L5
The Labyrinth of Time, A L5
The Little Island, A A3
The Minet, A L5
Mistress Frances, A L6
The Myth, A L5, A M15, A O7.1
No Men for the Poncho Weavers, A L5
On the Other Side of the Shore, A L5
The Other Shoes, A L5
The Pale Rose of Soho, A L5
Penetrating a Dream, A L5
Residuum, A L5
A Singular Couple, A L5
Sometime in Brussels, A L5
The Two Siblings, A L5
The Two Siblings and Other Stories, A L5
Ursula and the Hanged Man, A L5

With Passion and Compassion, A L5

Levis Levine, Ester (Cuba)
My Cuban Story, A A1.7

Liberman, Gloria (Chile)
La confesión, A G7

Lima, Chely (Cuba)
Common Stories, A S15
Monologue with Rain, A S15

Limpias Chávez, Viviana (Bolivia)
Copper Pumpkins, A R5

Lira (Lyra), Carmen (Costa Rica)
Bananas and Men (1931), A H8
The Bird of Sweet Charm, A H8
Brer Rabbit, Businessman, A D7
Coming Out with a Sunday Seven, A H8
The Cothnejo-Fishy District, A H8
The Cotton Guy, A H8
Dark-haired Girl, Fair-haired Girl, A H8
The Devil's Mother-in-Law, A H8
Estefanía, A J4, A P3, A Y5
The Flowering Olive Tree, A H8
The Fool of the Riddles, A H8
Front-row Seat in Heaven (1936), A H8
Golden Bean: The Coffee Bean and the Laborer (1933), A H8
The House of French Toast, A H8
How Uncle Rabbit Got Out of a Fix, A H8
How Uncle Rabbit Played a Trick on Aunt Whale and Uncle Elephant, A H8
Juan, the One with the Little Load of Firewood, A H8
Jump on It, Stick, A H8
La cucharachita Mandinga, A H8
The Monkey, A H8
Pastor's Ten Little Old Men, A H8, A R4
Ramona, Woman of the Ember, A J4
Silhouettes from the Maternal School (1929), A H8
The Subversive Voice of Carmen Lyra: Selected Work, A H8
The Tales of My Aunt Panchita, A D7
The Tales of My Aunt Panchita (prologue), A A14
Uncle Rabbit and Brother Juan Piedra's Horse, A H8

Uncle Rabbit and His Granny's Scuffed Sandals, A H8
Uncle Rabbit and the Cheeses, A H8
Uncle Rabbit and the Stream, A H8
Uncle Rabbit and Uncle Coyote, A H8
Uncle Rabbit, Businessman, A H8
Uncle Rabbit Get the Girl, A H8
Uvieta, Carmen Lira, A H8, A J7, A J9.1
Why Uncle Rabbit Has Such Long Ears, A H8

Lispector, Clarice (Brazil)
The Apple in the Dark, N L3
The Apple in the Dark (excerpt, chapter four, part one), A D11
An Apprenticeship, or, The Book of Delights, N L3.1
Beauty and the Beast, or, The Wound Too Great, A J1, A R17
Beginnings of a Fortune, A A14, A L7
The Besieged City, N L3.2
Better Than to Burn, A F9, A L7.2
The Body, A G4, A J1, A L7.2
The Breaking of the Bread, A J1
The Buffalo, A J1
But It's Going to Rain, A L7.2
The Chicken, A J1, A K2, A L7
A Complicated Case, A L7.2
The Conjurations of Dona Frozina, A L7.2
The Crime of the Mathematics Professor, A G10, A G13, A L7
Day by Day, A L7.2
The Daydreams of a Drunk Woman, A K2.1, A L7
The Dead Man in the Sea at Urea, A L7.2
The Departure of the Train, AI1, A L7.2
The Dinner, A L4
Discovering the World, N L3.3
Dry Point of Horses, A L7.2
The Egg and the Chicken, A L7.1
An Emptying, A L7.2
Evolution of Myopia, A L7.1
Explanation, A B4, A L7.2
Family Ties, A L7
Family Ties, A L7, A P7
The Fifth Story, A J1, A L7.1, A S10
The Flight, A S1
Footsteps, A L7.2
For the Time Being, A L7.2
The Foreign Legion, A L7.1

The Way of the Cross, A L7.2
Where You Were at Night, A L7.2

Lispector, Elisa (Brazil)
The Flight, A S1
The Fragile Balance, A S1

Llano, María Elena (Cuba)
In the Family, A C27, A F5
The Two of Us, A C7
Japanese Daisies, A Y2

Loaeza, Guadalupe (Mexico)
Oh, Polanco!, A M10

Loayza Millán, Beatriz (Bolivia)
The Mirror, A B8

Lobo, Tatiana (Chile)
Assault on Paradise, N L4

Lohman, Catalina (Peru)
The Red Line, A B8

Lojo, María Rosa (Argentina)
Compound Eyes, A C11

Lopes de Almeida, Júlia (Brazil)
He and She (excerpt), A S1

López, Griselda (Panama)
I'll Eat the Land, A J4
One Minute, A J4

López Gonzáles, Pilar (Cuba)
It Was All Mamá's Fault, A B24

López Kónina, Verónica (Cuba)
How Do You Know, Vivian?, A F3.1

Lorca de Tagle, Lillian (Chile)
Honorable Exiles: A Chilean Woman in the 20th Century, AB T1

Lorenzini, María Eugenia (Chile)
Bus Stop #4, A L4

Lubitch Domecq, Alcina (Guatemala)
Bottles, A M12.1, A P9, A S18.1, A S20
La Llorona, A S18.2

Luft, Lya Fett (Brazil)
The Island of the Dead, N L5
The Left Wing of the Angel (excerpt), A S1
The Red House, N L5.1

Lugo Filippi, Carmen (Puerto Rico)
Milagros, on Mercurio Street, A R19, A V4
Pilar, Your Curls, A V4, A Y5
Recipes for the Gullible, A M19

Lynch, Marta (Argentina)
Bedside Story, A L6
Hotel Taormina, A M15
Latin Lover, A L6, A M8.6

Macaya, Emilia (Costa Rica)
Alcestis, A J4
Eva, A J4

Machado, Ana María (Brazil)
At the Bottom of a Little Box, A M1
Chubby-cheeked Jelly Donut, A M1
Invisible Tattoo, A M1
Me in the Middle, A M1
Old-fashioned Conversations, A M1
People Braids, A M1
A Sneeze and a Tragedy, A M1
The Source of the Mysterious Voice, A M1
Whistling Girls, A M1

Maldonado, Clara Isabel (Bolivia)
Arcoiris de sueños (Retazos de una vida). Rainbow of Dreams (Patchwork of a Life),
    A M5
21 Years, A M5

Malinow, Inés (Argentina)
Fixed Distance, A M15

Mallet, Marilú (Chile)
Blind Alley, A M6
How Are You?, A M6
The Loyal Order of the Time-clock, A H3, A M6
The Vietnamese Hats, A M6
Voyage to the Other Extreme, A M6
Voyage to the Other Extreme: Five Stories, A M6

Mansour, Mónica (Mexico)
In Secret, A G5

Manzano, Sonia (Ecuador)
George, A R9

Marrero, Teresa (Cuba)
Ghost Limbs, A B6

Martín, Rita (Cuba)
Elisa, or the Price of Dreams, A B6

Martínez, Nela (Ecuador)
La Machorra, A B8

Mastretta, Ángeles (Mexico)
Aunt Clemencia Ortega, A D4
Aunt Concha Esparza, A C25.1
Aunt Cristina Martínez, A D4
Aunt Elena, A M10
Aunt Elvira, A P9
Aunt Leonor, A G2
Aunt Mariana, A H13
Aunt Natalia, A G2
Big-eyed Women (excerpt), A F10, A G5
Lovesick, N M1
Mal de amores (excerpt), A L1
Memory and Precipice, A D4
Mexican Bolero, N M1.1
Tear This Heart Out, N M1.2
White Lies, A A2, A B18
Women with Big Eyes, N M1.3

Matto de Turner, Clorinda (Peru)
Birds without Nests (excerpt from *Aves sin nido*), A A14, A J9
Birds without a Nest; a Story of Indian Life and Priestly Oppression in Peru, N M2
Torn from the Nest, N M2.1

Maturana, Andrea (Chile)
Cradle Song, A L3
Out of Silence, A L3

Mayo, C. M. (Mexico)
Mexico: A Traveler's Literary Companion, A M10
Rancho Santa Inés: Fast, A M10

Medina, C. C. (Cuba)
A Little Love, N M3

Medina, Eufelia (Mexico)
Me and My Helper, the Autobiography of Eufelia Medina 1914-1976, AB M3

Mellet, Viviana (Peru)
Good Night Air, A L3
The Other Mariana, A L3

Mellibovsky, Matilde (Argentina)
Circle of Love over Death: The Story of the Mothers of the Plaza de Mayo, AB M4

Melo, Patricia (Brazil)
Black Waltz, N M4
The Killer, N M4.1

Mendoza, María Luisa (Mexico)
Ausencia's Tale (excerpt), A F3, A G9.1

Menchú, Rigoberta (Guatemala)
Crossing Borders, AB M5
The Girl from Chimel, AB M6
The Honey Jar, AB M5.1
I, Rigoberta Menchú: An Indian Woman of Guatemala, AB M5.2
Maise, A H6
The Quincentenary Conference and the Earth Summit, 1992, A B22

Menéndez, Ana (Cuba)
Baseball Dreams, A M13

Confusing the Saints, A M13
Her Mother's House, A M13
Hurricane Stories, A M13
In Cuba I Was a German Shepherd, A G2.1
In Cuba I Was a German Shepherd, A M13
The Last Rescue, A M13
Loving Che, N M5
Miami Relatives, A M13
The Party, A M13
The Perfect Fruit, A M13
Story of a Parrot, A M13
Why We Left, A M13

Mercader, Martha (Argentina)
The Postponed Journey, A C11

Mercado, Tununa (Argentina)
In a State of Memory, AB M7

Miraglia, Liliana (Ecuador)
The Living Room, A R9

Miranda, Ana (Brazil)
Bay of All Saints and Every Conceivable Sin, N M6

Mistral, Gabriela (Chile)
Alfonsina Storni, A T1
Alfonso Reyes, A T1
The Alpaca, A A1.2, A T1
Art, A T1
The Body, A A1.2
Bread, A A1.2, A T1
Castile (An Imaginary Encounter with Saint Theresa), A F9
Children's Hair, A T1
Chile, A T1
The Coconut Palms, A A1.2
Commentary on Poems by Rabindranath Tagore, A T1
Decalogue of the Artist, A T1
The Enemy, A R18
The Fig, A A1.2, A T1
Flour, A A1.2
The Forbidden Word, A T1
Four, A T1

    AB H6
The Thistle, A T1
Thoughts on Teaching, A T1
To Declare the Dream, A T1
The Tortoise, A T1
Why Bamboo Canes Are Hollow, A T1
Why Roses Have Thorns, A T1
Why Reeds Are Hollow, A H12.1
The Zebra, A T1

Mohr, Nicolasa (Puerto Rico)
The Artist (Inéz), A M17.3
Aunt Rosana's Rocker (Zoraida), A K4.1, A M17.3
An Awakening...Summer 1956, A V6
Blessed Divination, A M17.1
Brief Miracle (Virginia), A M17.3
Christmas Was a Time of Plenty, A T2
Coming to Terms, A M17.2
El Bronx Remembered: A Novella and Stories, A M17
The English Lesson, A M17.2
Esperanza (excerpt from *Nilda*), A T2
Happy Birthday (Lucía), A M17.3
Herman and Alice, a Novella, A M17
I Never Seen My Father, A G9, A M17.2
In Another Place in a Different Era, A M17.1
In New York, A M17.2
Lali, A M17.2
A Lesson in Fortune-Telling, A M17
Love with Aleluya, A M17
A Matter of Pride, A M17.1
A Matter of Pride and Other Stories, A M17.1
Memories: R. I. P., A M17.1
Mr. Mendelsohn, A M17, A T8
My Newest Triumph, A M17.1
A New Window Display, A M17
Nilda (excerpt), A A16
Old Mary, A M17.2
Once Upon a Time..., A M17
The Operation, A M17.2
The Perfect Little Flower Girl, A M17.2
Princess, A M17
Rituals of Survival: A Woman's Portfolio, A M17.3
The Robbery, A M17.2

Rosalina de los Rosarios, A M17.1
Shoes for Hector, A M17
Tell the Truth, A M17
Ten Hispanic Authors, AB H2
A Thanksgiving Celebration (Amy), A M17.3
A Time with a Future (Carmela), A K4, A M17.3
Uncle Claudio, A M17
Utopia, and the Super Estrellas, A M17.1
A Very Special Pet, A M17, A T2
The Wrong Lunch Line, A M11, A M17, A T8

Molina, Silvia (Mexico)
Autumn, A R17
Gray Skies Tomorrow: A Novel, N M7
The Love You Promised Me, N M7.1
The New House, A D4
An Orange is an Orange, A B18
The Problem, A D4
Starting Over, A G5
Sunday, A A2
What Would You Have Done?, A D4

Molloy, Sylvia (Argentina)
Certificate of Absence, N M8
Certificate of Absence (excerpt), A H7
Sometimes in Illyria, A R17
Women's Writing in Latin America: An Anthology, A C10

Moncorva Bandeira de Mello, Emilia (pseud. Carmen Dolores) (Brazil)
Aunt Zézé's Tears, A J1

Mondragón Aguirre, Magdalena (Mexico)
Someday the Dream, N M9

Montecinos, Sonia (Chile)
Hualpín, A A1.8

Montero, Mayra (Cuba)
Captain of the Sleepers, N M10
Dancing to Almendra, N M10.1
Deep Purple: A Novel, N M10.2
El hombre Pollack, A M20
In the Palm of Darkness: A Novel, N M10.3

Last Night at Dawn, A V4
The Last Night I Spent with You, N M10.4
The Messenger, N M10.5
The Moon Line, N M10.6
The Red of His Shadow, N M10.7
That Man, Pollack, A C25.1
Thirteen and a Turtle, A V4
Under the Weeping Willow, A F3.1
You, Darkness, N M10.8

Morales, Rosario (Puerto Rico)
Bad Communist, A L4
Birth, A L4
Century Plant, A L4
Concepts of Pollution, A L4
Cosecha, A R19
Destitution, A T8
Diary Queen, A T8
The Dinner, A T8
Double Allegiance, A L4
El Salvador, A L4
Getting Home Alive, A L4
The Grandmother Time, A L4
Hace tiempo, A L4
I Am the Reasonable One, A L4
I Didn't Go Home (Christmas 1941), A S3
I Didn't Hear Anything, A R19
I Recognize You, A L4
I'm on Nature's Side, A L4
Memory, A L4
Nostalgia, A L4
Of Course She Read, A L4
Old, A L4
The Other Heritage, A T8
Puerto Rico Journal, A L4
Sketch, A T8
Synagogue, A L4
Trees, A L4

Morejón, Nancy (Cuba)
Attributed City, A G2.1
Love, A G2.1
Myth and Reality in Cecilia Valdés (excerpt), A D5

Richard Bought His Flute, A R19.1

Mouján Otaño, Magdalena (Argentina)
Gu Ta Butarrak (We and Our Own), A B7

Mujica, Barbara Louise (Chile)
Fairy Tale, A C6
Frida: A Novel, AB M9
Gotlib, Bombero, A A1.4
Mitrani, A A1.8

Muñiz (Muñiz-Huberman), Angelina (Mexico)
Abbreviated World, A A2
Brief World, A M22
The Cabalist, A S11
The Chrysalis of Clay Will Give Birth to a Butterfly, A M22
The Dream Curtain, A M22
El Cabalista, A S11
Enclosed Garden, A M22
Enclosed Garden, A M22
The Fortunes of the Infante Arnaldos, A M22
Gentlemen, A M22
The Grand Duchess, A M22
In the Name of His Name, A B10, A M22, A S18.1
Jocasta's Confession, A M22
Life Has No Plot, A M22
Longing, A M22
The Minstrel, A M22
The Most Precious Offering, A M22
On the Unicorn, A M22
The Portuguese Synagogue, A A1.4
The Prisoner, A A1.6, A M22
Retrospection, A M22
Rising, Mournful from the Earth, A M15, A M22
Salicio and Amarylis, A M22
The Sarcasm of God, A M22
The Swallows of Cuernavaca, A A2
Tlamapa, A M22
Vaguely, at Five in the Afternoon, A M22

Naranjo, Carmen (Costa Rica)
And We Sold the Rain, A S5, A Y5
Believe It or Not, A R4

The Compulsive Couple of the House on the Hill, A A1.5, A O6
Eighteen Ways to Make a Square, A N1
Everybody Loves Clowns, A N1
Five Women Writers of Costa Rica: Short Stories, A N2
*Five Women Writers of Costa Rica: Short Stories by Carmen Naranjo, Eunice Odio,
    Yolanda Oreamuno, Victoria Urbano, and Rima de Vallbona*, A U1
Floral Caper, A J5
The Flowery Trick, A N2, A U1
The Game That Is Only Played Once, A N1
Inventory of a Recluse, A N2, A U1
It Happened One Day, A N1
The Journey and the Journeys, A N2, A U1
Maybe the Clock Played with Time, A N1
My Byzantine Grandmother's Two Medieval Saints, A J4
Old Cat Meets Young Cat, A N1
Ondina, A P7
Over and Over, A P9
Symbiotic Encounter, A C27
Tell Me a Story, Olo, A N1
There Never Was a Once Upon a Time, A N1
Walls, A P3
When I Invented Butterflies, A N1
When New Flowers Bloomed, A J4, A R4
Why Kill the Countess?, A P7
A Woman at Dawn, A R17

Nery, Adalgisa (Brazil)
Premeditated Coincidence, A S1

Nicastro, Laura (Argentina)
Haguit, A C11

Niemeyer, Margarita (Chile)
The House, A A1.8

Nissan, Rosa (Mexico)
May You Make a Good Bride (excerpt), A A1.4

Nolla, Olga (Puerto Rico)
No Dust Is Allowed in This House, A E4
Macaroons, Eyes of Sea and Sky, A R19
Requiem for a Wreathless Corpse, A F3.1
A Tender Heart, A R17

The Fury, A O3
The Guests, A O3
The House of Sugar, A A3, A O3
Icera, A O3
The Inextinguishable Race, A K6, A R16
Leopoldina's Dream, A O3
Leopoldina's Dream, A O3
Livio Roca, A O3
Lovers, A O3
Magush, A O3
The Mastiffs of Hadrian's Temple, A M15
Mimoso, A O3
The Mortal Sin, A C10, A O3
The Music of the Rain, A S18
The Objects, A O3
The Perfect Crime, A O3
The Photographs, A O3
The Prayer, A L6, A O3
The Punishment, A O3
Report on Heaven and Hell, A O3
The Revelation, A O3
The Servant's Slaves, A A1.5, A C19
The Sibyl, A O3
Things, A A3
Thus Were Their Faces, A A3, A O3
Two Reports, A M8.6
The Velvet Dress, A A3, A O3
Visions, A O3
Voice on the Telephone, A O3
The Wedding, A O3

Ocampo, Victoria (Argentina)
The Archipelago (excerpt from *Archipiélago*), A A12, A C10
Emily Brönte, A C10
From Primer to Book (excerpt from *De la cartilla al libro*), A C10
The Insular Empire (excerpt from *El imperio insular*), A C10
Misfortunes of an Autodidact, M15
Terra incógnita (excerpt from the novel), A C10, A M15
This America of Ours: The Letters of Gabriela Mistral and Victoria Ocampo,
    AB H46

Odio, Eunice (Costa Rica)
Five Women Writers of Costa Rica: Short Stories by Carmen Naranjo, Eunice Odio,

Yolanda Oreamuno, Victoria Urbano, and Rima de Vallbona, A U1
A Homeless Writer, A N2
Once There Was a Man, A N2, A U1
The Trace of the Butterfly, A N2, U1
The Vestige of the Butterfly, A J4

O'Hara, Maricarmen (Bolivia)
The Bet, A O4
Cuentos para todos/Tales for Everybody, A O4
The Diamond, A O4
The Divine Language, A O4
The Grasshopper, A O4
He and She, A O4
Heddy the Airhead, A O4
The House that Jack Built, A O4
Hunger Strike, A O4
International Buffet, A O4
The King's Peaches, A O4
Little Joe Sticks, A O4
A Man and a Woman, A O4
Marcelino's Job, A O4
The Miser's Money, A O4
The Moon's Husband, A O4
Mr. Slowly Slow, A O4
Mr. Turista's Breakfast, A O4
The Old Peasant, A O4
Olga's Diet, A O4
Pay Me!, A O4
The Peacock's Voice, A O4
Questions and Answers, A O4
The 'Screaming Bag,' A O4
A Simple Story, A O4
The Smuggler, A O4
The Stronger, A O4
The Student Prince, A O4
Truth, A O4
The Two Kings, A O4
Wooden Spoon, A O4

Oreamuno, Yolanda (Costa Rica)
Five Women Writers of Costa Rica: Short Stories by Carmen Naranjo, Eunice Odio,
    Yolanda Oreamuno, Victoria Urbano, and Rima de Vallbona, A U1
High Valley, A N2, A U1

The Lizard with the White Belly, A R4
Of Their Obscure Family, A J4
The Spirit of My Land, A R4
The Tide Returns at Night, A N2, A U1
Urban Wake, A J4

O'Reilly Herrera, Andrea (Cuba)
The Homecoming, A P10.1
The Pearl of the Antilles, N H1
*A Secret Weaver's Anthology: Selections from the White Pine Press Secret Weaver's
    Series: Writing by Latin American Women*, A O6

Orfanoz, Luz (Chile)
Accelerated Cycle, A A1.8
Insignificance, A A1.8

Orozco, Olga (Argentina)
And the Wheel Still Spins, A A3
For Friends and Enemies, A A3
The Midgets, A C27

Orphée, Elvira (Argentina)
Angel's Last Conquest (excerpt from the novel), A P7
The Beguiling Ladies, A A1.5
Do Not Mistake Eternities, A C10
El Angel's Last Conquest, N O2
An Eternal Fear, A A3
How the Little Crocodiles Cry, A A3
I Will Return, Mommy, A A3
The Journey of Amatista and the Dirty Prince, A C11
Silence, A C10
The Silken Whale, A P7
Voices That Grew Old, A C10

Ortiz Cofer, Judith (Puerto Rico)
Abuela Invents the Zero, A O7
Advanced Biology, A O7.1
American History, A A16, A P10, A O7.1
Arturo's Flight, A O7
Bad Influence, A O7
Beauty Lessons, A O7
The Black Virgin, A F7, A G9, A O5, A O7.3
By Love Betrayed, A O7.1

The Paterson Public Library, A O7.1
Primary Lessons, A O7.2, A O7.3
Quinceañera, A O7.3
Riding Low on the Streets of Gold: Latino Literature for Young Adults, A O7.2
Silent Dancing, A A17, A D6, A K4.1, A N3, A O7.3
Silent Dancing (excerpts), A K2, A M12
Silent Dancing: A Partial Remembrance of a Puerto Rican Childhood, A O7.3,
    AB O3
Sleeping with One Eye Open: Women Writers and the Art of Survival, A O7.3,
    AB K1
Some of the Characters A O7.3
The Story of My Body, A O7.1
Tales Told under the Mango Tree, A C28, A K3, A O7.3
Talking to the Dead A O7.3
Ten Hispanic Authors, AB H2
Twist and Shout, A O7.1
Vida, A O7.4, A T2
Volar, A K9, A O7.2, A O7.4
White Balloons, A O7
The Witch's Husband, A G9, A O7.1
Woman in Front of the Sun: On Becoming a Writer, AB O3.1
The Year of Our Revolution, AB O3.2
The Year of Our Revolution: New and Selected Stories and Poems, A O7.4

Ortiz Salas, Mónica (Ecuador)
Mery Yagual (Secretary), A B8

Osorio, Elsa (Argentina)
My Name Is Light, N O4

Pacheco, Cristina (Mexico)
Noodle Soup, A A2, A O6

Pagano, Mabel (Argentina)
A Death in June, A C11

Palacios, Antonia (Venezuela)
A Gentleman on the Train, A C27, A G9.1

Pallotini, Renata (Brazil)
Woman Sitting on the Sand, A F3

Pantoja, Antonia (Puerto Rico)
Memoir of a Visionary: Antonia Pantoja, AB P1

Partnoy, Alicia (Argentina)
Around the Table, A P2
A Beauty Treatment, A P2
Benja's First Night, A P2
Birthday, A P2
Bread, A P2
A Conversation under the Rain, A P2
The Denim Jacket, A P2
Form of Address, A P2
Graciela, A P2
Latrine, A P2
The Little School: Tales of Disappearance and Survival in Argentina, A P2
My Names, A P2
My Nose, A P2
Nativity, A P2
On Being Shorter: How Our Testimonial Texts Defy the Academy, AB 22
The One-flower Slippers, A P2, A V5
Poetry, A P2
A Puzzle, A P2
Rain, A D13
Religion, A P2
Ruth v. the Torturer, A D13
Ruth's Father, A P2
The Small Box of Matches, A P2
Telepathy, A P2
Toothbrush, A P2
You Can't Drown the Fire: Latin American Women Writing in Exile, A P2.1

Partnoy, Raquel (Argentina)
Silent Witness, A B22

Paz, Blanca Elena (Bolivia)
The Light, A B8, A R5
Three Rains, A R5
Sacraments by the Hour, A S5.1
Symmetry, A R5

Peralta, Bertalicia (Panama)
Elio, A J4
The Guayacán Tree, A P3

A March Guayacán, A P4, A S5, A Y5
The Village Virgin, A J5

Pereira, Teresinka (Brazil)
Help, I'm Drowning, A P5
Little Man, A P5
Solitude, A P5
The Train and the Flowers, A P5

Pérez, Loida Maritza (Dominican Republic)
Geographies of Home, N P1
Geographies of Home (excerpt), A B13

Peri Rossi, Cristina (Uruguay)
The Acrobats, A P6.2
Airports, A P6.1
The Annunciation, A A3, A P9
The Art of Loss, A P6, A R17
As I was walking along, A P6.2
At the corner bar, A P6.2
At the Hairdresser, A P6.1
Atlas, A P6
The Avenues of Language, A P6.1
The Bathers, A P6.1
The Bell Ringer, A P6
Besieged, A P6.2
Between a Rock and a Hard Place, A P6.1
Breaking the Speed Record, A C27
The Bridge, A P6
Ca Foscar, A F3
Casting Daisies to the Swine, A P6.1
The Cavalcade, A A1.1
The City, A P6.1
The Crack, A P6.1
Deaf as a Doorknob, A P6.1
Desertion, A P6.2
Dialogue with the Writer, A P6.2
Disobedience and the Bear Hunt, A P6.2
Dostoevsky's Last Night, N P2
The Effect of Light on Fish, A P6.1
The Fallen Angel, A P6
The Fencesitters Society, A A1.1
Final Judgement, A H7, A P6

You are very beautiful, A P6.2

Perrera, Hilda (Cuba)
Paco, A H10

Petit, Magdalena (Chile)
La quintrala, N P3

Pinto, Julieta (Costa Rica)
The Blue Fish, A R4
The Country Schoolmaster, A J4
Disobedience, A J5
The Meeting, A J4

Piñón, Nélida (Brazil)
Adamastor, A I1, A M15
Big-bellied Cow, A C27, A J1, A S7.2
Bird of Paradise, A A14, A P7
Brief Flower, A C19, A J1
Caetana's Sweet Song, N P4
Fourteen Female Voices from Brazil: Interviews and Works, AB S6
The Heat of Things, A R17
House of Passion, A F10, A R13
I Love My Husband, A A1.5, A C10, A E3, A S21
Near East, A S1
The New Kingdom, A P7
Procession of Love, A H13
The Republic of Dreams: A Novel, N P4.1
The Shadow of the Prey, A V2.1
The Warmth of Things, A G10, A M12.1

Pizarnik, Alejandra (Argentina)
Alejandra Pizarnik: A Profile, A G12
Blood Bath (excerpt from *The Bloody Countess*), A G12
Blood Baths, A A3
The Bloody Countess, A B3, A F3, A M8.6, A M8.7
Desire of the Word, A G12
A Dream Where Silence Is Made of Gold, A G12
The End (excerpt from *Texts of Shadow and Last Poems),* A G12
Extraction of the Stone of Folly, A G12
Fragments for Dominating Silence, A G12
Fundamental Stone, A G12
House of Favors (excerpt from *Texts of Shadow and Last Poems*), A G12

The Iron Virgin (excerpt from *The Bloody Countess*), A G12
The Lady Buccaneer of Pernambuco or Hilda the Polygraph (excerpt from *Texts of Shadow and Last Poems)*, A F3, A G12
L'obscurité des eaux, A G12
The Mirror of Melancholy, A A3, A G12
The Mirror of Melancholy (excerpt from *The Bloody Countess*), a G12
The Musical Hell (excerpts), A G12
A Mystical Betrayal (excerpt from *Texts of Shadow and Last Poems),* A G12
Names and Figures, A G12
Night Shared in the Memory of an Escape, A G12
Nocturnal Singer, A G12
On Time and Not (excerpt from *Texts of Shadow and Last Poems*), A G12
Portrait of Voices (excerpt from *Texts of Shadow and Last Poems),* A G12
The Possessed among Lilacs, A G12
Roads of the Mirror, A G12
Severe Measures, A A3
Severe Measures (excerpt from *The Bloody Countess*), A G12
Small Poems in Prose (excerpt from *Texts of Shadow and Last Poems*), A G12
Sorceries, A G12
Tangible Absence (excerpt from *Texts of Shadow and Last Poems*), A G12
The Understanding (excerpt from *Texts of Shadow and Last Poems)*, A G12
The Word that Cures, A G12
Words, A F3, A O6
Words (excerpt from *Texts of Shadow and Last Poems*), A G12

Pizarro, Ana (Chile)
The Journey, A A1.8
The Moon, the Wind, the Year, the Day (excerpt), A A1.1, A A1.6

Pla, Josefina (Paraguay)
To Seize the Earth, A C27

Plager, Silvia (Argentina)
A Change of Heart, A C11
Empty Shell, A G3
No One Will Take Her Place, A G3

Poletti, Syria (Argentina)
The Final Sin, A L6
The King Who Forbade Balloons, N P5

Pollarolo, Giovanna (Peru)
The Grocer's Dream, A B1

Ponce, Mary Helen (Puerto Rico)
Blizzard!!!, A P10
La Doctora Barr, A V6
Recuerdo: How I Changed the War and Won the Game, A V6
Recuerdo: Los Piojos, A V6

Poniatowska, Elena (Mexico)
Compañeras de Mexico: Women Photograph Women, AB P3
Dear Diego, N P6
Don't Go Away, I'm Going to Bring You Something, A C9
El niño: Children of the Streets, Mexico City, AB P5
Frida Kahlo: The Camera Seduced, AB A1
The Gift, A J7
Happiness, A F3, A G9.1, A O6
Here's to You, Jesusa!, N P6.1
Here's to You, Jesusa! (introduction), A G2
Little House of Celluloid, A B18
Love Story, A A14, A H13, A P6.1
A Massacre in Mexico, A B22
Massacre in Mexico, N P6.2
The Message, A A1.5
Mexican Color, AB P4
The Night Visitor, A M8.6
Nothing, Nobody: The Voices of the Mexico City Earthquake, N P6.3
Park Cinema, A C27, A M8.4, A M12.1
The Rupture, A P9
The Skin of the Sky, N P6.4
Slide In, My Dark One, between the Crosstie and the Whistle, A E3
Soldaderas: Women of the Mexican Revolution, AB P3.1
State of Siege, A A2
Tinísima (excerpt), A B13
Tinismia: A Novel, N P6.5
Until We Meet Again, N P6.6

Ponte Landa, Miguelina (Cuba)
Blind Madness, A R10
Portela, Ena Lucía (Cuba)
At the Back of the Cemetery, A B9
The Urn and the Name (A Lighthearted Tale), A Y2

Porzecanski, Teresa (Uruguay)
Dying of Love, A K2.1
Parricide, A K2

Rojl Eisips, A A1.4
A Story in Episodes, A A1.7
The Story of a Cat, A C27
Sun Inventions and Perfumes of Carthage: Two Novellas, N P7

Posadas, Carmen (Uruguay)
The Nubian Lover, A C25.1

Puga, María Luisa (Mexico)
The Guests, A D4
Lucrecia, A D4
Memories on the Oblique, A R17
The Natural Thing to Do, A G5
Naturally, A F10
One, A D4
The Trip, A B18 , A C2.1
Young Mother, A A2

Puig Zaldívar, Raquel (Cuba)
Nothing in Our Hands but Age, N P8
Women Don't Need to Write, N P8.1

Quevedo, Violeta (Chile)
The Pilgrim's Angel, A A1.8

Quiroga, María Soledad (Bolivia)
The Tree That Produces Cups of Tea, A A1.1

Remba Nurko, Natania (Cuba)
My Cuban Story, A A1.7

Rendic, Amalia (Chile)
A Child, a Dog, the Night, A A 1.5, A A1.8, A O6

Restrepo, Laura (Colombia)
The Angel of Galilea, N R1
The Dark Bride, N R1.1
Delirium, N R1.2
Isle of Passion, N R1.3
Leopard in the Sun, N R1.4
Leopard in the Sun (excerpt), A B13
Scent of Invisible Roses, A C25.1
A Tale of the Dispossessed, N R1.5

Reyes, Sandra (Bolivia)
Oblivion and Stone: A Selection of Contemporary Bolivian Poetry and Fiction, A R5
One More Stripe to the Tiger: A Selection of Contemporary Chilean Poetry and Fiction, A R5.1

Reyna, Bessy (Cuba/Panama)
And This Blue Surrounding Me Again, A F2, A J4
The Clean Ashtrays, A P3

Rheda, Regina (Brazil)
The Cat Girl, A R6
Dry Spell, A R6
The Enchanted Princess (1997), A R6
First World Third Class (1996), A R6
First World Third Class and Other Tales of the Global Mix, A R6, N R2
The Front (2003), A R6
The Ghost, A R6
Girlfriends, A R6
The Neighbor from Hell, A R6
The Prostitute, A R6
The Sanctuary (2002), A R6
The Voyeuse, A R6
The Woman in White, A R6

Ribeiro, Stella Car (Brazil)
Sambaqui: A Novel of Pre-history, N R3

Riesco, Laura (Peru)
The Headache, A A1.1
Jimena's Fair, A A1.5
The Twins of Olmedo Court, A B8
Ximena at the Crossroads, N R4
Ximena at the Crossroads (excerpt), A O6

Ríos, Mi-Chelle L. (Mexico)
Chola, N R5

Ríos, Soleida (Cuba)
Life, A D5
Untitled, A D5

Rivera, Beatriz (Cuba)
Midnight Sandwiches at the Mariposa Express, N R6
Paloma, A P10.1
Playing with Light: A Novel, N R6.1
Shango's Rest, A F7

Rivera, Martha (Dominican Republic)
I've Forgotten Your Name, N R7

Rivera Marín, Guadalupe (Mexico)
Diego Rivera the Red, AB R2

Rivera Valdés, Sonia (Cuba)
Adela's Beautiful Eyes, A R11
Between Friends, A R11
The Fifth River, A R11
Five Windows on the Same Side, A R11
Little Poisons, A R10, A R11
Lunacy; Catching On, A R11
The Most Forbidden of All, A R11
The Scent of Wild Desire, A R11
A Whiff of Wild Desire, A Y2

Rivero Santa Cruz, Giovanna (Bolivia)
Barking Softly, A R12
The Day of Atonement, A S5.1
Final Countdown, A R12
An Imperfect Day, A R12
In Your Very Footsteps, A R12
Lava, A R12
Like a Vulture, A R12
Little Goddess, A G9
Masters of the Sand, A R12
Mulatta Moon, A R12
Player, A R12
Sangre Dulce/Sweet Blood: Cuentos, A R12
The Smell of Something New, A R12
Sweet Blood, A R12
Tita, A R12
Time to Dance!, A R12
Twin Beds, A R12
Warmi, A G9
Waves of Satin, A R12

The Widow, A R12

Ro, Mirta (Cuba)
Tania, the Unforgettable Guerrilla, AB R4

Robles, Mireya (Cuba)
Hagiography of Narcisa the Beautiful, N R8
In the Other Half of Time, A M16

Rodríguez, Aleida (Cuba)
A Month in a Nutshell, A G7
Sleeping with One Eye Open: Women Writers and the Art of Survival, AB K1

Rodríguez-Cabral, Cristina (Uruguay)
August 25, 1988, A B12, A D5

Roffé, Mercedes (Argentina)
From Morrocco to Buenos Aires, A A1.7

Roffé, Reina (Argentina)
Exotic Birds, A A1.4
Let's Hear What He Has to Say, A L6
Transforming the Desert, A C11

Roffiel, Rosamaría (Mexico)
Amora (excerpt), A F3
Forever Lasts Only a Full Moon, A H7

Rojas, Marta (Cuba)
Dead Man's Cave, N R9
Holy Lust or White Papers (excerpt), A D5
The *Sweet Enigma* of a Writer's Life: A Personal Narrative, A D5
Tania, the Unforgettable Guerrilla, AB R4

Rojas Sucre, Graciela (Panama)
On Account of the Piñata (excerpt from *Terruñadas de lo chico)*, A M18
Wings, A J4

Romo-Carmona, Mariana (Chile)
Contraband, A R15
Cuentos: Stories by Latinas, A G7
Disco Nights, A F8
Dream of Something Lost, A R15

Fear: Cuento de Jalohuín, A R15
Gabriela, A R3
Idilio, A R15
Kissing Susan, A R15
La bruja pirata de Chiloé, A R15
La virgen en el desierto, A G7
Living at Night, N R10
Love Story, A R15
The Meal, A R15
New England Reconsidered, A R15
Orphans, A R15
Speaking Like an Immigrant, A R15
Speaking Like an Immigrant: A Collection, A R15
2280, A R15
The Virgin in the Desert, A R15
The Web, A R15
Welcome to America, A R15

Rosel, Sara (Cuba)
El viaje, A G7

Rossel Huicí, Gladys (Peru)
Light and Shadow, A B8

Ruiz de Burton, María Amparo (Mexico)
Conflicts of Interest: The Letters of María Amparo Ruiz de Burton, AB R6
The Squatter and the Don (excerpt), A A16

Ruiz Rosas, Teresa (Peru)
Santa Catalina, Arequipa, A H13

Rumazo, Lupe (Ecuador)
The March of the Batrachians, A R9

Safranchik, Graciela (Argentina)
Kaddish, A A1.4

Sala, Mariella (Peru)
From Exile, A R17

Sánchez, Magaly (Cuba)
Catalina in the Afternoons, A Y2

Sánchez-Bello, Bertha (Cuba)
Family Portrait: Reflection on Interior Decoration, A H9

Santiago, Esmeralda (Puerto Rico)
Almost a Woman, AB S2
A Baby Doll Like My Cousin Jenny's, A S3
First Born, A S3.1
Las Christmas: Favorite Latino Authors Share Their Holiday Memories, A S3
Las Mamis: Favorite Latino Authors Remember Their Mothers, A S3.1, AB S3
Latina Self-Portraits: Interviews with Contemporary Women Writers. AB H1
Ten Hispanic Authors, AB H2
The Turkish Lover, AB S2.1
When I Was Puerto Rican, AB S2.2

Santos, Beatriz (Uruguay)
Chulin's Fantasy, A D5
Tía Coca, A D5

Santos-Febres, Mayra (Dominican Republic)
Abnel, Sweet Nightmare, A S6
Any Wednesday I'm Yours, N S1
Brine Mirror, A S6
Broken Strand, A S6
Dilcia M. Act of Faith, A S6
Flight I, A C25.1
A Little Bit of Bliss, A S3
Marina's Fragrance, A D5, A S6
Mystic Rose, A S6
Night Stand, A S6
A Normal Day in the Life of Couto Seducción, A S6
Oso Blanco, A S6
The Park, A S6
Resins for Aurelia, A S6
Sirena Selena, N S1.1
Stained Glass Fish, A S6
Tren, A S16
Urban Oracles, A S6
Urban Oracles: Stories, A S6
The Writer, A S6

Santos Silva, Loreina (Puerto Rico)
This Eye That Looks at Me: First Cycle, Memoirs, AB S4

São Paulo Penna e Costa, Marília (Brazil)
The Happiest Couple in the World, A G13

Sapia, Yvonne V. (Puerto Rico)
Sofia, A D6

Saralegui, Cristina (Cuba)
Cristina! My Life as a Blonde, AB S5

Saris, Lake (Chile)
The March, A G7

Schroeder, Agustina (Uruguay)
Mother of Fair, N S2

Seligson, Esther (Mexico)
Annunciation, A A2
Gypsy Curse, A A1.1
The Invisible Hour, A S18.1
Luz de dos, A K2
A Wind of Dry Leaves, A K2

Sepúlveda-Pulvirenti, Emma (Chile)
Amigas: Letters of Friendship and Exile, AB A3
From Border Crossings to Campaign Trail: Chronicle of a Latina in Politics,
    AB S6

Serrano, Marcela (Chile)
Antigua and My Life Before, N S3

Shapiro Rok, Ester Rebeca (Cuba)
Belarus to Bolondro: A Daughter's Dangerous Passage (excerpt), A A1.4

Shua, Ana María (Argentina)
The Ancient God of Fire, A A1.1
Bad Advice, A A1.1
The Book of Memories, N S34
The Book of Memories (excerpt), A A1.4
Cultural Taboo, A A1.1
Day of Final Judgement, A A1.1
Excesses of Passion, A A1.1
Family Chronicle, A D10.1
Farewell, My Love, A H13

Fishing Days (excerpt from *Dream Time*), A A3
Founding Fathers on the Blackboard, A A1.1
A Good Mother, A S18
Man on the Rug, A A1.1
Minor Surgery, A L3
Other/Other (excerpt from *Dream Time*), A A3
Patient, N S4.1
A Profession Like Any Other, A L3
Romance between Guard and Magnolia, A A1.1
Time Travel, A A1.1
The Unsurpassable Art of Wang Fo, A A1.1
The White Guanaco in the Middle of France, A C11
With All That I Am, A A1.7

Silva Ossa, María (Chile)
The Ship from Far Away (El barco de más allá), A R2

Silveira de Queiroz, Dinah (Brazil)
Christ's Memorial, N S5
Guidance, A E1, A G13, A M8.6
Jovita, A S1
Tarciso, H12.1
The Women of Brazil, N 5.1

Simo, Ana María (Cuba)
Aunt Albertina's Last Party, A C7
A Deathly Sameness, A C24
Growth of the Plant, A C24

Solá, Marcela (Argentina)
The Condemned Dress in White, A A3
Happiness, A A3
Invisible Embroidery, A A3

Solari, María Teresa (Peru)
Death and Transfiguration of a Teacher, A C27

Solís, Bernarda (Mexico)
Art and Monsters, A G5

Solís de King, Fabiola (Ecuador)
Before It's Time, A B8

Somers, Armonía (Argentina)
The Burial, A F5, A P7
The Fall, A H13, A M8.4, A M8.6, A S2
The Immigrant, A A7, A E3
Madness, A H12.1
Plunder, A P7
The Teacher, A S2
The Tunnel, A P7
Waiting for Polidoro, A C25

Steimberg, Alicia (Argentina)
Call Me Magdalena, N S6
Cecilia's Last Will and Testament, A A1.5, A S18.1
Fleur-de-Lis, A D10.1
García's Thousandth Day, A A3
Musicians and Watchmakers, N S6.1
Musician and Watchmakers (excerpt), A A1.4, A G3, A K2
Of Musicians and Watchmakers, A G3
The Rainforest, S6.2
Segismundo's Better World, A A3
Viennese Waltz, A A3
Young Amatista, A H13

Stolk, Gloria (Venezuela)
Crickets and Butterflies, A E3

Strauss de Milz, Ivonne (Dominican Republic)
A Tale of Courage and Fortitude, A A1.7

Strejilevich, Nora (Argentina)
A Single, Numberless Death, N S7
A Single, Numberless Death (excerpt), A M4
Too Many Names, A A1.7

Suárez, Karla (Cuba)
Anniversary, A B9
Eye of the Night, A B9
Open Your Eyes and Soar: Cuban Women Writing Now, A B9

Subercaseaux, Elizabeth (Chile)
Because We're Poor, A A1.8
Enedina, A A3
Francisco, A A3

Juana, A A3
Silendra (excerpts), A A3
The Song of the Distant Root, N S8
Tapihue (from *Silendra*), A A3

Swain, Regina (Mexico)
The Devil Also Dances in the Aloha, A J3
Señorita Supermán and the Instant Soup Generation, A J3

Szoka, Elzbieta (Brazil)
Fourteen Female Voices from Brazil: Interviews and Works, A S21

Tamayo, Evora (Cuba)
Sylvia, A C7

Tejeira, Isis (Panama)
The Birth, A J4
The Piano of My Desire, A J4

Toledo, Mirta (Argentina)
The Hunchback, A L3
In Between, A L3

Torres, Anabel (Colombia)
A Small Miracle, A O6

Torres, Lidia (Puerto Rico)
Three Keys, A D2

Torres, Olga Beatriz (Mexico)
Memorias de mi viaje/Recollections of My Trip, AB T2

Traba, Marta (Argentina)
All in a Lifetime, A P7
Conformity, A P7
The Day Flora Died, A P2.1
Mothers and Shadows, N T1
Mothers and Shadows (excerpt from the novel), A P7
The Tale of the Velvet Pillows, A C27

Tula, María Teresa (El Salvador)
Hear My Testimony: Maria Teresa Tula, Human Rights Activist of El Salvador,
    AB T3

Ulla, Noemí (Argentina)
Waking Up Alive, A D10.1

Umpierre, Luz María (Puerto Rico)
La veintiuna, A G7

Urbano, Victoria (Costa Rica)
Avery Island, A N2, A U1
The Creative Philosophy of Carmen Naranjo, A N2
Death in Mallorca, A J4
The Face, A J5
Five Women Writers of Costa Rica: Short Stories, A N2
On High Valley, A N2
Triptych, A N2, A U1

Valdés, Ana (Uruguay)
The Peace of the Dead, A C2

Valdés, Zoe (Cuba)
Dear First Love, N V1
I Gave You All I Had, N V1.1
The Ivory Trader and the Red Melons, A B25, A G2.1
Yocandra in the Paradise of Nada: A Novel of Cuba, N V1.2

Valdés-Rodríguez, Alisa (Cuba)
The Dirty Girls Social Club, N V2

Valdivieso, Mercedes (Chile)
Breakthrough, N V3

Valencia, Tita (Mexico)
Video: Zoom in to Close-up, A M15
Zoom Back: Visions of Taking Flight, A M15

Valenzuela, Luisa (Argentina)
Addendum, A V1.5
All about Suicide, A V1.2, A V1.4
All about Suicide (Pavada de suicidio), A V1
The Alphabet, A V1.1
Argentina, Here Innocence Is Born, A V1.4
The Attainment of Knowledge (Para alcanzar el conocimiento), A V1.2
Avatars, A V1.5
Bedside Manners, N V4

The Best Shod, A V1.2, A V1.4
The Best Shod (Los mejor calzados), A V1
Black Novel (with Argentines), N V4.1
The Blue Water Man, A F5, A P7, A V1.2
The Blue Water Man (El fontanero azul), A V1
Cat's Eye, A V1.2
Cat's Eye (Pantera ocular), A V1
The Celery Munchers, A V1.2, A V1.4
The Censors, A V1
The Censors, A A1.6, A B11, A H11, A M21, A V1.2
The Censors (Los censores), A V1
Change of Guard, A L6
The Charm against Storms, A V1.5
City of the Unknown, A V1.1, A V1.2
Clara, N V4.2
Clara, a Novel, A V1.1
Clara, Thirteen Short Stories and a Novel, N V4.3
Common Transport, A V1.4
Country Carnival, A A3, A V1.2
Country Carnival (Carnival campero), A V1
The Density of Words, A V1.5
Desire Makes the Matter Rise, A V1.5
Dirty Words, A F3, A O6
The Discovery, A V1.4
The Door, A S7, A V1.1, A V1.2
The Door (La puerta), A V1
El Es Di, A V1.4
The Encounter, A V1.4
End of the Millennium, A H1
The Envoy, A V1.5
A Family for Clotilde, A V1.1, A V1.2
Flea Market, A V1.2
Forsaken Woman, A V1.1
4 Prince 4, A V1.5
Fourth Version, A V1.3
The Fucking Game (excerpt from *The Efficacious Cat*), A F3
Generous Impediments Float Down the River, A M15
The Gift of Words, A V1.2, A V1.4
Grimorium, A V1.4
He Who Searches, N V4.4
If This Is Life, I'm Red Riding Hood, A V1.5
I'm Your Horse in the Night, A G4, A H1.1, A P7, A V1.3
The Invisible Mender, A V1.5

Strange Things Happen Here: Twenty-six Short Stories and a Novel, A V1.4, N V4.6
Sursum Corda, A V1.4
Symmetries, A V1.5
Symmetries, A V1.5
Tango, A R17, A V1.4, A V1.5
The Teacher, A S2, A V1.1
Technique, A K8
Three Days, A C2, A V1.5
Transparency, A V1.5
Trial of the Virgin (Proceso a la virgen), A V1, A V1.1, A V1.2
Two Foreign Women, A K8
United Rapes Unlimited, A V1.4
Up among the Eagles, A B4, A C2.1, A C27, A E3, A V1.2
Up among the Eagles (excerpt), A B1
Up among the Eagles (Donde viven las águilas), A V1
The Verb *To Kill*, A B14, A S10, A V1.2, A V1.4
Vision Out of the Corner of One Eye, A T3, A V1.2, A V1.4
Vision Out of the Corner of One Eye (Visión de reojo), A V1
Void and Vacuum, A V1.4
Void and Vacuum (Vacío era el de antes), A V1
Who, Me a Bum?, A H1, A V1.4
The Word "Killer," A V1.3
Writers on Writing: The Best of the Review of Contemporary Fiction, AB 01
You Can't Stop Progress, A V1.5
The Zombies, A V1.4

Valle, Carmen (Puerto Rico)
Diary Entry #1, A V4
Diary Entry #6, A V4

Vallejo, Gaby (Bolivia)
Sabina, A I2
Son of the Murdered Maid, N V5

Van Steen, Edla (Brazil)
Apartment for Rent, A V2
A Bag of Stories, A V2
The Beauty of the Lion, A V2
Before the Dawn, A V2
CAROL head LINA heart, A V2
Carol Head Lina Heart, A J1, A V2.1
A Day in Three Movements, A V2
Early Mourning, N V6

Forever After, A V2
Good Enough to Sing in a Choir, A V2
In Spite of Everything, A V2
Intimacy, A V2
Less than the Dream, A V2.2
Love Stories: A Brazilian Collection, A V2.1
The Misadventures of João, A V2
Mr. and Mrs. Martins, A S10
Nostalgia Row, A V2
Period, A V2
The Pledge, A V2
Queen of the Abyss, A V2.2
The Return, A V2
Scent of Love, A V2.2
Scent of Love (novella), A V2.2
The Sleeping Beauty (Script of a Useless Life), A S1
Village of the Ghost Bells, N V6.1

Varsavsky, Paula (Argentina)
No One Said a Word, N V7

Vásquez, Ana (Chile)
Elegance, A A1.8, A O6
The Sign of the Star, A A1.4

Vásquez, María Esther (Argentina)
Returning by Train with Borges, A C11

Veciana Suárez, Ana (Cuba)
Birthday Parties in Heaven: Thoughts of Love, Life, Grief, and Other Matters of the Heart, AB V2
The Chin Kiss King, N V8

Vega, Ana Lydia (Puerto Rico)
ADJ, Inc, A C19, A E4, A V4
Aerobics for Love, A S3, A V3
Below, A S15
The Blind Buffalo, A F3.1
Caribbean, A C27
Cloud Cover Caribbean, A B21, A M19
Communist, A H5
Consolation Prize, A V3
The Day It All Happened, A S15

Vidal, Virginia (Chile)
Journey of the Watermelon, A A1.8

Vilar, Irene (Puerto Rico)
A Message from God in the Atomic Age: A Memoir, AB V3
The Ladies' Gallery: A Memoir of Family Secrets, AB V3.1

Villegas de Magnón, Leonor (Mexico)
The Rebel, AB L3
The Rebel (excerpt), A A16
The Rebellious Woman (excerpt), A A14

Viramontes, Helena María (Mexico)
Birthday, A V7
The Broken Web, A V6
The Cariboo Café, A C18, A V7
Growing, A O7.2, A V7
Latina Self-Portraits: Interviews with Contemporary Women Writers, AB H3
The Long Reconciliation, A V7
Miss Clairol, A F7
The Moths, A A16, A A17, A C13, A K4, A K4.1, A V7
The Moths and Other Stories, A V7
Neighbors, A C18, A V7
Snapshots, A V7
Tears on My Pillow, A G9
Viteri, Eugenia (Ecuador)
The Ring, A B8

Yáñez, María Flora (Chile)
The Pond, A A1.8

Yáñez, Mirta (Cuba)
Cubana: Contemporary Fiction by Cuban Women, A Y2
Dust to Dust, A Y2
Fifita Calls Us in the Morning, A B9
Go Figure, A P9
Of Natural Causes, A E4
Past Meets Present, Old Tales Out of School, A B9
Public Declaration of Love, A F3.1
Split in Two, A B25
We Blacks All Drink Coffee, A M19

Yánez Cossío, Alicia (Ecuador)
Bruna and Her Sisters in the Sleeping City, N Y1
The IWM 1000, A C27
The Mayor's Wife, A B8
The Potbellied Virgin, N Y1.1
Sabotage, A I1, A M15

Zapata Pérez, Edelma (Colombia)
The Consciousness-raising of an Afro-Indio Mulatto, A D5
Woman Writer in Colombia's Multiethnic Society, A D5

Zavala, Iris (Puerto Rico)
Kiliagonia, A G7

Titles of Work/Authors

This index lists titles of all work contained in this book (anthologies, short stories, novela, novellas, novel excerpts, biographies, autobiographies, and other narrative) followed by the author's or editor's last name and the alpha-numeric code that refers to the type of work and where it can be found in this volume. "A" refers to the Anthologies index where authors and editors are listed alphabetically and where authors whose works are included in those anthologies may also be found. For example, "A A1" is the first entry in the index titled Anthologies, referring to Agosín, Marjorie, the author. "N" indicates the Novel and Novellas in Alphabetical Order by Author index and "AB" indicates the Autobiographies/Biographies and Other Narrative index.

A

A Mulher de Aleduma (excerpt), Aline França, A B24
Abbreviated World, Angelina Muñiz-Huberman, A A2
Abelardo, Pía Barros, A B5
Abnel, Sweet Nightmare, Mayra Santos-Febres, A S6
Above All, a Family Man, Achy Obejas, A O1, A O2
Absences, Aída Bahr, A B9
Abuela Invents the Zero, Judith Ortiz Cofer, A O7
Accelerated Cycle, Luz Orfanoz, A A1.8
Aceite guapo, Rosario Castellanos, A C8
The Acrobats, Cristina Peri Rossi, A P6.2
An Act of Vengeance, Isabel Allende, A C27, A S13
Adamastor, Nélida Piñón, A I1, A M15
Addendum, Luisa Valenzuela, A V1.5
Adela's Beautiful Eyes, Sonia Rivera Valdés, A R11
Adelina, Marjorie Agosín, A M16
ADJ, Inc, Ana Lydia Vega, A C19, A E4, A V4
Advanced Biology, Judith Ortiz Cofer, A O7.1
Adventures of Mariquita Samper, Giannina Braschi, N B8
The Adventures of Mariquita Samper, Giannina Braschi A B20
Aerobics for Love, Ana Lydia Vega, A S4, A V3

African Creation, Aurora Levins Morales, A R19
After Canaries, Martha Cerda, A C12
After Life: An Ethnographic Novel, Tobias Hecht (Bruna Verissimo), AB H2
Afternoon Tea, Marjorie Agosín, A A1
Agda, Hilda Hilst, A J1, A S1, A V2.1
The Agreement, Beatriz Kuramoto, B5
The Agüero Sisters, Cristina García, N G3
The Agüero Sisters (excerpt), Cristina García, A B13
Airports, Cristina Peri Rossi, A P6.1
AKUM: La magia de los sueños/The Magic of Dreams. A Bilingual Novel, Gloria
     Chávez-Vásquez, N C6
Albino Orma, Silvina Ocampo, A B8, A F3
Alcestis, Emilia Macaya, A J4
Alejandra Pizarnik: A Profile, Frank Graziano, A G12
Alfama, Marjorie Agosín, A A1.9
Alfonsina Storni, Gabriela Mistral, A T1
Alfonso Reyes, Gabriela Mistral, A T1
All about Suicide, Luisa Valenzuela, A V1.2, A V1.4
All about Suicide (Pavada de suicidio), Luisa Valenzuela, A V1
All in a Lifetime, Marta Traba, A P7
All Night Movie, Alicia Borinsky, N B6
All the Roses, Julieta Campos, A P7, A C4
Allegories, Julieta Campos, A P9
Allison, Marjorie Agosín, A A1.9
Alma-en-pena, Rima de Vallbona, A V6
Almost a Woman, Esmeralda Santiago, AB S2
Alongside the Track, Sylvia Iparraguierre, A D10.1
The Alpaca, Gabriela Mistral, A A1.2, A T1
The Alphabet, Marjorie Agosín, A A1.9
The Alphabet, Luisa Valenzuela, A V1.1
The Alphabet in My Hands: A Writing Life, Marjorie Agosín, A A1, AB A2
Altar, Kathleen Alcalá, A J6
Always from Somewhere Else (excerpt), Marjorie Agosín, A A1.4
Always from Somewhere Else: A Memoir of My Chilean Jewish Father, Marjorie
     Agosín, AB A2.1
Amalia, Rosario Ferré, A F4.1, A J2, A P9
Amanda's Motives, Martha Cerda, A C12
America and My Mother, Marjorie Agosín, A A1
America Street: A Multi cultural Anthology of Stories, Anne Mazer, A M11
American Chica: Two Worlds, One Childhood, Marie Arana, AB A8
American Fiction: States of the Art, Bradford Morrow and Walter Abish, A M20
American History, Judith Ortiz Cofer, A A16, A P10, A O7.1

The Apple in the Dark, Clarice Lispector, N L3

The Apple in the Dark (excerpt, chapter four, part one), Clarice Lispector, A D11

Appointment in Zinica, Claribel Alegría, A A8.1

Appraisals, Pía Barros, A B5

An Apprenticeship, or, The Book of Delights, Clarice Lispector, N L3.1

The Archipelago (excerpt from *Archipiélago*), Victoria Ocampo, A A12, A C10

The Archipelago: New Writing from and about the Caribbean, Robert Antoni and
    Bradford Morrow, A A12

*Arcoiris de sueños (Retazos de una vida). Rainbow of Dreams (Patchwork of a
    Life)*, Clara Isabel Maldonado, A M5

Argentina, Here Innocence Is Born, Luisa Valenzuela, A V1.4

Arrivals, Marjorie Agosín, A A1

Around the Table, Alicia Partnoy, A P2

Art, Gabriela Mistral, A T1

Art and Monsters, Bernarda Solís, A G5

The Art of Loss, Cristina Peri Rossi, A P6, A R17

*The Art of Peace: Nobel Peace Laureates Discuss Human Rights, Conflict and
    Reconciliation*, José Ramos-Horta, AB R1

The Art of the Story: An International Anthology of Contemporary Short Stories,
    Daniel Halpern, A H1

The Art of the Tale: An International Anthology of Short Stories 1945-1985, Daniel
    Halpern, A H1.1

Arthur Smith Finds Salvation, Rosario Castellanos, A C8

The Artist (Inéz), Nicholasa Mohr, A M17.3

Arturo's Flight, Judith Ortiz Cofer, A O7

As I was walking along, Cristina Peri Rossi, A P6.2

Ashes of Izalco, Claribel Alegría and Darwin J. Flakoll, N A5

Ask the Good Lord, Marilyn Bobes, A B25

Assault on Paradise, Tatiana Lobo, N L4

Assault on Time, Giannina Braschi, A B20

Asthmatic, Helena Araujo, A C27

The Astonishing Story of the Saint of Cabora, Brianda Domecq, N D9

At Face Value: Autobiographical Writing in Spanish America, Sylvia Molloy,
    AB M8

At First, Marjorie Agosín, A A1

At the Back of the Cemetery, Ena Lucía Portela, A B9

At the Baptismal Font, Martha Cerda, A C12

At the Bottom: A Woman's Life in Central America, Luisa González, AB G5

At the Bottom of a Little Box, Ana María Machado, A M1

At the Corner Bar, Cristina Peri Rossi, A P6.2

At the Hairdresser, Cristina Peri Rossi, A P6.1

Atlas, Cristina Peri Rossi, A P6

The Atonement, Silvina Ocampo, A B17

The Attainment of Knowledge, Luisa Valenzuela, A V1.2
The Attainment of Knowledge (Para alcanzar el conocimiento), Luisa Valenzuela,
A V1
Attributed City, Nancy Morejón, A G2.1
August 25, 1988, Cristina Rodríguez-Cabral, A B12, A D5
Aunt Albertina's Last Party, Ana María Simo, A C7
Aunt Clemencia Ortega, Ángeles Mastretta, A D4
Aunt Concha Esparza, Ángeles Mastretta, A C25.1
Aunt Elena, Ángeles Mastretta, A M10
Aunt Elsa and Cuis, Claribel Alegría, A A.8.1
Aunt Elvira, Ángeles Mastretta, A P9
Aunt Filiberta and Her Cretonnes, Claribel Alegría, A A8.1
Aunt Leonor, Ángeles Mastretta, A G2
Aunt Lucha, Marjorie Agosín, A A1
Aunt Luisita, Barbara Jacobs, A P9
Aunt Mariana, Ángeles Mastretta, A H13
Aunt Natalia, Ángeles Mastretta, A G2
Aunt Rosana's Rocker (Zoraida), Nicholasa Mohr, A K4.1, A M17.3
Aunt Zézé's Tears, Emilia Moncorva Bandeira de Mello (pseud. Carmen Dolores),
A G6, A J1
Aurora, Giancarla de Quiroga, N D4
Ausencia's Tale (excerpt), María Luisa Mendoza, A F3, A G9.1
The Autobiography of Irene, Silvina Ocampo, A O3
Autumn, Marjorie Agosín, A A1
Autumn, Silvia Molina, A R17
Autumn and Lovers, Marjorie Agosín, A A1
Autumn Memories: My New Mexican Roots and Traditions, Marie Oralia Durán
Trujillo, AB D7
Avatars, Luisa Valenzuela, A V1.5
The Avenues of Language, Cristina Peri Rossi, A P6.1
Avery Island, Victoria Urbano, A N2, A U1
An Avid One in Extremis, Hilda Hilst, A A1.5
The Awakening, Claribel Alegría, A R17
An Awakening...Summer 1956, Nicholasa Mohr, A V6
Azabache, Silvina Ocampo, A O3

B

A Baby Doll Like My Cousin Jenny's, Esmeralda Santiago, A S3
The Baby's Afternoon, Pía Barros, A B5
Back to School, Marjorie Agosín, A A1
The Backrooms, Marjorie Agosín, A A1
Bad Advice, Ana María Shua, A A1.1
Bad Communist, Rosario Morales, A L4

Bad Influence, Judith Ortiz Cofer, A O7
A Bag of Stories, Edla Van Steen, A V2
The Balcony, Marjorie Agosín, A A1
A Ballet for Girls, Cecilia Absatz, A L6
Ballet Dancers, Cecilia Absatz, A G3
Balún Canán, Rosario Castellanos, A A2
Balzac, Brianda Domecq, A D4
Bananas and Men (1931), Carmen Lyra, A H8
The Baptism, Julieta Campos, A C4
Baptisms, Marjorie Agosín, A A1
Barking Softly, Giovanna Rivero Santa Cruz, A R12
Barrio Boy: With Related Readings, Ernesto Galarza, A G1
Barrios and Borderlands: Cultures of Latinos and Latinas in the United States,
	Denis Lynn Daly Heyck, A D1
Baseball Dreams, Ana Menéndez, A M13
A Basket of Books, Marjorie Agosín, A A1
A Basket of Love, Marjorie Agosín, A A1
Basket of Water (excerpt from *Dreaming in Cuban*), Cristina García, A G9
The Bathers, Cristina Peri Rossi, A P6.1
The Battle of the Virgins, Rosario Ferré, A C9
Bay of All Saints and Every Conceivable Sin, Ana Miranda N M6
The Basement, Silvina Ocampo, A C10, A O3
The Beacon Best of 2000: Creative Writing by Women and Men of All Colors and
	Cultures, Edwidge Danticat, A D2
Beauty and the Beast, or, The Wound Too Great, Clarice Lispector, A J1, A R17
The Beauty of the Lion, Edla Van Steen, A V2
Beauty Lessons, Judith Ortiz Cofer, A O7
A Beauty Treatment, Alicia Partnoy, A P2
Because We're Poor, Elizabeth Subercaseaux, A A1.8
The Bed, Silvina Ocampo, A O3
Beds, Marjorie Agosín, A A1.3
Bedside Manners, Luisa Valenzuela, N V4
Bedside Story, Marta Lynch, A L6
Before It's Time, Fabiola Solís de King, A B8
Before the Dawn, Edla Van Steen, A V2
Before the Trojan War, Elena Garro, A C10
Before We Were Free, Julia Álvarez, N A7
The Beggar Woman, Marjorie Agosín, A A1
Beginnings of a Fortune, Clarice Lispector, A A14, A L7
The Beguiling Ladies, Elvira Orphée, A A1.5
Behind Bars, Amparo Dávila, A M15
Being Jewish, Marjorie Agosín, A A1

Birthday, Alicia Partnoy, A P2
Birthday, Helena María Viramontes, A V7
Birthday Parties in Heaven: Thoughts of Love, Life, Grief, and Other Matters of the Heart, Ana Veciana Suárez, AB V2
Bishop Berkeley or Mariana of the Universe, Liliana Heker, A C27, A H4
A Bit of Luck, Marjorie Agosín, A A1
The Bitches Colloquy, Rosario Ferré, A R19
Bitter Grounds, Sandra Benítez, N B2
Black Bird, Marta Brunet, A S12
The Black Glove, Juana Manuela Gorriti, A G11, A M9
Black Novel (with Argentines), Luisa Valenzuela, N V4.1
The Black Sheep, Margarita Aguirre, A R17
The Black Virgin, Judith Ortiz Cofer, A F7, A G9, A O5, A O7.3
Black Waltz, Patricia Melo, N M4
Black Water: Anthology of Fantastic Literature, Alberto Manguel, A M8
Black Water 2: More Tales of the Fantastic, Alberto Manguel, A M8.1
Blame It on Hormones, Martha Cerda, A C12
Blame the Tlaxcaltecs, Elena Garro, A C27
Blessed Divination, Nicholasa Mohr, A M17.1
Blessed Reality, Laura Esquivel, A C25.1
Blind Alley, Marilú Mallet, A M6
The Blind Buffalo, Ana Lydia Vega, A F3.1
Blind Madness, Miguelina Ponte Landa, A R10
Blizzard!!!, Mary Helen Ponce, A P10
Blood, Marjorie Agosín, A A1.3
Blood Bath (excerpts from *The Bloody Countess*), Alejandra Pizarnik, A G12
Blood Baths, Alejandra Pizarnik, A A3
The Blood of Conquistadores, Julia Álvarez, A C25.1
The Bloody Countess, Alejandra Pizarnik, A B3, A F3, A M8.6, A M8.7
The Book of Lamentations, Rosario Castellanos, N C4
Blow Up, Giannina Braschi, A S16
The Blue Fish, Julieta Pinto, A R4
The Blue Handkerchief, María del Carmen Garcés, A B8
Blue in the Family, Martha Cerda, A C12
Blue Lagoon, Alina Diaconú, A C11
The Blue Stone Emperor's Thirty Wives, Sara Gallardo, A A3
The Blue Teacups, Marjorie Agosín, A P2.1
The Blue Theatre, Claribel Alegría, A A8.1
The Blue Uniform, Marjorie Agosín, A A1
The Blue Water Man, Luisa Valenzuela, A F5, A P7, A V1.2
The Blue Water Man (El fontanero azul), Luisa Valenzuela, A V1
Boardinghouse, Claribel Alegría, A S5
The Body, Clarice Lispector, A G4, A J1, A L7.2

The Body, Gabriela Mistral, A A1.2
Boffil and Rivas de Santillana, Rosario Ferré, A A12
Bolivian Studies Journal: Issue Dedicated to Alcides Arguedas, Nelly S. González, A G8
The Bone Spoon, Luz Larraín, A A1.8
Bonfires, Marjorie Agosín, A A1, A A1.9
Book of Clowns and Buffoons, Giannina Braschi, A B20
A Book of Faces, Marjorie Agosín, A A1
The Book of Fantasy, Silvina Ocampo, A B17
The Book of God, Marjorie Agosín, A A1
The Book of Lamentations (exerpt), Rosario Castellanos, A G2
The Book of Memories, Ana María Shua, N S4
The Book of Memories (excerpt), Ana María Shua, A A1.4
Books, Marjorie Agosín, A A1
Bordering Fires: The Vintage Book of Contemporary Mexican and Chicana and Chicano Literature, Cristina García, A G2
Boricuas: Influential Puerto Rican Writings: An Anthology, Roberto Santiago, A S4
Borrowed Furniture, Marjorie Agosín, A A1
The Borzoi Anthology of Latin American Literature. Vol. 1 & 2, A R13
The Bottle, Marjorie Agosín, A A1.9
Bottles, Alcina Lubitch Domecq, A M12.1, A P9, A S18.1, A S20
Bougainvillaea Insomnia, Marjorie Agosín, A A1.9
The Boy, Luisa Mercedes Levinson, A L5
The Boy Swept Away in a Tree, Jacqueline Balcells, A B2
The Boy Who Saw God's Tears, Luisa Mercedes Levinson, A A3
The Boy Who Took Off in a Tree, Jacqueline Balcells, A A1.8
Braids, Marjorie Agosín, A A1.3
Braids, María Luisa Bombal, A A14, A B16
Brazilian Tales, Isaac Goldberg, A G6
Bread, Marjorie Agosín, A A1
Bread, Gabriela Mistral, A A1.2, A T1
Bread, Alicia Partnoy, A P2
The Breaking of the Bread, Clarice Lispector, A J1
Breaking Free: Women of Spirit at Midlife and Beyond, Marilyn Sewell, A S9
Breaking the Speed Record, Cristina Peri Rossi, A C27
Breakthrough, Mercedes Valdivieso, N V3
Brer Rabbit, Businessman, Carmen Lyra, A D7
The Bridge, Silvina Bullrich, A F9
The Bridge, Cristina Peri Rossi, A P6
Bridges: Literature across Cultures, Gilbreth Muller and John A. Williams, A M21
Bridges to Cuba. Puentes a Cuba, Ruth Behar, A B6
Brief Flower, Nélida Piñón, A C19, A J1

Brief Miracle (Virginia), Nicholasa Mohr, A M17.3
Brief World, Angelina Muñiz-Huberman, A M22
Brine Mirror, Mayra Santos-Febres, A S6
Broken Strand, Mayra Santos-Febres, A S6
A Broken Vase (Un búcaro roto), Gloria Chávez-Vásquez, A C15
The Broken Web, Helena María Viramontes, A V6
The Brothers, Inés Arredondo, A A15
Bruna and Her Sisters in the Sleeping City, Alicia Yánez Cossío, N Y1
Bubbeh, Sabina Bermin, N B3
The Buffalo, Clarice Lispector, A J1, A L7
The Building of the Waves of the Sea, Giannina Braschi, A B20
The Burden of Routine, Rima de Vallbona, A D8
The Burial, Armonía Somers, A F5, A P7
The Burial of Marisol, Hilma Contreras, A C26
The Buried Giant, Jacqueline Balcells, A B2
The Burning of Judas, Marjorie Agosín, A A1
Bus Stop # 46, María Eugenia Lorenzini, A L3
But It's Going to Rain, Clarice Lispector, A L7.2
But What If I Liked the Panchos, Not the Beatles, Magolo Cárdenas, A L9
Butterfly Man, Elena Aldunate, A A1.8
Buttons, Claudia Adriázola, A S5.1
By Love Betrayed, Judith Ortiz Cofer, A O7.1

C

Ca Foscar, Cristina Peri Rossi, A F3
The Cabalist, Angelina Muñiz-Huberman, A S11
Caetana's Sweet Song, Nélida Piñón, N P4
A Cafecito Story, Julia Álvarez, N A7.1
Cage Number One, Dora Alonso, A A1.5, A O6
Calama, Marjorie Agosín, A A1
California, Aurora Levins Morales, A L4
Call Me Magdalena, Alicia Steimberg, N S6
Call Me María: A Novel, Judith Ortiz Cofer, N O3
Callaloo: A Journal of African-American and African Arts and Letters, Charles H.
    Rowell, A R19
*Calyx: A Journal of Art and Literature by Women. Bearing Witness/Sobreviviendo,
    An Anthology of Native American/Latina Art and Literature*, Jo Cochar, A C22
Camera Obscura, Angélica Gorodischer, A A1.4, A R17
Captain Candelario's Heroic Last Stand, Rosario Ferré, A F4
Captain of the Sleepers, Mayra Montero, N M10
Caribbean, Ana Lydia Vega, A C27
Caribbean Siren, Fanny Buitrago, A B21
The Cariboo Café, Helena María Viramontes, A C18, A V7

The Cemetery, Marjorie Agosín, A B9
The Censors, Luisa Valenzuela, A V1
The Censors, Luisa Valenzuela, A A1.6, A B11, A H11, A M21, A V1, A V1.2
The Censors (Los censores), Luisa Valenzuela, A V1
A Century of Cuban Writers in Florida: Selected Prose and Poetry, Carolina
    Hospital, A H10
Century Plant, Rosario Morales, A L4
Certificate of Absence, Sylvia Molloy, N M8
Certificate of Absence (excerpt), Sylvia Molloy, A H7
Change of Guard, Luisa Valenzuela, A L6
A Change of Heart, Silvia Plager, A C11
The Charm against Storms, Luisa Valenzuela, A V1.5
Chepi, Marjorie Agosín, A A1
Chepita, Marjorie Agosín, A A1.9
The Chicken, Clarice Lispector, A J1, A K2, A L7
Chicago Noir, Neal Pollack, A P11
A Child, a Dog, the Night, Amalia Rendic, A A1.5, A A1.8, A O6
Child of the Americas, Aurora Levins Morales, A S18.2
Child of the Dark (excerpt), Carolina María de Jesús, A A14
Child of the Dark: The Diary of Carolina María de Jesús, Carolina María de Jesús,
    AB D3
The Child That Never Was, María Virginia Estenssoro, A C27
A Child's Christmas in Puerto Rico, Aurora Levins Morales, A T8
Chile, Gabriela Mistral, A T1
Chile: A Traveler's Literary Companion, Katherine Silver, A S12
Childhood, María Carolina de Jesús, A G7
Childhood Copybooks (excerpt from *Cuadernos de infancia*), Norah Lange, A C10
The Childhood Memories of Carolina María de Jesus, Robert M. Levine, AB L1
Children's Hair, Gabriela Mistral, A T1
The Chin Kiss King, Ana Veciana-Suárez, N V8
Chocolates, Marjorie Agosín, A A1.9
Chola, Mi-Chelle L. Ríos, N R5
Christmas Eve at the Pacific, Marjorie Agosín, A A1
A Christmas Like No Other, Gioconda Belli, A S3
Christmas Was a Time of Plenty, Nicholasa Mohr, A T2
Christ's Memorial, Dinah Silveira de Queiroz, N S5
The Chrysalis of Clay Will Give Birth to a Butterfly, Angelina Muñiz-Huberman,
    A M22
Chubby-Cheeked Jelly Donut, Ana María Machado, A M1
Chulin's Fantasy, Beatriz Santos, A D5
The Chumico Tree, Rima de Vallbona, A R4, A U1
Cipitio, Claribel Alegría, A A8.1
Circa 2000: Lesbian Fiction at the Millennium, Terry Wolverton and Robert Drake

A W2

Circle of Love over Death: The Story of the Mothers of the Plaza de Mayo, Matilde Mellibovsky, AB M4

Cities of Gold, Kathleen Alcalá, A L8

The City, Julieta Campos, A C4

The City, Cristina Peri Rossi, A P6.1

City of the Beasts, Isabel Allende, N A6.2

City of Children, Martha Cerda, A C12

City of Kings, Rosario Castellanos, A C8

The City of Strangers, Marjorie Agosín, A A1

City of the Unknown, Luisa Valenzuela, A V1.1, A V1.2

Clamor of Innocence: Central American Short Stories, Barbara Paschke, A P3

Cláper, Alicia Freilich de Segal, N F4

Cláper (excerpt), Alicia Freilich de Segal, A A1.4

Clara, Luisa Valenzuela, N V4.2

Clara, a Novel, Luisa Valenzuela, A V1.1

Clara, Thirteen Short Stories and a Novel, Luisa Valenzuela, A V1.1, N V4.3

Clarisa, Isabel Allende, A A9, A S17

Clark Central High, Marjorie Agosín, A A1

Claudina, Marjorie Agosín, A A1

The Clean Ashtrays, Bessy Reyna, A P3

Cleaning the Closet, Margarita Aguirre, A A1.8

The Clearing, Luisa Mercedes Levinson, A G10, A L6, A Y5

Cleopatra Dismounts, Carmen Boullosa, N B7

A Clinical Case, Guadalupe Dueñas, A C30

The Clock House, Silvina Ocampo, A O3

Closing the Circle That Began in Africa, Shirley Campbell, A D5

Cloud Cover Caribbean, Ana Lydia Vega, A B21, A M19

Coati 1950, Velia Calvimontes, A L3

Coatlicue Swept, Margo Glantz, A A2

Cobweb of Moons, Luisa Mercedes Levinson, A L5

The Coconut Palms, Gabriela Mistral, A A1.2

Cocuyo Flower, Magali García Ramis, A E4

Colita, Aída Cartagena Portalatín, A L9

The Color Black, Marjorie Agosín, A A1.9

Coming of the Eagle, Rosario Castellanos, A C8

Coming Out with a Sunday Seven, Carmen Lyra, A H8

Coming to Terms, Nicholasa Mohr, A M17.2

Commentary on Poems by Rabindranath Tagore, Gabriela Mistral, A T1

Common Stories, Chely Lima, A S15

Common Transport, Luisa Valenzuela, A V1.4

Communist, Ana Lydia Vega, A H5

The Companions, Lygia Bojunga Nunes, A B15, N N2

The Day of the Cross, Claribel Alegría, A A8.1
Day Off, Marjorie Agosín, A A1
The Day to Say "No!" Lygia Fagundes Telles, A S21
The Day We Were Dogs, Elena Garro, A I1, A M15
The Daydreams of a Drunk Woman, Clarice Lispector, A K2.1, A L7
The Days and Hours, Pilar Dughi, A B8
Days of Awe, Achy Obejas, N O1
The Dead, Marjorie Agosín, A A1.3
Dead Languages, Marjorie Agosín, A A1
The Dead Leaves, Barbara Jacobs, N J1
The Dead Man in the Sea at Urea, Clarice Lispector, A L7.2
Dead Man's Cave, Marta Rojas, N R9
The Deadman's Fiancee, Juana Manuela Gorriti, A G11, A M9
The Deaf, Marjorie Agosín, A A1
Deaf as a Doorknob, Cristina Peri Rossi, A P6.1
The Deaf Mutes of Ca'n Blau, Claribel Alegría, A A8.1
Dear Diego, Elena Poniatowska, N P6
Dear Editor, Lygia Fagundes Telles, A F1
Dear First Love, Zoe Valdés, N V1
Dear Joaquín, Judith Ortiz Cofer, A O7.1
Death, Marjorie Agosín, A A1
Death and Transfiguration of a Teacher, María Teresa Solari, A C27
Death in the Desert, Marjorie Agosín, A A1, A B22
A Death in June, Mabel Pagano, A C11
Death in Mallorca, Victoria Urbano, A J4
Death Lies on the Cots, Rosa María Britton, A P9
The Death of Fausto, Carolina Andrade, A R9
Death of Somoza, Claribel Alegría and Darwin Flakoll, AB A5
Death of the Tiger, Rosario Castellanos, A C8, A G4, A M8.6
Death Sounds, Marjorie Agosín, A A1.9
Death's Pure Fire, Ana Lydia Vega, A R17
A Deathly Sameness, Ana María Simo, A C24
Decade II: An Anniversary Anthology, Julián Olivares and Evangelina Vigil-Piñón,
    A O5
Decalogue of the Artist, Gabriela Mistral, A T1
Decision, Sonia Utrera Bravo, A B9
Deep Purple: A Novel, Mayra Montero, N M10.2
Delfina, Marjorie Agosín, A A1
Delfina Cuero: Her Autobiography, an Account of Her Last Years, and Her
    Ethnobotanic Contributions, Delfina Cuero and Florence Connolly Shipek,
    AB C6
Delirium, Laura Restrepo, N R1.2
Deliverance from Evil, Ana Lydia Vega, A V3

The Divorce, Silvina Bullrich, A M15
Do Not Mistake Eternities, Elvira Orphée, A C10
A Dog, a Boy and the Night, Amalia Rendic, A A1.8
The Doll, Silvina Ocampo, A O3
Dolores/Dolores, Cecilia Absatz, A S8
Don José of La Mancha, Judith Ortiz Cofer, A O7
Don Pascual Was Buried Alone, Concepción T. Alzola, A S7.1
Donna Summer, Aída Cartagena Portalatín, A E3
Don't Go Away, I'm Going to Bring You Something, Elena Poniatowska, A C9
Don't Look Back, Himilce Novas, N N1
Doña Ana, Rosario Aguilar, A A5
Doña Beatriz, Rosario Aguilar, A A5
Doña Carmelita, Aurora Levins Morales, A L4
Doña Isabel, Rosario Aguilar, A A5
Doña Leonor, Rosario Aguilar, A A5
Doña Luisa, Rosario Aguilar, A A5
Doña María, Rosario Aguilar, A A5
The Door, Luisa Valenzuela, A S7, A V1.1, A V1.2
The Door (La puerta), Luisa Valenzuela, A V1
Dora, Doralina, Rachel de Queiroz, N D3
Dorceli, Tania Jamardo Faillace, A S1
Dostoevsky's Last Night, Cristina Peri Rossi, N P2
Double Allegiance, Rosario Morales, A L4
Down River, Marta Brunet, A A1.8
Down the Tropical Path, Albalucía Angel, A R17
A Drama in the Countryside, Carmen Dolores, A S1
The Drawing Lesson, Silvina Ocampo, A D10
A Dream Compels Us: Voices of Salvadoran Women, New Americas Press, AB N1
The Dream Curtain, Angelina Muñiz-Huberman, A M22
Dream of Something Lost, Mariana Romo-Carmona, A R15
The Dream that Was Violated, Luisa Mercedes Levinson, A C1
Dream Tiger, Rosalba Campra, A C11
A Dream Where Silence Is Made of Gold, Alejandra Pizarnik, A G12
Dream with No Name: Contemporary Fiction from Cuba, Esteban Rivera, A R10
Dreamer of Fishes, Marjorie Agosín, A A1.9
The Dreamer's Portrait, Rosario Ferré, A C16, A F4.1
Dreaming in Cuban, Cristina García, N G3.1
Dreaming in Cuban (excerpt), Cristina García, A A16, A K1
Dreams and Realities: Selected Fiction of Juana Manuela Gorriti, Juana Manuela
    Gorriti, A G11, A M9
Dreams of the Abandoned Seducer, Alicia Borinsky, N B6.1
Dreams of the Heart: The Autobiography of President Violeta Barrios de
    Chamorro, Violeta Barrios de Chamorro, Guido Fernandez and Sonia Cruz de

False Limits, Vlady Kociancich, A S7.2, A T7
False Years, Josefina Vicens, N V9.1
Family Album, Claribel Alegría, A A8
Family Album: Three Novellas, Claribel Alegría, N A4
The Family Album, Ana María Güiraldes, A A1.8, A O6
Family Chronicle, Ana María Shua, A D10.1
A Family for Clotilde, Luisa Valenzuela, A V1.1, A V1.2
Family Life, Liliana Heker,A H4
A Family Man, Vlady Kociancich, A P9
Family Portrait: Reflection on Interior Decoration, Bertha Sánchez-Bello, A H9
Family Ties, Clarice Lispector, A L7, A P7
Family Ties, Clarice Lispector, A L7
The Family Tree (excerpt), Margo Glantz, A A1.4
The Family Tree: An Illustrated Novel, Margo Glantz, N G6
Fantasmas: Supernatural Stories by Mexican-American Writers, Rob Johnson,
    A J6
Far Away Where She Lived a Life Shattered by Rifles' Ravages (from *My Mother's
    Hands*), Nellie Campobello, A C3
Farabundo Marti, Claribel Alegría, A A8.1
Farewell, My Love, Ana María Shua, A H13
Fast Friends, Lygia Bojunga-Nunes, A B15
Fat, Marjorie Agosín, A A1.3
Fat Man from La Paz: Contemporary Fiction from Bolivia, Rosario Santos, A S5.1
Fear: Cuento de Jalohuín, Mariana Romo-Carmona, A R15
The Fear of Losing Eurydice: A Novel, Julieta Campos, N C2
Fearful of Valparaíso, Luisa Mercedes Levinson, A L5
The Feathered Serpent, Marcela Gutiérrez, A B8
Feiguele, Cecilia Absatz, A G3
Felix, Claribel Alegría, A A8.1
The Fencesitters Society, Cristina Peri Rossi, A A1.1
Fiction International 25. Special Issue: Mexican Fiction, Harold Jaffe, A J3
(Fidel) Castro's Daughter: An Exile's Memoir of Cuba, Alina Fernández, AB F1
The Fiesta, Marjorie Agosín, A A1.3
Fifita Calls Us in the Morning, Mirta Yáñez, A B9
The Fifth River, Sonia Rivera Valdés, A R11
The Fifth Story, Clarice Lispector, A J1, A L7.1, A S10
The Fig, Gabriela Mistral, A A1.2, A T1
Fill Your Heart with My Respect, Nellie Campobello, A C3
Final Act, Claribel Alegría, A A8.1
Final Countdown, Giovanna Rivero Santa Cruz, A R12
Final Judgement, Cristina Peri Rossi, A H7, A P6
The Final Mist, María Luisa Bombal, A B16
The Final Sin, Syria Poletti, A L6

Finally Us....: Contemporary Black Brazilian Women Writers, Miriam Alves, A A11

The Fire, Hilma Contreras, A C26

Fire from the Andes: Short Fiction by Women from Bolivia, Ecuador, and Peru, Susan Benner and Kathy S. Leonard, A B8

The Firefly and the Mirror (La luciérnaga y el espejo), Gloria Chávez-Vásquez, A C15

First Born, Esmeralda Santiago, A S3.1

First Communion, Marjorie Agosín, A A1.9

First Communion, Claribel Alegría, A A8.1

First Interlude, Rosario Aguilar, A A5

First Love, Judith Ortiz Cofer, A O7.4, A T2

First Love and Look for My Obituary: Two Novellas, Elena Garro, N G5

The First Months, Marjorie Agosín, A A1

The First Time, Martha Cerda, A C12

First Time to the Sea, Marjorie Agosín, A A1.3

First World Third Class (1996), Regina Rheda, A R6

First World Third Class and Other Tales of the Global Mix, Regina Rheda, A R6, N R2

The Fish Tank, Alejandra Farias, A A1.8

Fishing Days (excerpt from *Dream Time*), Ana María Shua, A A3

Fissures, Marjorie Agosín, A A1

5:00 A.M.: Writing as Ritual, Judith Ortiz Cofer, A O7.1

Five Windows on the Same Side, Sonia Rivera Valdés, A R11

Five Women Writers of Costa Rica: Short Stories, Carmen Naranjo and Victoria Urbano, A N2

Five Women Writers of Costa Rica: Short Stories by Carmen Naranjo, Eunice Odio, Yolanda Oreamuno, Victoria Urbano, and Rima de Vallbona, A U1

Fixed Distance, Inés Malinow, A M15

Flags, Cristina Peri Rossi, A P6.1

Flash Fiction. 72 Very Short Stories, James Thomas, Denise Thomas, and Tom Hazuka, A T3

Flea Market, Luisa Valenzuela, A V1.2

Fleeting Friendships, Rosario Castellanos, A A6

Fleur-de-Lis, Alicia Steinberg, A D10.1

Flight I, Mayra Santos-Febres A C25.1

The Flight, Clarice Lispector, A S1

Flight of the Swan, Rosario Ferré, A M20

Flight of the Swan, Rosario Ferré, N F3.1

The Floating Borderlands: Twenty-five Years of U.S. Hispanic Literature, Lauro Flores, A F7

The Flood, Claribel Alegría, A A8.1

Floral Caper, Carmen Naranjo, A J5

Flora's Complaint, Kathleen Alcalá, A S20

The Fragile Balance, Elisa Lispector, A S1
Fragment from a Lost Diary and Other Stories, Naomi Katz and Nancy Milton, A K5
Fragments for Dominating Silence, Alejandra Pizarnik, A G12
Francina, Marta Brunet, A J9.1
Francisco, Elizabeth Subercaseaux, A A3
Frida: A Novel, Barbara Louise Mujica, AB M9
Frida and Moises, Marjorie Agosín, A A1
Frida, Friduca, Mami, A S3.1
Frida Kahlo: The Camera Seduced, Ansel Adams & Elena Poniatowska, AB A1
The Friends, Silvina Ocampo, A M8, A O3
Fritters and Moons, Soledad Cruz, A F3.1
From Border Crossings to Campaign Trail: Chronicle of a Latina in Politics Emma Sepulveda-Pulvirenti, AB S6
From Exile, Mariella Sala, A R17
From Grandmother to Granddaughter: Salvadoran Women's Stories, Michae Gorkin, Marta Pineda, and Gloria Leal, AB G6
From La Alameda to New York (De La Alameda a Nueva York), Gloria Chávez-Vásquez, A C15
From Primer to Book (excerpt from *De la cartilla al libro*), Victoria Ocampo, A C10
From the Green Antilles: Writings of the Caribbean, Barbara Howes, A H12
From Morrocco to Buenos Aires, Mercedes Roffé, A A1.7
The Front (2003), Regina Rheda, A R6
Front-row Seat in Heaven (1936), Carmen Lyra, A H8
The Fucking Game (excerpt from *The Efficacious Cat*), Luisa Valenzuela, A F3
Fulana, Judith Ortiz Cofer, A O7.4
A Full Afternoon, Clarice Lispector, A L7.2
Full Stop, Cristina Peri Rossi, A P6.1
Fundamental Stone (excerpt from *The Musical Hell*), Alejandra Pizarnik, A G12
The Fury, Silvina Ocampo, A O3
Future Sorrows, Rima de Vallbona, A D8

G
Gabriela, Marjorie Agosín, A A1
Gabriela, Mariana Romo-Carmona, A R3
A Gabriela Mistral Reader, Marjorie Agosín, A A1.2
Gabriela Mistral: The Audacious Traveler, Marjorie Agosín, AB A2.4
Gabriela Mistral: Selected Prose and Prose-Poems, Stephen Tapscott, A T1
Galatea, Brianda Domecq, A D4
The Game That Is Only Played Once, Carmen Naranjo, A N1
Garabito the Indomitable, Delfina Collado, A J4
García's Thousandth Day, Alicia Steimberg, A A3

Happy Birthday, Clarice Lispector, A L7
Happy Birthday (Lucía), Nicholasa Mohr, A M17.3
Happy Days, Uncle Sergio, Magali García Ramis, A K1, N G4
Happy Days, Uncle Sergio (excerpt), Magali García Ramis, A O6
A Happy Family, Martha Cerda, A C12
Haute Cuisine, Amparo Dávila, A M8.6
Havana Split, Teresa Bevin, N B4
Havana USA: Cuban Exiles and Cuban Americans in South-Florida, 1959-1994,
    Cristina María García, AB G3
He and She (excerpt), Júlia Lopes de Almeida, A S1
He and She, Maricarmen O'hara, A O4
He Soaked Me Up, Clarice Lispector, A L7.2
He Who Searches, Luisa Valenzuela, N V4.4
The Headache, Laura Riesco, A A1.1
Hear My Testimony: Maria Teresa Tula, Human Rights Activist of El Salvador,
    María Teresa Tula and Lynn Stephen, AB T3
Heard in Passing, Martha Cerda, A C12
Heart of My Heart, Bone of My Bone, Aurora Levins Morales, A L4
The Heat of Things, Nélida Piñón, A R17
Hebrew, Marjorie Agosín, A A1
The Hebrew Institute, Marjorie Agosín, A A1
Heddy the Airhead, Maricarmen O'Hara, A O4
Helena of Vienna, Marjorie Agosín, A A1
Hell, Rima de Vallbona, A D8
Hell is bloody birds, Cristina Peri Rossi, A P6.2
"Hello, Dollinks," Mandalit del Barco, A S3.1
Help, I'm Drowning, Teresinka Pereira, A P5
The Hen, Marjorie Agosín, A A1.3
Henriqueta and I, Argentina Díaz Lozano, N D8.1
Her God, Nellie Campobello, A C3
Her Love, Nellie Campobello, A C3
Her Mother's House, Ana Menéndez, A M13
Her Skirt, Nellie Campobello, A C3
Her True-True Name: An Anthology of Women's Writing from the Caribbean,
    Pamela Mordecai and Betty Wilson, A M19
Herbarium, Lygia Fagundes Telles, A F1
Here I Am: Contemporary Jewish Stories from around the World, Marsha Lee
    Berkman and Elaine Marcus Starkman, A B10
Here's to You, Jesusa!, Elena Poniatowska, N P6.1
Here's to You, Jesusa! (introduction), Elena Poniatowska, A G2
Herman and Alice, a Novella, Nicholasa Mohr, A M17
The Hero, Cristina Peri Rossi, A P6.2
Hey Mama, Hilma Contreras, A C26

The House of the Angel (excerpt), Beatriz Guido, A F3
The House of the Spirits, Isabel Allende, N A6.6
The House of the Spirits (excerpt), Isabel Allende, A B1, A F3, A L1
The House on the Lagoon, Rosario Ferré, N F3.2
The House that Jack Built, Maricarmen O'hara, A O4
The House that Vanished, Rosario Ferré, A F4.1
Houses by the Sea, Marjorie Agosín, A A1.3
How Are You?, Marilú Mallet, A M6
How Do You Know, Vivian?,Verónica López Kónina, A F3.1
How Forgetfulness Began, Jacqueline Balcells, A B2
How I Write, Gabriela Mistral, A T1
How I Wrote "When Women Love Men" (essay), Rosario Ferré, A F4.1
How Milinco Escaped from School,Yolanda Bedregal, A L3
How the Garcia Girls Lost Their Accents, Julia Álvarez, N A7.2
How the Garcia Girls Lost Their Accents (excerpt), Julia Álvarez, A A13, A K1
How the Little Crocodiles Cry, Elvira Orphée, A A3
How the Monkey Lost the Fruit of His Labor, Lydia Cabrera, A H10, A M8.6
How Tía Lola Came to Visit/Stay, Julia Álvarez, N A7.3
How to Gather the Shadows of the Flowers, Ángela Hernández, A E4, A F3, A O6
How Uncle Rabbit Got Out of a Fix, Carmen Lyra, A H8
How Uncle Rabbit Played a Trick on Aunt Whale and Uncle Elephant, Carmen
      Lyra, A H8
Hualpín, Sonia Montecinos, A A1.8
A Huge Black Umbrella, Marjorie Agosín, A C6
The Human Virus (El virus humano), Gloria Chávez-Vásquez, A C15
The Hunchback, Mirta Toledo, A L3
Hunger Strike, Maricarmen O'hara, A O4
The Hunt, Lygia Fagundes Telles, A E3
Hurricane Stories, Ana Menéndez, A M13

I
I always imagine, Cristina Peri Rossi, A P6.2
I Am the Reasonable One, Rosario Morales, A L4, A T8
I am very interested in botany, Cristina Peri Rossi, A P6.2
I Came to Help, Julia Álvarez, A B22
I contribute to the general racket, Cristina Peri Rossi, A P6.2
I Didn't Go Home (Christmas 1941), Rosario Morales, A S3
I Didn't Hear Anything, Rosario Morales, A R19
I don't have it, and I wanted it (excerpt from *Empire of Dreams*), Giannina Braschi,
      A R19
I dreamt that I was, Cristina Peri Rossi, A P6.2
I Gave You All I Had, Zoe Valdés, N V1.1
I have a tiny apartment, Cristina Peri Rossi, A P6.2

Impossible Story, Carmen Boullosa, A H13
In a State of Memory, Mercado Tununa AB M7
In Another Place in a Different Era, Nicholasa Mohr, A M17.1
In Between, Mirta Toledo, A L3
In Cuba I Was a German Shepherd, Ana Menéndez, A M13
In Cuba I Was a German Shepherd, Ana Menéndez, A M13
In Florence Ten Years Later, Marilyn Bobes, A H13, A R10
In Heaven, Amparo Dávila, A C27
In Memoriam, Brianda Domecq, A D4
In My Grandmother's House, Aurora Levins Morales, A L4
In New York, Nicholasa Mohr, A M17.2
In Other Words: Literature by Latinas of the United States, Roberta Fernández, A F2
In Praise of Glass, Gabriela Mistral, A T1
In Praise of Gold, Gabriela Mistral, A A1.2
In Praise of Salt, Gabriela Mistral, A A1.2
In Praise of Sand, Gabriela Mistral, A T1
In Praise of Small Towns, Gabriela Mistral, A A1.2
In Praise of Stones, Gabriela Mistral, A A1.2
In Search of Dignity, ClariceLispector, A L7.2
In Secret, Mónica Mansour, A G5
In Short: A Collection of Brief Creative Nonfiction, Judith Kitchen and Mary Paumier Jones, A K9
In Spite of Everything, Edla Van Steen, A V2
In the Absence of Love, Ruth Behar, A A1.4
In the Dream Clock, Martha Cerda, A C12
In the Family, María Elena Llano, A C27, A F5
In the ghetto of my womb, Cristina Peri Rossi, A P6.2
In the Hero's Shadow, Eugenia Calny, A G3
In the Name of His Name, Angelina Muñiz-Huberman, A B10, A M22, A S18.1
In the Name of Salomé (excerpt), Julia Álvarez, A B13
In the Name of Salomé: A Novel, Julia Álvarez, N A7.4
In the Other Half of Time, Mireya Robles, A M16
In the Palm of Darkness: A Novel, Mayra Montero, N M10.3
In the Shadow of the Owl, Luisa Mercedes Levinson, N L2
In the Silence of the Big House, Emi Bulhões Carvalho da Fonseca, A S1
In the Time of the Butterflies, Julia Álvarez, N A7.5
In Your Very Footsteps, Giovanna Rivero Santa Cruz, A R12
The Inconclusive Journey, Cristina Peri Rossi, A P6.1
Indian Mother, Rosario Castellanos, A A1.6
The Indian Mummy, Delfina Collado, A J4
Indigenous Profile, María Cadilla de Martínez, A C28
Industrial Park: A Proletarian Novel, Patricia Galvão (Pagu), N G1

The Islet, Luisa Mercedes Levinson, A L5
Isolda's Mirror, Rosario Ferré, A F4
It Happened One Day, Carmen Naranjo, A N1
It Is Nothing of Mine, Araceli Ardó, A M10
It Was a Special Treat, Judith Ortiz Cofer, A K3
It Was All Mamá's Fault, Pilar López Gonzáles, A B24
Itinerants, Marjorie Agosín, A A1.3
It's a Good Thing, Marilyn Bobes, A B9
It's the Fault of the Tlaxcaltecas, Elena Garro, A M8.6
It's Their Fault, Martha Cerda, A C12
I've Forgotten Your Name, Martha Rivera, N R7
The Ivory Trader and the Red Melons, Zoe Valdés, A B25, A G2.1
The IWM 1000, Alicia Yánez Cossío, A C27

J
Jacinto's Deal, Nellie Campobello, A C3
Jamie in Poneloya, Claribel Alegría, A A8.1
Jane's Umbilical Cord, Claribel Alegría, A A8.1
Japanese Daisies, María Elena Llano, A Y2
Jazzbluesing, Regina Cohen, A J3
The Jewelry, Marjorie Agosín, A A1
The Jewish Cemetery in Guanabacoa, Ruth Behar, A S18.2
Jewish Dog, Marjorie Agosín, A A1
The Jewish White Slave Trade and the Untold Story of Raquel Liberman, Nora
     Glickman, AB G4
Jimena's Fair, Laura Riesco, A A1.5
A Job for Valentín, Judith Ortiz Cofer, A O7
Jocasta, Liliana Heker, A H4, A M8.3, A M8.4
Jocasta's Confession, Angelina Muñiz-Huberman, A M22
Joe, Julia Álvarez, A N4
José Martí, Gabriela Mistral, A T1
The Journey, Ana Pizarro, A A1.8
The Journey, Luisa Valenzuela, A V1.4
The Journey and the Journeys, Carmen Naranjo, A N2, A U1
The Journey of Amatista and the Dirty Prince, Elvira Orpheé, A C11
Journey of the Watermelon, Virgina Vidal, A A1.8
Journey to Pepe, Adelaida Fernández de Juan, A B9
Journey to Petrópolis, Clarice Lispector, A L7.1
Journey to the End of Coasts, Marjorie Agosín, A A1.3
Jovita, Dinah Silveira de Queiroz, A S1
Juan, the One with the Little Load of Firewood, Carmen Lyra, A H8
Juana, Elizabeth Subercaseaux, A A3
Juani en tres tiempos, Miriam Díaz-Diocaretz, A G7

The Judge's Wife, Isabel Allende, A A9, A C2.1, A E3
Jump on It, Stick, Carmen Lyra, A H8
June Gave Him the Voice, Josefina Estrada, A L2
Just a Saxophone, Lygia Fagundes Telles, A J1, A S1
Just a Woman, Gioconda Belli, A S3.1
Just One Small Detail, Ana Lydia Vega, A V3

K

Kaddish, Graciela Safranchik, A A1.4
Kalpa Imperial: The Greatest Empire That Never Was, Angélica Gorodischer,
    N G9
Keeping Track of Time, Cristina Peri Rossi A P6.1
Kennedy in the Barrio, Judith Ortiz Cofer, A O7.4, A S18.2, A S19
The Key, Lygia Fagundes Telles, A A1.5
The Key, Luisa Valenzuela, A V1.5
Kiliagonia, Iris Zavala, A G7
The Killer, Patricia Melo, N M4.1
King David's Harp: Autobiographical Essays by Jewish Latin American Writers,
    Stephen A. Sadow, AB S1
The King Who Forbade Balloons, Syria Poletti, N P5
Kingdom of the Golden Dragon, Isabel Allende, N A6.9
The King's Peaches, Maricarmen O'hara, A O4
The Kiss, Julia Álvarez, A M16
Kissing Susan, Mariana Romo-Carmona, A R15
Kitchens, Aurora Levins Morales, A G9, A L4, A T8
Knife and Mother, Luisa Valenzuela, A V1.5
Knight, Death, and the Devil, Vlady Kociancich, A C27, A M8.6
Kol Nidre, Marjorie Agosín, A A1

L

La bruja pirata de Chiloé, Mariana Romo-Carmona, A R15
La confesión, Gloria Liberman, A G7
La cucharachita Mandinga, Carmen Lyra, A H8
La Doctora Barr, Mary Helen Ponce, A V6
La hija del mashorquero/The Executioner's Daughter, Mercedes Cabello de
    Carbonera, A S8
La Llorona, Alcina Lubitch Domecq, A S18.2
La machorra, Nela Martínez, A B8
La quintrala, Magdalena Petit, N P3
La veintiuna, Luz María Umpierre, A G7
La virgen en el desierto, Mariana Romo-Carmona, A G7
The Labyrinth of Time, Luisa Mercedes Levinson, A L5
Ladders to Success, Luisa Valenzuela, A V1.2, A V1.4

Life Inside of Love, Marjorie Agosín, A A1.9
The Light, Blanca Elena Paz, A B8, A R5
Light and Shadow, Gladys Rossel Huicí, A B8
Like a Vulture, Giovanna Rivero Santa Cruz, A R12
Like Water for Chocolate (excerpt), Laura Esquivel, A B4, A B13, A L1
Like Water for Chocolate: A Novel in Monthly Installments, with Recipes, Romances, and Home Remedies, Laura Esquivel, N E4.1
Liliane's Sunday, Ana Lydia Vega, A D6, A R19
The Line of the Sun: A Novel, Judith Ortiz Cofer, N O3.1
Linked, Judith Ortiz Cofer, A G1
The Literature of Latin America. Volume I of the Series on Literature-Art-Music, L. S. Rowe and Pedro de Alba, A R18
Literatures of Asia, Africa, and Latin America from Antiquity to the Present, Willis Barnstone and Toni Barnstone, A B4.
A Little Bit of Bliss, Mayra Santos-Febres A S3
The Little Eastern Star, Cristina Ibarra, A J3
Little Girl in Red, on Her Way to the Moon, Marina Colasanti, A S1
Little Goddess, Giovanna Rivero Santa Cruz, A G9
Little Havana Blues: A Cuban-American Literature Anthology, Delia Poey and Virgil Suárez, A P10.1
Little Heart, Aída Bahr A B9
The Little Heidelberg, Isabel Allende, A A9
Little House of Celluloid, Elena Poniatowska, A B18
The Little Island, Luisa Mercedes Levinson, A A3
Little Joe Sticks, Maricarmen O'hara, A O4
A Little Love, C. C. Medina, N M3
Little Man, Teresinka Pereira, A P5
The Little New Moon, Gabriela Mistral, A A1.2
Little Poisons, Sonia Rivera Valdés, A R10, A R11
The Little School: Tales of Disappearance and Survival in Argentina, Alicia Partnoy, A P2
The Little Souls, Marjorie Agosín, A A1
Living at Night, Mariana Romo-Carmona, N R10
The Living Room, Liliana Miraglia, A R9
Livio Roca, Silvina Ocampo, A O3
The Lizard, Mónica Lavín, A G5
The Lizard Christmas, Cristina Peri Rossi, A P6.1
The Lizard's Tail, Luisa Valenzuela, N V4.5
The Lizard with the White Belly, Yolanda Oreamuno, A R4
L'obscurité des eaux (excerpt from *The Musical Hell*), Alejandra Pizarnik, A G12
Lol-Há: A Maya Tale, Ana María Gómez Rul, N G8
Longing, Angelina Muñiz-Huberman, A M22

Lullabies, Gabriela Mistral, A T1
Luminated (excerpt from the novel *Lumpérica*), Diamela Eltit, A C10
Luminescence, Clarice Lispector, A C10
Lunacy, Sonia Rivera Valdés, A R11
Luz de dos, Esther Seligson, A K2
Lydia, Judith Ortiz Cofer, A O7.1
Lyrics for a Salsa and Three Sonetos by Request, Ana Lydia Vega, A C17, A F3

M

Macaroons, Eyes of Sea and Sky, Olga Nolla, A R19
The Mad Woman of the Grand Armee, Claribel Alegría, A A8.1
Madness, Armonía Somers, A H12.1
*Madres del verbo/Mothers of the Word: Early Spanish-American Women Writers:
  A Bilingual Anthology*, Nina Scott, A S8
Maestra Arellano, Berta Hiriart, A R8
Magdalena, A Fable of Immortality, Beatriz Escalante, N E3
Magical Realist Fiction: An Anthology, David Young and Keith Hollaman, A Y4
Magical Sites: Women Travelers in 19th Century Latin America, Marjorie Agosín
  and Julie H. Levison, A A4
Magnolias, Marjorie Agosín, A A1
Magush, Silvina Ocampo, A O3
Making Callaloo: 25 Years of Black Literature, Charles H. Rowell, A R19.1
Making Love in Spanish, Judith Ortiz Cofer, Circa 1969, A O7.4
Mal de amores (excerpt), Ángeles Mastretta, A L1
Malinche, Laura Esquivel, AB E3.1
Malinche: Slave Princess of Cortez, Gloria Durán, AB D6
A Man of Mexico, Gabriela Mistral, A T1
Mama, Marjorie Agosín, A A1
Mama Blanca, Teresa de la Parra, A R18
Mama Blanca's Memoirs: The Classic Novel of a Venezuelan Girlhood, Teresa de
  la Parra, N D2.1
Mama Delfina, Marjorie Agosín, A A1
Mama's Farewell, Cristina Peri Rossi A P6.2
Mambrú Did Not Go to War, Hilma Contreras, A F3.1
A Man, a Woman (excerpt from *El muro de medio metro*), Omega Agüero, A B1,
  A M19
A Man and a Woman, Maricarmen O'hara, A O4
The Man in the Araucaria, Sara Gallardo, A A3, A O6
Man Oh Man, Achy Obejas, A O2
Man on the Rug, Ana María Shua, A A1.1
The Man Who Appeared, Clarice Lispector, A F9, A L7.2
The Man Who Died Facing the Sea, Hilma Contreras, A C26
Mangos, Bananas and Coconuts: A Cuban Love Story, Himilce Novas, N N1.1

A Manifesto of the City, Clarice Lispector, A L7.2

Manifesto on Poetic Eggs, Giannina Braschi, A B20

Man's Dwelling Place, Angélica Gorodischer, A M8.6

A Map of Hope: Women's Writing on Human Rights: An International Anthology, Marjorie Agosín, A A1.6

The Marble Dance, Lygia Fagundes Telles, N F1.1

Marcelino's Job, Maricarmen O'hara, A O4

March, Marjorie Agosín, A A1

The March, Lake Saris, A G7

The March, Luisa Valenzuela, A V1.5

A March Guayacán, Bertalicia Peralta, A P4, A S5, A Y5

The March of the Batrachians, Lupe Rumazo, A R9

The Marconi Theater, Marjorie Agosín, A A1

Margarita's Birthday, Claribel Alegría, A A8.1

María, Marjorie Agosín, A A1

María de Estrada: Gypsy Conquistadora, Gloria Durán, N D10

María Luisa, Marjorie Agosín, A A1

María Sabida, Judith Ortiz Cofer, A T2

Mariana, Mariana Alcorforado, AB V1

Mariana, Inés Arredondo, A A15

Mariana, Katherine Vaz, AB V1

Marina, Judith Ortiz Cofer, A O7.3

Marina and the Lion, Rosario Ferré, A F4.1

Marina's Fragrance, Mayra Santos-Febres, A D5, A S6

Mariquita and Me, Guadalupe Dueñas, A B18

Mariquita Samper's Childhood, Giannina Braschi, A B20

Marmosets, Clarice Lispector, A B4

Maruja, Elda L. C. de Crespo, A M18

Mary, Why Don't You? (Impossible Dialogue in One Act), Carmen Boullosa, A D4

Más allá de la máscaras. (Beyond the Masks), Lucía Guerra Cunningham, N G10

A Massacre in Mexico, Elena Poniatowska, A B22

Massacre in Mexico, Elena Poniatowska, N P6.2

The Master's Laugh, Luisa Valenzuela, A V1.5

Masters of the Sand, Giovanna Rivero Santa Cruz, A R12

The Mastiffs of Hadrian's Temple, Silvina Ocampo, A M15

Maternity, Marta Blanco, A A1.8, A O6

Matilde, Marjorie Agosín, A A1

Matoa's Mirror, Judith Ortiz Cofer, A O7, A O7.4

A Matter of Distance, Sonia González Valdenegro, A A1.8

A Matter of Pride, Nicholasa Mohr, A M17.1

A Matter of Pride and Other Stories, Nicholasa Mohr, A M17.1

May You Make a Good Bride (excerpt), Rosa Nissan, A A1.4

Mayapan, Argentina Díaz Lozano, N D8.2

Maybe the Clock Played with Time, Carmen Naranjo, A N1
The Mayor's Wife, Alicia Yánez, A B8
The Mazoquero's Daughter, Juana Manuela Gorriti, A G11
Me and My Helper, the Autobiography of Eufelia Medina 1914-1976, Eufelia
    Medina, AB M3
Me in the Middle, Ana María Machado, A M1
Me in the Middle, Ana María Machado, A M1
The Meal, Mariana Romo-Carmona, A R15
Mean Woman, Alicia Borinsky, N B6.2
The Meaning of Consuelo, Judith Ortiz Cofer, N O3.2
A Meaningless Story, Luisa Valenzuela, A V1.4
Meditation on the Dead, Marjorie Agosín, A A1.3
The Meeting, Julieta Pinto, A J4
The Mejia's Dogs, Claribel Alegría, A A8.1
The Melancholy of Black Panthers, Luisa Futoransky, A A1.4
Memoir of a Visionary: Antonia Pantoja, Antonia Pantoja, AB P1
Memorial of Oblivion, Marjorie Agosín, A A1
Memorias de mi viaje/Recollections of My T ip, Olga Beatriz Torres, AB T2
Memories, Marjorie Agosín, A A1
Memories of Clay, Cristina da Fonseca, A A1.8
Memories of Comings and Goings, Ethel Kosminsky, A A1.7
Memories on the Oblique, María Luisa Puga, A R17
Memories: R. I. P., Nicholasa Mohr, A M17.1
Memory, Rosario Morales, A L4
Memory Mambo, Achy Obejas, N O1.1
Memory, Oblivion, and Jewish Culture in Latin America, Marjorie Agosín,
    AB A2.5
The Men Left Their Mutilated Bodies Awaiting the Succor of These Simple
    Flowers, Nellie Campobello, A C3
Men of the North (excerpt from *Cartucho*), Nellie Campobello, A C3
The Men of the Troop, Nellie Campobello, A C3
Mercedes Benz 220 SL, Rosario Ferré, A E3, A F4.1, A F6, A G4
The Mermaids' Elixir, Jacqueline Balcells, A B2
Mery Yagual (Secretary), Mónica Ortiz Salas, A B8
The Message, Clarice Lispector, A L7.1
The Message, Elena Poniatowska, A A1.5
A Message about Pablo Neruda, Gabriela Mistral, A T1
A Message from God in the Atomic Age, Irene Vilar, AB V3
Messages, Pía Barros, A B5
The Messenger, Mayra Montero, N M10.5
The Messiah, Marjorie Agosín, A A1.9
Metonymy, or the Husband's Revenge, Rachel de Queiroz, A G13, A J1, A M8.2,
    A M8.6

The Moon, the Wind, the Year, the Day (excerpt), Ana Pizarro, A A1.1, A A1.6
The Moon's Husband, Maricarmen O'hara, A O4
The Moon's Not a Piece of Cake (La luna no es pan de horno), Laura Antillano, A P8.1
A Moral Lesson, Cristina Peri Rossi, A P6
The Morgue (excerpt from the novel *Bajo el oscuro sol*), Yolanda Bedregal, A L3
The Moribund, Guadalupe Dueñas, A T5
The Mortal Sin, Silvina Ocampo, A C10, A O3
Moshe, Marjorie Agosín, A A1
The Mosquito Net, Marisella Veiga, A H10
The Most Forbidden of All, Sonia Rivera Valdés, A R11
The Most Precious Offering, Angelina Muñiz-Huberman, A M22
Mother of Fair Love, Agustina Schroeder, N S2
A Mother to Be Assembled, Inés Fernández Moreno, A L3
Mothers & Daughters: An Anthology, Alberto Manguel, A M8.5
Mothers and Shadows, Marta Traba, N T1
Mothers and Shadows (excerpt from the novel), Marta Traba, A P7
Mothers of the Disappeared, Jo Fisher, AB F2
The Moths, Helena María Viramontes, A A16, A A17, A C13, A K4, A K4.1, A V7
The Moths and Other Stories, Helena María Viramontes, A V7
The Movies, Marjorie Agosín, A A1
Mr. and Mrs. Martins, Edla Van Steen, A S10
Mr. Mendelsohn, Nicholasa Mohr, A M17, A T8
Mr. Slowly Slow, Maricarmen O'hara, A O4
Mr. Turista's Breakfast, Maricarmen O'hara, A O4
Mr. Watson, Marjorie Agosín, A A1
Modesta Gómez, Rosario Castellanos, A C8
Monguí, Albalucía Angel, A M15
Monkey Hunting, Cristina García, N G3.3
Monkeys, Clarice Lispector, A L7.1
Monologue with Rain, Chely Lima, A S15
Monserrat Ordóñez, Marjorie Agosín, A A1.3
A Month in a Nutshell, Aleida Rodríguez, A G7
The Moon Line, Mayra Montero, N M10.6
More Room, Judith Ortiz Cofer, A O7.3
Motifs of Clay, Gabriela Mistral, A T1
Mulatta Moon, Giovanna Rivero Santa Cruz, A R12
Multiverse, Martha Cerda, A C12
Murder and Other Acts of Literature: Twenty-four Unforgettable and Chilling Stories by Some of the World's Best-loved, Most Celebrated Writers, Michel B. Slung, A S13
The Murmuring Coast, Lidia Jorge, N J2.1

The Muse in Mexico: A Mid-century Miscellany, Thomas Mabry Cranfill and George D. Schade, A C30

The Museum of Futile Endeavors, Cristina Peri Rossi, A A1.5

The Museum of Useless Efforts, Cristina Peri Rossi, A P6.1

The Museum of Useless Efforts, Cristina Peri Rossi, A P6.1

The Museum of Vain Endeavours, Cristina Peri Rossi, A C2.1

The Music of the Rain, Silvina Ocampo, A S18

The Musical Hell (excerpts), Alejandra Pizarnik, A G12

Musicians and Watchmakers, Alicia Steimberg, N S6.1

Musicians and Watchmakers (excerpt), Alicia Steimberg, A A 1.4, A G3, A K2

My Accent, Marjorie Agosín, A A1

My Apron, Marjorie Agosín, A A1

My Aunt, Esther Díaz Llanillo, A Y2

My Aunts, Marjorie Agosín, A A1

My Birthday, Marjorie Agosín, A A1

My Byzantine Grandmother's Two Medieval Saints, Carmen Naranjo, A J4

My Childhood, Marjorie Agosín, A A1

My Cousin Rafael, Marjorie Agosín, A A1

My Cuban Body, Carolina Hospital, A S18.2

My Cuban Story, Ester Levis Levine, A A1.7

My Cuban Story, Natania Remba Nurko, A A1.7

My Desk, Marjorie Agosín, A A1

My Everyday Colt, Luisa Valenzuela, A V1.2

My Friend the Painter, Lygia Bojunga-Nunes, A B15.1, N N2.1

My Grandfather, Marjorie Agosín, A A1

My Heart Lies South: The Story of My Mexican Marriage, Elizabeth Borton de Treviño, AB B5

My History Teacher, Marjorie Agosín, A A1

My House, Marjorie Agosín, A A1

My Invented Country: A Nostalgic Journey Through Chile, Isabel Allende, AB A6

My Mother's Hands, Nellie Campobello, A C3

My Name Is Light, Elsa Osorio, N O4

My Names, Alicia Partnoy, A P2

My Newest Triumph, Nicholasa Mohr, A M17.1

My Nose, Alicia Partnoy, A P2

My Social Beliefs, Gabriela Mistral, A T1

My Uncle Ricardo, Lúcia Benedetti, A S1

Mystery in São Cristóvão, Clarice Lispector, A L7

Mystery Stone, Rima de Vallbona, A R4

Mystic Rose, Mayra Santos-Febres, A S6

A Mystical Betrayal (excerpt from *Texts of Shadow and Last Poems*), Alejandra Pizarnik, A G12

The Myth, Luisa Mercedes Levinson, A L5, A M15, A O7.1

New Year's by the Sea, Marjorie Agosín, A A1
New Year's Eve, Inés Arredondo, A A15
The Nicaraguan Grandfather (2), Claribel Alegría, A A8.1
The Nicaraguan Grandfather (3), Claribel Alegría, A A8.1
The Nicaraguan Great Grandfather (1), Claribel Alegría, A A8.1
Nicolasa and the Lacework, Mónica Lavín, A A2
Nicolasa's Lace, Mónica Lavín, A J3
Night, Marjorie Agosín, A A1
Night of the Radishes, Sandra Benítez, N B2.1
Night Shared in the Memory of an Escape, Alejandra Pizarnik, A G12
Night Shift, Amalia Jamilis, A L6
Night Stand, Mayra Santos-Febres, A S6
The Night Visitor, Elena Poniatowska, A M8.6
Nightmare at Deep River, Lilia Algandona, A J4
Nightmare in Chinandega, Claribel Alegría, A A8.1
Nihil Obstat, Luisa Valenzuela, A V1.1, A V1.2
Nilda (excerpt), Nicholasa Mohr, A A16
The Nine Guardians, Rosario Castellanos, N C4.1
The Nine Guardians (excerpt from *Balún Canán*), Rosario Castellanos, A A10
1930, Aurora Levins Morales, A L4, A T8
No Circles, Pía Barros, A B5
No Dogs or Mexicans, Claribel Alegría, A A8.1
No Dust Is Allowed in this House, Olga Nolla, A E4
No-Man's-Land, Martha Cerda, A C12
No Men for the Poncho Weavers, Luisa Mercedes Levinson, A L5
No More Mill (excerpt from *Mama Blanca's Souvenirs*), Teresa de la Parra, A A14
No More Worries, Clairce Lispector, A A1.4
No One Knows for Whom One Works, Martha Cerda, A C12
No One Said a Word, Paula Varsavsky, N V7
No One Will Take Her Place, Silvia Plager, A G3
The Nocturnal Butterflies, Inés Arredondo, A A15
Nocturnal Singer, Alejandra Pizarnik, A G12
Nocturnal Visits, Claribel Alegría, A V5
Noodle Soup, Cristina Pacheco, A A2, A O6
A Normal Day in the Life of Couto Seducción, Mayra Santos-Febres, A S6
North, Marjorie Agosín, A A1.3
Nostalgia, Rosario Morales, A L4
Nostalgia Row, Edla Van Steen, A V2
Not for Sale, Judith Ortiz Cofer, A O7.1
Not without Her Glasses, Carmen Basáñez, A A1.8
Notes on a Journey, Cristina Peri Rossi, A P6.1
Nothing in Our Hands but Age, Raquel Puig Zaldívar, N P8

Photographs I, Marjorie Agosín, A A1
Photographs II, Marjorie Agosín, A A1
Photographs III, Marjorie Agosín, A A1
The Photographs, Silvina Ocampo, A O3
The Pianist, Ximena Arnal Franck, A S5.1
The Piano, Marjorie Agosín, A A1
The Piano of My Desire, Isis Tejeira, A J4
Pico Rico, Mandorico, Rosario Ferré, A V4
Pig Latin, Clarice Lispector, A C14, A L7.2
Pilar, Your Curls, Carmen Lugo Filippi, A V4, A Y5
The Pilgrim's Angel, Violeta Quevedo, A A1.8
Pine Trees, Marjorie Agosín, A A1.9
The Pineapple, Gabriela Mistral, A T1
Pisagua, Marjorie Agosín, A A1.3
The Place I Want to Die, Marjorie Agosín, A A1.9
The Place of Its Quietude, Luisa Valenzuela, A V1.2, A V1.4
The Place of Its Quietude (El lugar de su quietud), Luisa Valenzuela, A V1
The Place of Its Solitude, Luisa Valenzuela, A S18
A Place of Memories, Marjorie Agosín, A A1
A Place Where the Sea Remembers, Sandra Benítez, N B2.2
Planting Sticks and Grinding Yucca: On Being a Translated Writer, Julia Álvarez,
    A D2
Plash, Plash, Plash, Claribel Alegría, A A8.1
Player, Giovanna Rivero Santa Cruz, A R12
Playing with Light: A Novel, Beatriz Rivera, N R6.1
Plaza Mauá, Clarice Lispector, A A1.5, A J1, A L7.2
Plaza of the Lilacs, Nellie Campobello, A C3
Pleasure in the Word: Erotic Writing by Latin American Women, Margarite
    Fernández Olmos and Lizabeth Paravisini-Gebert, A F3
The Pledge, Edla Van Steen, A V2
A Plum for Coco, Laura del Castillo, A P12
Plunder, Armonía Somers, A P7
Poems for the Mothers, Gabriela Mistral, A T1
Poems of Ecstasy, Gabriela Mistral, A T1
Poems of the Home, Gabriela Mistral, A T1
Poems of the Saddest Mother, Gabriela Mistral, A T1
Poems of the World, or, The Book of Wisdom, Giannina Braschi, A B20
Poesía/Poetry, Sor Juana Inés de la Cruz, A S8
Poet, Claribel Alegría, A A8.1
Poetry, Marjorie Agosín, A A1
Poetry, Alicia Partnoy, A P2
Points of Departure: New Stories from Mexico, Mónica Lavín, A L2
The Poisoned Story, Rosario Ferré, A E4, A F4.1

The Poisoned Tale, Rosario Ferré, A C27
Politics, Luisa Valenzuela, A V1.4
The Politics of Exile, Claribel Alegría, A V5
The Pond, María Flora Yáñez, A A1.8
The Pool, Claribel Alegría, A A8.1
The Pools, Marjorie Agosín, A A1
Pork Sausages, Marjorie Agosín, A A1.3
Porno Flick, Luisa Valenzuela, A V1.4
Port-au-Prince, Ana Lydia Vega, A S15
Portal, Pía Barros, A B5
Portrait in Sepia, Isabel Allende, N A6.12
Portrait of Giannina Braschi, Giannina Braschi, A B20
Portrait of Voices (excerpt from *Texts of Shadow and Last Poems*), Alejandra
    Pizarnik, A G12
The Portuguese Synagogue, Angelina Muñiz-Huberman, A1.4
The Possessed among Lilacs (excerpt from *The Musical Hell*), Alejandra Pizarnik,
    A G12
Postcards, Marjorie Agosín, A A1.9
The Postponed Journey, Martha Mercader, A C11
The Potbellied Virgin, Alicia Yánez Cossío, N Y1.1
Potosí II: Address Unknown, Rosa Lleana Boudet, A Y2
Prairies, Marjorie Agosín, A A1.3
The Prayer, Silvina Ocampo, A L6, A O3
Prayer to the Goddesses, Virginia Ayllón Soria, A B8
Preciousness, Clarice Lispector, A L7, A M3
Premature Necrology, Claribel Alegría, A A8.1
Premeditated Coincidence, Adalgisa Nery, A S1
The Presence, Lygia Fagundes Telles, A F1
The President's Sheet, Claribel Alegría, A A8.1
Primary Lessons, Judith Ortiz Cofer, A O7.3
Princess, Nicholasa Mohr, A M17
The Princess and the Green Dwarf, Jacqueline Balcells, A B2
The Prisoner, Angelina Muñiz-Huberman, A A1.6, A M22
The Prize of Freedom, Lydia Cabrera, A C28, A E3
*Prize Stories from Latin America: Winner of the "A Life en español" Literary
    Contest*, A P12
The Problem, Silvia Molina, A D4
Procession of Love, Nélida Piñón, A H13
A Profession Like Any Other, Ana María Shua, A L3
Profile of Sor Juana Inés de la Cruz, Gabriela Mistral, A T1
The Proper Respect, Isabel Allende, A A9
Prophecy (1), Claribel Alegría, A A8.1
Prophecy (2), Claribel Alegría, A A8.1

Prospero's Mirror: A Translator's Portfolio of Latin American Short Fiction, Ilan Stavans, A S18
The Prostitute, Regina Rheda, A R6
Protection, Marjorie Agosín, A A1
Public Declaration of Love, Mirta Yáñez, A F3.1
The Puddle, Gabriela Mistral, A T1
Puerto Rican Writers at Home in the USA: An Anthology, Faythe Turner, A T8
Puerto Rico Journal, Rosario Morales, A L4
Puertoricanness, Aurora Levins Morales, A D1, A G9, A L4, A T8
Pulchritude, Marjorie Agosín, A A1
The Punishment, Silvina Ocampo, A O3
The Pushcart Prize XI: Best of the Small Presses with an Index to the First Eleven Volumes: An Annual Small Press Reader, Bill Henderson, A H5
A Puzzle, Alicia Partnoy, A P2
The Puzzle of the Broken Watch, María Elvira Bermúdez, A Y3
Puzzles, Inés Arredondo, A B18
Pythagoras' Illustrious Disciple, Rima de Vallbona, A D8

Q
The Queen of Beauty, Charm, and Coquetry, Giannina Braschi, A B20
Queen of the Abyss, Edla Van Steen, A V2.2
The Quena, Juana Manuela Gorriti, A G11, A M9
Questions and Answers, Maricarmen O'hara, A O4
The Quiet Café, Luisa Valenzuela, A V1.5
Quinceañera, Judith Ortiz Cofer, A O7.3

R
Rabbit Easter, Marjorie Agosín, A A1
The Raft Girl, Marjorie Agosín, A A1
Rage Is a Fallen Angel, Alba Ambert, A C18
Rain, Marjorie Agosín, A A1
Rain, Alicia Partnoy, A D13
The Rain on the Fire, Giovanna Benedetti, A J4
The Rainforest, Alicia Steimberg, N S6.2
The Raise, Giannina Braschi, A B20
Raising Raúl: Adventures Raising Myself and My Son, María Hinojosa, AB H5
Ramona, Woman of the Ember, Carmen Lyra, A J4
Rancho Santa Inés: Fast, C. C. Mayo, A M10
The Rat, Dora Alonso, A C7
Rat Seminar, Lygia Fagundes Telles, A F1
Reader Fill Your Heart with My Respect, Nellie Campobello, A C3
The Rebel, Clara Lomas, AB L4
The Rebel, Leonor Villegas de Magnón, AB L4

Shango's Rest, Beatriz Rivera, A F7
Shared Memories, Nedda G. de Anhalt, A A1.7
The Sharing of Bread, Clarice Lispector, A L7.1
She and Her Machine, Nellie Campobello, A C3
She brought me passionate presents, Cristina Peri Rossi, A P6.2
She had been brought from Peru, Cristina Peri Rossi, A P6.2
She hands me the scarf, Cristina Peri Rossi, A P6.2
She has given me happiness, Cristina Peri Rossi, A P6.2
She Has Reddish Hair and Her Name Is Sabina, A M10
She Has Reddish Hair and Her Name Is Sabina, Julieta Campos, N C2.1
She Is Here, Nellie Campobello, A C3
She Was (excerpt from *My Mother's Hands*), Nellie Campobello, A C3
The Ship from Far Away (El barco de más allá), María Silva Ossa, A R2
The Ship of Fools, Cristina Peri Rossi, N P2.1
Shoes, Pía Barros, A B5
Shoes, Margo Glantz, A A1.4
Shoes for Hector, Nicholasa Mohr, A M17
Shoes for the Rest of My Life, Amparo Dávila, A C27
Short Fiction by Hispanic Writers of the United States, Nicolas Kanellos, A K4.1
Short Fiction by Spanish-American Women, Evelyn Fishburn, A F6
Short-lived Summers, Pía Barros, A B5
Short Stories. An Anthology of the Shortest Stories, Irving Howe and Ilana Wiener
    Howe, A H11
Short Stories by Latin American Women: The Magic and the Real, Celia Correas
    de Zapata, A C27
Short Stories for Students, Jennifer Smith, A S14
Short Stories in Spanish, John R. King, A K7
Short Stories of Latin America, Arturo Torres-Rioseco, A T5
    Short Stories Written by Dominicans in the United States, Daisy Cocco de
    Fillippis and Franklin Gutiérrez, A C21
The Shrouded Woman, María Luisa Bombal, N B5.1, N B5.2
The Shunammite, Inés Arredondo, A A15, A M8.6
The Sibyl, Silvina Ocampo, A O3
Siesta, Eugenia Calny, A L6
The Sign, Inés Arredondo, A A15
The Sign of the Star, Ana Vásquez, A A1.4
The Sign of Winter, Magali García Ramis, A B21
Signs of Love, Marjorie Agosín, A A1.3
Silence, Clarice Lispector, A L7.2
Silence, Elvira Orphée, A C10
Silences, Marjorie Agosín, A A1, A A1.9
Silendra (excerpt), Elizabeth Subercaseaux, A A3
Silent Dancing, Judith Ortiz Cofer, A A17, A D6, A K4.1, A N3, A O7.3, A V5

Silent Dancing (excerpts), Judith Ortiz Cofer, A K1, A M12
Silent Dancing: A Partial Remembrance of a Puerto Rican Childhood, Judith Ortiz
    Cofer, A O7.3, AB O3
Silent Witness, Raquel Partnoy, A B22
The Silent Words, Inés Arredondo, A A15, A M10
Silhouettes from the Maternal School (1929), Carmen Lyra, A H8
The Silken Whale, Elvira Orphée, A P7
The Silver Candelabra & Other Stories: A Century of Jewish Argentine Literature,
    Rita Gardiol, A G3
Silvia, Ángela Hernández, A F3.1
Simple María, Isabel Allende, A A9
A Simple Story, Maricarmen O'hara, A O4
The Sin of the Apple, Luisa Valenzuela, A V1.1
Since One Has to Write (aphorisms and short prose), Clarice Lispector, A C10
A Sincere Friendship, Clarice Lispector, A L7.1
Sincronio, The Bird of Wonder (Sincronio, el ave fénix), Gloria Chávez-Vásquez,
    A C15
The Singer Machines, ClaribelAlegría, A A8.1
Singing in the Desert, Cristina Peri Rossi, A H7, A P6
Singing to Cuba, Margarita Engle, N E2
A Single, Numberless Death, Nora Strejilevich, N S7
A Single, Numberless Death (excerpt), Nora Strejilevich, A M4
A Singular Couple, Luisa Mercedes Levinson, A L5
Singular Like a Bird: The Art of Nancy Morejón, Miriam DeCosta-Willis, AB D1
Sirena Selena, Mayra Santos-Febres, N S1.1
Sister Orfelina (Sor Orfelina), Gloria Chávez-Vásquez, A C15
Sketch, Rosario Morales, A T8
The Skin of the Sky, Elena Poniatowska, N P6.4
Sky, Sea and Earth, María Luisa Bombal, A A1.5, A A1.9, A C19
Skywriting: A Novel of Cuba, Margarita Engle, N E2.1
Slaves, Marjorie Agosín, A A1.3
Sleeping Beauty, Rosario Ferré, A F4.1, A I1, A V4
The Sleeping Beauty (Script of a Useless Life), Edla Van Steen, A S1
Sleeping with One Eye Open: Women Writers and the Art of Survival, Marilyn
    Kallet and Judith Ortiz Cofer, AB K1
Slide In, My Dark One, between the Crosstie and the Whistle, Elena Poniatowska,
    A E3
The Small Box of Matches, Alicia Partnoy, A P2
Small Change, Marjorie Agosín, A A1
The Small Drawing Room, Guadalupe Amor, A C30
A Small Miracle, Anabel Torres, A O6
Small Poems in Prose (excerpt from *Texts of Shadow and Last Poems*), Alejandra
    Pizarnik, A G12

Souls, Marjorie Agosín, A A1
Soulstorm, Clarice Lispector, A L7.2
Soulstorm: Stories, Clarice Lispector, A L7.2
The Sound of Women, Marjorie Agosín, A A1
The Sound of Writing, Alan Cheuse and Caroline Marshall, A C16
The Source of the Mysterious Voice, Ana María Machado, A M1
South, Aurora Levins Morales, A L4, A T8
Spanish, Marjorie Agosín, A A1
Spanish American Literature in Translation: A Selection of Prose, Poetry, and Drama before 1888. Volume I, Willis Knapp Jones, A J9
Spanish American Literature in Translation: A Selection of Prose, Poetry, and Drama since 1888. Volume II, Willis Knapp Jones, A J9.1
The Spanish American Short Story: A Critical Anthology, Seymour Menton, A M14
Speaking Like an Immigrant, Mariana Romo-Carmona, A R15
Speaking Like an Immigrant: A Collection, Mariana Romo-Carmona, A R15
"*Special Latin American Fiction Issue.*" *Mundus Artium* 3.3 (1970), Rainer Schulte, A S7.2
Spick and Span, Liliana Heker, A H13
The Spirit of My Land, Yolanda Oreamuno, A R4
Spirits, Marjorie Agosín, A A1.9
Spirits of the Ordinary: A Tale of Casas Grandes, Kathleen Alcalá, N A3.1
Spiritual Readings, Gabriela Mistral, A T1
Split in Two, Mirta Yáñez, A B25
The Spotted Bird Perched High Above upon the Tall Green Lemon Tree (excerpt), Albalucía Angel, A F3
The Spouse, Achy Obejas, A O2
Spring, Marjorie Agosín, A A1
The Squatter and the Don (excerpt), María Amparo Ruiz de Burton, A A16
St. John's Eve, Marjorie Agosín, A A1
Stained Glass Fish, Mayra Santos-Febres A S6
The Stairway in the Gray Patio, Irma Verolín, A C11
Stalker, Hilma Contreras, A C26
The Stampede, Cristina Peri Rossi, A P6.2
The Star of David, Marjorie Agosín, A A1
Starting Over, Silvia Molina, A G5
The Statue, Cristina Peri Rossi, A P6.2
Statues, or, Being a Foreigner, Cristina Peri Rossi, A P6.1
Steps under Water, Alicia Kozameh, N K2
The Stolen Party, Liliana Heker, A H4, A M8.5, A M8.6
The Stolen Party and Other Stories, Liliana Heker, A H4
The Stone House, Marjorie Agosín, A A1
Stories from across the Globe, International Board on Books for Young People, A I2
The Stories of Eva Luna, Isabel Allende, A A9
Stories in the Stepmother Tongue, Josip Novakovich and Robert Shapard, A N4

The Storm, Alina Diaconú, A A3
Storms of Torment, Carmen Boullosa, A G5
A Story, Aurora Levins Morales, A L4
A Story about Greenery, Luisa Valenzuela, A V1.2, A V1.4
The Story and Its Writer: An Introduction to Short Fiction, Ann Charters, A C13
Story for a Window, Pía Barros, A B5
A Story in Episodes, Teresa Porzencanski, A A1.7
The Story of a Cat, Teresa Porzencanski, A C27
The Story of María Griselda, María Luisa Bombal, A A3
The Story of My Body, Judith Ortiz Cofer, A O7.1
Story of a Parrot, Ana Menéndez, A M13
The Story of Señorita Dust Grain, Ballerina of the Sun (Historia de la Señorita Grano
    de Polvo, bailarina del sol), Teresa de la Parra, A P8
Story-bound, Ana Lydia Vega, A C25
Storytelling, Aurora Levins Morales, A L4
The Strange Invasion that Rose from the Sea, Aminta Buenaño, A B8
Strange Things Happen Here, Luisa Valenzuela, A A14, A I1, A V1.2, A V1.4
Strange Things Happen Here: Twenty-six Short Stories and a Novel, Luisa
    Valenzuela, A V1.4, N V4.6
The Stream of Life, Clarice Lispector, N L3.7
The Street, Marjorie Agosín, A A1
The Street of Night, Lucía Guerra Cunningham, N G10.1
The Street of Night (excerpt), Lucía Guerra Cunningham, A B13
Strip Tease, Marjorie Agosín, A A1.9
The Stronger, Maricarmen O'hara, A O4
The Structure of the Soap Bubble, Lygia Fagundes Telles, A R17
The Student Prince, Maricarmen O'hara, A O4
Su vida/Her Life, Francisca Josefa de Castillo, A S8
Subterranean River, Inés Arredondo, A F10
The Subversive Voice of Carmen Lyra: Selected Work, Carmen Lyra, A H8
Subway, Ana María del Río, A A1.8
The Subwaynauts (Diario de un Subwaynauta), Gloria Chávez-Vásquez, A C15
Such apparent senselessness, Cristina Peri Rossi, A P6.2
Such Gentleness, Clarice Lispector, A L7.2
Sudden Fiction: 60 Short-Short Stories, Robert Shapard and James Thomas, A S10
The Sugar Island, Ivonne Lamazares, N L1
Sugarcane, Achy Obejas, A S18.2
Summer, Lygia Bojunga-Nunes, A B15
The Summer of the Future, Julia Álvarez, A C20
The Summer of the Future/El verano del futuro, Julia Álvarez, A C21
Summer's End in My Country, Marjorie Agosín, A A1
Summers of Syrup, Marjorie Agosín, A A1
The Sunflower, Gabriela Mistral, A T1
Sun Inventions and Perfumes of Carthage: Two Novellas, Teresa Porzecanski, N P7

Sunday, Silvia Molina, A A2
Sunday Siestas, Claribel Alegría, A A8.1
Sundays, Marjorie Agosín, A A1
Superstitions, Marjorie Agosín, A A1
Sursum Corda, Luisa Valenzuela, A V1.4
Survival Stories: Memories of Crisis, Kathryn Rhett, A R7
Susundamba Does Not Show Herself by Day, Lydia Cabrera, A R17
The Swallows of Cuernavaca, Angelina Muñiz-Huberman, A A2
Sweet Blood, Giovanna Rivero Santa Cruz, A R12
The Sweet Breathing of Plants: Women Writing on the Green World, Linda Hogan
    and Brenda Peterson, A H6
Sweet Companion, Marta Blanco, A R5.1
Sweet Diamond Dust (novel), Rosario Ferré, A F4
Sweet Diamond Dust: A Novel and Three Stories of Life in Puerto Rico, Rosario
    Ferré, A F4, N F3.3
The *Sweet Enigma* of a Writer's Life: A Personal Narrative, Marta Rojas, A D5
Swift as Desire, Laura Esquivel, N E4.2
Swift as Desire, Laura Esquivel, A M10
Switching to Santicló, Julia Álvarez, A S3
Sylvia, Evora Tamayo, A C7
Symbiotic Encounter, Carmen Naranjo, A C27
Symmetries, Luisa Valenzuela, A V1.5
Symmetries, Luisa Valenzuela, A V1.5
Symmetry, Blanca Elena Paz, A R5
Synagogue, Rosario Morales, A L4

T
Tag-sale, Nora Glickman, A T6
Takeover, Beatriz Guido, A L6
Taking Root: Narratives of Jewish Women in Latin America, Marjorie Agosín,
    A A1.7
Taking the Vows, Claribel Alegría, A A8.1
A Tale of Courage and Fortitude, Ivonne Strauss de Milz, A A1.7
A Tale of the Dispossessed, Laura Restrepo, N R1.5
The Tale of the Velvet Pillows, Marta Traba, A C27
Tales of Magic Realism by Women: Dreams in a Minor Key, Susana Sturgis, A S20
The Tales of My Aunt Panchita, Carmen Lyra, A D7
The Tales of My Aunt Panchita (prologue), Carmen Lyra, A A14
Tales of the Struggle in Northern Mexico (excerpt from *Cartridge*), Nellie
    Campobello, A A14
Tales Told under the Mango Tree, Judith Ortiz Cofer, A C28, A K3, A O7.3
The Talisman (novella), Claribel Alegría, A A8, N A4
Talking to the Dead, Judith Ortiz Cofer, A O7.3

A Thanksgiving Celebration (Amy), Nicholasa Mohr, A M17.3

That Man, Pollack, Mayra Montero, A C25.1

That's Where I'm Going, Clarice Lispector, A L7.2

There Never Was a Once upon a Time, Carmen Naranjo, A N1

There Never Was a Once upon a Time, Carmen Naranjo, A N1

They Called Her Aurora (A Passion for Donna Summer), Aída Cartagena, A E4

They Say, Marjorie Agosín, A A1

They Won't Take Me Alive: Salvadoran Women Struggle for National Liberation, Claribel Alegría, AB A4.

They're Cows, We're Pigs, Carmen Boullosa, N B7.3

Things, Silvina Ocampo, A A3

The Things that Happen to Men in New York!, Giannina Braschi, A B20

Thinking about Oblivion, Marjorie Agosín, A A1

Third Interlude, Rosario Aguilar, A A5

The Thirsty Little Fish, Jacqueline Balcells, A B2

Thirteen and a Turtle, Mayra Montero, A V4

This America of Ours: The Letters of Gabriela Mistral and Victoria Ocampo, Elizabeth Horan and Doris Meyer, AB H6

This Eye That Looks at Me: First Cycle, Memoirs, Loreina Santos Silva, AB S4

This Love, Marjorie Agosín, A A1.9

This Noise Was Different, Rosario Ferré, A F3.1

This Prison Where I Live: The PEN Anthology of Imprisoned Writers, Siobhan Dowd, A D13

This Time Listen Do What I Say, Marilyn Bobes, A B9

The Thistle, Gabriela Mistral, A T1

Those May Afternoons, Sonia Coutinho, A V2.1

Thou Shalt Not Deviate, Nancy Alonso, A B9

Thoughts on Teaching, Gabriela Mistral, A T1

III, Carmen Boullosa, A D4

Three Cronicas, Clarice Lispector, A E2

Three Days, Luisa Valenzuela, A C2, A V1.5

Three Keys, Lidia Torres, A D2

Three Knots in the Net, Rosario Castellanos, A A6, A A10

Three Love Aerobics, Ana Lydia Vega, A V4

The Three Marías, Rachel de Queiroz, N D3.1

The Three Marías (excerpt), Rachel de Queiroz, A A14

Three Rains, Blanca Elena Paz, A R5

The Threshold, Cristina Peri Rossi, A G10, A P6

Thus Were Their Faces, Silvina Ocampo, A A3, A O3

Tía Coca, Beatriz Santos A D5

Tickle of Love, Marjorie Agosín, A A1.9

Tidal Pools, Marjorie Agosín, A A1

The Tide Returns at Night, Yolanda Oreamuno, A N2, A U1

Tierra del fuego, Sylvia Iparraguierre, N I1

Translated Woman: Crossing the Border with Esperanza's Story, Ruth Behar, AB B3
Transparency, Luisa Valenzuela, A V1.5
The Trapeze Artists, Cristina Peri Rossi, A A14
The Traveler, Yolanda Bedregal, A B8
Travelers, Marjorie Agosín, A A1
Traveling the Length of My Country, Marjorie Agosín, A A1
Travels through Argentina, Peru, and Bolivia, Juana Manuela Gorriti, A A4
Travels through Cuba, María de la Merced Beltrán, A A4
Treasure of the Incas, Juana Manuela Gorriti, A G11, A M9
Treasures in Heaven, Kathleen Alcalá, N A3.2
The Tree, María Luisa Bombal, A B16, A C27, A G10, A H12.1, A M7, A M12, A M14, A R16, A T5
The Tree, Elena Garro, A P7
Tree Is Older Than You Are: A Bilingual Gathering of Poems & Stories from Mexico with Paintings by Mexican Artists, Naomi Shihad Nye, A S11
Tree Ducks, Cristina García, A A12
The Tree That Produces Cups of Tea, María Soledad Quiroga, A A1.1
Trees, Rosario Morales, A L4
Tren, Mayra Santos-Febres, A S16
Trial of the Virgin (Proceso a la virgen), Luisa Valenzuela, A V1, A V1.1, A V1.2
The Trip, Cristina Peri Rossi, A C2.1, A P6
The Trip, María Luisa Puga, A B18, A C2.1
Triptych, Victoria Urbano, A N2, A U1
The TriQuarterly Anthology of Contemporary Latin American Literature, José Donoso and William A. Henkin, A D11
Tropical Synagogues: Short Stories by Jewish-Latin American Writers, Ilan Stavans, A S18.1
The Truce, Rosario Castellanos, A C8
True and False Romances: Stories and a Novella, Ana Lydia Vega, A V3
True Romances (novella), Ana Lydia Vega, A V3
The True Story of a Princess, Inés Arredondo, A A2
Truth, Maricarmen O'hara, A O4
The Tunnel, Armonía Somers, A P7
The Turkish Lover, Esmeralda Santiago, AB S2.1
The Turtle, Brianda Domecq, A A2
Turtledove or a Love Story, Lygia Fagundes Telles, A V2.1
Turtle's Horse, Lydia Cabrera, A H12
25 August 1988, Cristina Rodríguez-Cabral, A D5
21 Years, Clara Isabel Maldonado, A M5
Twin Beds, Giovanna Rivero Santa Cruz, A R12
The Twins of Olmedo Court, Laura Riesco, A B8
Twist and Shout, Judith Ortiz Cofer, A O7.1
Two Foreign Women, Luisa Valenzuela, A K8

The Vintage Book of Latin American Stories, Carlos Fuentes and Julio Ortega, A F10
Violations: Stories of Love by Latin American Women, Psiche Hughes, A H13
Violeta, Marjorie Agosín, A A1
The Virgin in the Desert, Mariana Romo-Carmona, A R15
The Virgin's Passion, Lucía Guerra, A C27
Vision Out of the Corner of One Eye, Luisa Valenzuela, A T3, A V1.2, A V1.4
Vision Out of the Corner of One Eye (Visión de reojo), Luisa Valenzuela, A V1
Visions, Silvina Ocampo, A O3
The Visit, Nayla Chehade Durán, A L3
A Visit, Hilma Contreras, A C26
Voice on the Telephone, Silvina Ocampo, A O3
Voices that Grew Old, Elvira Orphée, A C10
Void and Vacuum, Luisa Valenzuela, A V1.4
Void and Vacuum (Vacío era el de antes), Luisa Valenzuela, A V1
Voyage to the Other Extreme, Marilú Mallet, A M6
Voyage to the Other Extreme: Five Stories, Marilú Mallet, A M6
The Voyeuse, Regina Rheda, A R6

W

Wachale! Poetry and Prose about Growing up Latino in America, Ilan Stavans, A S18.2
The Wait, Hilma Contreras, A C26
Waiting for Polidoro, Armonía Somers, A C25
Waiting Game, Pía Barros, A B5
The Wake, Margo Glantz, N G6.1
Waking Up Alive, Neomí Ulla, A D10.1
Walimai, Isabel Allende, A A9
The Wall, Rima de Vallbona, A J4
Walls, Carmen Naranjo, A P3
Walo-Wila, Lydia Cabrera, A A14, A H12
The Wanderer, Marjorie Agosín, A A1.9
Wanderings, Marjorie Agosín, A A1
Warmi, Giovanna Rivero Santa Cruz, A G9
The Warmth of Things, Nélida Piñón, A G10, A M12.1
Warnings, Marjorie Agosín, A A1.9
Wash Water, Ana María del Río, A R17
Wasted Effort, Aída Cartagena Portalatín, A D5
Water, Marjorie Agosín, A A1.3
Waters, Achy Obejas, A H7
Waters of the Sea, Clarice Lispector, A L7.2
Waves of Satin, Giovanna Rivero Santa Cruz, A R12
Wax Candles, Marjorie Agosín, A A1.3
The Way of the Cross, Clarice Lispector, A L7.2

Autobiographies/Biographies and Other Narrative

This index includes autobiographies, biographies, and other types of narrative, indicated by the letters "AB." The following letter represents the first letter of the author's last name. If there is more than one work per author, this is indicated by 1.1, 1.2, etc. These codes are used for cross-referencing in the other indices. Original titles are provided when available and appropriate.

AB A1
Adams, Ansel, and Elena Poniatowska, eds. *Frida Kahlo: The Camera Seduced.* San Francisco: Chronicle Books, 1992. 125 pp.
A memoir of Frida Kahlo, the Mexican artist, written by Elena Poniatowska as if she were Kahlo. Photographs by Ansel Adams, Imogen Cunningham, and Edward Weston. Essay by Carla Stellweg. Mexico.

AB A2
Agosin, Marjorie. *The Alphabet in My Hands: A Writing Life.* New Brunswick, NJ: Rutgers University Press, 2000. 187 pp.
A personal account of Agosín's life as a Jew in Chile. This work is fully annotated in the Anthology index. Chile.

AB A2.1
———. *Always from Somewhere Else: A Memoir of My Chilean Jewish Father.* Trans. Celeste Kostopulos Cooperman. New York: The Feminist Press at the City University of New York, 1999. 260 pp.
The story of the author's grandparents and parents who encountered anti-Semitism in Chile. Includes an introduction by Elizabeth Rose Horan. Chile.

AB A2.2
———. *Cartographies: Meditations on Travel.* Athens and London: The University of Georgia Press, 2004. 134 pp.
Agosin writes in lyrical form of the cities, towns, and villages on four continents that she has either visited or where she has lived.

AB A2.3

Agosín, Marjorie. *A Cross and a Star: Memories of a Jewish Girl in Chile.* Trans.
Celeste Kostopulos-Cooperman. Albuquerque: University of New Mexico
Press, 1995. 479 pp.

Agosín describes growing up in Chile as the daughter of Jewish immigrants. English
translation of *Sagrada memoria: reminiscencias de una niña judía en Chile.*
Includes an introduction by Celeste Kostopulos-Cooperman. Chile.

AB A2.4

———, ed. *Gabriela Mistral: The Audacious Traveler.* Athens: Ohio University
Press, 2003. 308 pp.

Essays by academics about the life of Gabriela Mistral, the Chilean writer.

AB A 2.5

———. *Memory, Oblivion, and Jewish Culture in Latin America.* Austin: University
of Texas Press, 2005. 248 pp.

Includes fifteen essays by people of various professions (writers, scholars, artists,
historians and social scientists) who write about Jewish life in Latin America.

AB A2.6

———, ed. *To Mend the World: Women Reflect on 9/11.* Buffalo, NY: White Pine
Press, 2002. 239 pp.

Essays by many Latin American women writers revealing their impressions and
thoughts on the attack on the World Trade Towers in New York on 9/11. Includes:
Marjorie Agosín, September 11 Arrived. Julia Alvarez, The Day After September
11; Ground Zero. Judith Ortiz Cofer, The Names of the Dead. Mirta Ojito, Through
the Prism of a Latin Past. Emma Sepúlveda, Can We Forget and Forgive?

AB A3

Agosín, Marjorie, and Emma Sepúlveda Pulvirenti. *Amigas: Letters of Friendship
and Exile.* Austin: University of Texas Press, 2001. 180 pp.

The correspondence between two Chilean friends, Marjorie Agosín and Emma
Sepúlveda-Pulvirenti. Letters date from their adolescence when both resided in
Chile through their adult years, as residents of the United States.

AB A4

Alegría, Claribel. *They Won't Take Me Alive: Salvadoran Women Struggle for
National Liberation.* Trans. Amanda Hopkinson. London: Women's Press,
1986. 145 pp.

Eugenia, a Salvadoran woman, tells the story of women's involvement in El
Salvador's military politics. Original title: *No me agarran viva: la mujer
salvadoreña en la lucha.*

AB A5

Alegria, Claribel and Darwin Flakoll. *Death of Somoza*. Willimantic, CT: Curbstone Press, 1996. 161 pp.

Based on interviews conducted in 1983 with the commando team that assassinated the deposed Nicaraguan President Somoza in Asunción, Paraguay. Original title: *Somoza: expediente cerrado, la historia de un ajusticiamiento*. El Salvador.

AB A6

Allende, Isabel. *My Invented Country: A Nostalgic Journey through Chile*. Trans. Margaret Sayers Peden. New York: HarperCollins Publishers, 2003. 199 pp.

A memoir of Chile where Allende recalls her native country and speaks about her adopted one. Original title: *Mi país inventado: un paseo nostálgico por Chile*.

AB A7

Álvarez, Julia. *Something to Declare*. Chapel Hill, NC: Algonquin Books, 1998. 300 pp.

Alvarez's insight into being a bi-cultural writer. Autobiographical essays: Part One: Customs. Grandfather's Blessing; Our Papers; My English; My Second Opera; I Want to Be Miss America; El Doctor; La Gringuita; Picky Eater; Briefly a Gardener; Imagining Motherhood; Genetics of Justice; Family Matters. Part Two: Declarations. First Muse; Of Maids and Other Muses; So Much Depends; Doña Aída, with Your Permission; Have Typewriter, Will Travel; A Vermont Writer from the Dominican Republic; Chasing the Butterflies; Goodbye, Ms. Chips; In the Name of the Novel; Ten of My Writing Commandments; Grounds for Fiction; Writing Matters. Dominican Republic.

AB A8

Arana, Marie. *American Chica: Two Worlds, One Childhood*. New York: Dial Press, 2001. 309 pp.

Arana, whose father is Peruvian and her mother American, tells the story of her parents' turbulent relationship when the family lived in Peru.

AB B1

Barrios de Chamorro, Violeta, Guido Fernández, and Sonia Cruz de Baltodano. *Dreams of the Heart: The Autobiography of President Violeta Barrios de Chamorro*. New York: Simon and Schuster, 1996. 352 pp.

The memoirs of the former president of Nicaragua, Violeta Barrios de Chamorro.

AB B2

Barrios de Chungará, Domitila. *Let Me Speak! Testimony of Domitila. A Woman of the Bolivian Mines*. With Moema Viezzer. Trans. Victoria Ortiz. New York: Monthly Review, 1978.

The testimony of Domitila, the wife of a Bolivian miner who organized other housewives to protest against the conditions in which miners lived.

AB B3

Behar, Ruth. *Translated Woman: Crossing the Border with Esperanza's Story.* Boston: Beacon Press, 1993. 369 pp.

The story of Esperanza Hernández, a Mexican street vendor, as translated from an oral interview with the author.

AB B4

Belli, Gioconda. *The Country under My Skin: A Memoir of Love and War.* Trans. Kristina Cordero with the author. New York: Alfred A. Knopf, 2002. 380 pp.

A memoir in which Belli relates her dissatisfaction with domestic life that led her to join the Sandinistas and her subsequent involvement with the group for many years. Original title: *El país bajo mi piel.* Nicaragua.

AB B5

Borton de Treviño, Elizabeth. *My Heart Lies South: The Story of My Mexican Marriage.* Bathgate, ND: Bethlehem Books, 2000. 228 pp.

Originally written in the 1950s, this edition has been edited to better appeal to adolescent readers. It's the story of a young American writer who travels to Mexico to work for the *Boston Herald* and who, a year later, returned to marry a Mexican.

AB B6

Boza, María del Carmen. *Scattering the Ashes: A Memoir.* Tempe, AZ: Bilingual Review Press, 1999. 320 pp.

A Cuban memoir in which the author details her family's exile in Miami.

AB B7

Browdy de Hernández, Jennifer. *Women Writing Resistance: Essays on Latin American and the Caribbean.* Cambridge: South End Press, 2005. 241 pp.

Includes essays by Aurora Levins Morales (Puerto Rico), Raquel Partnoy (Argentina), Ruth Behar (Cuba), Emma Sepúlveda (Chile), Rosario Castellanos (Mexico), Judith Ortiz Cofer (Puerto Rico), Rigoberta Menchú (Guatemala), Elena Poniatowska (Mexico), Alicia Partnoy (Argentina), Marjorie Agosín (Chile), and Julia Alvarez (Dominican Republic).

AB C1

Cerar, Melissa K., ed. *Teenage Refugees from Nicaragua Speak Out.* New York: Rosen Publishing Group, 1994. 64 pp.

Oral histories by Nicaraguan teenagers living in the United States and Canada.

AB C2

Codye, Corinn. *Vilma Martínez.* Trans. Alma Flor Ada. Austin, TX: Steck-Vaughn Co., 1990. 32 pp.

The biography of a woman who became a lawyer and challenged laws that discriminated against Latinos. Bilingual edition. Illustrated by Susi Kilgore.

AB C3

Corona, Ignacio, and Beth Ellen Jorgensen, eds. *The Contemporary Mexican Chronicle: Theoretical Perspectives on the Liminal Genre.* Albany: State University Press of New York, 2002. 266 pp.
Includes an essay by Elena Poniatowska, "How I started writing chronicles and why I never stopped," and "Cristina Pacheco's Narratives: Multimedia Chronicles" by Dawn Slack.

AB C4

Correas Zapata, Celia. *Isabel Allende: Life and Spirits.* Trans. Margaret Sayers Peden. Tempe, AZ: Arte Público Press, 2002. 228 pp.
The story of Isabel Allende's life through a series of interviews. Chile.

AB C5

Cruz, Celia, and Ana Cristina Reymundo. *Celia: My Life: An Autobiography.* New York: HarperCollins, 2004. 260 pp
The life story of Celia Cruz, the Cuban singer.

AB C6

Cuero, Delfina, and Florence Connolly Shipek. *Delfina Cuero: Her Autobiography, an Account of Her Last Years, and Her Ethnobotanic Contributions.* Menlo Park, CA: Ballena Press, 1991. 98 pp.
A detailed account of Delfina Cuero's work in ethnobotany.

AB D1

DeCosta-Willis, Miriam. *Singular Like a Bird: The Art of Nancy Morejón.* Washington, DC: Howard University Press, 1999. 363 pp.
Essays concerning the writing of Nancy Morejón, the Cuban author.

AB D2

De Ferrari, Gabriella. *Gringa Latina: Woman of Two Worlds.* New York: Kodansha International, 1996. 176 pp.
The life of the author who grew up in Peru as the daughter of foreigners.

AB D3

De Jesús, Carolina María. *Child of the Dark: The Diary of Carolina María de Jesús.* Trans. David St. Clair. New York: E. P. Dutton, 1962. 159 pp.
The story of Carolina María de Jesús, an impoverished woman who lived in the slums of Brazil, as told to a reporter and written in her personal diaries. Original title: *Quarto de despejo.* Brazil.

AB D4

de la Cruz, Sor Juana Inés. *A Woman of Genius/La respuesta a Sor Filotea: The Intellectual Autobiography of Sor Juana Inés de la Cruz.* Trans. Margaret Sayers Peden. Tempe, AZ: Bilingual Review Press, 1999. 108 pp.

The story of Sor Juana Inés de la Cruz, the Mexican nun. Spanish/English bilingual format.

AB D5

Dujovne Ortiz, Alicia. *Eva Perón.* Trans. Shawn Fields. New York: St. Martin's Griffin, 1997. 325 pp.

The story of Eva Perón, from her impoverished childhood to her marriage to the Argentine dictator Juan Perón.

AB D6

Durán, Gloria. *Malinche: Slave Princess of Cortez.* Hamden, CT: Linnet Books, 1993. 221 pp.

The biography of La Malinche who acted as Cortez's interpreter and helper in the conquest of Mexico by the Spanish conquistadores.

AB D7

Durán Trujillo, Marie Oralia. *Autumn Memories: My New Mexican Roots and Traditions.* Pueblo, CO: El Escritorio, 1999. 120 pp.

The story of the Durán family and their life in New Mexico.

AB E1

Eidse, Faith, and Nina Sichel, eds. *Unrooted Childhoods: Memoirs of Growing Up Global.* London: Nicholas Brealey, 2003. 375 pp.

Includes a memoir by Isabel Allende. Chile.

AB E2

Esquibel Tywoniak, Frances, and Mario T. García. *Migrant Daughter: Coming of Age as a Mexican-American Woman.* Berkeley: University of California Press, 2000. 237 pp.

Frances Esquibel Tywoniak's coming-of-age story as a Mexican-American dealing with two cultures.

AB E3

Esquivel, Laura. *Between Two Fires: Intimate Writings on Life, Love, Food and Flavor.* Trans. Stephen A. Lytle. New York: Crown Publishers, 2000. 153 pp.

Includes 14 short essays of recipes, memories, and stories. Mexico.

AB E3.1

——. *Malinche.* New York: Atria Books, 2006. 191 pp.

The story of Doña Marina, Hernán Cortés' interpreter and lover, who helped him in the conquest of Mexico. Illustrations by Jordi Castells. Original title: *Malinche.* Mexico.

AB F1

Fernández, Alina. *(Fidel) Castro's Daughter: An Exile's Memoir of Cuba.* New York: St. Martin's Press, 1998. 259 pp.
Fidel Castro's daughter tells the story of her life. Original title: *Alina: Memorias de la hija rebelde de Fidel Castro.* Cuba.

AB F2

Fisher, Jo. *Mothers of the Disappeared.* Cambridge: South End Press, 1989. 168 pp.
The story of the Mothers of the Plaza de Mayo in Argentina, and their struggle to find their lost children during the years of military rule.

AB G1

Galeana, Benita. *Benita.* Trans. Amy Diane Prince. Pittsburgh, PA: Latin American Literary Review Press, 1994. 176 pp.
The story of the Mexican political activist Benita Galeana who rose from humble beginnings to become an advocate for workers' rights.

AB G2

García, Cristina. *Cars of Cuba.* New York: H. N. Abrams, 1995. 64 pp.
A written and photographic account of the old American cars still in use in Cuba. Photographs by Joshua Greene, essay by Cristina García. Created by D. D. Allen. Cuba.

AB G3

García, María Cristina. *Havana USA: Cuban Exiles and Cuban Americans in South-Florida, 1959-1994.* Berkeley: University of California Press, 1996. 290 pp.
A reference guide to the successive waves of Cuban immigration to the United States and subsequent tensions between the Floridians and new immigrants. Includes information on writers and scholars in exile. Cuba.

AB G4

Glickman, Nora. *The Jewish White Slave Trade and the Untold Story of Raquel Liberman.* New York: Garland Publishers, 2000. 190 pp.
The story of Raquel Liberman, an immigrant to Argentina who was forced into prostitution and successfully fought against the violence and corruption associated with it.

AB G5

Gonzáles, Luisa. *At the Bottom: A Woman's Life in Central America.* Berkeley: New Earth Publications, 1994. 121 pp.
The autobiography of Luisa Gonzáles, a member of the Communist Party of Costa Rica. Original title: *A Ras del suelo.*

AB G6

Gorkin, Michael, Marta Pineda, and Gloria Leal, eds. *From Grandmother to Granddaughter: Salvadoran Women's Stories.* Berkeley: University of California Press, 2000. 260 pp.
Interviews revealing the life stories of nine Salvadoran women from different generations.

AB G7

Guillermoprieto, Alma. *Dancing with Cuba: A Memoir of the Revolution.* Trans. Esther Allen. New York: Pantheon Books, 2004. 290 pp.
Memories of the author's time spent teaching modern dance in Cuba. Original title: Unavailable. Mexico.

AB G8

———. *Samba.* New York: Knopf, 1990. 244 pp.
A description of the Brazilian samba as well as an interpretation of black Brazilian history and culture. Mexico.

AB H1

Hayden, Tom, ed. *The Zapatista Reader.* New York: Thunder's Mouth Press/Nation Books, 2002. 503 pp.
Material written by leading Zapatista supporters. Includes an essay by Elena Poniatowska, "Women's Battle for Respect Inch by Inch."

AB H2

Hecht, Tobias. *After Life: An Ethnographic Novel.* Durham, NC: Duke University Press, 2006. 144 pp.
The author interviewed Bruna Verissimo from Recife, Brazil, who related her horrendous childhood and her life as a prostitute. As the author was unable to confirm the veracity of Bruna's story, he ultimately wrote the work, based on her tales, as a novel.

AB H3

Heredia, Juanita, and Bridget A. Kevane, eds. *Latina Self-Portraits: Interviews with Contemporary Women Writers.* Albuquerque: University of New Mexico Press, 2000. 192 pp.
Authors interviewed: Julia Álvarez, Denise Chávez, Sandra Cisneros, Rosario Ferré, Christina García, Nicholasa Mohr, Cherríe Moraga, Judith Ortiz Cofer, Esmeralda

Santiago, and Helena María Viramontes. Also includes bibliographies for each of the writers.

AB H4

Hill, Christine M. *Ten Hispanic Authors*. Berkeley Heights, NJ: Enslow Publishers, 2002. 112 pp.
Includes biographies of Julia Álvarez, Sandra Cisneros, Judith Ortiz Cofer, Nicholasa Mohr, and Esmeralda Santiago.

AB H5

Hinojosa, María. *Raising Raúl: Adventures Raising Myself and My Son*. New York: Viking Press, 1999. 240 pp.
A memoir of a woman raising a child in the 1990s while struggling with her identity as a Mexican-American.

AB H6

Horan, Elizabeth, and Doris Meyer, eds. *This America of Ours: The Letters of Gabriela Mistral and Victoria Ocampo*. Austin: University of Texas Press, 2003. 377 pp.
Includes letters between Gabriela Mistral and Victoria Ocampo, a translation of Victoria Ocampo's essay "Gabriela Mistral en sus cartas," and excerpts from *Cartas a Angélica y otros* and *Correspondencia (1939-1978)*. Also includes a preface and an introduction by the editors, a chronology and a biographical dictionary.

AB K1

Kallet, Marilyn, and Judith Ortiz Cofer, eds. *Sleeping with One Eye Open: Women Writers and the Art of Survival*. Athens: University of Georgia Press, 1999. 221 pp.
Writers discuss their strategies for coping with life's demands and how this affects their writing. Essays by the Latina writers Judith Ortiz Cofer, Sandra Benítez, and Aleida Rodríguez. Includes bio-bibliographies for contributors.

AB L1

Levine, Robert M., ed. & intro. *Bitita's Diary: The Childhood Memories of Carolina Maria de Jesús*. Trans. Emanuelle Oliveira and Beth Joan Vinkler. Armonk, NY: M.E. Sharpe, 1997. 163 pp.
The autobiographical memoir of Carolina María de Jesús, a black Brazilian woman who lived in poverty. The book describes her early life in the 1920s and 30s.

AB L2

Levine, Robert M., and José Carlos Ebe Bom Meihy. *The Unedited Diaries of Carolina Maria de Jesús*. Trans. Nancy P. S. Naro and Cristina Mehrtens. New Brunswick, NJ: Rutgers University Press, 1999. 233 pp.
The diaries of Carolina María de Jesus, a black Brazilian women who lived in

poverty and described her situation in personal diaries.

AB L3

Lispector, Clarice. *Selected Cronicas.* Trans. Giovanni Pontiero. New York: New
    Directions Pub. Corp., 1996. 212 pp.

A selection of translated chronicles which were originally published as part of
Lispector's weekly column for the Brazilian newspaper *Jornal do Brasil.* Also
included is the translation of *Descoberta do mundo,* translated with the title
Discovering the World. Brazil.

AB L4

Lomas, Clara, ed. *The Rebel.* Houston, TX: Arte Público Press, 1994. 297 pp.

The memoirs of Leonor Villegas de Magnón (1876-1955), a woman opposed to the
dictatorship of Porfirio Díaz in Mexico. Originally written in the 1920s, this is the
work's first publication. Mexico.

AB M1

McNeese, Tim. *Isabel Allende.* New York: Chelsea House, Facts on File, 2006.

A biography of Isabel Allende, the Chilean author.

AB M2

Main, Mary. *Isabel Allende: Award-winning Latin American Author.* Berkeley
    Heights, NY: Enslow Publishers, 2005.

A biography of Isabel Allende, the Chilean writer.

AB M3

Medina, Eufelia. *Me and My Helper, the Autobiography of Eufelia Medina 1914-
    1976.* Denver, CO: Western History/Genealogy Dept., Denver Public Library,
    1970. 7 pp. and related papers.

The story of Eufelia Medina. Includes a typed autobiography, poems, clippings,
photographs, a family tree, and copies of letters.

AB M4

Mellibovsky, Matilde. *Circle of Love Over Death: The Story of the Mothers of the
    Plaza de Mayo.* Trans. Matthew and María Proser. Willimantic, CT: Curbstone
    Press, 1998. 254 pp.

Interviews with the mothers of the Plaza de Mayo who continue to search for their
disappeared family members after the Dirty Wars in Argentina. Mellibovksy is one
of the founding members of the Mothers of the Plaza de Mayo.

AB M5

Menchú, Rigoberta. *Crossing Borders.* Trans. Ann Wright. London: Verso, 1998.
    242 pp.

Menchú explores the themes of exile and return and discusses Guatemala's political situation.

AB M5.1

Menchú, Rigoberta. *The Honey Jar*. Trans. David Unger. Toronto: Groundwood
   Books/House of Anansi Press, 2006. 56 pp.
Menchú retells the Mayan stories told to her by her grandparents. Juvenile
literature. Original title: *El vaso de miel*. Guatemala.

AB M5.2

———. *I, Rigoberta Menchú: An Indian Woman of Guatemala*. Trans. Ann Wright.
   London: Verso, 1984. 251 pp.
The Quiché-Mayan human rights advocate gives testimony to the abuses inflicted
on her people by the Guatemalan government. Menchú received the Nobel Peace
Prize in 1992. Edited with an introduction by Elisabeth Burgos Debray. Original
title: *Me llamo Rigoberta Menchú y así me nació la conciencia*. Guatemala.

AB M6

Menchú, Rigoberta, and Dante Liano. *The Girl from Chimel*. Trans. David Unger.
   Toronto: Groundwood Books/House of Anansi Press, 2005. 54 pp.
The biography of Rigoberta Menchú, the Guatemalan peace activist and Nobel
Peace Prize winner, as told for young audiences. Original title: *Una niña de Chimel*.
Guatemala.

AB M7

Mercado, Tununa. *In a State of Memory*. Trans. Peter Kahn. Lincoln: University of
   Nebraska Press, 2001. 156 pp.
This novelistic memoir traces the author's exile and return to Argentina. She details
the psychological and physical effects exile has taken on her through the narrator's
voice. Original title: *El estado de memoria*. Argentina.

AB M8

Molloy, Sylvia. *At Face Value: Autobiographical Writing in Spanish America*.
   Cambridge: Cambridge University Press, 1991. 273 pp.
The author examines the genre of autobiography from the 19th and 20th centuries.
Includes the Argentine writer Victoria Ocampo.

AB M9

Mujica, Barbara Louise. *Frida: A Novel*. New York: Plume, 2002. 366 pp.
A fictionalized account of the life of Frida Kahlo, the Mexican artist, as told by
Frida's younger sister. Mexico.

AB N1

New Americas Press. eds. *A Dream Compels Us: Voices of Salvadoran Women*.
   Cambridge: South End Press, 1989. 246 pp.

Interviews, testimonies, and articles about women involved in the revolutionary movements in El Salvador.

AB O1

O'Brien, John, et al., eds. *Writers on Writing: The Best of the Review of Contemporary Fiction.* Normal, IL: The Review of Contemporary Fiction, 1999. 197 pp.

Includes essays from authors who write on the aesthetic, cultural, social, and political aspects of writing fiction. This volume includes an essay by Luisa Valenzuela (Argentina).

AB O2

O'Neil, Patrick M. *Great World Writers: Twentieth Century.* New York: Marshall Cavendish, 2004. 13 vols.

Includes a profile of the Chilean writer Isabel Allende with facts on her life and works.

AB O3

Ortiz Cofer, Judith. *Silent Dancing: A Partial Remembrance of a Puerto Rican Childhood.* Houston, TX: Piñata Books, 1991. 168 pp.

Autobiographical stories. This volume is fully annotated in the Anthologies index. Puerto Rico.

AB O3.1

——. *Woman in Front of the Sun: On Becoming a Writer.* Athens: University of Georgia Press, 2000. 127 pp.

A collection of prose and poetry that relates how Ortiz Cofer became a writer. Puerto Rico.

AB O3.2

——. *The Year of Our Revolution.* Houston, TX: Arte Público Press, 1998. 128 pp.

The process of growing up viewed through a young woman's eyes. Puerto Rico.

AB P1

Pantoja, Antonia. *Memoir of a Visionary: Antonia Pantoja.* Houston, TX: Arte Público Press, 2002. 218 pp.

Antonia Pantoja, who won the Presidential Medal of Freedom in 1996, was a teacher in Puerto Rico who then moved to New York to work as an engineer. Includes a foreword by Henry A. J. Ramos.

AB P2

Pérez-Mejía, Angela. *A Geography of Hard Times: Narratives about Travel to South America, 1780-1849.* Trans. Dick Cluster. Albany: State University of New York Press, 2002. 167 pp.

Includes essays about Flora Tristán (France/Peru) as well as an excerpt from Tristán's writing. Original title: *La geografía de los tiempos difíciles: escritura de viajes a Sur America durante los procesos de independencia 1780-1849.*

AB P3

Poniatowska, Elena, et al., eds. *Compañeras de Mexico: Women Photograph Women.* Riverside, CA: Sweeney Art Gallery, 1990. 80 pp.
Includes text by Poniatowska. The photographers are Graciela Iturbide, Mariana Yampolsky, Lourdes Grobet, Laura Cohen, and Eugenia Vargas. Mexico.

AB P3.1

Poniatowska, Elena. *Soldaderas: Women of the Mexican Revolution.* Trans. David Dorado Romo. El Paso, TX: Cinco Puntos Press, 2006.
The story of the Mexican women who followed and fought with the men in the Mexican Revolution. Original title: *Soldaderas.* Mexico.

AB P4

Poniatowska, Elena, and Amanda Holmes. *Mexican Color.* New York: Stewart, Tabori and Chang, 1998. 160 pp.
Poniatowska writes of the historical and contemporary uses of color in Mexico. Accompanied by 200 color photographs by Amanda Holmes.

AB P5

Poniatowska, Elena, and Kent Klich. *El niño: Children of the Streets, Mexico City.* Syracuse, NY: Syracuse University Press, 1999. 167 pp.
Poniatowska wrote the text to accompany the 70 photographs of street children taken by documentary photographer Kent Klich.

AB P6

Prentice Hall Literature Library, ed. *Biography and Autobiography.* Upper Saddle River, NJ: Prentice-Hall, Inc., 2000. 154 pp.
Includes various writers whose work is of an autobiographical nature. Includes bio-bibliographies of contributors.

AB R1

Ramos-Horta, José, ed. *The Art of Peace: Nobel Peace Laureates Discuss Human Rights, Conflict and Reconciliation.* Ithaca, NY: Snow Lion Publications, 2000. 233 pp.
Includes an essay by the Guatemalan Rigoberta Menchú: "Role of Indigenous People in a Democratic Guatemala."

AB R2

Rivera Marín, Guadalupe. *Diego Rivera the Red.* Trans. Dick Gerdes. Tempe, AZ: Arte Público Press, 2004. 256 pp.

The life story of the Mexican muralist Diego Rivera, written by his daughter.

AB R3
Roden, John, ed. *Conversations with Isabel Allende*. Austin: University of Texas Press, 1999.
Isabel Allende tells what it takes to be a writer. Chile.

AB R4
Rojas, Marta, and Mirta Ro. *Tania, the Unforgettable Guerrilla*. London: Ocean Books, 1973. 137 pp.
The story of the East German-born woman who died with Che Guevara in Bolivia. Includes letters, photographs, and memoirs. Original title: *Tania, la guerrillera inolvidable*.

AB R5
Ryan, Bryan. *Hispanic Writers: A Selection of Sketches from Contemporary Authors*. New York: Gale Group, 2000. 514 pp.
Includes more than 400 entries on twentieth-century Hispanic writers.

AB R6
Ruiz de Burton, María Amparo, Rosaura Sánchez, and Beatrice Pita. *Conflicts of Interest: The Letters of María Amparo Ruiz de Burton*. Houston, TX: Arte Público Press, 2001. 647 pp.
Edited and with a commentary by Rosaura Sánchez and Beatrice Pita.

AB S1
Sadow, Stephen A. *King David's Harp: Autobiographical Essays by Jewish Latin American Writers*. Albuquerque: University of New Mexico Press, 1999. 290 pp.
Includes essays by Alcina Lubitch Domecq, Margo Glantz, and Marjorie Agosín.

AB S2
Santiago, Esmeralda. *Almost a Woman*. New York: Vintage Books, 1999. 320 pp.
Sequel to *When I Was Puerto Rican*. The author's life after she arrives in Brooklyn at the age of 13.

AB S2.1
——. *The Turkish Lover.* Cambridge: Da Capo Press, 2004. 341 pp.
The autobiographical story of a young Esmeralda Santiago who ran away from home to be with her older lover who ultimately abused her. Puerto Rico.

AB S2.2
——. *When I Was Puerto Rican*. New York: Vintage Books, 1993. 274 pp.
The author recalls her childhood in Puerto Rico and Brooklyn. Includes a glossary

of Spanish terms.

AB S3

Santiago, Esmeralda, and Joie Davidow, eds. *Las Mamis: Favorite Latino Authors Remember Their Mothers*. New York: Knopf, 2000. 189 pp.
Fourteen authors talk about their mothers and their effect on their lives. This volume is fully annotated in the Anthologies index.

AB S4

Santos Silva, Loreina. *This Eye That Looks at Me: First Cycle, Memoirs*. Trans. Carys Evans-Corrales. Pittsburgh, PA: Latin American Literary Review Press, 2000. 106 pp.
A memoir of the Puerto Rican author. She explores her life in vignettes, beginning with her birth and ending with her escape to the United States. Original title: *Este ojo que me mira: ciclo 1 memorias*. Puerto Rico.

AB S5

Saralegui, Cristina. *Cristina! My Life as a Blonde*. Trans. Margaret Sayers Peden. New York: Warner Books, 1998. 273 pp.
The author, the host of "El Show de Cristina," offers her opinions on a variety of topics. Cuba.

AB S6

Sepúlveda-Pulvirenti, Emma. *From Border Crossings to Campaign Trail: Chronicle of a Latina in Politics*. Falls Church, VA: Azul Editions, 1998. 268 pp.
The Argentine-born author who grew up in Chile documents the trials and tribulations of running for the Nevada Senate.

AB S7

Shapiro, Michael. *A Sense of Place: Great Travel Writers Talk about Their Craft, Lives, and Inspiration*. San Francisco: Travelers' Tales, 2004. 399 pp.
Includes "At Home with the Spirits" by Isabel Allende (Chile).

AB S8

Sinclair, Minor, ed. *The New Politics of Survival: Grassroots Movements in Central America*. New York: Monthly Review Press, 1995. 301 pp.
Includes an essay by Rigoberta Menchú (Guatemala), "Weaving our future: campesino struggles for land."

AB S9

Stavans, Ilan. *Conversations with Ilan Stavans*. Tucson: University of Arizona Press, 2005. 255 pp.
Includes interviews with Isabel Allende (Chile), Marjorie Agosín (Chile), Elena Poniatowska (Mexico), and Esmeralda Santiago (Puerto Rico).

AB S10
Szoka, Elzbieta, ed. *Fourteen Female Voices from Brazil: Interviews and Works.* Austin, TX: Host Publications, Inc., 2002. 309 pp.
Includes: Nélida Piñón, Interview; I Love My Husband and Lygia Fagundes Telles, Interview; The Day to Say "No!" Also includes an introduction by Jean Franco and works of poetry and drama.

AB T1
Tagle, Lillian, Joy Bellington, and Chris Lucas, eds. *Honorable Exiles: A Chilean Woman in the 20th Century.* Austin: University of Texas Press, 2000. 232 pp.
Lillian Lorca de Tagle's memoir, detailing her privileged life in Chile and other countries and her eventual exile to the United States.

AB T2
Torres, Olga Beatriz. *Memorias de mi viaje/Recollections of My Trip.* Trans. Juanita Luna-Lawhn. Albuquerque: University of New Mexico Press, 1994. 156 pp.
Originally published in 1919, this is a collection of letters from a young Mexican girl to her aunt. Bilingual format, designed by Juan Bruce-Novoa.

AB T3
Tula, María Teresa, and Lynn Stephen. *Hear My Testimony: Maria Teresa Tula, Human Rights Activist of El Salvador.* Cambridge: South End Press, 1994. 240 pp.
The autobiography of the human rights activist and her involvement in the political strife in El Salvador.

AB V1
Vaz, Katherine. *Mariana.* London: Flamingo, 1997. 325 pp.
Based on the true story of Mariana Alcoforado, a nun who had a love affair with a French mercenary in the 17th century during Portugal's fight for independence.

AB V2
Veciana Suárez, Ana. *Birthday Parties in Heaven: Thoughts of Love, Life, Grief, and Other Matters of the Heart.* New York: Plume, 2000. 117 pp.
Autobiographical essays by the *Miami Herald* columnist. Cuba.

AB V3
Vilar, Irene. *A Message from God in the Atomic Age.* Trans. Gregory Rabassa. New York: Pantheon Books, 1996. 324 pp.
The author's true account of attempted suicide and subsequent confinement to a psychiatric hospital. Original title: unavailable. Puerto Rico.

AB V3.1

Vilar, Irene. *The Ladies' Gallery: A Memoir of Family Secrets.* Trans. Gregory Rabassa. New York: Vintage Books, 1996. 324 pp.

The author's true account of attempted suicide and subsequent confinement to a psychiatric hospital. This is Vintage's title for *A Message from God in the Atomic Age: A Memoir.* Original title: unavailable. Puerto Rico.

AB W1

Whitson, Kathy J. *Encyclopedia of Feminist Literature.* Westport, CT: Greenwood Press, 2004. 300 pp.

Includes entries on Isabel Allende (Chile), Judith Ortiz Cofer (Puerto Rico), and Clarice Lispector (Brazil).

AB Z 1

Zavella, Patricia. *Telling to Live: Latina Feminist Testimonies.* Durham, NC: Duke University Press, 2001.

Stories, poems, and memoirs of 18 Latina feminists who describe their struggle to become writers and to succeed in academia. Includes: Luz del Alba Acevedo, Norma Alarcón, Celia Álvarez, Ruth Behar, Rina Benmayor, Norma E. Cantú, Daisy Cocco De Filippis, Gloria Holguín Cuadraz, Liza Fiol-Matta, Yvette Flores-Ortiz, Inés Hernández-Avila, Aurora Levins Morales, Clara Lomas, Iris Ofelia López, Mirtha N. Quintanales, Eliana Rivero, and Caridad Souza.

Anthologies

The letter "A" indicates that the work is an anthology and the following letter represents the first letter of the author's or editor's last name. If there is more than one work per author or editor this is indicated by 1.1, 1.2, etc. These codes are used for cross-referencing in the other indices.

A A1

Agosín, Marjorie. The *Alphabet in My Hands: A Writing Life*. Trans. Nancy Abraham Hall. New Brunswick, NJ: Rutgers University Press, 2000. 187 pp. *Short fiction:*
Part I: Childhood
Chapter 1: Calendar. Spring; Birth; Passover; Back to School; March; The Blue Uniform; My Apron; My Desk; Rabbit Easter; St. John's Eve; My Birthday; Soledad; Rain; The Beggar Woman; Long Live Saint Peter!; September 18; The Marconi Theater; Rosh Hashanah; Kol Nidre; A Day of Atonement; Christmas Eve at the Pacific; New Year's by the Sea; Summers of Syrup; Tidal Pools; Gypsy Woman; The Movies; The Island of Swallows; Guardian Angels.
Chapter 2: Being Jewish. Identities; Arrivals; Names; Last Names; The Goyim; Being Jewish; Religious Education; Frida and Moises; Sundays; Pulchritude; Tell Me a Story, Papa; Jewish Dog; The Hebrew Institute; My History Teacher; Hebrew; Dead Languages; The Book of God; Shabbat; My Grandfather; Train Station; Aunt Lucha; Dinner with the Aristocrats; The Star of David; Thinking about Oblivion; A Glorious Body; They Say; Confessions; The Godmothers; Photographs I; Photographs II; Photographs III.
Chapter 3: The Women. The Jewelry; Looking-Glass Memory; Helena of Vienna; A Book of Faces; Autumn; Omama Helena; A Bit of Luck; Grandmother's Shoes; Chepi; Travelers; The Deaf; My Aunts; Tamara; Small Change; My Cousin Rafael; You'll Learn It Tomorrow; Superstitions; To Breathe.
Chapter 4: The Guardians of Childhood. Happiness; The Servants; Afternoon Tea; Women Friends/Comadres; The Other Women; Day Off; Claudina; A Corsage of Happiness; Delfina; Souls; Sacred Song; Nape; Nana; Wisdom; Mama Delfina; Carmen Carrasco; Baptisms; The Burning of Judas; The Little Souls; A Cat and a Chicken; Protection; Bread; With the Nanas; The Backrooms.
Part 2: Journey to the Other America

Chapter 5: Time of Ire. Autumn and Lovers; Israel; Jerusalem 1973; Moshe; God's Place; The Balcony; White; Curfew; Dark Silence; The Texture of Fear; Disappeared; The House; The Wind.

Chapter 6: Pilgrimages. The Gringos; Exile Begins; To Set Foot in America; A Foreigner's Nights; The First Months; The Flying Squirrel; Berkeley; Memories; Clark Central High; Mr. Watson; At First; Halloween; The Amusement Park; The Immigrant Girls; Neighbors and Friends; Of Parties and Other Audacities; Borrowed Furniture; The Piano; The Georgia House; Fissures; Gardens; Magnolias; Letters to Be Answered; America and My Mother; Wanderings; Georgian Soil; Country; The Exile; Wellesley College; Russian Lady; Matilde; Snow; Laura; The Raft Girl; Molly McArthur; Birthday; Mama; My House.

Chapter 7: Words. A Basket of Love. A Basket of Books; Books; Silences; Languages; Spanish; My Accent; Why Do I Write?; The Leper Colony; Poetry; Words; To Know the Night; Anne; Gabriela; María Luisa; Sonia Helena; Isla Negra; Pablo Neruda; Goodbye, Pablo Neruda; The Stone House.

Chapter 8: Returns. Memorial of Oblivion; Homecoming; The Street; To Be a Stranger; Escape; With My Children; An Invitation to Travel; My Childhood; Sonia Helena; I Tell Them We Are from Here; The Pools; Traveling the Length of My Country; Calama; Desert Light; The Bonfires; The City of Strangers; High Treason; María; Cecilia; Violeta; The Sound of Women; A Divided Heaven; Desire; Summer's End in My Country; New Year's Day 1997; A Place of Memories; Night; Old Age; Rice Powder; The Roommate; Death; The Last Goodbye; Copihue in Bloom; Guest. Includes an introduction by Nancy Abraham Hall.

Includes brief bio-bibliographic notes on contributors.

Chile.

A A1.1

——, ed. *The American Voice. New Voices from Latin America and Spain.* Louisville: The Kentucky Foundation for Women, 1997. 157 pp.

Short fiction:

Magali García Ramos (Dominican Republic), A Seven-Day Week. Cristina Peri Rossi (Uruguay), The Cavalcade; The Sentinel; The Uprooted; The Fencesitters Society. Ana Pizarro (Chile), The Moon, the Wind, the Year, the Day (excerpt from the novel). Ena Lucía Portela (Cuba), The Urn and the Name (A Comic Tale). Laura Riesco (Peru), The Headache. Ana María Shua (Argentina), Day of Final Judgement; Excesses of Passion; The Ancient God of Fire; Man on the Rug; Bad Advice; Romance between Guard and Magnolia; Founding Fathers on the Blackboard; Time Travel; The Unsurpassable Art of Wang Fo; Cultural Taboo. Ester Seligson (Mexico), Gypsy Curse. María Soledad Quiroga (Bolivia), The Tree That Produces Cups of Tea.

This is a special issue of the journal, no. 44. Includes brief bio-bibliographic notes on contributors.

A A1.2

Agosín, Marjorie, ed. and intro. *A Gabriela Mistral Reader*. Trans. Maria Giachetti. Fredonia, NY: White Pine Press, 1993. 227 pp.

Narrative:

The Sea; The Body; In Praise of Gold; The Lark; In Praise of Small Towns; In Praise of Stones; the Giraffe; An Owl; The Alpaca; The Coconut Palms; In Praise of Salt; Flour; The Little New Moon; Bread; The Fig; Chile; A Profile of the Mexican Indian Woman; Something about the Quechuan People; The Chilean *Copihue*; Alfonsina Storni; Gabriels Thinks about Her Absent Mother; The Tropical Destiny of South America; An American Myth: Chile's *El Caleuche;* The Argentine Pampa; A Word That We Have Stained: Tropicalism; An Invitation to the Work of Rainer Maria Rilke; A Message about Pablo Neruda; How I Write.

This volume also includes poetry and essays written by Mistral. Agosín's introduction titled "Gabriela Mistral, the Restless Soul," deals with Mistral's life and works. Includes notes on the translator and editor.

Chile.

A A1.3

——. *Happiness: Stories by Marjorie Agosín*. Trans. and intro. Elizabeth Horan. Fredonia, NY: White Pine Press, 1993. 237 pp.

Short stories:

Slaves; Happiness; Fat; Braids; An Immense Black Umbrella; Adelina; Nana; Monserrat Ordóñez; Emma; Wax Candles; Gypsy Women; North; Photographs; The Gold Bracelet; The Fiesta; Orphanages; The Seamstress from Saint Petersburg; The Eiderdown; Pisagua; The Hen; Pork Sausages; Itinerants; Water; Signs of Love; Love Letters; First Time to the Sea; Mirrors; Meditation on the Dead; Río de la Plata; Blood; Journey to the End of Coasts; Forests; Beds; Cartographies; The Dead; The Rubber Tree; Long Live Life; Prairies; Sargasso; Rivers; Distant Root of Autumn Loves; Naked; Houses by the Sea; The Dreams of Van Gogh.

Includes brief bio-bibliographic notes.

Chile.

A A1.4

——, ed. *The House of Memory: Stories by Jewish Women Writers of Latin America*. Trans. Elizabeth Rosa Horan. New York: The Feminist Press at the City University of New York, 1999. 246 pp.

Short stories:

Marjorie Agosín (Chile), *Always from Somewhere Else* (excerpt). Ruth Behar (Cuba), In the Absence of Love. Miriam Bornstein (Mexico), On the Border: Essential Stories. Luisa Futoransky (Argentina), The Melancholy of Black Panthers. Alicia Freilich de Segal (Venezuela), *Cláper* (excerpt). Margo Glantz (Mexico), *The Family Tree* (excerpt); Shoes. Angelina Gorodischer (Argentina), Camara Obscura. Sonia Guralnik (Chile), *Sailing Down the Rhine* (excerpt). Rosalina Kalina, (Costa Rica), Golem. Alicia Kozameh (Argentina), Alcira in Yellows. Clarice Lispector (Brazil), No More Worries. Barbara Mujica (Chile), Gotlib, Bombero. Angelina

Muñiz-Huberman (Mexico), The Portuguese Synagogue. Rosa Nissan (Mexico), *May You Make a Good Bride* (excerpt). Teresa Porzecanski (Uruguay), Rojl Eisips. Reina Roffé (Argentina), Exotic Birds. Graciela Safranchik (Argentina), Kaddish. Ana María Shua (Argentina), *The Book of Memories* (excerpt). Ester Rebeca Shapiro Rok (Cuba), Belarus to Bolondro: A Daughter's Dangerous Passage (excerpt). Alicia Steimberg (Argentina), *Musicians and Watchmakers* (excerpt). Ana Vásquez (Chile), The Sign of the Star.
Includes brief bio-bibliographies on contributors. The introduction by Marjorie Agosín traces the history of Latin American Jewish women writers.

A A1.5
Agosín, Marjorie, ed. and intro. *Landscapes of a New Land: Short Fiction by Latin American Women*. Fredonia, NY: White Pine Press, 1993. 193 pp.
Short stories:
Dora Alonso (Cuba), Cage Number One. Helena Araujo (Colombia), The Open Letter. Jacqueline Balcells (Chile), The Enchanted Raisin. Yolanda Bedregal (Bolivia), "Good Evening, Agatha." Patricia Bins (Brazil), Destination. María Luisa Bombal (Chile), Sky, Sea and Earth. Marta Brunet (Chile), Solitude of Blood. Lygia Fagundes Telles (Brazil), The Key. Margo Glantz (Mexico), Genealogies. Hilda Hilst (Brazil), An Avid One in Extremis; Natural Theology. Clarice Lispector (Brazil), Plaza Mauá. Carmen Naranjo (Costa Rica), The Compulsive Couple of the House on the Hill. Silvina Ocampo (Argentina), The Servant's Slaves. Elvira Orphée (Argentina), The Beguiling Ladies. Cristina Peri Rossi (Uruguay), The Museum of Futile Endeavors. Nélida Piñón (Brazil), I Love My Husband. Elena Poniatowska (Mexico), The Message. Amalia Rendic (Chile), A Child, a Dog, the Night. Laura Riesco (Peru), Jimena's Fair. Alicia Steimberg (Argentina), Cecilia's Last Will and Testament. Luisa Valenzuela (Argentina), The Snow White Guard.
Includes brief bio-bibliographic notes on authors and translators.

A A1.6
——, ed. *A Map of Hope: Women's Writing on Human Rights: An International Anthology.* New Brunswick, NJ: Rutgers University Press, 1998. 369 pp.
Short stories:
Claribel Alegría (El Salvador), The Writer's Commitment. Isabel Allende (Chile), The Hour of Truth. Rosario Castellanos (Mexico), Indian Mother. Matilde Mellibovsky (Argentina), Arriving at the Plaza. Angelina Muñiz Huberman (Mexico), The Prisoner. Ana Pizarro (Chile), The Moon, the Wind, the Year, the Day. Luisa Valenzuela (Argentina), The Censors.
Includes brief bio-bibliographic notes on contributors.

A A1.7
——, ed. and intro. *Taking Root: Narratives of Jewish Women in Latin America.* Athens: Ohio University Center for International Studies, Latin American Series No. 38, 2002. 299 pp.

Narrative:
Edna Aizenberg (Argentina/Venezuela), Latin American Jewishness, A Game with Shifting Identities. Fortuna Calvo-Roth (Peru), Growing up Sephardi in Peru. Joan E. Friedman (Venezuela), El Azar-Fate Put the Novel *Cláper* in My Hands. Ethel Kosminsky (Brazil), Memories of Comings and Goings. Ester Levis Levine (Cuba), My Cuban Story. Natania Remba Nurko (Cuba), My Cuban Story. Nedda G. de Anhalt (Cuba/Mexico), Shared Memories. Graciela Chichotky (Argentina), An Essential Tool. Sonia Guralnik (Chile), A Passion to Remember. Rosita Kalina de Piszk (Costa Rica), A Costa Rican Journey. Angelina Muñiz de Huberman (Mexico), A Story of Secrets. Teresa Porzecanski (Uruguay), A Story in Episodes. Mercedes Roffé (Argentina), From Morrocco to Buenos Aires. Ana María Shua (Argentina), With All That I Am. Ivonne Strauss de Milz (Dominican Republic), A Tale of Courage and Fortitude. Nora Strejilevich (Argentina), Too Many Names. Includes bio-bibliographic notes on contributors.

A A1.8
Agosín, Marjorie, ed. and intro. *What Is Secret: Stories by Chilean Women.* Fredonia, NY: White Pine Press, 1995. 303 pp.
Short stories:
Margarita Aguirre, Cleaning the Closet. Elena Aldunate, Butterfly Man. María Flor Aninat, The Department Store. Jacqueline Balcells, The Boy Who Took Off in a Tree. Pía Barros, Scents of Wood and Silence. Carmen Basáñez, Not without Her Glasses. Alejandra Basualto, A Requiem for Hands. Marta Blanco, Maternity. María Luisa Bombal, The Secret. Marta Brunet, Down River. Elena Castedo, The White Bedspread. Cristina da Fonseca, Memories of Clay; Endless Flight. María Asunción De Fokes, Vanessa and Victor. Ana María del Río, Subway. Alejandra Farias, The Fish Tank. Agata Gligo, The Bicycles. Sonia González Valdenegro, A Matter of Distance. Lucía Guerra, Encounter on the Margins. Ana María Güiraldes, Up to the Clouds; The Family Album. Sonia Guralnik, Sailing Down the Rhine. Marta Jara, The Dress; The Englishwoman. Luz Larraín, The Bone Spoon. Sonia Montecinos, Hualpín. Barbara Mujica, Mitrani. Margarita Niemeyer, The House. Luz Orfanoz, Insignificance; Accelerated Cycle. Ana Pizarro, The Journey. Violeta Quevedo, The Pilgrim's Angel. Amalia Rendic, A Dog, a Boy, and the Night. Elizabeth Subercaseaux, Because We're Poor. Ana Vásquez, Elegance. Virginia Vidal, Journey of the Watermelon. María Flora Yáñez, The Pond.
Includes bio-bibliographic notes on authors and translators.

A A1.9
——. *Women in Disguise: Stories by Marjorie Agosín.* Trans. Diane Russell Pineda. Falls Church, VA: Azul Editions, 1996. 164 pp.
Short stories:
Chapter I, Women Potters: Curriculum Vitae (poem); Last Names; Silences; Convents; Strip Tease; Olga; Letters; Bonfires; Guillermina Aguilar; The Cemetery; Alfama.
Chapter II, Ritural: First Communion; Women in Disguise; Cousins; The Messiah;

Chepita; Birthday; Weddings.
Chapter III, In September, When the Rains Stop: The Alphabet; Dunedin; Ireland; Chocolates; The Wanderer; Islands; Ocean Retreats; Allison.
Chapter IV, Death Sounds: The Place I Want to Die; Lady Death; Rivers; Antigua; Warnings; Spirits; House of Lights; Widowhood; Appointment; Death Sounds; The Color Black.
Chapter V, Tickle of Love: Revenge; Fingertips (poem); This Love; A Scented Love Letter; The Bottle; A Recent Nakedness; Life Inside of Love; Tickle of Love.
Chapter VI, Bougainvilla Insomnia: Dreamer of Fishes; Pine Trees; The Tower; Postcards; Mists; Bougainvillaea Insomnia; Witches; Wine.
This volume is a reworking of Agosín's book *Las alfareras*. Some texts have been added, others deleted. Includes a foreword by Patricia Rubio.
Chile.

A A2
Agosín, Marjorie, and Nancy Abraham Hall, eds. and intro. *A Necklace of Words: Stories by Mexican Women*. Fredonia: White Pine Press, 1997. 148 pp.
Short stories:
I. Recollections of Things to Come: Nelly Campobello, General Rueda. Elena Garro, Recollections of Things to Come. Inés Arredondo, The True Story of a Princess.
II. Coatlicue Swept: Marcela Guijosa, Regarding My Mestiza Self. Esther Seligson, Annunciation. Sara Sefchovich, Too Much Love. Margo Glantz, Coatlicue Swept. Rosario Castellanos, Balún Canán.
III. Where Things Fly: Silvia Molina, Sunday. Mónica Lavín, Nicolasa and the Lacework. Angeles Mastretta, White Lies. Cristina Pacheco, Noodle Soup. Brianda Domecq, The Turtle. Ethel Krauze, Where Things Fly.
IV. Beyond the Gaze: Angelina Muñiz-Huberman, Abbreviated World; The Swallows of Cuernavaca. Elena Poniatowska, State of Siege. Guadalupe Dueñas, The Guardian Angel. María Luisa Puga, Young Mother. Martha Cerda, Birthday. Akline Petterson, Beyond the Gaze. Nedda G. De Anhalt, A Concealing Nakedness.

A A3
Agosín, Marjorie, and Celeste Kostopulos-Cooperman, eds. *Secret Weavers: Stories of the Fantastic by Women of Argentina and Chile*. Fredonia, NY: White Pine Press, 1993. 339 pp.
Short fiction:
Isabel Allende (Chile), Two Words. María Luisa Bombal (Chile), The Story of María Griselda. Alina Diaconú (Argentina), The Storm; Welcome to Albany; The Widower. Marosa Di Giorgio (Uruguay), excerpts from *The Wild Papers*. Sara Gallardo (Argentina), The Man in the Araucaria; The Blue Stone Emperor's Thirty Wives. Angélica Gorodischer (Argentina), The Perfect Married Woman; Letters From an English Lady; Under the Flowering Juleps; The Resurrection of the Flesh. Liliana Hecker (Argentina), When Everything Shines. Luisa Mercedes Levinson (Argentina), The Little Island; The Boy Who Saw God's Tears. Silvina Ocampo

(Argentina), The Compulsive Dreamer; Things; The Velvet Dress; The House of Sugar; Thus Were Their Faces. Olga Orozco (Argentina), For Friends and Enemies; And the Wheel Still Spins. Elvira Orphée (Argentina), An Eternal Fear; I Will Return, Mommy; How the Little Crocodiles Cry. Cristina Peri Rossi (Uruguay), The Annunciation. Alejandra Pizarnik (Argentina), The Mirror of Melancholy; Blood Baths; Severe Measures. Ana María Shua (Argentina), excerpts from Dream Time: Other/Other; Fishing Days. Marcela Solá (Argentina), The Condemned Dress in White; Happiness; Invisible Embroidery. Alicia Steimberg (Argentina), Viennese Waltz; García's Thousandth Day; Segismundo's Better World. Elizabeth Subercaseaux (Chile), Selections from Silendra: Tapihue; Enedina; Juana; Silendra; Francisco. Luisa Valenzuela (Argentina), Country Carnival; Legend of the Self-Sufficient Child.
Includes an introduction by Marjorie Agosín, "Reflections on the Fantastic."

A A4

Agosín, Marjorie, and Julie H. Levison. *Magical Sites: Women Travelers in 19th Century Latin America.* Buffalo, NY: White Pine Press, 1999. 234 pp.
Prose selections:
Juana Manuela Gorriti (Argentina), Travels through Argentina, Peru, and Bolivia. María de la Merced Beltrán (Cuba/France), Travels through Cuba.
Includes bio-bibliographic notes on contributors.

A A5

Aguilar, Rosario. *The Lost Chronicles of Terra Firma.* Trans. Edward Waters Hood. Fredonia: White Pine Press, 1997. 186 pp.
Short stories:
Doña Isabel; First Interlude; Doña Luisa; Second Interlude; Doña Beatriz; Doña Leonor; Third Interlude; Doña Ana; Fourth Interlude; Doña María; Epilogue. Colombia.

A A6

Ahern, Maureen, ed. and intro. *A Rosario Castellanos Reader.* Austin: University of Texas Press, 1988. 378 pp.
Short fiction:
The Eagle; Three Knots in the Net; Fleeting Friendships; *The Widower Román* (novella); Cooking Lesson.
Includes brief bio-bibliographic notes on the editor and the translators. Mexico.

A A7

Ahern, Tom, ed. *Diana's Second Almanac.* Providence, RI: Diana's Bimonthly Press, 1980. 88 pp.
Short stories:
Armonía Somers (Uruguay), The Immigrant.

A A8

Alegría, Claribel. *Family Album*. Trans. Amanda Hopkinson. Willimantic, CT: Curbstone Press, 1991. 191 pp.

Novellas:

The Talisman; Family Album; Village of God and the Devil.

El Salvador.

A A8.1

——. *Luisa in Realityland*. Trans. Darwin J. Flakoll. Willimantic, CT: Curbstone Press, 1987. 152 pp.

Short stories:

Wilf (1); Luisa's Litanies; Wilf (2); Luisa and the Gypsy; Wilf (3); Aunt Elsa and Cuis; I'm a Whore: Are You Satisfied?; The Ancestor Room; Taking the Vows; The Versailles Tenement; The President's Sheet; The Nicaraguan Great-Grandfather (1); First Communion; The Nicaraguan Grandfather (2); Aunt Filiberta and Her Cretonnes; The Nicaraguan Grandfather (3); The Myth-making Uncles (1); Rene; Margarita's Birthday; Felix; Jane's Umbilical Cord; Cipitio; Jamie in Poneloya; The Day of the Cross; The Gypsy (1); Luisa's Paintings; The Gypsy (2); Premature Necrology; The Deaf Mutes of Ca'n Blau; The Flood; Sunday Siestas; The Mad Woman of the Grand Armee; Roque's Via Crucis; The Myth-making Uncles (2); Farabundo Marti; Nightmare in Chinandega; Granny and the Golden Bridge; Prophecy (1); The Singer Machines; The Blue Theatre; Eunice Aviles; Appointment in Zinica; The Gypsy (3); The Pool; Salarrue; Plash, Plash, Plash; No Dogs or Mexicans; The Mejia's Dogs; Carmen Bomba; Poet; Prophecy (2); The Gypsy (4); Final Act.

This volume also includes poetry and brief bio-bibliographic notes on the author. El Salvador.

A A9

Allende, Isabel. *The Stories of Eva Luna*. Trans. Margaret Sayers Peden. New York: Atheneum, 1991. 331 pp.

Short stories:

Two Words; Wicked Girl; Clarisa; Toad's Mouth; The Gold of Tomás Vargas; If You Touched My Heart; Gift for a Sweetheart; Tosca; Wilimai; Ester Lucero; Simple María; Our Secret; The Little Heidelberg; The Judge's Wife; The Road North; The Schoolteacher's Guest; The Proper Respect; Interminable Life; A Discreet Miracle; Revenge; Letters of Betrayed Love; Phantom Palace; And of Clay Are We Created.

Includes a prologue by Rolf Carlé.

Chile.

A A10

Allgood, Myralyn F., ed., preface, intro., and trans. *Another Way to Be: Selected Works of Rosario Castellanos*. Athens: The University of Georgia Press, 1990. 146 pp.

Short fiction:
Three Knots in the Net; The Nine Guardians (excerpt from *Balún Canán*); The Luck of Teodoro Méndez Acúbal; The Cycle of Hunger; Tenebrae Service (excerpt from *Oficio de tinieblas*); Cooking Lesson.
Includes a foreword by Edward D. Terry and an extensive bibliography of primary and secondary works for Rosario Castellanos in Spanish and English.
Mexico.

A A11
Alves, Miriam, ed. *Finally Us...: Contemporary Black Brazilian Women Writers.*
     Trans. Carolyn R. Durham. Colorado Springs, CO: Three Continents Press,
     1995. 258 pp.
Short stories:
Miriam Alves, Words.
The only short story in the collection is listed above. The remainder of the book contains poetry. Includes bio-bibliographic information on authors as well as a photograph of each and a glossary of Brazilian terminology. Bilingual Portuguese-English.

A A12
Antoni, Robert, and Bradford Morrow, eds. *The Archipelago: New Writing from
     and about the Caribbean.* Annandale-on-Hudson, NY: Bard College, 1996.
     352 pp.
Short fiction:
Julia Álvarez (Dominican Republic), Consuelo's Letter. Rosario Ferré (Puerto Rico), *Eccentric Neighborhoods* (excerpt); Fording Río Loco; Boffil and Rivas de Santillana. Cristina García (Cuba), *A Natural History* (excerpt); Tree Ducks; The Leatherback; The Nature of Parasites.
This is no. 27 of the biannual journal *Conjunctions.* Includes brief bio-bibliographies for contributors.

A A13
Aparicio, Frances, ed. *Latino Voices.* Brookfield, CT: Writers of America, 1994.
     143 pp.
Short fiction:
Julia Álvarez (Dominican Republic), *How the Garcia Girls Lost Their Accents* (excerpt). Judith Ortiz Cofer (Puerto Rico), Casa.
Includes brief bio-bibliographies for contributors and a bibliography for further reading.

A A14
Arkin, Marian, and Barbara Shollar, eds. *Longman Anthology of Literature by
     Women, 1875-1975.* New York: Longman, 1989. 1274 pp.
Short fiction:
María Luisa Bombal (Chile), Braids. Lydia Cabrera (Cuba), Walo-Wila. Nellie

Campobello (Mexico), excerpt from *Cartridge: Tales of the Struggle in Northern Mexico*. Carolina María de Jesús (Brazil), Child of the Dark (excerpt). Teresa de la Parra (Venezuela), No More Mill, excerpt from *Mama Blanca's Souvenirs*. Rachel de Queiroz (Brazil), *The Three Marías* (excerpt). Rosario Ferré (Puerto Rico), *The Youngest Doll* (excerpt). Luisa Josefina Hernández (Mexico), Florinda and Don Gonzalo. Clarice Lispector (Brazil), The Beginnings of a Fortune. Carmen Lyra (Costa Rica), prologue to *The Tales of My Aunt Panchita*. Clorinda Matto de Turner (Peru), *Birds Without a Nest* (excerpt). Cristina Peri Rossi (Uruguay), The Trapeze Artists. Nélida Piñón (Brazil), Bird of Paradise. Elena Poniatowska (Mexico), Love Story. Luisa Valenzuela (Argentina), Strange Things Happen Here. Leonor Villegas de Magnón (Mexico), *The Rebellious Woman* (excerpt).

Includes a lengthy introduction concerning women's literature. The appendices contain essays dealing with women's literary traditions from each country represented in the anthology; the essay on Spanish America was written by Margarite Fernández Olmos. Includes an index of writers and selections by region.

A A15

Arredondo, Inés. *Underground River and Other Stories*. Trans. and intro. Cynthia Steele. Lincoln: University of Nebraska Press, 1996. 128 pp.

Short stories:

The Shunammite; Mariana; The Sign; New Year's Eve; Underground River; The Silent Words; Orphanhood; The Nocturnal Butterflies; The Brothers; The Mirrors; On Love; Shadow in the Shadows.

Includes a foreword by Elena Poniatowska.

Mexico.

A A16

Augenbraum, Harold, and Margarite Fernández, eds. and intro. *The Latino Reader: An American Literary Tradition from 1542 to the Present*. Boston: Houghton Mifflin Company, 1997. 502 pp.

Short fiction:

Cristina García (Cuba), *Dreaming in Cuban* (excerpt). Nicholasa Mohr (Puerto Rico), *Nilda* (excerpt). Judith Ortiz Cofer (Puerto Rico), American History. María Amparo Ruiz de Burton (Mexico), *The Squatter and the Don* (excerpt). Leonor Villegas de Magnón (Mexico), *The Rebel* (excerpt). Helena María Viramontes (Mexico), The Moths.

The anthology is organized into three parts: Encounters, Prelude, and Latino United States, each with its own introduction which includes historical and thematic context. Includes notes on the editors.

A A17

Augenbraum, Harold, and Ilan Stavans, eds. and intro. *Growing Up Latino: Memories and Stories*. New York: Houghton Mifflin Company, 1993. 344 pp.

Short fiction:

Julia Álvarez (Dominican Republic), Daughter of Invention. Judith Ortiz Cofer

(Puerto Rico), Silent Dancing. Helena María Viramontes (Mexico), The Moths. Includes brief bio-bibliographies for contributors, a bibliography of suggestions for future reading, an introduction titled "Soldier of the Culture Wars" by Harold Augenbraum, and a foreword by Ilan Stavans.

A A17.1

Augenbraum, Harold, and Ilan Stavans, eds. *Lengua Fresca: Latinos Writing on the Edge.* Boston: Houghton Mifflin Co., 2006.
Includes work by Ana Lydia Vega. Not available for annotation.

A B1

Baird, Vanessa, ed. *Eye to Eye Women: Their Words and Worlds. Life in Africa, Asia, Latin America and the Caribbean as Seen in Photographs and in Fiction by the Region's Top Women Writers.* Toronto: Second Story Press, 1997. 127 pp.
Short fiction:
Omega Agüero (Cuba), A Man, A Woman. Isabel Allende (Chile), *Eva Luna* (excerpt); *The House of the Spirits* (excerpt). Domitila Barrios de Chungará, (Bolivia), *Let Me Speak* (excerpt). Fanny Fierro (Ecuador), Hidden Pleasure. Clarice Lispector (Brazil), *The Hour of the Star* (excerpt). Giovanna Pollarolo (Peru), The Grocer's Dream. Luisa Valenzuela (Argentina), Up among the Eagles (excerpt).
Includes an introduction by Anita Desai, photographs of the authors, and bio-bibliographies for contributors. Each piece of writing is accompanied by a photograph of a woman reflected in the literature.

A B2

Balcells, Jacqueline. *The Enchanted Raisin.* Trans. Elizabeth Gamble Miller. Pittsburgh, PA: Latin American Literary Review Press, 1988. 103 pp.
Short stories:
The Enchanted Raisin; The Mermaids' Elixir; The Buried Giant; The Princess and the Green Dwarf; How Forgetfulness Began; The Boy Swept Away in a Tree; The Thirsty Little Fish.
Children's stories and fairy tales.
Chile.

AB3

Baldick, Chris, ed. *The Oxford Book of Gothic Tales.* Oxford: Oxford University Press, 2001. 560 pp.
Short stories:
Isabel Allende (Chile), If You Touched My Heart. Alejandra Pizarnik (Argentina), The Bloody Countess.
Includes bio-bibliographic information on contributors.

A B4

Barnstone, Willis, and Toni Barnstone, eds. and intro. *Literatures of Asia, Africa, and Latin America from Antiquity to the Present.* Upper Saddle River, NJ: Prentice Hall, 1999. 1990 pp.

Narrative:

Isabel Allende (Chile), Gift for a Sweetheart. Giannina Braschi (Puerto Rico), *Empire of Dreams* (excerpt). Laura Esquivel (Mexico), *Like Water for Chocolate* (excerpt). Clarice Lispector (Brazil), Marmosets; Explanation. Luisa Valenzuela (Argentina) Up among the Eagles.

Each section (geographical region as well as time period) contains its own introduction. Includes bio-bibliographic on contributors.

A B5

Barros, Pía. *Transitory Fears.* Trans. Diane Russell-Pineda and Martha Manier. Santiago, Chile: Asterión Publishers, 1989. 176 pp.

Short stories:

Abelardo; Story for a Window; Estanvito; Appraisals; Coup; No Circles; Waiting Game; Short-lived Summers; The Baby's Afternoon; Windows; Horses are a Gringo Invention; Portal; When the Patagoni. 1s Hunted Stars; Routine Inspection; Messages; Looking at Manet; Núñez from Over Here; The Inheritor of Wisdom; Shoes.

Bilingual edition. Includes bio-bibliographic notes on author and translators. Chile.

A B6

Behar, Ruth, ed. and intro. *Bridges to Cuba. Puentes a Cuba.* Ann Arbor: University of Michigan Press, 1995. 421 pp.

Short fiction:

Teresa Marrero, Ghost Limbs. Rita Martín, Elisa, or the Price of Dreams. Includes brief bio-bibliographic information on contributors.

Cuba.

A B7

Bell, Andrea L., and Yolanda Molina-Gavilán, eds., trans. and intro. *Cosmos Latinos: An Anthology of Science Fiction from Latin America and Spain.* Middletown, CT: Wesleyan University Press, 2003. 352 pp.

Short stories:

Diana Chaviano (Cuba), The Annunciation. Angélica Gorodishcer (Argentina), The Voilet's Embryos. Magdalena Mouján Otaño (Argentina), Gu Ta Butarrak (We and Our Own).

Includes a selected bibliography and bio-bibliographic information on contributors.

A B8

Benner, Susan, and Kathy S. Leonard, eds., trans., and intro. *Fire from the Andes: Short Fiction by Women from Bolivia, Ecuador, and Peru.* Albuquerque:

University of New Mexico Press, 1997.

Short fiction:
Virginia Ayllón Soria (Bolivia), Prayer to the Goddesses. Yolanda Bedregal (Bolivia), The Traveler. Mónica Bravo (Ecuador), Wings for Dominga. Erika Bruzonic (Bolivia), Inheritance. Aminta Buenaño (Ecuador), The Strange Invasion that Rose from the Sea. Gaby Cevasco (Peru), Between Clouds and Lizards. Giancarla de Quiroga (Bolivia), Of Anguish and Illusions. Elsa Dorado de Revilla Valenzuela (Bolivia), The Parrot. Pilar Dughi (Peru), The Days and Hours. María del Carmen Garcés (Ecuador), The Blue Handkerchief. Carmen Luz Gorriti (Peru), The Legacy (A Story from Huancayo). Bethzabé Guevara (Peru), The Señorita Didn't Teach Me. Marcela Gutiérrez (Bolivia), The Feathered Serpent. Beatriz Kuramoto (Bolivia), The Agreement. Beatriz Loayza Millán (Bolivia), The Mirror. Catalina Lohman (Peru), The Red Line. Nela Martínez (Ecuador), La Machorra. Mónica Ortiz Salas (Ecuador), Mery Yagual (Secretary). Blanca Elena Paz (Bolivia), The Light. Laura Riesco (Peru), The Twins of Olmedo Court. Gladys Rossel Huicí (Peru), Light and Shadow. Fabiola Solís de King (Ecuador), Before It's Time. Eugenia Viteri (Ecuador), The Ring. Alicia Yánez Cossío (Ecuador), The Mayor's Wife.
Includes biographic information, a photograph, and a primary and secondary bibliography for each author. Also includes an extensive bibliography titled "Short Story Collections by or Including Women Authors from Bolivia, Ecuador, and Peru." Foreword by Marjorie Agosín and notes on the editors/translators.

A B9
Berg, Mary G., and Karla Suárez, eds. *Open Your Eyes and Soar: Cuban Women Writing Now.* New York: White Pine Press, 2003. 188 pp.
Narrative:
Nancy Alonso, Seventh Thunderbolt; Thou Shalt Not Deviate. Aída Bahr, Little Heart; Absences. Marilyn Bobes, This Time Listen to What I Say; It's a Good Thing. Sonia Bravo Utrera, Decision. Adelaida Fernández de Juan, Oh Life; Journey to Pepe. Mylene Fernández Pintado, Mare Atlanticum; Anteater. Ena Lucía Portela, At the Back of the Cemetery. Karla Suaréz, Eye of the Night; Anniversary. Ana Lidia Vega Serova, Peter Piper Picked a Peck; Russian Food.
Mirta Yáñez, Fifita Calls Us in the Morning; Past Meets Present, Old Tales Out of School.
Includes bio-bibliographic information on contributors.

A B10
Berkman, Marsha Lee, and Elaine Marcus Starkman, eds., and intro. *Here I Am: Contemporary Jewish Stories from around the World.* Philadelphia, PA: Haddon Craftsmen, Inc., 1998. 466 pp.
Short stories:
Marjorie Agosín (Chile), Osorno (excerpt). Nora Glickman (Argentina), The Last Emigrant. Angelina Muñiz Huberman (Mexico), In The Name of His Name. Includes brief bio-bibliographies on authors and translators and bibliographical

references on Jewish writing and critical works. Works by authors included in the volume are divided by country; also included are anthologies and holocaust tales.

A B11
Biddle, Arthur, ed., intro., and preface. *Global Voices: Contemporary Literature from the Non-western World.* Englewood Cliffs, NJ: Prentice Hall, A Blair Press Book, 1995. 845 pp.
Short stories:
Rosario Ferré (Puerto Rico), The Youngest Doll. Luisa Valenzuela (Argentina), The Censors.

A B12
Birmingham-Pokorny, Elba D., ed. *An English Anthology of Afro-Hispanic Writers of the Twentieth Century.* Miami: Ediciones Universal, 1995. 126 pp.
Narrative:
Luz Argentina Chiriboga (Ecuador), Under the Skin of the Drums. Cristina Rodríguez-Cabral (Uruguay), August 25, 1988.
Includes bio-bibliographic information on authors and a primary and secondary bibliography for each author.

A B13
Blair, J. M., ed. *Caliente! The Best Erotic Writing in Latin American Fiction.* New York: Berkley Trade, Penguin Group, 2002. 203 pp.
Short stories:
Isabel Allende (Chile), *The Infinite Plan* (excerpt). Julia Álvarez (Dominican Republic), *In the Name of Salomé* (excerpt). Laura Esquivel (Mexico), *Like Water for Chocolate* (excerpt). Rosario Ferré (Puerto Rico), *Eccentric Neighborhoods* (excerpt). Cristina García (Cuba), *The Agüero Sisters* (excerpt). Lucia Guerra (Chile), *The Street of Night* (excerpt). Loida Maritza Pérez (Dominican Republic), *Geographies of Home* (excerpt). Elena Poniatowska (Mexico), *Tinísima* (excerpt). Laura Restrepo (Colombia), *Leopard in the Sun* (excerpt).
Includes brief bio-bibliographic information on contributors and an introduction by the editor.

A B14
Bohner, Charles H., ed. and intro. *Short Fiction: Classic and Contemporary.* 3rd. ed. Englewood Cliffs, NJ: Prentice Hall, 1994. 1183 pp.
Short stories:
Luisa Valenzuela (Argentina), The Verb to Kill.
Includes bio-bibliographic notes on authors. This volume is intended for use in college courses.

A B15
Bojunga-Nunes, Lygia. *The Companions.* Trans. Ellen Watson. New York: Farrar, Straus & Giroux, 1984. 58 pp.

Short stories:
Fast Friends; A Time of Trouble; Summer. Children's stories.
Illustrated by Larry Wilkes.
Brazil.

A B15.1
Bojunga-Nunes, Lygia. *My Friend the Painter*. Trans. Giovanni Pontiero. San
    Diego, CA: Harcourt Brace Jovanovich, Publishers. 85 pp.
A children's story.
Brazil.

A B16
Bombal, María Luisa. *New Islands and Other Stories*. Trans. Richard and Lucía
    Cunningham. New York: Farrar, Straus & Giroux, 1982. 112 pp.
Short stories:
The Final Mist; The Tree; Braids; The Unknown; New Islands.
Includes a brief preface by Jorge Luís Borges.
Chile.

A B17
Borges, Jorge Luís, Silvina Ocampo, and Adolfo Bioy Cásares, eds. *The Book of
    Fantasy*. New York: Viking, 1988. 384 pp.
Short stories:
Elena Garro (Mexico), A Secure Home. Delia Ingenieros and Jorge Luís Borges
(Argentina), Odin. Silvina Ocampo (Argentina), The Atonement.
Includes a brief introduction by Ursula K. Le Guin and very brief bio-bibliographic
notes on authors.

A B18
Bowen, David, and Juan A. Ascencio, eds. *Pyramids of Glass: Short Fiction from
    Modern Mexico*. San Antonio, TX: Corona Publishing Co., 1994. 244 pp.
Short stories:
Inés Arredondo, Puzzles. Marta Cerda, Mirror of a Man. Guadalupe Dueñas,
Mariquita and Me. Silvia Molina, An Orange Is an Orange. Angeles Mastretta,
White Lies. Elena Poniatowska, Little House of Celluloid. María Luisa Puga, The
Trip.
Includes an introduction by Ilan Stavans and bio-bibliographic notes on contributors.

A B19
Boyce Davies, Carole E., and 'Molara Ogundipe-Leslie, eds and intro. *Moving
    beyond Boundaries. Volume 1: International Dimensions of Black Women's
    Writing*. New York: New York University Press, 1995. 252 pp.
Short stories:
Luz Argentina Chiriboga (Ecuador), *Under the Skin of the Drums* (excerpt).
Includes a brief preface by Carole Boyce Davies, bio-bibliographic notes on authors,

and two introductions: "Hearing Black Women's Voices: Transgressing Imposed Boundaries," by Carole E. Boyce Davies, and "Women in Africa and Her Diaspora: From Marginality to Empowerment," by 'Molara Ogundipe-Leslie. Bio-bibliographic notes on authors.

A B20

Braschi, Giannina. *Empire of Dreams*. Trans. Tess O'Dwyer. New Haven and
  London: Yale University Press, 1994. 220 pp.
Short fiction:
Assault on Time; Book of Clowns and Buffoons; Poems of the World; or, The Book of Wisdom; Pastoral; or, The Inquisition of Memories; Song of Nothingness; Epilogue; The Adventures of Mariquita Samper; The Life and Works of Berta Singerman; The Things That Happen to Men in New York!; The Queen of Beauty, Charm, and Coquetry; Gossip; Portrait of Giannina Braschi; Mariquita Samper's Childhood; The Raise; Manifesto on Poetic Eggs; The Building of the Waves of the Sea; Requiem for Solitude.
Includes an introduction by Alicia Ostriker and translator's note by Tess O'Dwyer. Puerto Rico.

A B21

Breton, Marcela, ed. and intro. *Rhythm and Revolt: Tales of the Antilles*. New York:
  Penguin, 1995. 278 pp.
Short stories:
Fanny Buitrago (Colombia), Caribbean Siren. Lydia Cabrera (Cuba), The Hill of Mambiala. Magali García Ramis (Puerto Rico), The Sign of Winter. Ana Lydia Vega (Puerto Rico), Cloud Cover Caribbean.
Includes brief bio-biographic notes on authors.

A B22

Browdy de Hernández, Jennifer, ed. *Women Writing Resistance: Essays on Latin
  America and the Caribbean*. Cambridge: South End Press, 2003. 241 pp.
Contents:
Aurora Levins Morales (Puerto Rico), Revision. Raquel Partnoy (Argentina), The Silent Witness. Ruth Behar (Cuba) Everything I Kept: Reflections on an "Anthropoeta." Emma Sepúlveda (Chile), The Dream of *Nunca Más*: Healing the Wounds. Rosario Castellaños (Mexico), Language as an Instrument of Domination. Ruth Irupé Sanabria (Argentina) Las Aeious. Judith Ortiz Cofer (Puerto Rico), The Myth of the Latin Woman. Rigoberta Menchú (Guatemala), The Quincentenary Conference and the Earth Summit, 1992. Elena Poniatowska (Mexico), A Massacre in Mexico. Alicia Partnoy (Argentina), On Being Shorter: How Our Testimonial Texts Defy the Academy. Marjorie Agosín (Chile), Death in the Desert: The Women of Ciudad Juárez. Julia Álvarez (Dominican Republic), I Came to Help: Resistance Writ Small.
Includes a preface by Elizabeth Martínez and an introduction by Jennifer Browdy de Hernández.

A B23

Brown, Stewart, and John Wickham, eds. *The Oxford Book of Caribbean Short Stories.* Oxford: Oxford University Press, 1999. 475 pp.

Short stories:

Rosario Ferré (Puerto Rico), When Women Love Men. Ana Lydia Vega (Puerto Rico), Eye-openers.

Includes an excellent introduction on the history of Caribbean literature by Stewart Brown; also contains bio-bibliographies on contributors and suggestions for wider reading.

A B24

Busby, Margaret, ed. and intro. *Daughters of Africa: An International Anthology of Words and Writings by Women of African Descent: From the Ancient Egyptian to the Present.* New York: Pantheon Books, 1992. 1089 pp.

Short stories:

Carolina María de Jesús (Brazil), Diary: 1955 (excerpt from *Beyond all Pity*). Aline França (Brazil), *A Mulher de Aleduma* (excerpt). Pilar López Gonzáles (Cuba), It Was All Mamá's Fault.

Includes brief bio-bibliographic notes on authors, a bibliography of primary and secondary sources for authors as well as an extensive bibliography of further reading.

A B 25

Bush, Peter, ed. and intro. *The Voice of the Turtle: An Anthology of Cuban Stories.* New York: Grove Press, 1997. 383 pp.

Short stories:

Marilyn Bobes, Ask the Good Lord. Lydia Cabrera, Daddy Turtle and Daddy Tiger. Lourdes Casal, The Founders: Alfonso. Uva de Aragón, Round Trip. Zoe Valdés, The Ivory Trader and the Ted Melons. Mirta Yáñez, Split in Two.

Includes brief bio-bibliographic notes on the contributors.

A C1

Caillois, Roger, ed. *The Dream Adventure.* New York: Orion Press, 1963. 285 pp.

Short stories:

Luisa Mercedes Levinson (Argentina), The Dream That Was Violated.

A C2

Caistor, Nick, ed. and intro. *Columbus' Egg. New Latin American Stories on the Conquest.* Boston: Faber & Faber, 1992. 162 pp.

Short stories:

Ana Valdés (Uruguay), The Peace of the Dead. Luisa Valenzuela (Argentina), Three Days. Ana Lydia Vega (Puerto Rico), Pateco's Little Prank.

A C2.1

Caistor, Nick, ed. and intro. *The Faber Book of Contemporary Latin American Short Stories.* London: Faber & Faber, 1989. 188 pp.

Short stories:

Isabel Allende (Chile), The Judge's Wife. María Luisa Puga (Mexico), The Trip. Cristina Peri Rossi (Uruguay), The Museum of Vain Endeavours. Luisa Valenzuela (Argentina), Up among the Eagles.

Includes brief bio-bibliographic notes on authors.

A C3

Campobello, Nellie. *Cartucho and My Mother's Hands.* Trans. Doris Meyer and Irene Matthews. Austin: University of Texas Press, 1988. 129 pp.

Narrative:

Cartucho: Men of the North; The Executed; Under Fire. My Mother's Hands: She Was; Once I Sought Her, Far Away Where She Lived a Life Shattered by Rifles' Ravages; Reader, Fill Your Heart with My Respect; She Is Here; You and He; Her Love; Our Love; Her Skirt; Her God; The Men Left Their Mutilated Bodies Awaiting the Succor of These Simple Flowers; The Men of the Troop; The Dumb One; A Villa Man Like So Many Others; She and Her Machine; Jacinto's Deal; Plaza of the Lilacs; When We Came to a Capital City; A Letter for You.

Includes an introduction by Elena Poniatowska and translators' notes from both Meyer and Matthews. *Cartucho* is often called a novel, but consists of 56 sketches made up of autobiography, history, and poetry. *My Mother's Hands* is described as a poem by the translator. However, its format is that of short fictional pieces. Mexico.

A C4

Campos, Julieta. *Celina or the Cats.* Trans. Leland Chambers and Kathleen Ross. Pittsburgh, PA: Latin American Literary Review Press, 1995. 140 pp.

Short fiction:

On Cats and Other Worlds; Celina or the Cats; The Baptism: All the Roses; The House; The City.

Includes brief bio-bibliographic notes on the author and the translators. Mexico.

A C5

Canfield, Cass Jr., ed. *Masterworks of Latin American Short Fiction: Eight Novellas.* New York: Icon Editions, 1996. 385 pp.

Short fiction:

Ana Lydia Vega (Puerto Rico), *Miss Florence's Trunk.*

Includes an introduction by Ilan Stavans and short bio-bibliographies of the authors.

A C6

Carlson, Lori M., and Cynthia L. Ventura, eds. *Where Angels Glide at Dawn: New Stories from Latin America.* New York: J. B. Lippincott, 1990. 114 pp.

Short stories:
Marjorie Agosín (Chile), A Huge Black Umbrella. María Rosa Fort (Peru), Tarma.
Barbara Mujica (Chile), Fairy Tale.
Includes an introduction by Isabel Allende, a glossary, and bio-bibliographic
information on authors. Many of the stories are adaptations for young readers.
Illustrations by José Ortega.

A C7
Carranza, Sylvia, and María Juana Cazabón, eds. *Cuban Short Stories, 1959-1966.*
    Havana: Book Institute, 1967. 229 pp.
Short stories:
Dora Alonso, The Rat. María Elena Llano, The Two of Us. Ana María Simo, Aunt
Albertina's Last Party. Evora Tamayo, Sylvia.
Includes brief bio-bibliographic notes on contributors, a photograph of each author,
and a Spanish/English glossary.

A C8
Castellanos, Rosario. *City of Kings.* Trans. Robert S. Rudder and Gloria Chacón de
    Arjona. Pittsburgh, PA: Latin American Literary Review Press, 1992. 143 pp.
Short stories:
Death of the Tiger; The Truce; Aceite guapo; The Luck of Teodoro Méndez Acúba;
Modesta Gómez; Coming of the Eagle; The Fourth Vigil; The Wheel of Hunger; The
Gift, Refused; Arthur Smith Finds Salvation.
Includes an introduction by Claudia Schaefer, bio-bibliographic notes on the author
and editors, and a Spanish-English glossary.
Mexico.

A C9
Castillo, Ana, ed. and intro. *Goddess of the Americas/La Diosa de las Américas:*
    Writings on the Virgin Guadalupe. New York: Riverhead Books, 1996. 231 pp.
Short stories:
Rosario Ferré (Puerto Rico) The Battle of the Virgins. Elena Poniatowska (Mexico)
Don't Go Away, I'm Going to Bring You Something.
Includes bio-bibliographies on contributors.

A C10
Castro-Klarén, Sara, and Sylvia Molloy, eds. *Women's Writing in Latin America:*
    An Anthology. Boulder, CO: Westview Press, 1991. 362 pp.
Short fiction:
Diamela Eltit (Chile), Luminated (excerpt from the novel *Lumpérica*). Elena Garro
(Mexico), Before the Trojan War. Lygia Fagundes Telles (Brazil), The Sauna. Norah
Lange (Argentina), Childhood Copybooks (excerpt from *Cuadernos de infancia*).
Clarice Lispector (Brazil), Luminescence; Since One Has to Write (aphorisms and
short prose). Silvina Ocampo (Argentina), The Basement; The Mortal Sin. Victoria
Ocampo (Argentina), Emily Bronte; Terra incognita (excerpt from same); From

Primer to Book (excerpt from *De la cartilla al libro*), The Archipelago (excerpt from *Archipiélago*), The Insular Empire (excerpt from El imperio insular). Elvira Orphée (Argentina), Silence; Do Not Mistake Eternities; Voices That Grew Old. Cristina Peri Rossi (Uruguay), The Nature of Love. Nélida Piñón (Brazil), I Love My Husband.

Includes an extensive introduction by Sara Castro-Klarén, brief bio-bibliographic notes on authors, and primary and secondary bibliographies for each author.

A C11

Casaubon Hermann, Eliana, ed. Trans. Sally Webb Thornton. *English Translation of Short Stories by Contemporary Argentine Women Writers.* Lewiston, NY: Edwin Mellen Press, 2002. 187 pp.

Short stories:

Chapter I: Realism

María Isabel Clucella, Tango and Feathers. Alicia Jurado, Saying Goodbye through Twenty-five Centuries. Martha Mercader, The Postponed Journey. Laura Nicastro, Haguit. Flaminia Ocampo, Crossing Oceans. Mabel Pagano, A Death in June. Silvia Plager, A Change of Heart. Reine Roffé, Transforming the Desert. María Esther Vázquez, Returning by Train with Borges.

Chapter 2: Magic Realism

Elvira Orpheé, The Journey of Amatista and the Dirty Prince. Irma Verolín, The Stairway in the Gray Patio.

Chapter 3: The Fantastic

Rosalba Campra, Dream Tiger. Alina Diaconú, Blue Lagoon. María Rosa Lojo, Compound Eyes. Ana María Shúa, the White Guanaco in the Middle of France.

Includes bio-bibliographic information on contributors.

A C12

Cerda, Martha. *Señora Rodríguez and Other Worlds.* Trans. Sylvia Jiménez-Andersen. Durham, NC: Duke University Press, 1997. 134 pp.

Short fiction:

One; Multiverse; Two; After Canaries; Three; A Happy Family; Four; Good Habits; Five; The First Time; Six; City of Children; Seven; In the Dream Clock; Eight; Last Night at Night; Nine; Hide-and-Seek; The Best Night; Eleven; No One Knows for Whom One Works; Twelve; Blue in the Family; Thirteen; German Dollars; Fourteen; Between the Lines; Fifteen; With Respect to the Sky; Sixteen; Without Knowing That It Is You; Seventeen; Office Machine; Eighteen; Geography Lesson; Nineteen; The Congregation in the Park; Twenty; No-Man's-Land; Twenty-one; And the Crows Cawed; Twenty-two; Heard in Passing; Twenty-three; The Same Stock; Twenty-four; At the Baptismal Font; Twenty-five; A Time of Mourning; Last Night, Mariana; Twenty-seven; It's Their Fault; Twenty-eight; Right Place, Wrong Time; Twenty-nine; Blame It on Hormones; Thirty; Amanda's Motives; Epilogue.

Mexico.

A C13

Charters, Ann, ed. *The Story and Its Writer: An Introduction to Short Fiction.*
Boston: Bedford/Saint Martin's, 2003. 1801 pp.
Short stories:
Isabel Allende (Chile), And of Clay Are We Created. Clarice Lispector (Brazil), The
Smallest Woman in the World. Helena María Viramontes (Mexican), The Moths.
Includes writer commentaries and editorial features. Created for students.

A C14

Charyn, Jerome. *The Crime Lover's Casebook: The International Association of
Crime Writers' Essential Crime Writing of the Late 20th Century.* New York:
Signet, Penguin Books USA, Inc., 1996. 400 pp.
Short stories:
Clarice Lispector (Brazil), Pig Latin.
Includes bio-bibliographic information on contributors.

A C15

Chávez-Vásquez, Gloria. *Opus Americanus: Short Stories.* Trans. Gloria Chávez-
Vásquez. Brooklyn, NY: White Owl Editions, 1993. 189 pp.
Short stories:
The Firefly and the Mirror (La luciérnaga y el espejo); The Termites (Las termitas);
Sincronio, the Bird of Wonder (Sincronio, el ave fénix); The Subwaynauts (Diario
de un subwaynauta); From La Alameda to New York (De La Alameda a Nueva
York); A Broken Vase (Un búcaro roto); A Consulate's Tale (Un cuento de
consulado); The Human Virus (El virus humano); The American Legend of the
Creation of the Brain (La leyenda americana de la creación del cerebro); The
Origins of Bureaucracy (Orígenes de la burocracia); The Lookout (El mirador);
Sister Orfelina (Sor Orfelina).
Includes a brief introduction by Mario Sandoval. Bilingual edition.
Colombia.

A C16

Cheuse, Alan, and Caroline Marshall, eds. *The Sound of Writing.* New York: Anchor
Books, 1991. 239 pp.
Short stories:
Rosario Ferré (Puerto Rico), The Dreamer's Portrait.
Includes a preface by Caroline Marshall and bio-bibliographic notes on authors.

A C17

Chipps, Genie D., and Bill Henderson, eds. and intro. *Love Stories: For the Rest of
Us.* Wainscott, NY: Pushcart Press, 1994. 399 pp.
Short stories:
Ana Lydia Vega (Puerto Rico), Lyrics for a Salsa and Three Sonetos by Request.

A C18

Christie, John S., and Jose B. Gonzalez, eds. *Latino Boom: An Anthology of US Latino Literature.* New York: Pearson/Longman, 2006. 567 pp.

Short fiction:

Helena María Viramontes (Mexico), The Cariboo Café; Neighbors. Cristina García (Cuba), Tito's Goodbye. Alba Ambert (Puerto Rico), Rage Is a Fallen Angel. Achy Objeas (Cuba), We Came All the Way from Cuba So You Could Dress Like This? Includes introductions to Latino narrative and poetry. Also includes resources for writing and class discussions. This volume is intended for use as a reader in university courses.

A C19

Clerk, Jayana, and Ruth Siegel, eds. and preface. *Modern Literatures of the Non-Western World. Where the Waters Are Born.* New York: HarperCollins College Division, 1995. 1223 pp.

Short stories:

Isabel Allende (Chile), Our Secret. María Luisa Bombal (Chile), Sky, Sea and Earth. Rachel de Queiroz (Brazil), Tangerine Girl. Lygia Fagundes Telles (Brazil), The Ants. Rosario Ferré (Puerto Rico), The Youngest Doll. Silvina Ocampo (Argentina), The Servant's Slaves. Gabriela Mistral (Chile), Song. Nélida Piñón (Brazil), Brief Flower. Ana Lydia Vega (Puerto Rico), ADJ, Inc.

The appendices include general bio-bibliographic references as well as alternate tables of contents by theme, country, and genre. Besides Latin American and Caribbean literature, this volume also includes literatures from Africa, the Middle East, East, South, and Southeast Asia, as well as aboriginal literatures from Australia and New Zealand. Each selection is followed by a set of questions titled "Discussion and Writing" and suggestions for "Research and Comparison." This volume is intended for use as a reader in university courses.

A C20

Cocco de Fillippis, Daisy, ed. *Tertuliando: Dominicanas y amiga(o)s/ Hanging Out: Dominican Women and Friends: Bilingual Text(o)s bilinguales, 1994-1996.* Santo Domingo: Comisión Permanenete de la Feria Nacional del Libro, 1997.

Short fiction:

Julia Álvarez, The Summer of the Future.

Includes an introduction by Daisy Cocco de Filippis and bio-bibliographies for contributors. Bilingual edition.

A C21

Cocco de Fillippis, Daisy, and Franklin Gutiérrez, eds. *Short Stories Written by Dominicans in the United States.* Bronx, NY: Latino Press, 1994. 204 pp.

Short stories:

Julia Álvarez, The Summer of the Future; El Verano del Futuro.

Includes bio-bibliographic information on contributors and introduction by Daisy

Cocco de Filippis.
Bilingual edition.

A C22
Cochar, Jo, et al., eds. *Calyx: A Journal of Art and Literature by Women. Bearing Witness/Sobreviviendo, An Anthology of Native American/Latina Art and Literature*. Corvallis: University of Oregon, 1984. 128 pp.
Short fiction:
Julia Álvarez (Dominican Republic), New World.
This is a special issue of the journal, vol. 8 no. 2. Includes bio-bibliographic information on the contributors and an introduction by Margarita Connelly.

A C23
Coelho Pinto, José Saldanha da Gama, ed. *Contistas brasileiros. New Brazilian Short Stories*. Trans. Rod W. Horton. Rio de Janeiro: Revista Branca, 1957. 238 pp.
Short stories:
Lygia Fagundes Telles, Happiness.
Includes very brief bio-bibliographic notes on authors. Bilingual edition.

A C24
Cohen, J. M., ed. *Writers in the New Cuba: An Anthology*. Harmondsworth, UK. and Baltimore, MD: Penguin, 1967. 191 pp.
Short stories:
Ana María Simo, A Deathly Sameness; Growth of the Plant.
Includes bio-bibliographic notes on authors.

A C25
Colchie, Thomas, ed. and intro. *A Hammock Beneath the Mangoes: Stories from Latin America*. New York: Penguin, 1994. 430 pp.
Short stories:
Isabel Allende (Chile), Toad's Mouth. Lygia Fagundes Telles (Brazil), The Corset. Rosario Ferré (Puerto Rico), The Gift. Clarice Lispector (Brazil), Love. Armonía Somers (Uruguay), Waiting for Polidoro. Ana Lydia Vega (Puerto Rico), Story-Bound.
Includes bio-bibliographic notes on authors and editor.

A C25.1
——, ed. *A Whistler in the Nightworld: Short Fiction from the Latin Americas*. New York: A Plume Book, 2002. 410 pp.
Short stories:
Julia Álvarez (Dominican Republic), The Blood of Conquistadores. Mayra Santos-Febres (Dominican Republic), Flight I. Laura Restrepo (Colombia), The Scent of Invisible Roses. Anna Kazumi Stahl (Argentina), Natural Disasters. Angeles Mastretta (Mexico), Aunt Concha Esparza. Carmen Posadas (Uruguay), The

Nubian Lover. Laura Esquivel (Mexico), Blessed Reality. Mayra Montero (Cuba), That Man, Pollack.
Includes bio-bibliographic notes on authors and editor.

A C26
Contreras, Hilma. *Between Two Silences*. Trans. and ed. Paulette Ramsay and
  Anne-Maria Bankay. Kingston, Jamaica: Arawak Publications, 2004. 56 pp.
Short stories:
Now We Will Be Happy; Stalker; The Burial of Marisol; A Visit; Plenitude; The Fire; Hey Mama; The Wait; The Window; Hair; The Man Who Died Facing the Sea. Dominican Republic.

A C27
Correas de Zapata, Celia, ed. and intro. *Short Stories by Latin American Women:*
  The Magic and the Real. Houston, TX: Arte Público Press, 1990. 224 pp.
Short stories:
Isabel Allende (Chile), An Act of Vengeance. Dora Alonso (Cuba), Sophie and the Angel. Helena Araujo (Colombia), Asthmatic. María Luisa Bombal (Chile), The Tree. Rosario Castellanos (Mexico), Culinary Lesson. Amparo Dávila (Mexico), In Heaven; Shoes for the Rest of My Life. Rima de Vallbona (Costa Rica), Penelope's Silver Wedding Anniversary. María Virginia Estenssoro (Bolivia), The Child That Never Was. Rosario Ferré (Puerto Rico), The Poisoned Tale. Elena Garro (Mexico), Blame the Tlaxcaltecs. Nora Glickman (Argentina), The Last Emigrant. Lucía Guerra (Chile), The Virgin's Passion. Liliana Heker (Argentina), Bishop Berkeley or Mariana of the Universe. Vlady Kociancich (Argentina), Knight, Death and the Devil. Luisa Mercedes Levinson (Argentina), The Cove. Clarice Lispector (Brazil), Looking for Some Dignity. María Elena Llano (Cuba), In the Family. Carmen Naranjo (Costa Rica), Symbiotic Encounter. Olga Orozco (Argentina), The Midgets. Antonia Palacios (Venezuela), A Gentleman on the Train. Cristina Peri Rossi (Uruguay), Breaking the Speed Record. Nélida Piñón (Brazil), Big-bellied Cow. Josefina Pla (Paraguay), To Seize the Earth. Elena Poniatowska (Mexico), Park Cinema. Teresa Porzecanski (Uruguay), The Story of a Cat. María Teresa Solari (Peru), Death and Transfiguration of a Teacher. Marta Traba (Argentina), The Tale of the Velvet Pillows. Luisa Valenzuela (Argentina), Up among the Eagles. Ana Lydia Vega (Puerto Rico), Caribbean. Alicia Yánez Cossío (Ecuador), The IWM 1000.
Includes a foreword by Isabel Allende and brief bio-bibliographical notes on the authors and translators.

A C28
Cortina, Rodolfo, ed. and intro. *Hispanic American Literature: An Anthology.*
  Lincolnwood, IL: NTC Publishing Group, 1998. 414 pp.
Short fiction:
María Cadilla de Martínez (Puerto Rico), Indigenous Profile. Lydia Cabrera (Cuba), The Prize of Freedom. Evangelina Cossío y Cisneros (Cuba), To Free Cuba. Judith

Ortiz Cofer (Puerto Rico), Tales Told under the Mango Tree. Includes a foreword by Rolando Hinojosa-Smith. This volume is arranged according to major themes in the Hispanic American experience. It is designed to be used as a classroom text and contains bio-bibliographic information on the contributors and discussion questions and writing topics.

A C 29
Coverdale Sumrall, Amber, ed. and preface. *Lover: Stories by Women.* Freedom, NY: The Crossing Press, 1992. 432 pp.
Short stories:
Isabel Allende (Chile), Our Secret.

A C30
Cranfill, Thomas Mabry, and George D. Schade, eds. *The Muse in Mexico: A Mid-century Miscellany.* Austin: University of Texas Press 1959. 179 pp.
Short stories:
Guadalupe Amor, The Small Drawing Room. Guadalupe Dueñas, A Clinical Case. Includes a brief preface by Thomas Mabry Cranfill.

A D1
Daly Heyck, Denis Lynn. *Barrios and Borderlands: Cultures of Latinos and Latinas in the United States.* New York: Routledge, 1994. 485 pp.
Short stories:
Aurora Levins Morales (Puerto Rico), Puertoricanness.
Includes a glossary of Spanish terms used in the selections. The lengthy introduction is titled "Latinos, Past and Present" and details the history of Mexican-Americans, Puerto Ricans, and Cubans. Includes bio-bibliographic information on contributors and a photograph of each.

A D2
Danticat, Edwidge, ed. *The Beacon Best of 2000: Creative Writing by Women and Men of All Colors and Cultures.* Boston: Beacon Press, 2000. 232 pp.
Narrative:
Julia Álvarez (Dominican Republic), Planting Sticks and Grinding Yucca: On Being a Translated Writer. Lidia Torres (Puerto Rico), Three Keys.

A D3
Datlow, Ellen, Kelly Link, and Gavin J. Grant, eds. *The Year's Best Fantasy and Horror 2006.* New York: Griffin, Godalming, Melia, 2006. 480 pp.
Short stories:
Isabel Allende (Chile), Guggenheim Lovers.

A D4
de Beer, Gabriella, ed. *Contemporary Mexican Women Writers: Five Voices.* Austin: University of Texas Press, 1996. 266 pp.

Short fiction:
Carmen Boullosa, III; Mary, Why Don't You? (Impossible Dialogue in One Act). Brianda Domecq, Balzac; In Memoriam; Galatea. Ángeles Masstretta, Aunt Clemencia Ortega; Aunt Cristina Martínez; Memory and Precipice. Silvia Molina, The New House; What Would You Have Done?; The Problem. María Luisa Puga, One; Lucrecia; The Guests.
Includes a photograph and a primary bibliography for each author as well as a bibliography titled "On Mexican Literature and Women's Writing."

A D5
DeCosta-Willis, Miriam, ed. *Daughters of the Diaspora: Afra-Hispanic Writers.* Kingston, Miami: Ian Randle Publishers, 2003. 500 pp.
Narrative:
Aída Cartagena Portalatín (Dominican Republic), Wasted Effort. Marta Rojas (Cuba), The *Sweet Enigma* of a Writer's Life: A Personal Narrative; *Holy Lust or White Papers* (excerpt). Lourdes Casal (Cuba), The Founders: Alfonso. Argentina Chiriboga (Ecuador), *Drums under My Skin* (excerpt). Nancy Morejón (Cuba), Myth and Reality in Cecilia Valdés (excerpt). Beatriz Santos (Uruguay), Chulin's Fantasy; Tía Coca. María Nsue Angüe (Equatorial Guinea), *Ekomo* (excerpt). Sherezada (Chiqui) Vicioso (Dominican Republic), An Oral History (Testimonio); Julia de Burgos, Our Julia. Soleida Ríos (Cuba), Untitled; Life. Edelma Zapata Pérez (Colombia), The Consciousness-Raising of an Afro-Indio Mulatto; Woman Writer in Colombia's Multiethnic Society. Cristina Cabral (Uruguay), 25 August 1988. Shirley Campbell (Costa Rica), Closing the Circle That Began in Africa. Mayra Santos-Febres (Dominican Republic), Marina's Fragrance.
Includes an introduction titled: "This Voyage toward Words: Mapping the Routes of the Writers" by the editor. Also includes essays by experts for each author included in the volume. Includes a photograph and a primary and secondary bibliography for each author.

A D6
De Jesús, Joy L., ed. *Growing Up Puerto Rican: An Anthology.* New York: William Morrow and Company, Inc., 1997. 233 pp.
Short fiction:
Alba Ambert, A Perfect Silence. Rosario Ferré, The Gift. Aurora Levins Morales, Immigrants. Judith Ortiz Cofer, Silent Dancing. Yvonne V. Sapia, Sofia. Ana Lydia Vega, Liliane's Sunday.
Includes bio-bibliographies for contributors and a foreword by Ed Vega.

A D7
de Onis, Harriet, ed., trans., and foreword. *The Golden Land. An Anthology of Latin American Folklore in Literature.* New York: Alfred A. Knopf, 1948. 395 pp.
Short stories:
Carmen Lyra (Costa Rica), The Tales of My Aunt Panchita; Brer Rabbit, Businessman.

A D8

de Vallbona, Rima. *Flowering Inferno: Tales of Sinking Hearts.* Trans. Lillian Lorca de Tagle. Pittsburgh, PA: Latin American Literary Review Press, 1994. 92 pp.
Short stories:
The Word Weaver; The Secret Life of Grandma Anacleta; History's Editor; The Burden of Routine; Future Sorrows; The Peace Brigade; Hell; An Ephemeral Star; The Libel of Dismissal; Pythagoras' Illustrious Disciple; Intergalactic Crusade; Once More Cain and Abel; Confirmation of the Obvious; Distributive Justice. Costa Rica.

A D9

Diaz, Tony, ed. *Latino Heretics.* Normal, IL: Fiction Collective Two, 1999. 215 pp.
Short fiction:
Judith Ortiz Cofer (Puerto Rico), Gravity.
Includes bio-bibliographies for contributors.

A D10

di Giovanni, Norman Thomas, and Susan Ashe, eds. and trans. *Celeste Goes Dancing and Other Stories: An Argentine Collection.* San Francisco: North Point Press, 1990. 184 pp.
Short stories:
Estela dos Santos, Celeste Goes Dancing. Liliana Heker, The Letter to Ricardo. Silvina Ocampo, The Drawing Lesson.
Includes an introduction by Norman Thomas di Giovanni and bio-bibliographic notes on authors and editors.

A D10.1

———, eds. and trans. *Hand in Hand Alongside the Track: and Other Stories (Contemporary Argentine Stories).* London: Constable and Company Limited, 1992. 172 pp.
Short stories:
Sylvia Iparraguirre, Alongside the Track. Vlady Kociancich, An Englishman in Mojacár. Ana María Shua, Family Chronicle. Alicia Steimberg, Fleur-de-Lis. Noemí Ulla, Waking Up Alive.
Includes complete bio-bibliographic notes on contributors.

A D11

Donoso, José, and William A. Henkin, eds. *The TriQuarterly Anthology of Contemporary Latin American Literature.* New York: E. P. Dutton, 1969. 496 pp.
Short stories:
Clarice Lispector (Brazil), excerpt from *The Apple in the Dark* (chapter four, part one).
Includes two introductory articles: "A Literature of Foundations" by Octavio Paz

and "The New Latin American Novelists" by Rodríguez Monegal.

A D 12

Doty, Mark, ed. and intro. *Open House: Writers Redefine Home.* Saint Paul, MN: Graywolf Press, 2003. 236 pp.
Narrative:
Carmen Boullosa (Mexico), Seeing Is Believing.
Includes bio-bibliographic notes on contributors.

A D 13

Dowd, Siobhan, ed. and intro. *This Prison Where I Live: The PEN Anthology of Imprisoned Writers.* London: Cassell, 1993. 192 pp.
Short stories:
Alicia Partnoy (Argentina), Rain; Ruth v. the Torturer.
Foreword by Joseph Brodsky.

A E1

Eagleton, Sandra, ed., preface, and intro. *Women in Literature: Life Stages through Stories, Poems, and Plays.* Englewood Cliffs: Prentice-Hall Inc., 1988. 472 pp.
Short stories:
Dinah Silveira de Queiroz (Brazil), Guidance.
Includes brief bio-bibliographic notes on contributors.

A E2

Epler, Barbara, ed. *Terrestrial Intelligence: International Fiction from New Directions.* New York: New Directions Publishing Corp., 2006. 256 pp.
Short stories:
Clarice Lispector (Brazil), Three Cronicas.
Includes bio-bibliographic notes on contributors.

A E3

Erro-Peralta, Nora, and Caridad Silva-Núñez, eds. and intro. *Beyond the Border: A New Age in Latin American Women's Fiction.* Pittsburgh, PA: Cleis Press, 1991. 223 pp.
Short stories:
Isabel Allende (Chile), The Judge's Wife. Lydia Cabrera (Cuba), The Prize of Freedom. Aída Cartagena Portalatín (Dominican Republic), Donna Summer. Rima de Vallbona (Costa Rica), The Secret World of Grandmamma Anacleta. Lygia Fagundes Telles (Brazil), The Hunt. Rosario Ferré (Puerto Rico), Mercedes Benz 220 SL. Lucía Fox (Peru), The Wedding. Elena Garro (Mexico), Perfecto Luna. Angélica Gorodischer (Argentina), Under the Yubayas in Bloom. Sylvia Lago (Uruguay), Homelife. Elena Poniatowska (Mexico), Slide In, My Dark One, Between the Crosstie and the Whistle. Armonía Somers (Uruguay), The Immigrant. Gloria Stolk (Venezuela), Crickets and Butterflies. Luisa Valenzuela (Argentina), Up among the Eagles.
Includes primary and secondary bibliographies for each author and brief

biographical notes. The appendix includes "The Short Story, Feminism and Latin American Women Writers: A Bibliography."

A E4

Esteves, Carmen C., and Lizabeth Paravisini-Gebert, eds. and intro. *Green Candy and Juicy Flotsam: Short Stories by Caribbean Women*. New Brunswick, NJ: Rutgers University Press, 1991. 273 pp.

Short stories:

Dora Alonso (Cuba), Cotton Candy. Aída Cartagena Portalatín (Dominican Republic), They Called Her Aurora (A Passion for Donna Summer). Hilma Contreras (Dominican Republic), Hair. Rosario Ferré (Puerto Rico), The Poisoned Story. Magali García Ramis (Puerto Rico), Cocuyo Flower. Angela Hernández (Dominican Republic), How to Gather the Shadows of the Flowers. Olga Nolla (Puerto Rico), No Dust Is Allowed in this House. Ana Lydia Vega (Puerto Rico), ADJ, Inc. Mirta Yáñez (Cuba), Of Natural Causes.

Includes bio-bibliographic notes and primary and secondary bibliographies for each author. Also includes stories by francophone and anglophone writers.

A F1

Fagundes Telles, Lygia. *Tigrela and Other Stories*. Trans. Margaret A. Neves. New York: Avon Books, 1986. 152 pp.

Short stories:

The Ants; Rat Seminar; The Consultation; Yellow Nocturne; The Presence; The Touch on the Shoulder; The X in the Problem; Crescent Moon in Amsterdam; Lovelorn Dove (A Story of Romance); WM; The Sauna; Herbarium; Tigrela; Dear Editor.

Includes brief bio-bibliographic notes on the authors.

Brazil.

A F2

Fernández, Roberta, ed., preface, and intro. *In Other Words: Literature by Latinas of the United States*. Houston, TX: Arte Público Press, 1994. 554 pp.

Short fiction:

Elena Castedo (Spain/Chile), excerpt from Paradise. Nora Glickman (Argentina), A Day in New York. Aurora Levins Morales (Puerto Rico), A Remedy for Heartburn. Bessy Reyna (Cuba/Panama), And This Blue Surrounding Me Again. Each selection is preceded by bio-bibliographic notes on the author and a photograph. Includes a foreword by Jean Franco, a selected bibliography of Latina literature of the United States, and brief bio-bibliographic notes on the translators and the critic (Jean Franco).

A F3

Fernández Olmos, Margarite, and Lizabeth Paravisini-Gebert, eds. and intro. *Pleasure in the Word: Erotic Writing by Latin American Women*. Fredonia. NY: White Pine Press, 1994. 284 pp.

Short fiction:
Isabel Allende (Chile), excerpt from The House of the Spirits. Albalucía Angel (Colombia), excerpt from The Spotted Bird Perched High Above Upon the Tall Green Lemon Tree.... Pía Barros (Chile), Foreshadowing of a Trace; A Smell of Wood and of Silence. María Luisa Bombal (Chile), excerpt from *The Last Mist.* Matilde Daviú (Venezuela), The Woman Who Tore Up the World. Rosario Ferré (Puerto Rico), Rice and Milk. Beatriz Guido (Argentina), excerpt from *The House of the Angel.* Angela Hernández (Dominican Republic), How to Gather the Shadows of the Flowers. María Luisa Mendoza (Mexico), excerpt from *Ausencia's Tale.* Silvina Ocampo (Argentina), Albino Orma. Renata Pallotini (Brazil); Woman Sitting on the Sand. Cristina Peri Rossi (Uruguay), The Witness; Ca Foscar. Alejandra Pizarnik (Argentina); Words, The Lady Buccaneer of Pernambuco or Hilda the Polygraph; The Bloody Countess. Elena Poniatowska (Mexico), Happiness. Rosamaría Roffiel (Mexico), excerpt from *Amora.* Luisa Valenzuela (Argentina), Dirty Words; excerpt from *The Efficacious Cat:* The Fucking Game. Ana Lydia Vega (Puerto Rico), Lyrics for a Salsa and Three Sonetos by Request. Includes brief preface by Marjorie Agosín, bio-bibliographic notes on editors and authors, and a bibliography of original works in Spanish and Portuguese.

A F3.1
Fernández Olmos, Margarite, and Lizabeth Paravisini-Gebert, eds. and intro. *Remaking a Lost Harmony: Stories from the Hispanic Caribbean.* Fredonia, NY: White Pine Press, 1995. 249 pp.
Short stories:
Aída Cartagena Portalatín (Dominican Republic), The Path to the Ministry. Hilma Contreras (Dominican Republic), Mambrú Did Not Go to War. Soledad Cruz (Cuba), Fritters and Moons. Rosario Ferré (Puerto Rico), This Noise Was Different. Magali García Ramis (Puerto Rico), Corinne, Amiable Girl. Angela Hernández (Dominican Republic), Silvia. Verónica López Kónina (Russia-Cuba), How Do You Know, Vivian? Mayra Montero (Cuba), Under the Weeping Willow. Olga Nolla (Puerto Rico), Requiem for a Wreathless Corpse. Ana Lydia Vega (Puerto Rico), The Blind Buffalo. Mirta Yáñez (Cuba), Public Declaration of Love.
Includes a brief bio-bibliographic notes on editors, authors, translators, and cover artist.

A F4
Ferré, Rosario. *Sweet Diamond Dust: A Novel and Three Stories of Life in Puerto Rico.* Trans. Rosario Ferré. New York: Ballantine Books, 1988. 198 pp.
Narrative:
Sweet Diamond Dust (novel); The Gift; Isolda's Mirror; Captain Candelario's Heroic Last Stand.
Puerto Rico.

A F4.1
——. *The Youngest Doll.* Trans. Rosario Ferré. Lincoln: University of Nebraska Press, 1991. 169 pp.

Short stories:
The Youngest Doll; The Poisoned Story; The Dust Garden; The Glass Box; The Fox Fur Coat; The Dreamer's Portrait; The House that Vanished; Amalia; Marina and the Lion; The Seed Necklace; The Other Side of Paradise; Sleeping Beauty; Mercedes Benz 220 SL; When Women Love Men; How I Wrote "When Women Love Men" (essay); On Destiny, Language, and Translation; or, Ophelia Adrift in the C &O Canal (essay).
Includes a foreword by Jean Franco and a bibliography of major works by Rosario Ferré.
Puerto Rico.

A F5
Figes, Kathy, ed. and intro. *The Penguin Book of International Women's Stories.* New York: Penguin Book USA Inc., 1996. 462 pp.
Short stories:
Isabel Allende (Chile), Two Words. María Elena Llano (Cuba), In the Family. Armonía Somers (Uruguay), The Burial. Luisa Valenzuela (Argentina), Blue Water-man.
Includes bio-bibliographic notes on the authors.

A F6
Fisburn, Evelyn, ed. and intro. *Short Fiction by Spanish-American Women.* Manchester & New York: Manchester University Press, 1998. 126 pp.
Short fiction:
Rosario Ferré (Puerto Rico), Mercedes Benz 220 SL.
Includes a critical introduction to each story, a select bibliography for contributors, "Temas de discusión" and "Temas de debate" for each story, and a Spanish glossary. Stories are in Spanish.

A F7
Flores, Lauro. *The Floating Borderlands: Twenty-five Years of U.S. Hispanic Literature.* Seattle: University of Washington Press, 1998. 432 pp.
Narrative:
Alba Ambert, (Puerto Rico). Losses. Sandra Benítez (Mexico), El pajarero. Julia Álvarez (Dominican Republic), El Doctor. Beatriz Rivera, (Cuba), Shango's Rest. Judith Ortiz Cofer (Puerto Rico), The Black Virgin. Helena María Viramontes (Mexico), Miss Clairol.

A F8
Foster, Nicole. *Electric: Best Lesbian Erotic Fiction.* Los Angeles: Alyson Books, 1999. 314 pp.
Short fiction:
Mariana Romo-Carmona (Chile), Disco Nights.
Includes bio-bibliographies for contributors.

A F9

Fremantle, Anne, ed. and preface. *Latin American Literature Today.* New York: New American Library, 1977. 342 pp.

Short stories:

Silvina Bullrich (Argentina), The Bridge. Rosario Castellanos (Mexico), excerpt from Office of Tenebrae. Kitzia Hoffman (Mexico), Old Adelina. Clarice Lispector (Brazil), The Man Who Appeared; Better Than to Burn. Gabriela Mistral (Chile), Castile (An Imaginary Encounter with Saint Theresa).

Includes brief bio-bibliographic notes on the authors.

A F10

Fuentes, Carlos, and Julio Ortega, eds. *The Vintage Book of Latin American Stories.* New York: Vintage Books, 2000. 380 pp.

Short stories:

Inés Arredondo (Mexico), Subterranean River. Clarice Lispector (Brazil), Love. Nélida Pinón (Brazil), House of Passion. María Luisa Puga (Mexico), Naturally. Angeles Mastretta (Mexico), *Big-Eyed Woman* (excerpt). Luisa Valenzuela (Argentina), Panther Eyes.

Includes bio-bibliographic notes on the authors.

A G1

Galarza, Ernesto. *Barrio Boy: With Related Readings.* New York: Glencoe/McGraw-Hill, 2002. 263 pp.

Short fiction:

Judith Ortiz Cofer (Puerto Rico), An Hour with Abuelo; A Day in the Barrio; Linked.

A G2

García, Cristina, ed. *Bordering Fires: The Vintage Book of Contemporary Mexican and Chicana and Chicano Literature.* New York: Vintage; Knopf Publishing Group, 2006. 384 pp.

Elena Poniatowska (Mexico), Introduction from *Here's to You, Jesusa!* Angeles Mastretta (Mexico), Aunt Leonor; Aunt Natalia. Rosario Castellanos (Mexico), *The Book of Lamentations* (excerpt).

A G2.1

——, ed. and intro. *Cubanísimo: The Vintage Book of Contemporary Cuban Literature.* New York: Vintage Books, 2002. 373 pp.

Narrative:

Nancy Morejón, Love; Attributed City. Lourdes Casal, The Founders: Alfonso. Zoé Valdés, The Ivory Trader and the Red Melons. María Elena Cruz Varela, Love Song for Difficult Times; The Exterminating Angel. Ana Menéndez, In Cuba I Was a German Shepherd.

Includes bio-bibliographic notes on contributors.

A G3

Gardiol, Rita, ed., intro., and trans. *The Silver Candelabra and Other Stories: A Century of Jewish Argentine Literature*. Pittsburgh, PA: Latin American Literary Review Press, 1997. 187 pp.

Short stories:

Cecilia Absatz, Feiguele; Ballet Dancers. Eugenia Calny, Drifting Balloons; In the Hero's Shadow. Alicia Steimberg, Of Musicians and Watchmakers. Silvia Plager, Empty Shell; No One Will Take Her Place.

Includes bio-bibliographic notes on authors and selected works of Jewish Argentine history and literature. Also includes a preface by Darrell B. Lockhart and a brief overview of Argentine history relative to its Jewish population.

A G4

Geok-Lin Lim, Shirley, and Norman Spencer, eds. *One World of Literature*. Boston: Houghton Mifflin Co., 1993. 1182 pp.

Short stories:

Isabel Allende (Chile), Phantom. Rosario Castellanos (Mexico), Death of the Tiger. Rosario Ferré (Puerto Rico), Mercedes Benz 220 SL. Clarice Lispector (Brazil), The Body. Luisa Valenzuela (Argentina), I'm Your Horse in the Night.

Includes a brief introduction to literature from every continent. The appendix includes bibliographies organized into general bibliographies and by country (critical studies).

A G5

Gibbons, Reginald, ed. *New Writing from Mexico. A Special Issue of TriQuarterly Magazine*. Evanston, IL: TriQuarterly and Northwestern University, 1992. 420 pp.

Short fiction:

Carmen Boullosa, Storms of Torment. Barbara Jacobs, The Time I Got Drunk. Mónica Lavín, The Lizard. Mónica Mansour, In Secret. Angeles Mastretta, *Big-Eyed Women* (excerpt). Silvia Molina, Starting Over. María Luisa Puga, The Natural Thing to Do. Bernarda Solís, Art and Monsters. Gloria Velázquez, Temptress of the Torch-Pines.

Includes brief bio-bibliographic notes on authors and translators.

A G6

Goldberg, Isaac, ed. *Brazilian Tales*. Boston: Four Seas, 1921. 149 pp.

Short stories:

Carmen Dolores, Aunt Zeze's Tears.

Includes preliminary remarks by Isaac Goldberg.

A G7

Gómez, Alma, Cherríe Moraga, and Mariana Romo-Carmona, eds. and intro. *Cuentos: Stories by Latinas*. New York: Kitchen Table, Women of Color Press, 1983. 241 pp.

Short stories:
María Carolina de Jesús (Brazil), Childhood. Miriam Díaz-Diocaretz (Chile), Juani en tres tiempos. Cicera Fernándes de Oliveira (Brazil), We Women Suffer More than Men. Aurora Levins Morales (Puerto Rico), El bacalao viene de más lejos y se come aquí. Gloria Liberman (Chile), La confesión. Aleida Rodríguez (Cuba), A Month in a Nutshell. Mariana Romo-Carmona (Chile), La virgen en el desierto. Sara Rosel (Cuba), El viaje. Lake Saris (Chile), The March. Luz María Umpierre (Puerto Rico), La Veintiuna. Iris Zavala (Puerto Rico), Kiliagonia.
Includes a Spanish/English glossary.

A G8
Gonzalez, Nelly S. *Bolivian Studies Journal: Issue Dedicated to Alcides Arguedas* Vol. II (2004). 214 pp.
Short stories:
Giovanna Rivero Santa Cruz (Bolivia), Little Goddess; Warmi.
Includes contributor information.

A G9
González, Ray, ed. *Currents from the Dancing River: Contemporary Latino Fiction, Nonfiction and Poetry.* New York: A Harvard Original Harcourt Brace & Company, 1994. 573 pp.
Short fiction:
Cristina García (Cuba), Basket of Water (excerpt from *Dreaming in Cuban*). Aurora Levins Morales (Puerto Rico), Puertoricanness; Immigrants; Kitchens. Nicholasa Mohr (Puerto Rico), I Never Seen My Father. Judith Ortiz Cofer Puerto Rico), The Black Virgin; The Witch's Husband. Helena María Viramontes (Mexico), Tears on My Pillow.
Includes bio-bibliographies for contributors.

A G9.1
——, ed. *Under the Pomegranate Tree: The Best New Latino Erotica.* New York: Washington Square Press, 1996. 362 pp.
Short stories:
María Luisa Mendoza, (Mexico) Ausencia's Tales. Antonia Palacios, (Venezuela) A Gentleman on the Train. Elena Poniatowska (Mexico), Happiness.

A G10
González Echeverría, Roberto, ed., preface and intro. *Latin American Short Stories.* New York: Oxford University Press, Inc., 1997. 481 pp.
Short stories:
Nélida Piñón (Brazil), The Warmth of Things. María Luisa Bombal (Chile), The Tree. Rosario Castellanos (Mexico), Cooking Lesson. Juana Manuela Gorriti (Peru), To His Regret: Confidence of a Confidence. Luisa Mercedes Levinson (Argentina), The Clearing. Clarice Lispector (Brazil), The Crime of the Mathematics Professor. Christina Peri Rossi (Uruguay), The Threshold. Rosario Ferré (Puerto Rico), When Women Love Men.

Includes bio-bibliographic notes, sources in English about Latino American literature, and author studies.

A G11

Gorriti, Juana Manuela. *Dreams and Realities: Selected Fiction of Juana Manuela Gorriti.* Trans. Sergio Gabriel Waisman. New York: Oxford University Press, 2003. 270 pp.

Short fiction:
The Quena; Treasure of the Incas; The Deadman's Fiancee; The Mazoquero's Daughter; The Black Glove; If You Do Wrong Expect No Good; Gubi Amaya: A Year in California.
Edited and with an introduction, chronology, and critical notes by Francine Masiello.
Peru.

A G12

Graziano, Frank, ed. and intro. *Alejandra Pizarnik: A Profile.* Durango, CO: Logbridge-Rhodes, Inc., 1987. 143 pp.

Short prose:
Alejandra Pizarnik, Nocturnal Singer; Fragments for Dominating Silence; Sorceries; Roads of the Mirror; A Dream Where Silence Is Made of Gold; Extraction of the Stone of Folly; Night Shared in the Memory of an Escape; excerpts from The Musical Hell: Fundamental Stone; Desire of the Word; L'obscurité des eaux; The Word that Cures; Names and Figures; The Possessed among Lilacs; *Texts of Shadow and Last Poems: Words* (excerpts); Small Poems in Prose; On Time and Not; The Understanding; Tangible Absence; A Mystical Betrayal; House of Favors; The Lady Buccaneer of Pernambuco or Hilda the Polygraph; The End; Portrait of Voices. Excerpts from The Bloody Countess: The Iron Virgin; The Mirror of Melancholy; Blood Bath; Severe Measures.
Includes notes on the author and a bibliography of her works.
Argentina.

A G13

Grossman, William L., ed., trans., and intro. *Modern Brazilian Short Stories.* Berkeley: University of California Press, 1967. 167 pp.

Short stories:
Rachel de Queiroz, Metonymy, or the Husband's Revenge. Clarice Lispector, The Crime of the Mathematics Professor. Marília São Paulo Penna e Costa, The Happiest Couple in the World. Dinah Silveira de Queiroz, Guidance.
Includes bio-bibliographic notes on authors.

A H1

Halpern, Daniel, ed. *The Art of the Story: An International Anthology of Contemporary Short Stories.* New York: Viking, 1999. 667 pp.

Short stories:
Luisa Valenzuela (Argentina), Who, Me a Bum?
Includes bio-bibliographic notes on authors.

A H1.1

Halpern, Daniel, ed. *The Art of the Tale: An International Anthology of Short Stories 1945-1985.* New York: Viking Penguin Books, 1986. 818 pp.
Short stories:
Luisa Valenzuela (Argentina), I'm Your Horse in the Night.
Includes bio-bibliographic notes on authors.

A H2

Hanson, Ron, and Jim Shepard, eds. and intro. *You've Got to Read This: Contemporary American Writers Introduce Stories that Held Them in Awe.* New York: Harper Perennial, 1994. 630 pp.
Short stories:
Clarice Lispector (Brazil), The Smallest Woman in the World.
Includes an introduction to the story written by Julia Álvarez.

A H3

Hazelton, Hugh, and Gary Geddes, eds. and intro. *Compañeros: An Anthology of Writings about Latin America.* Ontario: Cormorant Books, 1990. 320 pp.
Short stories:
Marilú Mallet (Chile), The Loyal Order of the Time-Clock. Edith Velásquez (Venezuela), Una comedia no muy divina (excerpt in English).
Includes brief bio-bibliographic notes on authors.

A H4

Heker, Liliana. *The Stolen Party and Other Stories.* Trans. and afterword, Alberto Manguel. Toronto: Coach House Press, 1994. 136 pp.
Short stories:
Georgina Requeni or the Chosen One; Early Beginnings or Ars Poética; Family Life; Bishop Berkeley or Mariana of the Universe; Jocasta; The Stolen Party.
These stories were taken from three of Heker's other collections: Aquarius (1972), Resplandor que se apagó en el mundo (1977), and Peras del mal (1982).
Argentina.

A H5

Henderson, Bill, ed. *The Pushcart Prize XI: Best of the Small Presses with an Index to the First Eleven Volumes: An Annual Small Press Reader.* New York: Pushcart Press, 1986. 245 pp.
Short stories:
Ana Lydia Vega (Puerto Rico), Communist.
Includes bio-bibliographic information on the contributors and an introduction by Cynthia Ozick.

A H6

Hogan, Linda, and Brenda Peterson, eds. *The Sweet Breathing of Plants: Women Writing on the Green World.* New York: North Point Press, 2001. 288 pp.

Narrative:
Isabel Allende (Chile), The Language of Flowers. Rigoberta Menchú (Guatemala), Maise.
Includes a preface by the editors and bio-bibliographic information on the contributors.

A H7
Holoch, Naomi, and Joan Nestle, eds. *The Vintage Book of International Lesbian Fiction.* New York: Vintage Books, 1999. 348 pp.
Short stories:
Sylvia Molloy (Argentina), Certificate of Absence (excerpt). Achy Obejas (Cuba), Waters. Cristina Peri Rossi (Uruguay), Final Judgement; Singing in the Desert. Rosamaría Roffiel (Mexico), Forever Lasts Only a Full Moon.
Includes brief bio-bibliographic information on contributors.

A H8
Horan, Elizabeth Rosa, ed. and trans. *The Subversive Voice of Carmen Lyra: Selected Works.* Gainesville: University Press of Florida, 2000. 224 pp.
Narrative:
I. From Modernism to Critical Realism (1923-1936)
The Cothnejo-Fishy District; Silhouettes from the Maternal School (1929); Bananas and Men (1931); Golden Bean: The Coffee Bean and the Laborer (1933); Front-Row Seat in Heaven (1936); Pastor's Ten Little Old Men (1936).
II. Tales from My Aunt Panchita (1920-1926)
The Fool of the Riddles; Uvieta; Juan, the One with the Little Load of Firewood; Jump on It, Stick; The Monkey; The Cotton Guy; La cucharachita Mandinga; The Devil's Mother-in-Law; The House of French Toast; The Flowering Olive Tree; Dark-haired Girl, Fair-haired Girl; The Bird of Sweet Charm; Coming Out with a Sunday Seven.
III. Tales of Uncle Rabbit (1920-1926)
Uncle Rabbit and Uncle Coyote; Why Uncle Rabbit Has Such Long Ears; How Uncle Rabbit Played a Trick on Aunt Whale and Uncle Elephant; How Uncle Rabbit Got Out of a Fix; Uncle Rabbit, Businessman; Uncle Rabbit and the Cheeses; Uncle Rabbit and His Granny's Scuffed Sandals; Uncle Rabbit and the Stream; Uncle Rabbit and Brother Juan Piedra's Horse; Uncle Rabbit Get the Girl.
Includes a chronology titled: A The Life of Carmen Lyra/María Isabel Carvajal of Costa Rica and an introduction "May She Rest in Peace" by the editor. Includes bio-bibliographies of the editor and author and family photographs of the author. Costa Rica.

A H9
Hospital, Carolina, ed. and intro. *Cuban American Writers: Los atrevidos.* Princeton, NJ: Ediciones Ellas/Linden Lane Press in Association with Co/Works, Inc., 1998. 169 pp.

Short fiction:
Bertha Sánchez-Bello, Family Portrait: Reflection on Interior Decoration.
Includes bio-bibliographic notes on contributors.

A H10
Hospital, Carolina, and Jorge Cantera, eds. and intro. *A Century of Cuban Writers*
    in Florida: Selected Prose and Poetry. Sarasota, FL: Pineapple Inc., 1996.
    237 pp.
Short stories:
Lydia Cabrera, How the Monkey Lost the Fruit of His Labor; Animals in Cuban
Folklore & Magic. Ivone Lamazares, Cousin Sarita. Hilda Perrera, Paco. Marisella
Veiga, The Mosquito Net.
Includes bio-bibliographic notes on contributors and a preface by Carolina Hospital.
Also includes an extensive introduction by the editors dealing with Cuba and Cuban
immigration to Florida.

A H11
Howe, Irving, and Ilana Wiener Howe, eds. *Short Stories. An Anthology of the*
    Shortest Stories. Boston: David R. Grodine Publisher, 1982. 262 pp.
Short stories:
Luisa Valenzuela (Argentina), The Censors.
Includes an introduction by Irving Howe.

A H12
Howes, Barbara, ed. and intro. *From the Green Antilles: Writings of the Caribbean.*
    New York: Macmillan, 1966. 368 pp.
Short stories:
Lydia Cabrera (Cuba), Turtle's Horse; Walo-Wila.
Includes bio-bibliographic notes on authors. Also includes work of English, French,
and Dutch-speaking authors. A brief introduction precedes each language group.

A H12.1
——, ed. and intro. *The Eye of the Heart: Short Stories from Latin America.* New
    York: Avon Books, 1973. 576 pp.
Short stories:
María Luisa Bombal (Chile), The Tree. Clarice Lispector (Brazil), The Smallest
Woman in the World. Gabriela Mistral (Chile), Why Reeds Are Hollow. Dinah
Silveira de Queiroz (Brazil), Tarciso. Armonía Somers (Uruguay), Madness.
Includes bio-bibliographic notes on authors and translators.

A H13
Hughes, Psiche, ed. *Violations: Stories of Love by Latin American Women.* Lincoln:
    University of Nebraska Press, 2005. 208 pp.
Short stories:
Cristina Peri Rossi (Uruguay),To Love or Ingest. Margo Glantz (Mexico), English
Love. Armonía Somers (Uruguay),The Fall. Fanny Buitrago (Colombia), The Sea

from the Window. Alicia Steimberg (Argentina),Young Amatista. Ana María Shua (Argentina), Farewell, My Love. Andrea Blanqué (Uruguay), Immensely Eunice. Sylvia Lago (Uruguay), Golden Days of a Queen of Diamonds. Marilyn Bobes (Cuba), In Florence Ten Years Later; Elena Poniatowska (Mexico), Love Story. Angeles Mastretta (Mexico), Aunt Mariana. Nélida Piñón (Brazil), Procession of Love. Teresa Ruiz Rosas (Peru), Santa Catalina, Arequipa. Carmen Boullosa (Mexico), Impossible Story. Liliana Heker (Argentina), Spick and Span. Luisa Valenzuela (Argentina), End of the Millennium.
Includes bio-bibliographic notes on authors and translators.

A I1
Ibieta, Gabriella, ed. and intro. *Latin American Writers: Thirty Stories*. New York: St. Martin's Press, 1993. 355 pp.
Short stories:
María Luisa Bombal (Chile), New Islands. Lydia Cabrera (Cuba), The Hill Called Mambiala. Rosario Castellanos (Mexico), Cooking Lesson. Rosario Ferré (Puerto Rico), Sleeping Beauty. Elena Garro (Mexico), The Day We Were Dogs. Clarice Lispector (Brazil), The Imitation of the Rose; The Departure of the Train. Cristina Peri Rossi (Uruguay), The Influence of Edgar Allan Poe on the Poetry of Raimundo Arias. Nélida Piñón (Brazil), Adamastor. Luisa Valenzuela (Argentina), Strange Things Happen Here. Alicia Yánez Cossío (Ecuador), Sabotage.
Includes bio-bibliographic notes on authors.

A I2
International Board on Books for Young People, ed. *Stories from across the Globe*. Gurgaon: Scholastic India, 2002. 131 pp.
Short stories:
Gaby Vallejo (Bolivia), Sabina.
Created for young readers.

A J1
Jackson, David K., ed. *Oxford Anthology of the Brazilian Short Story*. Oxford; New York: Oxford University Press, 2006. 523 pp.
Narrative:
Emilía Moncorva Bandeira de Mello (pseud. Carmen Dolores), Aunt Zézé's Tears. Rachel de Queiroz, Metonymy, or The Husband's Revenge. Clarice Lispector, The Buffalo; The Chicken; The Smallest Woman in the World; The Breaking of the Bread; The Fifth Story; Miss Algrave; The Body; Plaza Mauá; Beauty and the Beast, or, The Wound Too Great. Nélida Piñón, Big-Bellied Cow; Brief Flower. Lygia Fagundes Telles, Just a Saxophone. Hilda Hilst, Agda. Edla Van Steen, Carol head Lina heart.
Includes a lengthy introduction on the Brazilian short story, a bibliography on Brazil and on Brazilian literature, and bio-bibliographic notes on authors and translators.

A J2

Jacobsen McLennan, Karen, ed. and intro. *Nature's Ban. Women's Incest Literature.* Boston: Northeastern University Press, 1996. 394 pp.

Short stories:

Rosario Ferré (Puerto Rico), Amalia.

Includes brief bio-bibliographic notes on authors and a select bibliography consisting of: Literature by and about Selected Authors; Critical, Historical, and Clinical References (about incest); and Additional Literature about Incest: Fiction, Poetry, Memoir, and Drama.

A J3

Jaffe, Harold, ed. *Fiction International 25. Special Issue: Mexican Fiction.* San Diego, CA: San Diego State University Press, 1994. 277 pp.

Short stories:

Acela Bernal, The Taste of Good Fortune. Silvia Castillejos Peral, Tomorrow the World Ends. Ana Clavel, Dark Tears of a Mere Sleeper. Regina Cohen, Jazzbluesing. Hilda Rosina Conde Zambada, Sonatina. Josefina Estrada, Women in Captivity. Cristina Ibarra, The Little Eastern Star. Patricia Laurent Kullick, Crazy Cuts. Mónica Lavín, Nicolasa's Lace. Regina Swain, The Devil Also Dances in the Aloha; Señorita Supermán and the Instant Soup Generation.

Includes an introduction by Gabriel Trujillo Muñoz, "Turn-of-the-Century Mexican Narrative: A Tourist Guide."

A J4

Jaramillo, Enrique Levi, ed. *When New Flowers Bloomed: Short Stories by Women Writers from Costa Rica and Panama.* Pittsburgh, PA: Latin American Literary Review Press, 1991. 208 pp.

Short stories:

Lilia Algandona (Panama), Nightmare at Deep River. Giovanna Benedetti (Panama), The Rain on the Fire; The Scent of Violets. Rosa María Britton (Panama), The Wreck of the Enid Rose. Delfina Collado (Costa Rica), Garabito the Indomitable; The Indian Mummy. Rima de Vallbona (Costa Rica), The Good Guys; The Wall. Griselda López (Panama), One Minute; I'll Eat the Land. Carmen Lyra (Costa Rica), Ramona, Woman of the Ember; Estefania. Emilia Macaya (Costa Rica), Alcestis; Eva. Carmen Naranjo (Costa Rica), My Byzantine Grandmother's Two Medieval Saints; When New Flowers Bloomed. Eunice Odio (Costa Rica), The Vestige of the Butterfly. Yolanda Oreamuno (Costa Rica), Urban Wake; Of Their Obscure Family. Bertalicia Peralta (Panama), Elio. Julieta Pinto (Costa Rica), The Country Schoolmaster; The Meeting. Bessy Reyna (Panama), And This Blue Surrounding Me Again. Graciela Rojas Sucre (Panama), Wings. Isis Tejeira (Panama), The Birth; The Piano of My Desire. Victoria Urbano (Costa Rica), Death in Mallorca.

Includes bio-bibliographic notes on authors, translators, and the editor. Also includes the bibliographies: "Studies on Literature from Costa Rica: A General Bibliography," "Studies on Literature from Panama: A General Bibliography," "Anthologies of (or including) Latin American Women Writers in English and Spanish," and "General Bibliographies of (or including) Latin American Women

Writers."

A J5
Jaramillo, Enrique, and Leland Chambers, eds. and intro. *Contemporary Short Stories from Central America.* Austin: University of Texas Press, 1994. 275 pp.
Short stories:
Rosa María Britton (Panama), Love Is Spelled with a "G." Carmen Naranjo (Costa Rica), Floral Caper. Bertalicia Peralta (Panama), The Village Virgin. Julieta Pinto (Costa Rica), Disobedience. Victoria Urbano (Costa Rica), The Face.
Includes a bibliography for each country represented in the book and brief bio-bibliographic notes on authors and translators.

A J6
Johnson, Rob, ed. *Fantasmas: Supernatural Stories by Mexican-American Writers.* Tempe, AZ: Bilingual Review Press, 2001. 176 pp.
Short fiction:
Kathleen Alcalá (Mexico).
Includes an introduction by Kathleen Alcalá.

A J7
Jones, Earl, ed. *Selected Latin American Literature for Youth.* College Station: Texas A & M University Press, 1968. 152 pp.
Short stories:
Carmen Baez (Mexico), The Cylinder. Carmen Lira (Costa Rica), Uvieta. Elena Poniatowska (Mexico), The Gift.
Includes brief bio-bibliographic notes on authors.

A J8
Jones, Richard Gly, and A. Susan Williams, eds. *The Penguin Book of Erotic Stories by Women.* New York: Penguin, 1995. 416 pp.
Short stories:
Isabel Allende (Chile), Our Secret.
Includes bio-bibliographic notes on authors.

A J9
Jones, Willis Knapp, ed. and intro. *Spanish American Literature in Translation: A Selection of Prose, Poetry, and Drama Before 1888. Volume I.* New York: Frederick Ungar, 1966. 356 pp.
Short stories:
Clorinda Matto de Turner (Peru), Birds without Nests (excerpt from Aves sin nido).

A J9.1
——, ed. and preface. *Spanish American Literature in Translation: A Selection of Prose, Poetry, and Drama since 1888. Volume II.* New York: Frederick Ungar, 1963. 469 pp.

Short stories:
Marta Brunet (Chile), Francina. Carmen Lira (Costa Rica), Uvieta.
Includes a lengthy introduction outlining the history of Latin American literature since 1888.

A K1
Kafka, Phillipa, ed. *"Saddling La Gringa." Gatekeeping in Literature by Contemporary Latina Writers.* Westport, CT: Greenwood Press, 2000. 192 pp.
Narrative:
Julia Álvarez (Domincan Republic), *How the Garcia Girls Lost Their Accents.* Rosario Ferré (Puerto Rico), *The Youngest Doll.* Cristina García (Cuba), *Dreaming in Cuban.* Magali García Ramis (Puerto Rico), *Happy Days, Uncle Sergio.* Judith Ortiz Cofer (Puerto Rico), *Silent Dancing.* All excerpts from the novels.

A K2
Kalechofsky, Robert, and Roberta Kalechofsky, eds. *Echad: An Anthology of Latin American Jewish Writings.* Marblehead, MA: Micah Publications, 1980. 281 pp.
Short stories:
Clarice Lispector (Brazil), Love; The Chicken. Teresa Porzecanski (Uruguay), Parricide. Esther Seligson (Mexico), A Wind of Dry Leaves; Luz de dos. Alicia Steimberg (Argentina), *Musicians and Watchmakers* (excerpt).
Includes a brief introduction by Roberta Kalechofsky and brief bio-bibliographic notes on authors and translators.

A K2.1
——, eds. *Echad 5: The Global Anthology of Jewish Women Writers.* Marblehead, MA: Micah Publications, 1990. 426 pp.
Short fiction:
Luisa Futoransky (Argentina), *Son cuentos chinos* (excerpts). Clarice Lispector (Brazil), The Smallest Women in the World, The Daydreams of a Drunk Woman. Teresa Porzecanski (Uruguay), Dying of Love.
Includes an introduction by Roberta Kalechofsky and brief bio-bibliographic notes on authors.

A K3
Kallet, Marilyn, and Patricia Clark, eds. *Worlds in Our Words: Contemporary American Women Writers.* Englewood Cliffs, NJ: Prentice Hall, 1996. 770 pp.
Short fiction:
Judith Ortiz Cofer (Puerto Rico), Tales Told under the Mango Tree; The Latin Deli; It Was a Special Treat.
Includes brief bio-bibliographies for contributors, along with contextual notes for each reading selection.

A K4
Kanellos, Nicolas, ed. and intro. *The Hispanic Literary Companion.* Detroit, MI: Visible Ink, 1997. 408 pp.

Short fiction:
Cristina García (Cuba), Inés in the Kitchen. Nicholasa Mohr (Puerto Rico), A Time with a Future (Carmela). Judith Ortiz Cofer (Puerto Rico), Casa. Helena María Viramontes (Mexico), The Moths.
A brief bio-bibliography for each author precedes their selection and a primary bibliography follows. Photographs are included for most contributors as well as addresses where authors may be contacted.

A K4.1
Kanellos, Nicolas, ed. *Short Fiction by Hispanic Writers of the United States.* Houston, TX: Arte Público Press, 1993. 285 pp.
Short fiction:
Nicholasa Mohr (Puerto Rico), Aunt Rosana's Rocker. Judith Ortiz Cofer (Puerto Rico), Silent Dancing. Helena Maria Viramontes (Mexico), The Moths.
Includes entries on each author detailing their historical and cultural context.

A K5
Katz, Naomi, and Nancy Milton, eds. *Fragment from a Lost Diary and Other Stories.* New York: Pantheon Books, 1973. 318 pp.
Short stories:
Dora Alonso (Cuba), Times Gone By.
Includes bio-bibliographic information on authors and editors.

A K6
Kerrigan, Anthony, ed. *Extraordinary Tales.* New York: Herder and Herder, 1971. 144 pp.
Short stories:
Delia Ingenieros (with Jorge Luís Borges) (Argentina), Odin. Silvina Ocampo (Argentina), The Inextinguishable Race.
Includes preliminary notes by Jorge Luís Borges and Adolfo Bioy Casares.

A K7
King, John R., ed. *Short Stories in Spanish.* New York: Penguin, 1999. 256 pp.
Short stories:
Isabel Allende (Chile), Walimai.
Includes bio-bibliographic information on authors and editors. Parallel text in Spanish and English.

A K8
Kingston, Maxine, and Luisa Valenzuela. *Two Foreign Women.* Leichhardt, N.S.W., Australia: Pluto Press, 1990. 45 pp.
Short stories:
Luisa Valenzuela (Argentina), Technique.

A K9

Kitchen, Judith, and Mary Paumier Jones, eds. and intro. *In Short: A Collection of Brief Creative Nonfiction*. New York: W. W. Norton & Company, 1996. 334 pp.

Short fiction:

Judith Ortiz Cofer (Puerto Rico), Volar.

Includes brief bio-bibliographies for contributors and a preface titled "The Disproportionate Power of the Small" by Bernard Cooper.

A L1

Lambert Ortiz, Elisabeth, ed. *A Taste of Latin America: Recipes and Stories*. New York: Interlink Books, 1999. 121 pp.

Short fiction:

Isabel Allende (Chile), *House of the Spirits* (excerpt). Laura Esquivel (Mexico), *Like Water for Chocolate* (excerpt). Angeles Mastretta (Mexico), *Mal de amores* (excerpt).

This volume contains recipes, anecdotes, and prose excerpts.

A L2

Lavín, Mónica, ed. *Points of Departure: New Stories from Mexico*. Trans. Gustavo V. Segade. San Francisco: City Lights, 2001. 159 pp.

Short stories:

Rosa Beltrán, Scheheresade. Rosina Conde, Morente. Josefina Estrada, June Gave Him the Voice. Ethel Krauze, Isaiah VII, 14. Mónica Lavín, Why Come Back? Includes bio-bibliographies of contributors.

A L3

Leonard, Kathy S., ed., trans., and intro. *Cruel Fictions, Cruel Realities: Short Stories by Latin American Women Writers*. Pittsburgh, PA: Latin American Literary Press, 1997. 134 pp.

Short fiction:

Gloria Artigas (Chile), Corners of Smoke. Yolanda Bedregal (Bolivia), How Milinco Escaped from School; The Morgue (excerpt from the novel *Bajo el oscuro sol*). Velia Calvimontes (Bolivia), Coati 1950. Nayla Chehade Durán (Colombia), The Vigil; The Visit. Silvia Diez Fierro (Chile), The Sailor's Wife; We Must Keep Fanning the Master. Inés Fernández Moreno (Argentina), A Mother to Be Assembled. Gilda Holst (Ecuador), The Competition. María Eugenia Lorenzini (Chile), Bus Stop #46. Andrea Maturana (Chile), Cradle Song; Out of Silence. Viviana Mellet (Peru), Good Night Air; The Other Mariana. Ana María Shua (Argentina), A Profession Like Any Other; Minor Surgery. Mirta Toledo (Argentina), The Hunchback; In Between.

Includes biographic information and a complete primary and secondary bibliography for each author. Foreword by Ana María Shua and notes on the editor/translator. Also includes a selected bibliography of anthologies in English containing short fiction by Latin American women writers.

A L4
Levins Morales, Aurora, and Rosario Morales. *Getting Home Alive.* Ithaca, NY:
    Firebrand Books, 1986. 213 pp.
Short fiction:
Aurora Levins Morales, Immigrants; Kitchens; 1930; South; Distress Signals;
Puertoricanness; Old Countries; A Story; Heart of My Heart, Bone of My Bone;
Tito; Doña Carmelita; Gardens; Letter to a Compañero; Storytelling; The Flute; And;
In My Grandmother's House; California; If I Forget Thee; Oh Jerusalem. Rosario
Morales, Hace tiempo; The Dinner; The Other Heritage; Concepts of Pollution; I'm
on Nature's Side; El Salvador; Puerto Rico Journal; Nostalgia; Destitution; Diary
Queen; Birth; The Grandmother Time; Of Course She Read; Synagogue; Trees;
Memory; I Am What I Am; Sketch; I Recognize You; I Am the Reasonable One;
Century Plant; Double Allegiance; Bad Communist; Old.
Includes family photographs of the authors.
Puerto Rico.

A L5
Levinson, Luisa Mercedes. *The Two Siblings and Other Stories.* Trans. Sylvia
    Ehrlich Lipp. Pittsburgh, PA: Latin American Literary Review, 1996. 157 pp.
Short stories:
Sometime in Brussels; Penetrating a Dream; The Pale Rose of Soho; On the Other
Side of the Shore; The Castle; The Girl with the Grey Woolen Gloves; The Two
Siblings; Beyond the Grand Canyon; No Men for the Poncho Weavers; Ursula and
the Hanged Man; Cobweb of Moons; The Islet; Fearful of Valparaíso; The Angel;
The Minet; The Myth; With Passion...and Compassion; The Labyrinth of Time; A
Singular Couple; The Boy; Residuum; The Other Shoes; The Cove.
Includes a prologue by Luisa Valenzuela and notes on the author and translator.
Argentina.

A L6
Lewald, Ernest, ed., trans. and intro. *The Web: Stories by Argentine Women.*
    Washington, DC: Three Continents Press, 1983. 170 pp.
Short stories:
Cecilia Absatz, A Ballet for Girls. María Angélica Bosco, Letter from Ana Karenina
to Nora; Letter from Nora to Ana Karenina. Silvina Bullrich, The Lover; Self Denial.
Eugenia Calny, Siesta. Beatriz Guido, Ten Times around the Block; Takeover.
Amalia Jamilis, Night Shift; Department Store. Luisa Mercedes Levinson, The
Clearing; Mistress Frances. Marta Lynch, Bedside Story; Latin Lover. Silvina
Ocampo, The Prayer. Syria Poletti, The Final Sin. Reina Roffé, Let's Hear What He
Has to Say. Luisa Valenzuela, Change of Guard.
Includes bio-bibliographic notes on contributors and author photographs.

A L7
Lispector, Clarice. *Family Ties.* Trans. and intro. Giovanni Pontiero. Austin:
    University of Texas Press, 1972. 156 pp.

Short stories:
The Daydreams of a Drunk Woman; Love; The Chicken; The Imitation of the Rose; Happy Birthday; The Smallest Woman in the World; The Dinner; Preciousness; Family Ties; Beginnings of a Fortune; Mystery in São Cristóvão; The Crime of the Mathematics Professor; The Buffalo.
Brazil.

A L7.1
Lispector, Clarice. *The Foreign Legion: Stories and Chronicles.* Trans. and afterword Giovanni Pontiero. Manchester: Carcanet, 1986. 219 pp.
Short stories:
The Misfortunes of Sofia; The Sharing of Bread; The Message; Monkeys; The Egg and the Chicken; Temptation; Journey to Petrópolis; The Solution; The Evolution of Myopia; The Fifth Story; A Sincere Friendship; The Obedient; The Foreign Legion.
Chronicles:
Includes arts criticism, character sketches, travel notes, conversations with her children, aphorisms, and personal reflections.
Brazil.

A L7.2
———. *Soulstorm: Stories.* Trans. and afterword Alexis Levitin. New York: New Directions Publications, 1989. 175 pp.
Short stories:
Explanation; Miss Algrave; The Body; The Way of the Cross; The Man Who Appeared; He Soaked Me Up; For the Time Being; Day by Day; Footsteps; A Complicated Case; Plaza Mauá; Pig Latin; Better than to Burn; But It's Going to Rain; In Search of Dignity; The Departure of the Train; Dry Point of Horses; Where You Were at Night; A Report on a Thing; A Manifesto of the City; The Conjurations of Dona Frozina; That's Where I'm Going; The Dead Man in the Sea at Urea; Silence; An Emptying; A Full Afternoon; Such Gentleness; Waters of the Sea; Soulstorm; Life au naturel.
Includes an introduction by Grace Paley.
Brazil.

A L8
Loring, Nigel, ed. *The Pen and the Key: 50th Anniversary Anthology of Pacific Northwest Writers.* Seattle: 74th St. Productions, 2005. 257 pp.
Short fiction:
Kathleen Alcalá (Mexico), Cities of Gold.

A L9
Luby, Barry J., and Wayne H. Finke, eds. and intro. *Anthology of Contemporary Latin American Literature, 1960-1984.* Rutherford, NJ: Fairleigh Dickinson University Press, 1986. 309 pp.
Short stories:
Magolo Cárdenas (Mexico), But What If I Liked the Panchos, Not the Beatles. Aída

Cartagena Portalatín (Dominican Republic), Colita. Matilde Daviú (Venezuela), Ofelia's Transfiguration. Margot Glantz (Mexico), Genealogies (excerpt). Includes brief bio-bibliographic notes on authors.

A M1

Machado, Ana María. *Me in the Middle*. Trans. David Unger. Toronto: Groundwood Books, 2002. 110 pp.

Short fiction:
Me in the Middle; At the Bottom of a Little Box; Chubby-Cheeked Jelly Donut; Invisible Tattoo; Old-Fashioned Conversations; Whistling Girls; A Sneeze and a Tragedy; The Source of the Mysterious Voice; People Braids.
Young adult literature.
Brazil.

A M2

MacShane, Frank, and Lori M. Carlson, eds. *Return Trip Tango and Other Stories from Abroad*. New York: Columbia University Press, 1992. 255 pp.

Short stories:
Cristina Peri Rossi (Uruguay), The Rebellious Sheep.
Includes an introduction by Anthony Burgess, "A Celebration of Translation," and brief bio-bibliographic notes on contributors.

A M3

Madison, Soyini, ed. *The Woman That I Am: The Literature and Culture of Contemporary Women of Color*. New York: St Martin's Press, Inc., 1994. 709 pp.

Short stories:
Clarice Lispector (Brazil), Preciousness.
Includes an introduction by Angela de Hoyos.

A M4

Maier, Linda S., and Isabel Dulfano, eds. *Woman as Witness: Essays on Testimonial Literature by Latin American Women*. New York: Peter Lang, 2004. 218 pp.

Narrative:
Nora Strejilevich (Argentina), *A Single, Numberless Death* (excerpt).

A M5

Maldonado, Clara Isabel. *Arcoiris de sueños (Retazos de una vida). Rainbow of Dreams (Patchwork of a Life)*. Trans. Clara Isabel Maldonado. Sydney: Cervantes Publishing, 1993. 93 pp.

Short stories:
21 Years.
Also includes poetry.
Bolivia.

A M6

Mallet, Marilú. *Voyage to the Other Extreme: Five Stories*. Trans. Alan Brown. Montreal: Vehicule, 1985. 105 pp.

Short stories:

The Loyal Order of the Time-Clock; Blind Alley; Voyage to the Other Extreme; How Are You?; The Vietnamese Hats.

Includes brief bio-bibliographic notes on author and translator.

Chile.

A M7

Mancini, Pat McNees, ed. and intro. *Contemporary Latin American Short Stories*. New York: Ballantine Books, 1974. 479 pp.

Short stories:

María Luisa Bombal (Chile), The Tree. Clarice Lispector (Brazil), The Imitation of the Rose.

Includes brief bibliography for further reading in English translation.

A M8

Manguel, Alberto, ed. *Black Water: Anthology of Fantastic Literature*. New York: Clarkson N. Potter Publishers, Inc., 1983. 967 pp.

Short stories:

Silvina Ocampo (Argentina), The Friends.

Includes bio-bibliographic notes on authors.

A M8.1

——, ed. *Black Water 2: More Tales of the Fantastic*. New York: Clarkson N. Potter Publishers Inc., 1990. 941 pp.

Short stories:

Isabel Allende (Chile), Two Words.

Includes bio-bibliographic notes on authors.

A M8.2

——, ed. *Dark Arrows: Chronicles of Revenge*. New York: Penguin Books Ltd., 1985. 219 pp.

Short stories:

Rachel de Queiroz (Brazil), Metonymy, or the Husband's Revenge.

Includes brief bio-bibliographic notes on the authors and the editor.

A M8.3

——, ed. *Evening Games: Tales of Parents and Children*. New York: Clarkson N. Potter Publishers, Inc., 1987. 353 pp.

Short stories:

Liliana Heker (Argentina), Jocasta.

Includes bio-bibliographic notes on authors.

A M8.4

Manguel, Alberto, ed. *The Gates of Paradise: The Anthology of Erotic Short Fiction.* New York: Clarkson N. Potter Publishers, Inc., 1993. 689 pp.
Short stories:
Isabel Allende (Chile), Wicked Girl. Liliana Heker (Argentina), Jocasta. Elena Poniatowska (Mexico), Park Cinema. Armonía Somers (Uruguay), The Fall. Includes bio-bibliographic notes on contributors.

A M8.5

——, ed. *Mothers and Daughters: An Anthology.* San Francisco: Chronicle Books, 1998. 359 pp.
Short stories:
Liliana Heker (Argentina), The Stolen Party.
Includes bio-bibliographic notes on the authors.

A M8.6

——, ed. and intro. *Other Fires: Short Fiction by Latin American Women.* New York: Clarkson N. Potter Publishers, Inc., 1986. 222 pp.
Short stories:
Albalucía Angel (Colombia), The Guerrillero. Inés Arredondo (Mexico), The Shunammite. Lydia Cabrera (Cuba), How the Monkey Lost the Fruit of His Labor. Rosario Castellanos (Mexico), Death of the Tiger. Amparo Dávila (Mexico), Haute Cuisine. Rachel de Queiroz (Brazil), Metonymy, or The Husband's Revenge. Lygia Fagundes Telles (Brazil), Tigrela. Elena Garro (Mexico), It's the Fault of the Tlaxcaltecas. Angélica Gorodischer (Argentina), Man's Dwelling Place. Beatriz Guido (Argentina), The Usurper. Liliana Heker (Argentina), The Stolen Party. Vlady Kociancich (Argentina), Knight, Death, and the Devil. Clarice Lispector (Brazil), The Imitation of the Rose. Marta Lynch (Argentina), Latin Lover. Silvina Ocampo (Argentina), Two Reports. Alejandra Pizarnik (Argentina), The Bloody Countess. Elena Poniatowska (Mexico), The Night Visitor. Dinah Silveira de Queiroz (Brazil), Guidance. Armonía Somers (Uruguay), The Fall.
Includes a foreword by Isabel Allende and bio-bibliographic notes on authors.

A M8.7

——, ed. and intro. *The Second Gates of Paradise: The Anthology of Erotic Short Fiction.* New York: Clarkson N. Potter Publishers, Inc., 1996. 692 pp.
Short stories:
Alejandra Pizarnik (Argentina), The Bloody Countess.
Includes bio-bibliographic notes on contributors.

A M8.8

——, ed. and intro. *Soho Square III.* London: Bloomsbury Publishing Ltd., 1990. 287 pp.
Short fiction:
Liliana Heker (Argentina), Early Beginnings or Ars Poética. Amparo Dávila (Mexico), Welcome to the Chelsea.

Includes extremely brief bio-bibliographic notes on authors.

A M9

Masiello, Francine, ed. and intro. Trans. Sergio Waisman. *Dreams and Realities: Selected Fiction of Juana Manuela Gorriti.* New York: Oxford University Press, 2003. 270 pp.
Short fiction:
The Quena; Treasure of the Incas; The Deadman's Fiancée; The Mazorquero's Daughter; The Black Glove; If You Do No Wrong, Expect No Good; Gubi Amaya; A Year in California.
Includes an introduction and notes on contributors by Francine Masiello.

A M10

Mayo, C. M., ed. *Mexico: A Traveler's Literary Companion.* Berkeley: Whereabouts Press, 2006. 238 pp.
Narrative:
Inés Arredono, The Silent Words. C. M. Mayo, Rancho Santa Inés: Fast. Guadalupe Loaeza, Oh, Polanco! Mónica Lavín, Day and Night. Angeles Mastretta, Aunt Elena. Martha Cerda, And One Wednesday. Araceli Ardó, It Is Nothing of Mine. Julieta Campos, She Has Reddish Hair and Her Name Is Sabina. Rosario Castellanos, Tenebrae Service. Laura Esquivel, Swift as Desire.
Includes bio-bibliographic notes on authors.

A M11

Mazer, Anne, ed. and intro. *America Street: A Multicultural Anthology of Stories.* New York: Persea Books, 1993. 152 pp.
Short fiction:
Nicholasa Mohr (Puerto Rico), The Wrong Lunch Line.

A M12

McDougal Littell Publishers, ed. *Great Expectations and Related Readings.* Evanston, IL: McDougal Littell, 1998. 699 pp.
Short fiction:
Judith Ortiz Cofer (Puerto Rico), *Silent Dancing* (selection).
Includes bio-bibliographic notes on contributors.

A M12.1

——, ed. *Latin American Writers: A Literary Reader.* Evanston, IL: McDougal Littell Publishers, 2001. 224 pp.
Short stories:
Isabel Allende (Chile), Two Words. Nélida Piñón (Brazil), the Warmth of Things. Maria Luisa Bombal (Chile), The Tree. Alcina Lubitch Domecq (Guatemala), Bottles. Clarice Lispector (Brazil), Looking for Some Dignity. Elena Poniatowska (Mexico), Park Cinema.
Intended for use as a text. Includes glossaries for English words and content questions following each piece. Also includes brief bio-bibliographic notes on

authors.

A M13

Menéndez, Ana. *In Cuba I Was a German Shepherd*. New York: Grove Press, 2001. 229 pp.
Short fiction:
In Cuba I Was a German Shepherd; Hurricane Stories; The Perfect Fruit; Why We Left; Story of a Parrot; Confusing the Saints; Baseball Dreams; The Last Rescue; Miami Relatives; The Party; Her Mother's House.

A M14

Menton, Seymour, ed. and preface. *The Spanish American Short Story: A Critical Anthology*. Trans. Seymour Menton. Berkeley: University of California Press, 1980. 496 pp.
Short stories:
María Luisa Bombal (Chile), The Tree.
Includes brief bio-bibliographic notes on authors, a bibliography of anthologies of the Spanish-American short story (works in Spanish), and a bibliography of historical critical works.

A M15

Meyer, Doris, and Margarita Fernández Olmos, eds. and preface. *Contemporary Women Authors of Latin America: New Translations*. Brooklyn, NY: Brooklyn College Press, 1983. 331 pp.
Short stories:
Albalucía Angel (Colombia), Monguí. Silvina Bullrich (Argentina), The Divorce. Lydia Cabrera (Cuba), Obbara Lies But Doesn't Lie; The Hill Called Mambiala. Rosario Castellanos (Mexico), Cooking Lesson. Amparo Dávila (Mexico), Behind Bars. Rosario Ferré (Puerto Rico), When Women Love Men. Elena Garro (Mexico), The Day We Were Dogs. Luisa Mercedes Levinson (Argentina), The Myth. Marta Lynch (Argentina), Hotel Taormina. Inés Malinow (Argentina), Fixed Distance. Angelina Muñiz (Mexico), Rising, Mournful from the Earth. Silvina Ocampo (Argentina), The Mastiffs of Hadrian's Temple; Ana Valerga. Victoria Ocampo (Argentina), Misfortunes of an Autodidact. Cristina Peri Rossi (Uruguay), The Influence of Edgar Allan Poe on the Poetry of Raimundo Arias. Nélida Piñón (Brazil), Adamastor. Tita Valencia (Mexico), Video: Zoom in to Close-up; Zoom Back: Visions of Taking Flight. Luisa Valenzuela (Argentina), Generous Impediments Float Down the River. Alicia Yánez Cossío (Ecuador), Sabotage.
Includes bio-bibliographic notes on editors and translators and a selected bibliography.

A M16

Milligan, Bryce, Mary Guerrero Milligan, and Angela de Hoyos, eds. and intro. *Daughters of the Fifth Sun: A Collection of Latina Fiction and Poetry*. New York: Riverhead Books, 1995. 284 pp.

Short Stories in Translation:
Marjorie Agosín (Chile), Adelina. Rosario Ferré (Puerto Rico), The Glass Box.
Mireya Robles (Cuba), In the Other Half of Time. Julia Álvarez (Dominican
Republic), The Kiss. Margarita Engle (Cuba), Uncle Teo's Shorthand Cookbook.
Judith Ortiz Cofer (Puerto Rico), Nada.
Includes a foreword by María Hinojosa and bio-bibliographic notes on authors. This
collection includes Latin American, Latina, and Chicana writers.

A M17
Mohr, Nicholasa. *El Bronx Remembered: A Novella and Stories.* New York: Harper
     & Row Publishers, 1975. 179 pp.
Short fiction:
A Very Special Pet; A New Window Display; Tell the Truth; Shoes for Hector; Once
Upon a Time...; Mr. Mendelsohn; The Wrong Lunch Line; A Lesson in Fortune-
Telling; Uncle Claudio; Princess; Herman and Alice, a Novella; Love with Aleluya.
Short stories about Puerto Rican immigrants and their struggles for survival in New
York. Includes a preface by the author.
Puerto Rico.

A M17.1
———. *A Matter of Pride and Other Stories.* Houston, TX: Arte Público Press, 1997.
     191 pp.
Short Stories:
A Matter of Pride; In Another Place in a Different Era; My Newest Triumph;
Memories: R.I.P.; Rosalina de los Rosarios; Blessed Divination; Utopia, and the
Super Estrellas.
Puerto Rico.

A M17.2
———. *In New York.* New York: Dial Press, 1977. 192 pp.
Short fiction:
Old Mary; I Never Seen My Father; The English Lesson; The Perfect Little Flower
Girl; The Operation; Lali; The Robbery; Coming to Terms.
Includes a brief bio-bibliography on the author.
Puerto Rico.

A M17.3
———. *Rituals of Survival: A Woman's Portfolio.* Houston, TX: Arte Público Press,
     1994. 158 pp.
Short fiction:
Aunt Rosana's Rocker (Zoraida); A Time with a Future (Carmela); Brief Miracle
(Virginia); A Thanksgiving Celebration (Amy); Happy Birthday (Lucía); The Artist
(Inéz).
Puerto Rico.

A M18

Moore, Evelyn, ed. and intro. *Sancocho: Stories and Sketches of Panama.*
Panama: Panama American Publishing Co., 1938. 194 pp.
Short stories:
Elda L. C. de Crespo, Village Fiesta; Maruja; Seña Paula. Graciela Rojas Sucre, On
Account of the Piñata (excerpt from *Terruñadas de lo chico*).
Includes bio-bibliographic notes on authors.

A M19

Mordecai, Pamela, and Betty Wilson, eds. and intro. *Her True-True Name: An
    Anthology of Women's Writing from the Caribbean.* Oxford: Heinemann, 1989.
    202 pp.
Short stories:
Omega Agüero (Cuba), A Man, a Woman (excerpt from *El muro de medio metro*)
Hilma Contreras (Dominican Republic), The Window. Rosario Ferré (Puerto Rico),
The Youngest Doll. Magali García Ramis (Puerto Rico), Every Sunday. Carmen
Lugo Filippi (Puerto Rico), Recipes for the Gullible. Ana Lydia Vega (Puerto Rico),
Cloud Cover Caribbean. Mirta Yáñez (Cuba), We Blacks All Drink Coffee.
Includes bio-bibliographic notes on authors. Also includes Anglophone and
Francophobe authors from the Caribbean.

A M20

Morrow, Bradford, and Walter Abish, eds. *American Fiction: States of the Art.*
    Annandale-on-Hudson, NY: Bard College, 2000. 481 pp.
Short stories:
Julia Álvarez (Dominican Republic), Our Father. Rosario Ferré (Puerto Rico), Flight
of the Swan. Mayra Montero (Cuba), El hombre Pollack.
Includes bio-bibliographic references for contributors.

A M21

Muller, Gilberth, and John A. Williams, eds. and preface. *Bridges: Literature across
    Cultures.* New York: McGraw Hill, Inc., 1994. 1048 pp.
Short stories:
Luisa Valenzuela (Argentina), The Censors.
Includes bio-bibliographic notes on authors. This is a text suited for use in
composition and introductory literature courses.

A M22

Muñiz-Huberman, Angelina. *Enclosed Garden.* Trans. and preface Lois Parkinson
    Zamora. Pittsburgh, PA: Latin American Literary Review Press, 1988. 103 pp.
Short stories:
On the Unicorn; In the Name of His Name; The Sarcasm of God; The Most Precious
Offering; The Grand Duchess; Jocasta's Confession; Tlamapa; Salicio and Amarylis;
Rising, Mournful, from the Earth; Gentlemen; The Fortunes of the Infante Arnaldos;
The Minstrel; The Prisoner; Brief World; The Dream Curtain; Enclosed Garden;

Longing; Vaguely, at Five in the Afternoon; Life Has No Plot; The Chrysalis of Clay
Will Give Birth to a Butterfly; Retrospection.
Includes an afterword by Elena Poniatowska, "Meditation on the Enclosed Garden
of Exile: A Conversation with Angelina Muñiz-Huberman."
Mexico.

A N1

Naranjo, Carmen. *There Never Was a Once Upon a Time.* Trans. and foreword
    Linda Britt. Pittsburgh, PA: Latin American Literary Review Press, 1989. 94 pp.
Short stories:
There Never Was a Once Upon a Time; Eighteen Ways to Make a Square; It
Happened One Day; The Game That Is Only Played Once; Everybody Loves
Clowns; Maybe the Clock Played with Time; When I Invented Butterflies; Old Cat
Meets Young Cat; Tell Me a Story, Olo.
Costa Rica.

A N2

Naranjo, Carmen, and Victoria Urbano, eds. *Five Women Writers of Costa Rica:*
    Short Stories. Beaumont, TX: Asociación de Literatura Femenina Hispánica,
    1978. 131 pp.
Narrative:
Carmen Naranjo, The Flowery Trick; The Journey and the Journeys; Inventory of a
Recluse. Victoria Urbano, The Creative Philosophy of Carmen Naranjo. C. Matheiu,
Commentary on the Flowery Trick. Eunice Odio, Once There Was a Man; The Trace
of the Butterfly. Rima Vallbona, Eunice Odio, A Homeless Writer. Yolanda
Oremuno, High Valley; The Ride Returns at Night. Victoria Urbano, On High
Valley; Avery Island; Triptych. C. G. Bellver, On the Tide Returns at Night.

A N3

Norris, Gloria, ed. and intro. *The Seasons of Women: An Anthology.* New York: W.
    W. Norton & Company, 1996. 464 pp.
Short fiction:
Judith Ortiz Cofer (Puerto Rico), Silent Dancing.

A N4

Novakovich, Josip, and Robert Shapard, eds. and intro. *Stories in the Stepmother*
    Tongue. Buffalo, NY: White Pine Press, 2000. 254 pp.
Short fiction:
Julia Álvarez (Domincan Republic), Joe. Judith Ortiz Cofer (Puerto Rico), Not for
Sale.
Includes a brief bio-bibliography and a personal statement from each contributor.

A O1

Oard Warner, Sharon. *The Way We Write Now: Short Stories from the AIDS Crisis.*
    Secaucus, NJ: Carol Publishing Group, 1995. 294 pp.
Short fiction:
Achy Obejas (Cuba), Above All, a Family Man.
Includes bio-bibliographic references for contributors.

N O2

Obejas, Achy. *We Came All the Way from Cuba So You Could Dress Like This?* San
    Francisco: Cleis Press, 1994. 133 pp.
Short fiction:
Wrecks; The Cradleland; Above All, a Family Man; Man Oh Man; The Spouse;
Forever; We Came All the Way from Cuba So You Could Dress Like This?
Includes a brief bio-bibliography for the author.

A O3

Ocampo, Silvina. *Leopoldina's Dream.* Trans. Daniel Balderston. London and New
    York: Penguin, 1988. 205 pp.
Short stories:
Thus Were Their Faces; Lovers; Revelation; The Fury; The Photographs; The Clock
House; Mimoso; The Velvet Dress; The Objects; The Bed; The Perfect Crime;
Azabache; Friends; The House of Sugar; Visions; The Wedding; Voice on the
Telephone; Icera; The Autobiography of Irene; The Sibyl; Report on Heaven and
Hell; The Mortal Sin; The Expiation; Livio Roca; The Doll; The Punishment; The
Basement; The Guests; Carl Herst; Magush; The Prayer; Leopoldina's Dream.
Includes a brief preface by Jorge Luís Borges and an introduction by the author.
Contains thirty-two short stories chosen from four of Ocampo's books: *Autobiografía
de Irene*, *La furia y otros cuentos*, *Las imitadas*, and *Los días de la noche*.
Includes brief bio-bibliographic notes on author and translator.
Argentina.

A O4

O'Hara, Maricarmen. *Cuentos para todos/Tales for Everybody.* Trans. Maricarmen
    O'Hara. Ventura: Alegría Hispana Publications, 1994. 176 pp.
Short stories:
He and She; A Simple Story; Mr. Turista's Breakfast; Little Joe Sticks; Olga's Diet;
Mr. Slowly Slow; The Student Prince; A Man and a Woman; The Old Peasant; The
Stronger; The "Screaming Bag"; The Diamond; International Buffet; Questions and
Answers; Truth; Hunger Strike; The Moon's Husband; Heddy the Airhead; The
Peacock's Voice; The King's Peaches; The Smuggler; The Miser's Money;
Marcelino's Job; The Divine Language; Pay Me!; The Grasshopper; The Bet; The
House that Jack Built; Wooden Spoon; The Two Kings.
Bilingual edition. These stories are intended to be used to teach Spanish to English

speakers. Each story is accompanied by a list of Spanish/English vocabulary. Bolivia.

A O5

Olivares, Julián, and Evangelina Vigil-Piñón, eds. *Decade II: An Anniversary Anthology.* Houston, TX: Arte Público Press, 1993. 255 pp.
Short fiction:
Judith Ortiz Cofer (Puerto Rico), The Black Virgin. Rima de Vallbona (Costa Rica), La tejedora de palabras.
Includes an introduction by Evangelina Vigil-Piñón. This volume contains a selection from *Revista Chicano-Riqueña/The Americas Review* from 1983-1992 and was published in celebration of the twentieth anniversary of the founding of the journal.

A O6

O'Reilly Herrera, Andrea, ed. *A Secret Weaver's Anthology: Selections from the White Pine Press Secret Weaver's Series: Writing by Latin American Women.* Fredonia, NY: White Pine Press, 1998. 225 pp.
Short fiction:
Rosario Aguilar (Nicaragua), *The Lost Chronicles of Terra Firma* (excerpt). Dora Alonso (Cuba), Cage Number One. Marta Blanco (Chile), Maternity. Marta Brunet (Chile), Solitude of Blood. Sara Gallardo (Argentina), The Man in the Araucaria. Magali García Ramis (Puerto Rico), *Happy Days, Uncle Sergio* (excerpt). Marcela Guijosa (Mexico), Regarding My Mestiza Self. Ana María Güiraldes (Chile), The Family Album. Liliana Heker (Argentina), When Everything Shines. Ángela Hernández (Dominican Republic), How to Gather the Shadows of the Flowers. Marta Jara (Chile), The Englishwoman. Gabriela Mistral (Chile), The Lark. Carmen Naranjo (Costa Rica), The Compulsive Couple of the House on the Hill. Cristina Pacheco (Mexico), Noodle Soup. Alejandra Pizarnik (Argentina), Words. Elena Poniatowska (Mexico), Happiness. Amalia Rendic (Chile), A Boy, a Dog, the Night. Laura Riesco (Peru), *Ximena at the Crossroads* (excerpt). Anabel Torres (Colombia), A Small Miracle. Luisa Valenzuela (Argentina), Dirty Words. Ana Vásquez (Chile), Elegance.

A O7

Ortiz Cofer, Judith. *An Island Like You: Stories of the Barrio.* New York: Orchard Books, 1995. 165 pp.
Short fiction:
Bad Influence; Arturo's Flight; Beauty Lessons; Catch the Moon; An Hour with Abuelo; The One Who Watches; Matoa's Mirror; Don José of La Mancha; Abuela Invents the Zero; A Job for Valentín; Home to El Building; White Balloons. Puerto Rico.

A O7.1
Ortiz Cofer, Judith. *The Latin Deli: Prose and Poetry.* Athens: The University of
   Georgia Press, 1993. 170 pp.
Short fiction:
American History; Not for Sale; Twist and Shout; By Love Betrayed; The Witch's
Husband; Nada; Letter from a Caribbean Island; Dear Joaquín; Lydia; Corazón's
Café; Advanced Biology; The Paterson Public Library; The Story of My Body; The
Myth of the Latin Women; I Just Met a Girl Named María; 5:00 A.M.: Writing as
Ritual.
Puerto Rico.

A O7.2
——, ed. *Riding Low on the Streets of Gold: Latino Literature for Young Adults.*
   Houston, TX: Piñata Books, 2003. 198 pp.
Short fiction:
Helena Maria Viramontes (Mexico), Growing. Judith Ortiz Cofer (Puerto Rico),
Primary Lessons; Volar.
Includes an introduction by Judith Ortiz Cofer.

A O7.3
——. *Silent Dancing: A Partial Remembrance of a Puerto Rican Childhood.*
   Houston, TX: Arte Público Press, 1990. 167 pp.
Short fiction:
Casa; More Room; Talking to the Dead; The Black Virgin; Primary Lessons; One
More Lesson; Tales Told under the Mango Tree; Silent Dancing; Some of the
Characters; The Looking-Glass Shame; Quinceañera; Marina; The Last Word.
Puerto Rico.

A O7.4
——. *The Year of Our Revolution: New and Selected Stories and Poems.* New
   York: Puffin, 2001. 131 pp.
Short fiction:
Origen; Volar; Fulana; Kennedy in the Barrio; Lost Relatives; Gravity Making
Love in Spanish, Circa 1969; The Year of Our Revolution; El Olvido; The One
Peso Prediction; First Love; Vida.
Adolescent literature, addresses the issue of living in two cultures. First published
by Piñata Books in 1998.
Puerto Rico.

A P1
Paretsky, Sara, ed. and intro. *Women on the Case.* New York: Delacorte Press,
   1996. 367 pp.
Short stories:
Myriam Laurini (Argentina), Lost Dreams.

A volume of short fiction by women crime writers.

A P2

Partnoy, Alicia. *The Little School: Tales of Disappearance and Survival in Argentina*. Trans. Alicia Partnoy with Lois Athey and Sandra Braunstein. San Francisco: Cleis Press, 1986. 136 pp.

Short stories:

The One-flower Slippers; Latrine; Birthday; My Names; Benja's First Night; Telepathy; Graciela; Around the Table, My Nose; Religion; A Conversation under the Rain; A Puzzle; Toothbrush; Bread; The Small Box of Matches; Ruth's Father; Form of Address; Poetry; The Denim Jacket; A Beauty Treatment; Nativity.

Includes a brief preface by Bernice Johnson Reagon, introduction by Alicia Partnoy, and bio-bibliographic notes on the author. Appendices include "Cases of the Disappeared at the Little School" and "Descriptions of the Guards at the Little School."

Argentina.

A P2.1

———, ed. *You Can't Drown the Fire: Latin American Women Writing in Exile*. San Francisco: Cleis Press, 1988. 258 pp.

Short stories:

Marjorie Agosín (Chile), The Blue Teacups. Alicia Dujovne Ortiz (Argentina), Courage or Cowardice? Cristina Peri Rossi (Uruguay), The Influence of Edgar A. Poe on the Poetry of Raimundo Arias. Marta Traba (Argentina), The Day Flora Died. Luisa Valenzuela (Argentina), On the Way to the Ministry.

Includes notes on contributors.

A P3

Paschke, Barbara, and Davis Volpendesta, eds. *Clamor of Innocence: Central American Short Stories*. San Francisco: City Lights Books, 1988. 174 pp.

Short stories:

Rima de Vallbona (Costa Rica), Penelope on Her Silver Wedding Anniversary. Carmen Lyra (Costa Rica), Estefanía. Carmen Naranjo (Costa Rica), Walls. Bertalicia Peralta (Panama), The Guayacan Tree. Bessy Reyna (Panama), The Clean Ashtrays.

Includes brief bio-bibliographic notes on authors and translators.

A P4

Penelope Julia, and Sarah Valentine, eds. *International Feminist Fiction*. Freedom, CA: The Crossing Press, 1992. 333 pp.

Short stories:

Rosario Ferré (Puerto Rico), The Youngest Doll. Bertalicia Peralta (Panama), A March Guayacán.

Includes brief notes on contributors and a brief introduction by Valerie Miner.

A P5

Pereira, Teresinka. *Help, I'm Drowning.* Trans. Angela de Hoyos. Chicago: Palos
Heights Press, 1975. 18 pp.
Short stories:
The Train and the Flowers; Solitude; Little Man.
Includes bio-bibliographic notes on the author and translator.
Brazil.

A P6

Peri Rossi, Cristina. *A Forbidden Passion.* Trans. Mary Jane Treacy. San Francisco:
Cleis Press, 1993. 148 pp.
Short stories:
The Fallen Angel; A Forbidden Passion; The Bridge; Atlas; Guilt; The Trip;
Patriotism; Gratitude Is Insatiable; The Nature of Love; The Parable of Desire; The
Revelation; Final Judgement; A Moral Lesson; The Threshold; The Art of Loss; A
Useless Passion; The Mirror Maker; The Bell Ringer; The Sentence; Singing in the
Desert.
Includes a brief introduction by Cristina Peri Rossi and bio-bibliographic notes on
the author and translator.
Uruguay.

A P6.1

———. *The Museum of Useless Efforts.* Lincoln: University of Nebraska Press, 1983.
156 pp.
Short stories:
The Museum of Useless Efforts; Up on the Rope; Mona Lisa; The Runner
Stumbles; Tarzan's Roar; The Session; the Lizard Christmas; The Crack; The
Rebellious Sheep; Deaf as a Doorknob; Full Stop; The Inconclusive Journey;
Letters; Flags; The Avenues of Language; Instructions for Getting Out of Bed;
Airports; Time Heals All Wounds; Love Story; A Sense of Duty; Between a Rock
and a Hard Place; The Effect of Light on Fish; Keeping Track of Time; Statues, or,
Being a Foreigner; At the Hairdresser; Wednesday; The Bathers; Notes on a
Journey; The City; Casting Daisies to the Swine.
Uruguay.

AP6.2

———. *Panic Signs.* Trans. Mercedes Rowinksy-Geurts and Angelo A. Borras.
Waterloo, Ontario, Canada: Wilfrid Laurier University Press, 2002. 114 pp.
Short narrative:
I am very interested in botany; I live in a country of old people; I have never been
in Vermont; We have not gone to the moon; For more than twenty-five years;
Sometimes my mother consoles me; I spent many years caressing statues; I always
imagine; She brought me passionate presents; She hands me the scarf; I contribute
to the general racket; She had been brought from Peru; I have a tiny apartment; She

has given me happiness; Dialogue with the Writer; For many years I lived; When I was mature enough; Hell is bloody birds; "You are very beautiful"; I will till no more; In the ghetto of my womb; I dreamt that I was: Desertion; What is happening?; As I was walking along; The Acrobats; Besieged; The minister called me; "What are you doing?"; Disobedience and the Bear Hunt; The Statue; I possessed her when I was eight; Mama's Farewell; I started to feel your absence; At the corner bar; When the bishops rebelled; A Great Family; Such apparent senselessness; I was enjoying an ice cream cone; Selene I; Selene II; I have come by train; Urgent Messages for Navigators; The Social Contract; The Stampede; The Hero.

These short texts foreshadow life in Uruguay after the military coup of 1972. Uruguay.

A P7

Picon Garfield, Evelyn, ed. and intro. *Women's Fiction from Latin America: Selections from Twelve Contemporary Authors.* Detroit: Wayne State University Press, 1988. 355 pp.

Short fiction:

Isabel Allende (Chile), Rosa the Beautiful (excerpt from *The House of the Spirits*). Lydia Cabrera (Cuba), The Mire of Almendares; Tatabisako. Julieta Campos (Cuba/Mexico), *A Redhead Named Sabina* (excerpts from the novel); All the Roses. Elena Garro (Mexico), The Tree. Clarice Lispector (Brazil), Love; Family Ties. Carmen Naranjo (Costa Rica), Ondina; Why Kill the Countess? Elvira Orphée (Argentina), *Angel's Last Conquest* (excerpt from the novel); The Silken Whale. Nélida Piñón (Brazil), Bird of Paradise; The New Kingdom. Armonía Somers (Uruguay), The Tunnel; The Burial; Plunder. Marta Traba (Argentina), *Mothers and Shadows* (excerpt from the novel); Conformity; All in a Lifetime. Luisa Valenzuela (Argentina), Blue Water Man; Other Weapons; I'm Your Horse in the Night.

Includes bio-bibliographic notes, a photograph, and a primary and secondary bibliography for each author.

A P8

Pocaterra, Jose Rafael, ed. *Venezuelan Short stories: Cuentos venezolanos.* Trans. Seymour Menton. Caracas: Monte Ávila Editores, 1992. 275 pp.

Short stories:

Laura Antillano, The Moon's Not a Piece of Cake (La luna no es pan de horno). Teresa de la Parra, The Story of Señorita Dust Grain, Ballerina of the Sun (Historia de la Señorita Grano de Polvo, bailarina del sol).

Includes a prologue by Lydia Aponte de Zacklin and brief bio-bibliographic notes on authors. Bilingual edition.

A P9

Poey, Delia, ed. *Out of the Mirrored Garden: New Fiction by Latin American Women.* New York: Anchor Books, 1996. 222 pp.

Short stories:
Carmen Boullosa (Mexico), So Disappear. Rosa María Britton (Panama), Death Lies on the Cots. Julieta Campos (Mexico), Allegories. Elena Castedo (Spain/Chile), Ice Cream. Marta Cerda (Mexico), A Time of Mourning. Diamela Eltit (Chile), Even if I Bathed in the Purest Waters. Rosario Ferré (Puerto Rico), Amalia. Magali García Ramis (Puerto Rico), A Script for Every House. Angela Hernández (Dominican Republic), Teresa Irene. Barbara Jacobs (Mexico), Aunt Luisita. Vlady Kociancich (Argentina), A Family Man. Alcina Lubitch Domecq (Guatemala), Bottles. Angeles Mastretta (Mexico), Aunt Elvira. Carmen Naranjo (Costa Rica), Over and Over. Cristina Peri Rossi (Uruguay), The Annunciation. Elena Poniatowska (Mexico), The Rupture. Mirta Yáñez (Cuba), Go Figure.
Includes bio-bibliographic notes on the authors and the editor, a brief selected bibliography of related anthologies, and a bibliography of authors' work in translation.

A P10
Poey, Delia, and Virgil Suárez, eds. *Iguana Dreams.* New York: Harper Perennial, 1992. 376 pp.
Short fiction:
Julia Álvarez (Dominican Republic), Customs. Elena Castedo (Chile), The White Bedspread. Cristina García (Cuba), Tito's Good-bye. Judith Ortiz Cofer (Puerto Rico), American History. Mary Helen Ponce (Puerto Rico), Blizzard!!!
Includes a brief bio-bibliography and a black and white photograph for each author.

A P10.1
———, eds. *Little Havana Blues: A Cuban-American Literature Anthology.* Houston, TX: Arte Público Press, 1996. 444 pp.
Short stories:
Margarita Engle, On the Morning of His Arrest. Cristina García, Inés in the Kitchen. Andrea O'Reilly Herrera, The Homecoming. Beatriz Rivera, Paloma. Marisella Veiga, Liberation in Little Havana.
Includes a bibliography on Cuban-American literature and bio-bibliographic information on contributors. Also includes poetry, drama, and essay.

A P11
Pollack, Neal, ed. *Chicago Noir.* New York: Akashic Books, 2005. 252 pp.
Short fiction:
Achy Obejas (Cuba), Destiny Returns.

A P12
Prize Stories from Latin America: Winner of the "A Life en español" Literary Contest. Garden City: Doubleday, 1963. 398 pp.
Short stories:
Laura del Castillo (Argentina), A Plum for Coco.

Includes a brief preface by Arturo Uslar Pietro and brief bio-bibliographic notes on authors.

A R1

Rafkin, Louise, ed. *New Women's Fiction. Unholy Alliances.* San Francisco: Cleis Press, 1988. 160 pp.
Short fiction:
Julia Álvarez (Dominican Republic), Daughter of Invention.
Includes bio-bibliographies for contributors.

A R2

Ramírez, Anthony, ed. and trans. *The Best of Latin American Short Stories. Los mejores cuentos hispanoamericanos.* Los Angeles: Bilingual Book Press, 1994. 114 pp.
Short stories:
María Silva Ossa (Chile). The Ship from Far Away (El barco de más allá).
Side by side Spanish-English bilingual edition. Includes a brief introduction, bio-bibliographic notes on authors, and a Spanish-English glossary.

A R3

Ramos, Juanita, ed. *Compañeras: Latina Lesbians.* New York: Routledge, 1994. 276 pp.
Short fiction:
Mariana Romo-Carmona (Chile), Gabriela.
Includes an introduction by Mariana Romo-Carmora, brief bio-bibliographic notes for contributors, and a selected bibliography on Latina lesbian resources.

A R4

Ras, Barbara, ed. *Costa Rica: A Traveler's Literary Companion.* San Francisco: Whereabouts Press, 1994. 238 pp.
Short stories:
Rima de Vallbona, The Chumico Tree; Mystery Stone. Carmen Lyra, Pastor's Ten Little Old Men. Carmen Naranjo, Believe It or Not; When New Flowers Bloomed. Yolanda Oreamuno, The Lizard with the White Belly; The Spirit of My Land. Julieta Pinto, The Blue Fish.
Includes a foreword by Oscar Arias, brief bio-bibliographic notes on authors and translators, and a glossary of Spanish terms.

A R5

Reyes, Sandra, ed. *Oblivion and Stone: A Selection of Contemporary Bolivian Poetry and Fiction.* Trans. John DuVal et al. Fayetteville: University of Arkansas, 1998. 273 pp.
Short stories:
Blanca Elena Paz, Symmetry; The Light; Three Rains. Viviana Limpias Chávez,

Copper Pumpkins.
Includes brief biographic notes on authors.

A R5.1
Reyes, Sandra, ed., intro., and trans. *One More Stripe to the Tiger: A Selection of Contemporary Chilean Poetry and Fiction.* Fayetteville: University of Arkansas Press, 1989. 311 pp.
Short stories:
Cecilia Casanova, The Unmarriage. Marta Blanco, Sweet Companion.
Includes brief biographic notes on authors.

A R6
Rheda, Regina. *First World Third Class and Other Tales of the Global Mix.* Trans. Adria Frizzi et al. Austin: University of Texas Press, 2005. 304 pp.
Short stories:
I. Stories from the Copan Building (1994): The Neighbor from Hell; The Cat Girl; Dry Spell; The Ghost; The Woman in White; Girlfriends; The Voyeuse; The Prostitute.
II. First World Third Class (1996).
III. A Trio of Tales: The Enchanted Princess (1997); The Sanctuary (2002); The Front (2003).
Includes an introduction by David Coles.
Brazil.

A R7
Rhett, Kathryn, ed. and intro. *Survival Stories: Memories of Crisis.* New York: Doubleday, 1997. 397 pp.
Short stories:
Isabel Allende (Chile), *Paula* (excerpt).
Includes brief bio-bibliographic notes on contributors.

A R8
Rieder, Inés, ed. and preface. *Cosmopolis: Urban Stories by Women.* Pittsburgh, PA: Cleis Press, 1990. 196 pp.
Short stories:
Silvia Fanaro (Brazil), The Day I Met Miss America. Berta Hiriart (Mexico), Maestra Arellano.
Includes brief bio-bibliographic notes on authors.

A R9
Rivas Iturralde, Vladimiro, ed. *Contemporary Ecuadorian Short Stories.* Trans. Mary Ellen Fieweger. Quito: Paradiso Editores, 2002. 353 pp.
Narrative:
Lupe Rumazo, The March of the Batrachians. Sonia Manzano, George. Gilda Holst,

Reunión. Liliana Miraglia, The Living Room. Aminta Buenaño, Splendor in the Dark. Carolina Andrade, The Death of Fausto.
Includes brief bio-bibliographic notes on contributors.

A R10

Rivera, Esteban, and Juana Ponce de León, eds. *Dream with No Name: Contemporary Fiction from Cuba.* New York: Seven Stories Press, 1998. 303 pp.
Short stories:
Jacqueline Herranz Brooks, An Unexpected Interlude between Two Characters. Marilyn Bobes, Ten Years Later. Lourdes Casal, A Love Story According to Cyrano Prufrock. Miguelina Ponte Landa, Blind Madness. Sonia Rivera Valdés, Little Poisons.
Includes bio-bibliographies for contributors.

A R11

Rivera Valdés, Sonia. *The Forbidden Stories of Marta Veneranda.* Trans. Dick Cluster, Marina Harss, Mark Schafer, and Alan West Durán. New York: Seven Stories Press, 2001. 158 pp.
Narrative:
Five Windows on the Same Side; The Scent of Wild Desire; Between Friends; Lunacy; Catching On; Adelas Beautiful Eyes; Little Poisons; The Most Forbidden of All; The Fifth River.
True stories collected for a doctoral dissertation. Includes brief bio-bibliographies. Cuba.

A R12

Rivero Santa Cruz, Giovanna. *Sangre Dulce/ Sweet Blood: Cuentos.* Trans. Kathy S. Leonard. Santa Cruz, Bolivia: La Mancha Editorial, 2006. 256 pp.
Short stories:
Final Countdown; Twin Beds; Waves of Satin; Barking Softly; Sweet Blood; Tita; Masters of the Sand; An Imperfect Day; Mulatta Moon; Like a Vulture; Lava; Player; Time to Dance!; The Widow; In Your Very Footsteps; The Smell of Something New.
Includes a prologue by the Bolivian novelist Edmundo Paz Soldán, bio-bibliographic information on the contributors, and black and white photographs by Kathy S. Leonard to illustrate each story. Bilingual format.
Bolivia.

A R13

Rodríguez Monegal, Emir, and Thomas Colchie, eds. and intro. *The Borzoi Anthology of Latin American Literature. Vol. 1 and 2.* New York: Knopf, 1977. 982 pp.

Short stories in Volume 2:
Clarice Lispector (Brazil), The Passion According to G. H.; Nélida Piñón (Brazil),
House of Passion.
Volume 1 does not contain any short stories by Latin American women.

A R14

Rojo, Grinor, and Cynthia Steele, eds. *Ritos de iniciación: tres novelas cortas de*
Hispanoamérica. Boston: Houghton Mifflin, 1986. 233 pp.
Short fiction:
Rosario Ferré (Puerto Rico), Bella durmiente.
Bilingual format. Includes author bibliographies. Geared to intermediate and
advanced students of college Spanish.

A R15

Romo-Carmona, Mariana. *Speaking Like an Immigrant: A Collection.* Binghamton,
NY: Latina Lesbian History Project, 2000. 156 pp.
Short stories:
Speaking Like an Immigrant; The Virgin in the Desert; The Meal; Contraband;
Dream of Something Lost; New England Reconsidered; Orphans; Kissing Susan;
Gabriela; Love Story; Fear: Cuento de Jalohuínñ The Web; La bruja pirata de
Chiloé; 2280; Welcome to America; Idilio.
Includes an introduction by Elizabeth Crespo Kebler. Winner of the 2002 Lambda
Book Award.
Chile.

A R16

Rosenberg Donna, ed. *World Literature: An Anthology of Great Short Stories,*
Drama, and Poetry. Lincolnwood, IL: National Textbook Company, 1992. 884
pp.
Short stories:
María Luisa Bombal (Chile), The Tree. Rosario Catellanos (Mexico), Chess.
Silvina Ocampo (Argentina), The Inextinguishable Race.
Includes questions after each selection, and bio-bibliographies preceding each
selection.

A R17

Ross, Kathleen, and Yvette Miller, eds. *Scents of Wood and Silence: Short Stories*
by Latin American Women Writers. Pittsburgh, PA: Latin American Literary
Review Press, 1991. 218 pp.
Short stories:
Margarita Aguirre (Chile), The Black Sheep. Claribel Alegría (El Salvador), The
Awakening. Isabel Allende (Chile), Tosca. Albalucía Angel (Colombia), Down the
Tropical Path. Pía Barros (Chile), Scents of Wood and Silence. Lydia Cabrera
(Cuba), Susundamba Does Not Show Herself by Day. Julieta Campos (Mexico),

The House. Ana María del Río (Chile), Wash Water. Lygia Fagundes Telles (Brazil), The Structure of the Soap Bubble. Angélica Gorodischer (Argentina), Camera Obscura. Matilde Herrera (Argentina), Eduardito Doesn't Like the Police. Clarice Lispector (Brazil), Beauty and the Beast, or, The Wound Too Great. Silvia Molina (Mexico), Autumn. Sylvia Molloy (Argentina), Sometimes in Illyria. Carmen Naranjo (Costa Rica), A Woman at Dawn. Olga Nolla (Puerto Rico), A Tender Heart. Silvina Ocampo (Argentina), Creation (An Autobiographical Story). Cristina Peri Rossi (Uruguay), The Art of Loss. Nélida Piñón (Brazil), The Heart of Things. María Luisa Puga (Mexico), Memories on the Oblique. Mariella Sala (Peru), From Exile. Luisa Valenzuela (Argentina), Tango. Ana Lydia Vega (Puerto Rico), Death's Pure Fire.

Includes an introduction by Kathleen Ross and bio-bibliographic notes on authors and translators. Appendices include primary and secondary bibliographies for each author and bibliographies: "General Works on Women Writers and Feminist Literary Criticism," "Works on Latin American Women," "Anthologies of (or including) Latin American Women Writers in English and Spanish," and "General Bibliographies of (or including) Latin American Women Writers."

A R18
Rowe, L. S., and Pedro de Alba, eds. *The Literature of Latin America. Volume I of the Series on Literature-Art-Music.* Washington, DC: Pan American Union, 1944. 64 pp.
Short stories:
Teresa de la Parra (Venezuela), Mama Blanca. Gabriela Mistral (Chile), The Enemy.

A R19
Rowell, Charles H., ed. *Callaloo: A Journal of African-American and African Arts and Letters.* Baltimore, MD: The Johns Hopkins University Press, 1994. 954 pp.
Short fiction:
All Puerto Rican Authors
Giannina Braschi, I Don't Have It, and I Wanted It (excerpt from *Empire of Dreams*). Judith Ortiz Cofer, Corazón's Café. Rosario Ferré, The Bitches Colloquy. Carmen Lugo Filippi, Milagros, Mercurio Street. Liza Fiol Matta, Blanca (excerpt from Julia Rodríguez, MSW). Aurora Levins Morales, Hurricane; African Creation. Rosario Morales, I Didn't Hear Anything; Cosecha. Olga Nolla, Macaroons, Eyes of Sea and Sky. Magali García Ramis, Every Sunday. Ana Lydia Vega, Liliane's Sunday.
This is volume 17.3 of the journal. Includes an introduction by Consuelo López Springfield, the guest editor, and bio-bibliographies for the contributors.

A R19.1
Rowell, Charles H., ed. *Making Callaloo: 25 Years of Black Literature*. New York:
St. Martin's Press, 2002. 433 pp.
Short fiction:
Nancy Morejón (Cuba), Richard Bought His Flute.
Includes both poetry and fiction of Black writers.

A S1
Sadlier, Darlene J., ed., trans., and intro. *One Hundred Years after Tomorrow:
Brazilian Women's Fiction in the 20th Century*. Bloomington: Indiana University Press, 1992. 241 pp.
Short fiction:
Lúcia Benedetti, My Uncle Ricardo. Emi Bulhões Carvalho da Fonseca, In the
Silence of the Big House. Marina Colasanti, Little Girl in Red, on Her Way to the
Moon. Lia Correia Dutra, A Perfect World. Sonia Coutinho, Every Lana Turner
Has Her Johnny Stompanato. Rachel de Queiroz, excerpt from The Year Fifteen.
Márcia Denser, The Vampire of Whitehouse Lane. Carmen Dolores, A Drama in
the Countryside. Sra. Leando Dupré, excerpt from We Were Six. Lygia Fagundes
Telles, Just a Saxophone. Hilda Hilst, Agda. Tania Jamardo Faillace, Dorceli.
Clarice Lispector, The Flight. Elisa Lispector, The Fragile Balance. Júlia Lopes de
Almeida, excerpt from He and She. Lya Luft, excerpt from The Left Wing of the
Angel. Adalgisa Nery, Premeditated Coincidence. Nélida Piñón, Near East. Dinah
Silveira de Queiroz, Jovita. Edla Van Steen, The Sleeping Beauty (Script of a
Useless Life).
Includes bio-bibliographic notes on authors.

A S2
Salmonson, Jessica Amanda, ed. and preface. *What Did Miss Darrington See? An
Anthology of Feminist Supernatural Fiction*. New York: The Feminist Press,
1989. 263 pp.
Short stories:
Armonía Somers (Uruguay), The Fall. Luisa Valenzuela (Argentina), The Teacher.
Includes an introduction by Rosemary Jackson, bio-bibliographic notes on authors,
and a bibliography of recommended reading of women's fiction.

A S3
Santiago, Esmeralda, and Joie Davidow, eds. *Las Christmas: Favorite Latino
Authors Share Their Holiday Memories*. New York: Knopf, 1998. 198 pp.
Short fiction:
Julia Álvarez (Dominican Republic), Switching to Santicló. Gioconda Belli
(Nicaragua), A Christmas Like No Other. Aurora Levins Morales (Puerto Rico),
Dulce de Naranja. Rosario Morales (Puerto Rico), I Didn't Go Home (Christmas
1941). Judith Ortiz Cofer (Puerto Rico), The Gift of a Cuento. Esmeralda Santiago
(Puerto Rico), A Baby Doll Like My Cousin Jenny's. Mayra Santos Febres.

(Dominican Republic), A Little Bit of Bliss.
Includes bio-bibliographic information on the authors. Illustrated by José Ortega, introduction by Joie Davidow.

A S3.1
Santiago, Esmeralda, and Joie Davidow, eds. *Las Mamis: Favorite Latino Authors Remember Their Mothers*. New York: Alfred. A. Knopf, 2000. 189 pp.
Narrative:
Marjorie Agosín (Chile), Frida, Friduca, Mami. Alba Ambert (Puerto Rico), Persephone's Quest at Waterloo: A Daughter's Tale. Gioconda Belli (Nicaragua), Just a Woman. Mandalit del Barco (Peru), "Hello, Dollinks," Letters from Mom. Esmeralda Santiago (Puerto Rico), First Born.
Includes bio-bibliographic information on the authors and photographs of the authors' mothers.

A S4
Santiago, Roberto, ed. and intro. *Boricuas: Influential Puerto Rican Writings: An Anthology*. New York: One World Ballantine Books, 1995. 355 pp.
Short stories:
Ana Lydia Vega, Aerobics for Love.
Includes short stories by other Puerto Rican women writers (Nicholasa Mohr, Judith Ortiz Cofer, Esmeralda Santiago) which were originally written in English. Also includes poetry and essays by some forty Puerto Rican authors, male and female.

A S5
Santos, Rosario, ed. *And We Sold the Rain: Contemporary Fiction from Central America*. New York: Four Walls Eight Windows, 1988. 215 pp.
Short stories:
Claribel Alegría (El Salvador), Boardinghouse. Jacinta Escudos (El Salvador), Look at Lislique, See How Pretty It Is. Carmen Naranjo (Costa Rica), And We Sold the Rain. Bertalicia Peralta (Panama), A March Guayacán.
Includes an introduction by Jo Anne Engelbert and brief bio-bibliographic notes on authors and translators.

A S5.1
——, ed. *The Fat Man from La Paz: Contemporary Fiction from Bolivia*. New York: Seven Stories Press, 2000. 314 pp.
Short fiction:
Claudia Adriázola, Buttons. Ximena Arnal Franck, The Pianist. Virginia Ayllón Soria, Sisterhood. Giancarla de Quiroga, Celebration. Blanca Elena Paz, Sacraments by the Hour. Giovanna Rivero Santa Cruz, The Day of Atonement.
Includes bio-bibliographic information for the contributors and an introduction by Javier Sanjinés.

A S6

Santos-Febres, Mayra. *Urban Oracles: Stories*. Trans. Nathan Budoff and Lydia Platon Lázaro. Cambridge: Brookline Books Inc., 1997. 129 pp.
Short stories:
Broken Strand; Abnel, Sweet Nightmare; Night Stand; Resins for Aurelia; Urban Oracles; Marina's Fragrance; Brine Mirror; The Park; Stained Glass Fish; Dilcia M. Act of Faith; Oso Blanco; Mystic Rose; A Normal Day in the Life of Couto Seducción; The Writer.
Dominican Republic.

A S7

Schulte, Rainer, ed. *"International Short Fiction." Mundus Artium* 8.2 (1975). 156 pp.
Short stories:
Luisa Valenzuela (Argentina), The Door.
Includes a foreword by Lucia Getsi and bio-bibliographical notes on contributors.

A S7.1

Schulte, Rainer, ed. *"International Women's Issue." Mundus Artium* 7.2 (1974). 160 pp.
Short stories:
Concepción T. Alzola (Cuba), Don Pascual Was Buried Alone.

A S7.2

——, ed. *"Special Latin American Fiction Issue." Mundus Artium* 3.3 (1970). 124 pp.
Short stories:
Vlady Kociancich (Argentina), False Limits. Nélida Piñón (Brazil), Big-bellied Cow.
Includes bio-bibliographic notes on contributors.

A S8

Scott, Nina, ed. and trans. *Madres del verbo/Mothers of the Word: Early Spanish-American Women Writers: A Bilingual Anthology*. Albuquerque: University of New Mexico Press, 1999. 414 pp.
Short fiction:
Juana Inés de la Cruz (Mexico), Carta al R. P. M. Antonio Núñez / Letter to the R. P. M. Antonio Núñez ; Poesía / Poetry. Francisca Josefa de Castillo (Colombia), Su vida / Her Life. Juana Manuela Gorriti (Argentina/Peru), Cartas a Ignacio de Cepeda / Letters to Ignacio de Cepeda; Carta a Antonio Romero Ortiz / Letter to Antonio Romero Ortiz. Mercedes Cabello de Carbonera (Peru), La hija del mashorquero / The Executioner's Daughter. Teresa González de Fanning (Peru), Estudio comparativo de la inteligencia y la belleza en la mujer / A Comparative Study on Intelligence and Beauty in Women. Soledad Acosta de Samper

(Colombia), Trabajo para la mujer/Work for Women; Dolores/Dolores. Bilingual edition.

A S9
Sewell, Marilyn. *Breaking Free: Women of Spirit at Midlife and Beyond*. Boston: Beacon Press, 2004. 256 pp.
Narrative:
Isabel Allende (Chile), *Aphrodite: A Memoir of the Senses* (excerpt).
Includes bio-bibliographic notes on contributors.

A S10
Shapard, Robert, and James Thomas, eds. *Sudden Fiction: 60 Short-Short Stories*. New York: W. W. Norton and Co., Inc., 1989. 342 pp.
Short stories:
Clarice Lispector (Brazil), The Fifth Story. Luisa Valenzuela (Argentina), The Verb To Kill. Edla Van Steen (Brazil), Mr. and Mrs. Martins.
Includes an introduction by Charles Baxter.

A S11
Shihad Nye, Naomi, ed. and intro. *The Tree Is Older Than You Are: A Bilingual Gathering of Poems and Stories from Mexico with Paintings by Mexican Artists*. New York: Simon & Schuster for Young Readers, 1995. 111 pp.
Short stories:
Angelina Muñiz-Huberman (Mexico), The Cabalist; El Cabalista.
Includes bio-bibliographic notes on contributors.

A S12
Silver, Katherine, ed. *Chile: A Traveler's Literary Companion*. St. Paul, MN: Whereabouts Press, 2003.
Narrative:
Marjorie Agosín, Isla Negra. Marta Brunet, Black Bird. Beatriz García Huidobro, Until She Go No More.

A S13
Slung, Michel B. *Murder and Other Acts of Literature: Twenty-four Unforgettable and Chilling Stories by Some of the World's Best-loved, Most Celebrated Writers*. New York: St. Martin's Press, 1997. 345 pp.
Short stories:
Isabel Allende (Chile), An Act of Vengeance.

A S14
Smith, Jennifer. *Short Stories for Students*. Detroit: Gale Group, 2001. 328 pp.
Short stories:
Isabel Allende (Chile), And of Clay We Are Created.

Each story is accompanied by the author biography, plot summary, themes, characters, and other useful information.

A S15

Smorkaloff, Pamela María, ed. and intro. *If I Could Write This in Fire: An Anthology of Literature from the Caribbean.* New York: New Press, 1994. 374 pp.

Short stories:

Chely Lima (Cuba), Monologue with Rain; Common Stories. Ana Lydia Vega (Puerto Rico), The Day It All Happened; Port-au-Prince; Below.

A bibliography of prose works by the authors included in the volume.

A S16

Soldán, Edmundo Paz, and Alberto Fuguet, eds. *Se habla español: voces latinas en USA.* Miami: Alfaguara, 2000. 386 pp.

Short fiction:

Giannina Braschi (Puerto Rico), Blow Up. Mayra Santos-Febres (Dominican Republic), Tren.

Includes bio-bibliographic notes on the contributors.

A S17

Solomon, Barbara, ed. and intro. *Other Voices, Other Vistas. Short Stories from Africa, China, India, Japan, and Latin America.* New York: Penguin USA, 1992. 478 pp.

Short stories:

Isabel Allende (Chile), Clarisa. Luisa Valenzuela (Argentina), Papito's Story.

Includes bio-bibliographic notes on authors and a bibliography of selected Latin American anthologies in English.

A S18

Stavans, Ilan, ed. and intro. *Prospero's Mirror: A Translator's Portfolio of Latin American Short Fiction.* Willimantic, CT: Curbstone Press, 1998. 323 pp.

Short fiction:

Silvino Ocampo (Argentina), The Music of the Rain. Ana María Shua (Argentina), A Good Mother. Luisa Valenzuela (Argentina), The Place of Its Solitude.

Includes bio-bibliographic notes on contributors and an epilogue by Margaret Sayers Peden.

A S18.1

——, ed. and intro. *Tropical Synagogues: Short Stories by Jewish-Latin American Writers.* New York: Holmes & Meier, 1994. 239 pp.

Short stories:

Aída Bortnik (Argentina), Celeste's Heart. Margo Glantz (Mexico), Genealogies. Elisa Lerner (Venezuela), Papa's Friends. Clarice Lispector (Brazil), Love. Alcina

Lubitch Domecq (Guatemala), Bottles. Angelina Muñiz-Huberman (Mexico), In the Name of His Name. Esther Seligson (Mexico), The Invisible Hour. Alicia Steimberg (Argentina), Cecilia's Last Will and Testament.
Includes bio-bibliographic notes and a primary and secondary bibliography for each author.

A S18.2

Stavans, Ilan, ed. *Wachale! Poetry and Prose about Growing up Latino in America.*
      Chicago: Cricket Books, 2001. 146 pp.
Short fiction:
Judith Ortiz Cofer (Puerto Rico), Kennedy in the Barrio. Carolina Hospital (Cuba), My Cuban Body. Alcina Lubitch Domecq (Guatemala), La Llorona. Ruth Behar (Cuba), The Jewish Cemetery in Guanabacoa. Achy Obejas (Cuba), Sugarcane. Aurora Levins Morales (Puerto Rico), Child of the Americas.
A bilingual collection dealing with diversity among Latinos. Juvenile literature. Includes bio-bibliographic notes.

A S19

Stern, Jerome, ed. *An Anthology of Really Short Stories.* New York: W. W. Norton
      & Company, 1996. 141 pp.
Short fiction:
Judith Ortiz Cofer (Puerto Rico), Kennedy in the Barrio.
Includes brief bio-bibliographies for contributors.

A S20

Sturgis, Susana J., ed. *Tales of Magic Realism by Women: Dreams in a Minor Key.*
      Freedom: The Crossing Press, 1991. 235 pp.
Short fiction:
Kathleen Alcalá (Mexico), Flora's Complaint. Alcina Lubitch Domecq (Guatemala), Bottles.

A S21

Szoka, Elzbieta, ed. *Fourteen Female Voices from Brazil: Interviews and Works.*
      Austin, TX: Host Publications, Inc., 2002. 309 pp.
Short stories:
Nélida Piñón, I Love My Husband. Lygia Fagundes Telles, The Day to Say "No!"
Includes an introduction by Jean Franco. Works of poetry and drama are also included in the volume.

A T1

Tapscott, Stephen, ed. and trans. *Gabriela Mistral: Selected Prose and Prose-*
      Poems. Austin: University of Texas Press, 2002. 248 pp.
Contents:
Fables, Elegies, and Things of the Earth

The Sea; The Zebra; The Golden Pheasant; Four; In Praise of Salt; The Fig; The Pineapple: The Tortoise: Bread; The Giraffe; The Alpaca; The Sunflower; In Praise of Glass; In Praise of Sand; Second Praise-Song for the Sand.

Prose and Prose-Poems from Desolation (1922)
The Teacher's Prayer; Children's Hair; Poems fo the Mothers; Poems of the Saddest Mother; Lullabies; Motifs of Clay; The Four-Petaled Flower; Poems of Ecstasy; Art; Decalogue of the Artist; Commentary on Poems by Rabindranath Tagore; Spiritual Readings; Motifs of the Passion; Poems of the Home; Scholarly Prose/Stories for Schools; Why Bamboo Canes Are Hollow; Why Roses Have Thorns; The Root of the Rosebush; The Thistle; The Puddle.

1. Lyrical Biographies
Song to Saint Francis; Profile of Sor Juana Inés de la Cruz; To Declare the Dream; Thoughts on Teaching; Profile of the Mexican Indian Woman; Chile; A Man of Mexico: Alfonso Reyes; Alfonsina Storni; An Invitation to Read Rainer Maria Rilke; If Napoleon Had Never Existed; José Martí; A Message about Pablo Neruda; How I Write; On Four Sips of Water; The Forbidden Word; My Social Beliefs.

Includes the translator's remarks. Bilingual edition.
Chile.

A T2

Tashlik, Phyllis, ed. and intro. *Hispanic, Female and Young: An Anthology.* Houston, TX: Piñata Books, 1994. 217 pp.

Short fiction:
Nicholasa Mohr (Puerto Rico), A Very Special Pet; Esperanza (excerpt from *Nilda*); Christmas Was a Time of Plenty. Judith Ortiz Cofer (Puerto Rico), First Love; Vida; María Sabida.

A T3

Thomas, James, Denise Thomas, and Tom Hazuka, eds. *Flash Fiction. 72 Very Short Stories.* New York: W. W. Norton & Company, 1992. 224 pp.

Short stories:
Luisa Valenzuela (Argentina), Vision Out of the Corner of One Eye.
Brief introduction by James Thomas.

A T4

Thomas, Sue, ed. *Wild Women: Contemporary Short Stories by Women Celebrating Women.* Woodstock, NY: The Overlook Press, 1994. 368 pp.

Short stories:
Isabel Allende (Chile), Two Words.
Includes an introduction by Clarissa Pinkola Estés and bio-bibliographic notes on the authors.

A T5

Torres-Rioseco, Arturo, ed. and intro. *Short Stories of Latin America*. New York:
    Las Americas, 1963. 203 pp.

Short stories:

María Luisa Bombal (Chile), The Tree. Guadalupe Dueñas (Mexico), The
Moribund.

Includes brief bio-bibliographic notes on authors.

A T6

Torres-Saillant, Silvio, ed. and intro. *Hispanic Immigrant Writers and the
    Family/Escritores immigrantes hispanos y la familia*. Jackson Heights, NY:
    Ollantay Center for the Arts, Inc., 1989. 93 pp.

Short fiction:

Nora Glickman (Argentina), El último de los colonos; Tag-Sale; Dios salve a
América.

Includes a conversation with each writer and a foreword by Pedro R. Monge.

A T7

Troupe, Quincy, and Rainer Schulte, eds. and intro. *Giant Talk: An Anthology of
    Third World Writings*. New York: Random House, 1975. 547 pp.

Short stories:

Vlady Kociancich (Argentina), False Limits.

Includes brief bio-bibliographic notes on authors and editors and an extensive
bibliography divided into the following categories: African-American and Puerto
Rican-American Anthologies; African-American Literary Criticism; Anthologies
of African Poetry and Prose; Critical Books of Essays on African Literature; Latin
American Anthologies; and Periodicals, Journals, and Magazines.

A T8

Turner, Faythe, ed. and intro. *Puerto Rican Writers at Home in the USA: An
    Anthology*. Seattle, WA: Open Hand Publishing, 1991. 347 pp.

Short fiction:

Aurora Levins Morales, Immigrants; Puertoricanness; Kitchens; 1930; South; The
Other Heritage; Old Countries; A Child's Christmas in Puerto Rico. Nicholasa
Mohr, Mr. Mendelsohn; The Wrong Lunch Line. Rosario Morales, The Dinner; I
Recognize You; I Am the Reasonable One.

Includes a photo and a bio-bibliography for each author.

A U1

Urbano, Victoria, ed. *Five Women Writers of Costa Rica: Short Stories by Carmen
    Naranjo, Eunice Odio, Yolanda Oreamuno, Victoria Urbano, and Rima de
    Vallbona*. Beaumont: Asociación de Literatura Femenina Hispánica, 1978. 131
    pp.

Short stories:
Rima de Vallbona, Chumico Tree; Penelope's Silver Wedding Anniversary; Parable of the Impossible Eden. Carmen Naranjo, The Flowery Trick; The Journey and the Journeys; Inventory of a Recluse. Eunice Odio, Once There Was a Man; The Trace of the Butterfly. Yolanda Oreamuno, High Valley; The Tide Returns at Night. Victoria Urbano, Avery Island; Triptych.
Includes bio-bibliographic notes on contributors and a critical commentary on the authors and their works.

A V1
Valenzuela, Luisa. *The Censors.* Trans. Hortense Carpentier. Willimantic, CT: Curbstone Press, 1992. 255 pp.
Short stories:
The Best Shod (Los mejor calzados); The Snow White Watchman (El custodio blancanieves); The Censors (Los censores); Redtown Chronicles (Crónicas de pueblorrojo); Void and Vacuum (Vacío era el de antes); Papito's Story (La historia de Papito); Country Carnival (Carnival campero); The Blue Water Man (El fontanero azul); One Siren or Another (Unas y otras sirenas); Trial of the Virgin (Proceso a la virgen); The Minstrels (Los menestreles); The Son of Kermaria (El hijo de Kermaria); The Door (La puerta); Vision Out of the Corner of One Eye (Visión de reojo); All about Suicide (Pavada de suicidio); The Attainment of Knowledge (Para alcanzar el conocimiento); Legend of the Self-Sufficient Child (Leyenda de la criatura autosuficiente); Cat's Eye (Pantera ocular); Up among the Eagles (Donde viven las águilas); The Place of Its Quietude (El lugar de su quietud).
Side by side bilingual edition.
Argentina.

A V1.1
——. *Clara: Thirteen Short Stories and a Novel.* Trans. Hortense Carpentier and J. Jorge Castello. New York: Harcourt Brace Jovanovich, 1976. 233 pp.
Short fiction:
Nihil Obstat; The Door; Trial of the Virgin; City of the Unknown; The Minstrels; The Son of Kermaria; Forsaken Woman; The Teacher; Irka of the Horses; The Legend of the Self-sufficient Creature; The Sin of the Apple; The Alphabet; A Family for Clotilde; Clara, a Novel.
Argentina.

A V1.2
——. *Open Door.* Trans. Hortense Carpentier. San Francisco: North Point Press, 1988. 202 pp.
Short stories:
The Censors; The Snow White Watchman; Cat's Eye; Flea Market; Legend of the Self-Sufficient Child; Country Carnival; Generous Impediments Float Downriver;

The Redtown Chronicles; Up among the Eagles; The Attainment of Knowledge; One Siren or Another; The Blue Water Man; My Everyday Colt; Papito's Story; Strange Things Happen Here; The Best Shod; The Gift of Words; Love of Animals; The Verb *to Kill*; All about Suicide; The Celery Munchers; Vision Out of the Corner of One Eye; Ladders to Success; A Story about Greenery; The Place of Its Quietude; The Door; City of the Unknown; Nihil Obstat; A Family for Clotilde; Trial of the Virgin; The Son of Kermaria; The Minstrels.
Includes a brief preface by Luisa Valenzuela.
Argentina.

A VI.3
Valenzuela, Luisa. *Other Weapons*. Trans. Deborah Bonner. Hanover: Ediciones del Norte, 1985. 135 pp.
Short stories:
Fourth Version; The Word "Killer"; Rituals of Rejection; I'm Your Horse in the Night; Other Weapons.
Includes brief bio-bibliographic notes on author by Margo Glantz and Julio Cortázar.
Argentina.

A VI.4
———. *Strange Things Happen Here. Twenty-six Short Stories and a Novel*. Trans. Helen Lane. New York and London: Harcourt Brace Jovanovich, 1986. 220 pp.
Short fiction:
Strange Things Happen Here; The Best Shod; On the Way to the Ministry; Sursum Corda; The Gift of Words; Love of Animals; Common Transport; Vision Out of the Corner of One Eye; Porno Flick; United Rapes Unlimited; Argentina, Here Innocence Is Born; The Verb *to Kill*; All about Suicide; The Zombies; Who, Me a Bum?; Neither the Most Terrifying Nor the Least Memorable; A Meaningless Story; El Es Di; Grimorium; The Celery Munchers; Ladders to Success; Void and Vacuum; A Story about Greenery; The March; Politics; The Place of Its Quietude; The Discovery; The Loss; The Journey; The Encounter.
Argentina.

A VI.5
———. *Symmetries*. Trans. Margaret Jull Costa. London: Serpent's Tail, 1998. 167 pp.
Short stories:
Tango; Knife and Mother; Addendum; The Invisible Mender; The Quiet Café; Desire Makes the Matter Rise; Journey; Three Days; The Charm against Storms; Transparency; The Envoy; The Master's Laugh; If This Is Life, I'm Red Riding Hood; You Can't Stop Progress; 4 Prince 4; The Density of Words; Avatars; The Key; Symmetries.
Includes brief bio-bibliographic information on the author.

Argentina.

A V2

Van Steen, Edla. *A Bag of Stories.* Trans. and intro. David George. Pittsburgh, PA: Latin American Literary Review Press, 1991. 174 pp.

Short stories:

Period; Good Enough to Sing in a Choir; Intimacy; The Beauty of the Lion; The Pledge; Nostalgia Row; Before the Dawn; Forever After; Apartment for Rent; CAROL head LINA heart; A Day in Three Movements; In Spite of Everything; The Return; The Misadventures of João.

Brazil.

A V2.1

———, ed. *Love Stories: A Brazilian Collection.* Trans. Elizabeth Lowe. Rio de Janeiro: Gráfica Editora Hamburg Ltda., 1978. 192 pp.

Short stories:

Sonia Coutinho, Those May Afternoons. Lygia Fagundes Telles, Turtledove or A Love Story. Judith Grossman, On the Way to Eternity. Hilda Hilst, Agda. Nélida Piñón, The Shadow of the Prey. Edla Van Steen, Carol Head Lina Heart Includes an introduction by Fábio Lucas and illustrations by Italo Cencini.

A V2.2

———. *Scent of Love.* Trans. and foreword David S. George. Pittsburgh, PA: Latin American Literary Review Press, 1997. 110 pp.

Narrative:

Scent of Love (novella); Queen of the Abyss; Less than the Dream.

Received the Nestlé Award for Literature in 1997.

Brazil.

A V3

Vega, Ana Lydia. *True and False Romances: Stories and a Novella.* Trans. Andrés Hurley. London: Serpent's Tail, 1994. 261 pp.

Short fiction:

Aerobics for Love; Deliverance from Evil; Solutions, Inc.; Just One Small Detail; Série Noire; Consolation Prize; Eye-Openers; Miss Florence's Trunk; *True Romances* (novella).

Puerto Rico.

A V4

Vélez, Diana, ed., intro., and trans. *Reclaiming Medusa: Short Stories by Contemporary Puerto Rican Women.* San Francisco: Spinsters/Aunt Lute Book Co., 1988. 161 pp.

Short stories:

Rosario Ferré, The Youngest Doll; Sleeping Beauty; Pico Rico, Mandorico.

Carmen Lugo Filippi, Milagros, on Mercurio Street; Pilar, Your Curls. Mayra Montero, Thirteen and a Turtle; Last Night at Dawn. Carmen Valle, Diary Entry #6; Diary Entry #1. Ana Lydia Vega, Three Love Aerobics; ADJ, Inc.

Includes the original Spanish versions of "Pico Rico, Mandorico" and "Thirteen and a Turtle."

A V5

Ventura, Gabriela Baeza, ed. *US Latino Literature Today.* New York: Pearson/Longman, 2005. 324 pp.

Short fiction:

Marjorie Agosín (Chile), United States. Judith Ortiz Cofer (Puerto Rico), Silent Dancing. Claribel Alegría (El Salvador), Nocturnal Visits; The Politics of Exile. Julia Álvarez (Dominican Republic), Snow from *How the García Girls Lost Their Accents.* Aurora Levins Morales (Puerto Rico), Immigrants. Alicia Partnoy (Argentina), The One-flower Slippers from *The Little School.*

A V6

Vigil, Evangelina, ed. and intro. *Women of the Word: Hispanic Women Write.* Houston, TX: Arte Público Press, 1987. 180 pp.

Short fiction:

Rima de Vallbona (Costa Rica), Alma-en-pena. Nicholasa Mohr (Puerto Rico), An Awakening...Summer 1956. Mary Helen Ponce (Puerto Rico), La Doctora Barr; Recuerdo: How I Changed the War and Won the Game; Recuerdo: Los piojos. Helena María Viramontes (Mexico), The Broken Web.

Includes bio-bibliographies for contributors. This volume also contains poetry, criticism, and art.

A V7

Viramontes, Helena María. *The Moths and Other Stories.* Houston, TX: Arte Público Press, 1985. 118 pp.

Short fiction:

The Moths; Growing; Birthday; The Broken Web; The Cariboo Café; The Long Reconciliation; Snapshots; Neighbors.

Includes an introduction by Yvonne Yarbro-Bejarano and bio-bibliographic notes on contributors.

Mexico.

A W1

Waters, Erika J., ed. and intro. *New Writing from the Caribbean.* London: The Macmillan Press Ltd., 1994. 116 pp.

Short fiction:

Julia Álvarez (Dominican Republic), Anteojos.

Includes brief bio-bibliographies for contributors.

A W2

Wolverton, Terry, and Robert Drake, eds. *Circa 2000: Lesbian Fiction at the Millennium.* Los Angeles: Alyson, 2000. 331 pp.
Short fiction:
Achy Obejas (Cuba), Wrecks.
Includes brief bio-bibliographies for contributors.

A Y1

Yanes, Gabriela, Manuel Sorto, Horacio Castellanos Moya, and Lyn Sorto, eds. *Mirrors of War: Literature and Revolution in El Salvador.* Trans. and intro. Keith Ellis. New York: Monthly Review Press, 1985. 151 pp.
Short fiction:
Claribel Alegría, Tamales from Cambray (and other excerpts from the novel *Izalco Ashes*).
Includes brief bio-bibliographic notes on authors.

A Y2

Yáñez, Mirta, ed. *Cubana: Contemporary Fiction by Cuban Women.* Trans. Dick Cluster and Cindy Schuster. Boston: Beacon Press, 1998. 213 pp.
Short stories:
Marilyn Bobes, Somebody Has to Cry. María Elena Llano, Japanese Daisies. Josefina de Diego, Internal Monologue on a Corner in Havana. Nancy Alonso, A Tooth for a Tooth. Mylene Fernández Pintado, Anhedonia (A Story in Two Women). Aída Bahr, The Scent of Limes. Esther Díaz Llanillo, My Aunt. Ana Luz García Caizada, Disremembering a Smell. Magaly Sánchez, Catalina in the Afternoons. Rosa Lleana Boudet, Potosí II: Address Unknown. Sonia Rivera-Valdés, A Whiff of Wild Desire. Mirta Yáñez, Dust to Dust. Uva de Aragón, I Just Can't Take It. Adelaida Fernández de Juan, The Egyptians. Achy Obejas, We Came All the Way from Cuba So You Could Dress Like This? Ena Lucía Portela, The Urn and the Name (A Lighthearted Tale).
Includes a foreword by Ruth Behar and an introduction by Mirta Yáñez: "Women's Voices from the Great Blue River." Includes bio-bibliographic notes on contributors.

A Y3

Yates, Donald, ed. and intro. *Latin Blood: The Best Crime and Detective Stories of South America.* New York: Herder & Herder, 1972. 224 pp.
Short stories:
María Elvira Bermúdez (Mexico), The Puzzle of the Broken Watch.

A Y4

Young, David, and Keith Hollaman, eds. and intro. *Magical Realist Fiction: An Anthology.* New York and London: Longman Inc., 1984. 519 pp.

Short stories:
María Luisa Bombal (Chile), New Islands.
Includes bio-bibliographic notes on authors.

A Y5
Young-Bruehl, Elisabeth, ed. and intro. *Global Cultures. A Transnational Short Fiction Reader.* Hanover, NH: Wesleyan University Press, 1994. 509 pp.
Short stories:
Marta Brunet (Chile), Solitude of Blood. Aurora Levins Morales (Puerto Rico), El bacalao viene de más lejos y se come aquí. Luisa Mercedes Levinson (Argentina), The Clearing. Carmen Lugo Filippi (Puerto Rico), Pilar, Your Curls. Carmen Lyra (Costa Rica), Estefanía. Carmen Naranjo (Costa Rica), And We Sold the Rain. Bertalicia Peralta (Panama), A March Guayacán. Cristina Peri Rossi (Uruguay), The Influence of Edgar Allan Poe in the Poetry of Raimundo Arias.

Novels and Novellas in Alphabetical Order by Author

The letter "N" indicates that the work is a novel or novella and the following letter represents the first letter of the author's last name. If there is more than one work per author, this is indicated by 1.1, 1.2, etc. These codes are used for cross-referencing in the other indices. The country refers to the author's country of origin.

N A1
Aguilar, Rosario. *The Lost Chronicles of Terra Firma.* Trans. Edward Waters
    Hood. Fredonia, NY: White Pine Press, 1997. 186 pp.
An historical novel that deals with the conquest of Central America as seen through the eyes of both Spanish and indigenous women.
Original title: *La niña blanca y los pájaros sin pies.* Nicaragua.

N A2
Albues, Tereza. *Pedra Canga* Trans. Clifford Elanders. Los Angeles, CA: Green
    Integer, 2001. 153 pp.
The story of the inhabitants of Pedra Canga, a small and isolated village in the Brazilian Pantanal, who triumph against a powerful family who has oppressed them for many years.
Original title: *Pedra Canga.* Brazil.

N A3
Alcalá, Kathleen. *The Flower in the Skull.* San Diego, CA: Harcourt Brace, 1999.
    180 pp.
The second part of the trilogy that began with *Spirits of the Ordinary: A Tale of Casas Grandes.* Set in Mexico, this is the story of three women who struggle to adjust to their current lives while at the same time coming to terms with their past.
Originally written in English. Mexico.

N A3.1
——. *Spirits of the Ordinary: A Tale of Casas Grandes.* Trans. Eduardo Hojman.
    Buenos Aires: Emecé, 1998. 252 pp.

The author's first novel, set in Mexico in the 1870s. The story of a Jew who marries into a Catholic family and becomes estranged from both religions. Winner of the Pacific Northwest Booksellers Association Award.
Original title: *Espíritus de las pequeñas cosas.* Mexico.

N A3.2
Alcalá, Kathleen. *Treasures in Heaven.* San Francisco: Chronicle Books, 2000. 224 pp.
Set in Mexico City in the 1900s, the tale of a young mother and son caught up in the country's feminist movement. Sequel to *The Flower in the Skull.*
Originally written in English. Mexico.

N A4
Alegría, Claribel. *Family Album: Three Novellas.* Trans. Amanda Hopkinson. London: Women's Press, 1990. 170 pp.
Three novellas that explore the critical stages in a woman's life. Includes *The Talisman, Family Album,* and *Village of God and the Devil.*
Original title: *Pueblo de Dios y de Mandinga.* El Salvador.

N A4.1
——. *Luisa in Realityland.* Willimantic, CT: Curbstone Press, 1988.
A combination of prose and poetry dealing with Salvadoran politics.
Original title: *Luisa en el país de la realidad.* El Salvador.

N A5
Alegría, Claribel, and Darwin J. Flakoll. *Ashes of Izalco.* Trans. Darwin J. Flakoll. Willimantic, CT: Curbstone Press, 1993. 173 pp.
A love story set against the events of a massacre of thirty thousand Indians and peasants in Izalco.
Original title: *Cenizas de Izalco.* El Salvador.

N A6
Allende, Isabel. *Aphrodite: The Love of Food and the Food of Love.* London: Flamingo, 1999. 272 pp.
Combines personal narrative with erotic tales. Allende includes her mother's recipes, poems, and stories from a variety of sources.
Original title: *Afrodita: cuentos, recetas y otros afrodisíacos.* Chile.

N A6.1
——. *Aphrodite: A Memoir of the Senses.* Trans. Margaret Sayers Peden. New York: HarperCollins, 1998. 315 pp.
Combines personal narrative with erotic tales. Allende includes her mother's recipes, poems, and stories from a variety of sources.
Original title: *Afrodita: cuentos, recetas y otros afrodisíacos.* Chile.

N A6.2

Allende, Isabel. *City of the Beasts*. Trans. Margaret Sayers Peden. New York: HarperCollins, 2002. 406 pp.

Written for elementary and junior high school students. The story of Alexander Cold who travels with his grandmother to find a beast in the Amazon jungle.

Original title: *La ciudad de las bestias*. Chile.

N A6.3

——. *Daughter of Fortune*. Trans. Margaret Sayers Peden. London: Flamingo, 1999. 352 pp.

Set in the 1800s, a young woman follows her lover to California and searches for him in the midst of the Gold Rush.

Original title: *Hija de la fortuna*. Chile.

N A6.4

——. *Eva Luna*. Trans. Margaret Sayers Peden. New York: Knopf, 1988. 392 pp.

The story of Eva Luna, from her childhood through her later years, and the people she encounters in life's path.

Original title: *Eva Luna*. Chile.

N A6.5

——. *Forest of the Pygmies*. Trans. Margaret Sayers Peden. New York: HarperCollins, 2005. 296 pp.

Alexander Cold and his grandmother travel to Africa and find a world of poaching, corruption, and slavery.

Original title: *El bosque de los pigmeos*. Chile.

N A6.6

——. *The House of the Spirits*. Trans. Magda Bogin. New York: Knopf, 1985. 368 pp.

The story of three generations of a family in Chile during turbulent times. The author's first novel.

Original title: *La casa de los espíritus*. Chile.

N A6.7

——. *Inés of My Soul*. Trans. Margaret Sayers Peden. New York: HarperCollins Publishers, 2006. 321 pp.

The life of Inés Suárez, a Spaniard born in 1507, who became the lover of Chile's first governor and then helped defend Santiago against attacks by natives.

Original title: *Inés del alma mía*. Chile.

N A6.8

——. *The Infinite Plan: A Novel*. Trans. Margaret Sayers Peden. New York: HarperCollins Publishers, 1993. 382 pp.

Allende's first novel to be set in North America. The story of Gregory Reeves, the son of Charles Reeves, the "Doctor of Sciences" who travels the country revealing the secret of life: "The Infinite Plan."
Original title: *El plan infinito*. Chile.

N A6.9
Allende, Isabel. *Kingdom of the Golden Dragon*. Trans. Margaret Sayers Peden. New York: Harper Trophy, 2005. 437 pp.
The story of Alexander Cold and his best friend, Nadia, and her grandmother who travel to a remote part of the world to find the legendary Dragon of Gold. Written for secondary school students.
Original title: *El reino del Dragón de Oro*. Chile.

N A6.10
——. *Of Love and Shadows*. Trans. Margaret Sayers Peden. New York: Knopf, 1987. 274 pp.
A love story between the daughter of a wealthy family and the son of a Spanish exile. Original title: *De amor y de sombra*. Chile.

N A6.11
——. *Paula*. Trans. Margaret Sayers Peden. New York: HarperCollins, 1995. 330 pp.
The author tells stories to her daughter while she lies in her hospital bed in a coma.
Original title: *Paula*. Chile.

N A6.12
——. *Portrait in Sepia*. Trans. Margaret Sayers Peden. New York: HarperCollins, 2001. 304 pp.
Set in the 19th century, the story of Aurora, a young woman who returns to Chile.
Original title: *Retrato en sepia: una novela*. Chile.

N A6.13
——. *Zorro: A Novel*. Trans. Margaret Sayers Peden. New York: HarperCollins, 2005. 390 pp.
How the legend of Zorro was born. Diego de la Vega, the son of a Spanish father and a Shosone Indian mother, travels to California to aid the poor and helpless.
Original title: *Zorro: una novela*. Chile.

N A7
Álvarez, Julia. *Before We Were Free*. New York: Alfred A. Knopf, 2002.
A young Dominican girl discovers that her family is involved in bringing down Trujillo, the Dominican dictator. For adolescent readers.
Originally written in English. Dominican Republic.

N A7.1
Álvarez, Julia. *A Cafecito Story.* White River Junction, VT: Chelsea Green Publishing
    Co., 2001. 58 pp.
How a beverage united people in a variety of ways.
Originally written in English. Dominican Republic.

N A7.2
——. *How the Garcia Girls Lost Their Accents.* New York: A Plume Book,1992.
    290 pp.
Four sisters from the Dominican Republic embrace American life in Miami and attempt
to fully acculturate.
Originally written in English. Dominican Republic.

N A7.3
——. *How Tía Lola Came to Visit/Stay.* New York: Alfred A. Knopf, 2001. 145 pp.
Tía Lola comes to Vermont from the Dominican Republic to visit her family.
Originally written in English. Dominican Republic.

N A7.4
——. *In the Name of Salomé: A Novel.* Chapel Hill, NC: Algonquin Books, 2000.
    368 pp.
The story of the Dominican poet Salomé Ureña and her daughter Camila, who were
both revolutionaries.
Originally written in English. Dominican Republic.

N A7.5
——. *In the Time of the Butterflies.* New York: Plume, 1995. 325 pp.
Based on a true story, the tale of three sisters in the Dominican Republic who were
murdered for taking part in a plot to overthrow the government.
Originally written in English. Dominican Republic.

N A7.6
——. *Saving the World.* Chapel Hill, NC: Algonquin Books of Chapel Hill, 2006.
    368 pp.
A woman accompanies a shipload of homeless children from Spain to the New World.
The purpose of the trip was to bring the smallpox vaccine to the Americas and Asia.
Originally written in English. Dominican Republic.

N A7.7
——. *The Secret Footprints.* New York: Alfred Knopf, 2000. 40 pp.
The story of Ciguapas, a tribe of beautiful people who live under water. Dominican
folklore. Illustrations by Fabian Negrin.
Originally written in English. Dominican Republic.

N A7.8
Álvarez, Julia. *Yo!* New York: Plume, 1999. 414 pp.
The immigrant experience in New York. Sequel to *How the Garcia Girls Lost Their Accents*.
Originally written in English. Dominican Republic.

N A8
Arana, Marie. *Cellophane*. New York: Dial Books, 2006. 384 pp.
An eccentric engineer discovers the recipe for cellophane while working in the Peruvian rain forest. Strange events follow for his family.
Originally written in English. Peru.

N B1
Belli, Gioconda. *The Inhabited Woman*. Trans. Kathleen March. Willimantic, CT: Curbstone Press, 1993. 412 pp.
A love story that takes place during a revolution. An upper-class young woman is invaded by the spirit of an ancient woman warrior and joins in the effort to overthrow a military dictatorship.
Original title: *La mujer habitada*. Nicaragua.

N B2
Benitez, Sandra. *Bitter Grounds*. New York: Hyperion, 1997. 445 pp.
Three generations of women in El Salvador survive the decimation of the indigenous people in their country.
Originally written in English. Mexico.

N B2.1
——. *Night of the Radishes*. New York: Hyperion Press, 2005. 288 pp.
After the death of her mother, a woman travels to Mexico to look for her long lost brother.
Originally written in English. Mexico.

N B2.2
——. *A Place Where the Sea Remembers*. Minneapolis, MN: Coffee House Press, 1993. 163 pp.
The events that take place in the lives of villagers in a seaside town in Mexico.
Originally written in English. Mexico.

N B2.3
——. *The Weight of All Things*. New York: Hyperion, 2001. 256 pp.
A tale of a young boy in war-torn El Salvador.
Originally written in English. Mexico.

N B3

Bermin, Sabina. *Bubbeh.* Trans. Andrea G. Labinger. Pittsburgh, PA: Latin American
   Literary Review Press, 1998. 90 pp.
Set in a Jewish community is Mexico City in the 1960s, a young girl explores the
memories of her youth and the stories of three generations of women.
Original title: *Bobe.* Mexico.

N B4

Bevin, Teresa. *Havana Split.* Houston, TX: Arte Público Press, 1998. 368 pp.
A woman returns to Cuba and finds that it has dramatically changed since her departure.
Originally written in English. Cuba.

N B5

Bombal, María Luisa. *House of Mist.* Trans. María Luisa Bombal. New York: Farrar-
   Straus, 1947. 259 pp.
A young wife lives in a fantasy world due to her husband's negligence and
incomprehension of her needs.
Original title: *La última niebla.* Chile.

N B5.1

———. *House of Mist;* and *The Shrouded Woman.* Trans. María Luisa Bombal. Austin:
   University of Texas Press, 1995. 198 pp.
La última niebla: A young wife lives in a fantasy world due to her husband's negligence
and incomprehension of her needs. *La amortajada:* As a corpse views the mourners
at her wake, she thinks back on her life which she considers a failure. Includes a
foreword by Naomi Lindstrom.
Original titles: *La última niebla* and *La amortajada.* Chile.

N B5.2

———. *The Shrouded Woman.* Trans. María Luisa Bombal. New York: Farrar-Straus,
   1948. 198 pp.
As a corpse views the mourners at her wake, she thinks back on her life which she
considers a failure.
Original title: *La amortajada.* Chile.

N B6

Borinsky, Alicia. *All Night Movie.* Trans. Cola Franzen and Alicia Borinsky. Evanston,
   IL: Hydra Books/Northwestern University Press, 2002. 204 pp.
The author utilizes a variety of narrative techniques to tell a series of absurd events
involving an offbeat group of characters. A young woman attempts to kill a man she
loves then undergoes a series of transformations.
Original title: *Cine continuado.* Argentina.

N B6.1

Borinsky, Alicia. *Dreams of the Abandoned Seducer.* Trans. Cola Franzen and Alicia
    Borinsky. Lincoln: University of Nebraska Press, 1998. 211 pp.
A surreal novel comprised of short chapters describing a series of mistreated women.
Original title: *Sueños del seductor abandonado.* Argentina.

N B6.2

———. *Mean Woman.* Trans. Cola Franzen. Lincoln: University of Nebraska Press,
    1993. 179 pp.
A dark comedy set during the time of dictatorship when it is not uncommon for people
to disappear.
Original title: *Mina cruel.* Argentina.

N B7

Boullosa, Carmen. *Cleopatra Dismounts.* Trans. Geoff Hargreaves. New York: Grove
    Press, 2005. 240 pp.
The reconstruction of two possible lives of Cleopatra, the Queen of Egypt.
Original title: *De un salto descabalga la reina.* Mexico.

N B7.1

———. *Leaving Tabasco.* Trans. Geoff Hargreaves. New York: Grove Press, 1999.
    244 pp.
A coming-of-age story of Delmira Ulloa who grows up in a magical world and begins
a search for her unknown father.
Original title: *Treinta años.* Mexico.

N B7.2

———. *The Miracle-worker.* Trans. Amanda Hopkinson. London: Jonathan Cape, 1995.
    137 pp.
A woman has the power to make the dreams of others come true.
Original title: *La milagrosa.* Mexico.

N B7.3

———. *They're Cows, We're Pigs.* Trans. Leland Chambers. New York: Grove Press,
    1997. 180 pp.
Jean Smeeks is kidnapped at the age of 13 in Flanders and sold into slavery on Tortuga,
a mythical island where he becomes a medical officer with a band of pirates.
Original title: *Son vacas, somos puercos.* Mexico.

N B8

Braschi, Giannina. *Empire of Dreams.* Trans. Tess O'Dwyer. New Haven, CT: Yale
    University Press, 1994. 219 pp.
Stream-of-consciousness narrative on New York City. Includes the following pieces:
Assault on Time; Book of Clowns and Buffoons; Poems of the World; or, The Book

of Wisdom; Pastoral; or, The Inquisition of Memories; Song of Nothingness; Epilogue; The Adventures of Mariquita Samper; The Life and Works of Berta Singerman; The Things That Happen to Men in New York!; The Queen of Beauty, Charm, and Coquetry; Gossip; Portrait of Giannina Braschi; Mariquita Samper's Childhood; The Raise; Manifesto on Poetic Eggs; The Building of the Waves of the Sea; Requiem for Solitude.

Original title: *El Imperio de los sueños*. Puerto Rico.

N B8.1

Braschi, Giannina. *Yo-Yo Boing!* Pittsburgh, PA: Latin American Literary Review Press, 1998. 205 pp.

A story of cultural strife between Latino and American cultures in New York. Spanish and English version.

Orignal title: *Yo-Yo Boing*. Puerto Rico.

N B9

Buitrago, Fanny. *Señora Honeycomb*. Trans. Margaret Sayers Peden. New York: Harper Collins Publishers, 1996. 232 pp.

A rowdy fairy tale about Teodora Vencejos' sexual awakening. The heroine marries a man who squanders her inheritance forcing her to take a job in Madrid, far from her home in Colombia.

Original title: *Señora de la miel*. Colombia.

N B10

Bullrich, Silvina. *Tomorrow I'll Say Enough*. Trans. Julia Shirek Smith. Pittsburgh: Latin American Literary Review Press, 1996. 189 pp.

A Buenos Aires widow escapes the city to spend her 49th birthday alone in a remote village by the sea.

Original title: *Mañana digo basta*. Argentina.

N C1

Calderón, Sara Levi. *The Two Mujeres*. Trans. Gina Kaufer. San Francisco: Aunt Lute Books, 1991. 211 pp.

Valeria, the protagonist, falls in love with a woman and against all odds leaves her conventional life to become a writer.

Original title: *Las dos mujeres*. Mexico.

N C2

Campos, Julieta. *The Fear of Losing Eurydice: A Novel*. Trans. Leland H. Chambers. Normal, IL: Dalkey Archive Press, 1993. 121 pp.

The story of Monsier who teaches French in a tropical seaport. He becomes obsessed with love stories and is distracted from his work.

Original title: *Miedo de perder a Eurídice*. Mexico.

N C2.1

Campos, Julieta. *She Has Reddish Hair and Her Name Is Sabina.* Trans. Leland H.
    Chambers. Athens: University of Georgia Press, 1993. 135 pp.

A metafictional meditation on the creative process. Sabina is a character in the mind
of a writer who is seated on a balcony at an Acapulco hotel and represents the act
of creating fiction.

Original title: *Tiene los cabellos rojizos y se llama Sabina.* Mexico.

N C3

Castedo, Elena. *Paradise.* New York: Washington Square Press, 1990. 328 pp.

A young female refugee tells the story of the injustices in the class system of Latin
America.

Originally written in English and then translated into Spanish by the author with the
title: *El paraíso.* Chile

N C4

Castellanos, Rosario. *The Book of Lamentations.* Trans. Esther Allen. New York:
    Marsilio Publishing, 1996. 400 pp.

The story of a Mayan uprising in Chiapas, the southern Mexican state.

Original title: *Oficio de tinieblas.* Mexico.

N C4.1

———. *The Nine Guardians.* Trans. Irene Nicolson. New York: Vanguard, 1960;
    Colombia, LA: Readers International, 1992. 272 pp.

Related by a seven year-old girl, this is the story of a family attempting to hold on
to their property and way of life during the Mexican Revolution.

Original title: *Balún-Canán.* Mexico.

N C5

Cerda, Marta. *Señora Rodríguez and Other Worlds.* Trans. Sylvia Jiménez-Andersen.
    Durham and London: Duke University Press, 1997. 133 pp.

The story of a woman and her magical purse.

Original title: *La señora Rodríguez y otros mundos.* Mexico.

N C6

Chávez-Vásquez, Gloria. *AKUM: La magia de los sueños/The Magic of Dreams.*
    A Bilingual Novel. Trans. Gloria Chávez-Vásquez. Brooklyn, NY: White Owl
    Publications, 1996. 116 pp.

Chávez-Vásquez creates a world for children as seen through Mariel's eyes (the
protagonist). As the young heroine, she makes contact with nature through a fairy
tale book.

Original title: *AKUM: La magia de los sueños.* Colombia.

N C7
Cunha, Helena Parente. *Woman between Mirrors*. Trans. Fred P. Ellison and Naomi Lindstrom. Austin: University of Texas Press, 1989. 132 pp.
This work explores female identity and personality through an inner dialogue.
Original title: *Mulher no Espelho*. Brazil.

N D1
de la Cuesta, Barbara. *The Gold Mine*. Pittsburgh, PA: Latin American Literary Review Press, 1989. 160 pp.
A Latin American social reformer and an American school teacher fall in love and abandon their idealism to seek wealth in the gold mines of the Andes. Chapter I was originally published as "Ordóñez" in the *California Quarterly*, winter 1987, no. 30 (pages 68-77).
Originally written in English. United States.

N D1.1
——. *If There Weren't So Many of Them You Might Say They Were Beautiful*. Delhi, NY: Birch Bark Press, 1992. 60 pp.
The author tells the story of inmates at a nursing home in Massachusetts where she once worked. Includes original artwork by the author.
Originally written in English. United States.

N D2
de la Parra, Teresa. *Iphigenia: The Diary of a Young Lady Who Wrote Because She Was Bored*. Trans. Bertie Acker. Austin: University of Texas Press, 1994. 354 pp.
After a young girl's inheritance is stolen by a family member, she is forced to leave France where she was raised and travel to Venezuela. She describes her journey into adulthood.
Original title: *Ifigenia*. Venezuela.

N D2.1
——. *Mama Blanca's Memoirs: The Classic Novel of a Venezuelan Girlhood*. Trans. Harriet de Onís. Pittsburgh, PA: University of Pittsburgh Press, 1993: Washington, DC: Pan American Union, 1959. 183 pp.
Recollections of the author's childhood on a sugar plantation.
Original title: *Memorias de Mama Blanca*. Venezuela.

N D3
de Queiroz, Rachel. *Dora, Doralina*. Trans. Dorothy Scott Loos. New York: Avon, 1984. 281 pp.
The story of Dora, a Brazilian woman who attempts to find her independence when such efforts are difficult for women.
Original title: *Dôra, Doralina: romance*. Brazil.

N D3.1

de Queiroz, Rachel . *The Three Marías.* Trans. Fred P. Ellison. Austin: University of Texas Press, 1963. 178 pp.
The Marías of the title are three girls who were friends in the convent. They are María Augusta, the narrator, María José, and María Glória. This is the story about their time in school and their lives after they left.
Original title: *Tres Marías.* Brazil.

N D4

de Quiroga, Giancarla. *Aurora.* Trans. Kathy S. Leonard. Seattle, WA: Women in Translation, 1999. 178 pp.
Aurora, a young Bolivian girl, elopes with her lover and finds a new and challenging life in the Bolivian countryside. She grows from a timid and inexperienced girl to a strong and self-sufficient woman.
Original title: *La flor de "La Candelaria."* Bolivia.

N D5

del Río, Ana María. *Carmen's Rust.* Trans. Michael J. Lazzara. Woodstock, NY: Overlook Duckworth, 2003. 128 pp.
A political allegory dealing with General Augusto Pinochet's dictatorship in Chile.
Original title: *Óxido de Carmen.* Chile.

N D6

del Valle, Rosamel. *Eva, the Fugitive.* Trans. Anna Balakian. Berkeley: University of California Press, 1990. 105 pp.
Originally written in 1930 and published posthumously in 1970. This is the first translation of the work that is a first-person narrative in which the outside world intrudes on inner reality.
Original title: *Eva y la fuga.* Chile.

N D7

Delgado, Ana María. *The Room In-Between.* Trans. Sylvia Ehrlich Lipp. Pittsburgh, PA: Latin American Literary Review Press, 1996. 91 pp.
A woman confronts her fears stemming from her unhappy childhood as she waits at her dying mother's bedside. Winner of the 1988 Letras de Oro prize for fiction.
Original title: *La habitación de por medio.* Puerto Rico.

N D8

Díaz Lozano, Argentina. *And We Have to Live.* Trans. Lillian Sears. Palos Verdes, CA: Morgan Press, 1978. 181 pp.
A fictional account of Guatemalan history.
Original title: *Y tenemos que vivir.* Honduras.

N D8.1

Díaz Lozano, Argentina. *Henriqueta and I.* Trans. Harriet de Onis. London: D.
 Dobson, 1945. 152 pp.
The story of a young girl and her life in Honduras with her school-teacher mother.
Original Title: *Peregrinaje.* Honduras.

N D8.2

——. *Mayapan.* Trans. Lydia Wright. Indian Hills, CO: Falcon's Wing Press, 1955.
 185 pp.
A fictionalized version of Hernán Cortés' conquest of the new world. Based on the
true adventures of two survivors of the brigantine lost in the Caribbean in 1511,
Jerónimo de Aguiolar and Gonzalo Guyerrero.
Original title: *Mayapan.* Honduras.

N D9

Domecq, Brianda. *The Astonishing Story of the Saint of Cabora.* Trans. Kay García.
 Tempe, AZ: Bilingual Review Press, 1998. 304 pp.
A fictional recreation of the life of Teresa Urrea, a Mexican heroine who showed
healing powers at a young age.
Original title: *Insólita historia de la Santa de Cabora.* Mexico.

N D9.1

——. *Eleven Days.* Trans. Kay S. García. Albuquerque: University of New Mexico
 Press, 1995. 226 pp.
Based on the true story of Domecq's kidnapping when she was held for eleven days.
A psychological study of the effects of violent crime.
Original title: *Once días.* Mexico.

N D10

Durán, Gloria. *María de Estrada: Gypsy Conquistadora.* Pittsburgh, PA: Latin
 American Literary Review Press, 1999.
The fictionalized biography of a woman from Spain, trained in swordsmanship by
gypsies, who flees the Inquisition to then join forces with Hernán Cortés in his conquest
of Mexico.
Originally written in English.

N E1

Eltit, Diamela. *Custody of the Eyes.* Trans. Helen Lane and Ronald Christ. Santa Fe,
 NM: Lumen Books, 2006. 72 pp.
An exploration, in experiemental prose, of the climate of vigilance as it relates to
family relations as well as to societal norms disrupted by the dictatorship of Pinochet
in Chile.
Original title: *Los vigilantes.* Chile.

N E1.1

Eltit, Diamela. *E. Luminata.* Trans. Ronald Christ with the collaboration of Gene Bell-Villada, Helen Lane, and Catalina Parra. Santa Fe, NM: Lumen, Inc., 1997. 240 pp.

An experimental novel that portrays a series of scenes that raise issues of concern, such as how the dictatorship has affected individuals and society.

Original title: *Lumpérica.* Chile.

N E1.2

——. *The Fourth World.* Trans. Dick Gerdes. Lincoln: University of Nebraska Press, 1995. 113 pp.

The story of a Chilean family's disintegration mirrored by the breakdown of Chilean society under the rule of Pinochet. Includes an introduction by Dick Gerdes.

Original title: *El cuarto mundo.* Chile.

N E1.3

——. *Sacred Cow.* Trans. Amanda Hopkinson. London: Serpent's Tail, 1995. 106 pp.

Set in Santiago, Chile, with the backdrop of political repression, this is the story of Ana who questions the connection between her sexual cravings and the mistreatment of women in Chilean society.

Original title: *La vaca sagrada.* Chile.

N E2

Engle, Margarita. *Singing to Cuba.* Houston, TX: Arte Público Press, 1993. 164 pp.

A woman returns to Cuba to discover the truth about her family.

Originally written in English. Cuba.

N E2.1

——. *Skywriting: A Novel of Cuba.* New York: Bantam Books, 1996. 288 pp.

The attempts of the narrator's half-brother to flee Cuba and his subsequent imprisonment.

Originally written in English. Cuba.

N E3

Escalante, Beatriz. *Magdalena, A Fable of Immortality.* Trans. Jay Miskowiec. Minneapolis, MN: Aliform Publishing, 2002. 126 pp.

A fable that traces a metaphoric pilgrimage by María Magdalena as she searches for a secret paradise.

Original title: *Fábula de la inmortalidad.* Mexico.

N E4

Esquivel, Laura. *The Law of Love.* Trans. Margaret Sayers Peden. New York: Crown Publishers, 1996. 266 pp.

The story of Azucena who meets her soul mate, Rodrigo, and shares a night of passion. She then must search for him across the galaxy through past lives. The reader is cued to listen to music throughout the book. Accompanied by a CD of Puccini arias and Mexican danzones.
Original title: *La ley del amor.* Mexico.

N E4.1
Esquivel, Laura. *Like Water for Chocolate: A Novel in Monthly Installments, with Recipes, Romances, and Home Remedies.* Trans. Carol Christensen and Thomas Christensen. New York: Doubleday, 1992. 245 pp.
The story of Tita and Pedro in turn-of-the-century Mexico. Tita cannot marry Pedro as custom dictates the youngest daughter must care for her mother until her death.
Original title: *Como agua para chocolate.* Mexico.

N E4.2
————. *Swift as Desire.* New York: Anchor; Knopf Publishing Group, 2002. 208 pp.
The story of Júbilo, a man who is able to sense the feelings of others and bring them happiness. However, he is unable to do the same for his own wife.
Original title: *Tan veloz como el deseo.* Mexico.

N F1
Fagundes Telles, Lygia. *The Girl in the Photograph.* Trans. Margaret A. Neves. New York: Avon Books, 1982. 247 pp.
Narrated by three different girls, this is the story of Lia, who is in love with an imprisoned guerilla.
Original title: *As meninas.* Brazil.

N F1.1
————. *The Marble Dance.* Trans. Margaret A. Neves. New York: Avon Books, 1986. 184 pp.
The story of three sisters and their romantic relationships which include infidelity, adultery and moral conflict.
Original title: *Ciranda de pedra.* Brazil.

N F2
Felinto, Marilene. *The Women of Tijucopapo.* Trans. Irene Matthews. Lincoln and London: University of Nebraska Press, 1994. 132 pp.
A young woman wanders through the forest in an attempt to return to Tijucopapo where her mother was born and abandoned.
Original title: *Mulheres de Tijucopapo.* Brazil.

N F3
Ferré, Rosario. *Eccentric Neighborhoods.* New York: Farrar, Straus, and Giroux, 1998; New York: Plume, 1999. 336 pp.; London: Abacus, 2000. 352 pp.

Puerto Rico's transformation from an agricultural society to an industrial one. Original title: *Vecindarios eccéntricos*. Puerto Rico.

N F3.1

Ferré, Rosario. *Flight of the Swan*. New York: Plume; Penguin Group, 2002. 272 pp.
A Russian ballerina is stranded in Puerto Rico due to political events in her country; while there, she falls in love with a revolutionary. Originally written in English. Puerto Rico.

N F3.2

———. *The House on the Lagoon*. Trans. Rosario Ferré. New York: Farrar, Straus & Giroux, 1995. 407 pp.
The exploration of the antagonism as well as the mutual dependence between literature and history.
Original title: *La casa de la laguna*. Puerto Rico.

N F3.3

———. *Sweet Diamond Dust: A Novel and Three Stories of Life in Puerto Rico*. Trans. Rosario Ferré. New York: Ballantine Books, 1988. 197 pp.
Includes the novel *Sweet Diamond Dust* and the stories "The Gift," "Isolda's Mirror," and *Captain Candelario's Heroic Last Stand*.
Original title: *Maldito amor*. Puerto Rico.

N F4

Freilich de Segal, Alicia. *Cláper*. Trans. Joan E. Friedman. Albuquerque: University of New Mexico Press, 1998. 182 pp.
The story of a Jewish family in Venezuela as told by the father. The novel deals with the struggles between first- and second-generation family members.
Original title: *Cláper*. Venezuela.

N G1

Galvão, Patricia (Pagu). *Industrial Park: A Proletarian Novel*. Trans. Elizabeth and Kenneth David Jackson. Lincoln: University of Nebraska Press, 1993. 153 pp.
Originally published in 1933, this work was written as communist propaganda supporting the workers' movement in Brazil. Includes a translators' preface and afterword.
Original title: *Parque Industrial*. Brazil.

N G2

Gambaro, Griselda. *The Impenetrable Madam X*. Trans. Evelyn Picon Garfield. Detroit: Wayne State University Press, 1991. 149 pp.
Set in 19th century Spain, the author satirizes the battle of the sexes and explores the female libido.

Original title: *Lo impenetrable.* Argentina.

N G3
García, Cristina. *The Agüero Sisters.* New York: Alfred A. Knopf, 1997. 300 pp.
The story of two very different Cuban sisters who have been estranged for thirty years.
Originally written in English. Cuba.

N G3.1
———. *Dreaming in Cuban.* New York: Ballantine Books, 1992. 146 pp.
Set in Havana and Brooklyn, a chronicle of three generations of a Cuban family.
Originally written in English. Cuba.

N G3.2
———. *A Handbook to Luck.* New York: Random House, Inc., 2007. 288 pp.
A three-part story with three main characters, one based in Los Angeles and Las Vegas,
one in Iran, and one in El Salvador. All ultimately end up in Los Angeles.
Originally written in English. Cuba.

N G3.3
———. *Monkey Hunting.* New York: Ballantine Books, 2004. 269 pp.
Chen Pan leaves China to work in Cuba and finds himself a slave in the sugar cane
fields. The story of his family through various generations in Cuba, China, and the
United States.
Originally written in English. Cuba.

N G4
García Ramis, Magali. *Happy Days, Uncle Sergio.* Trans. Carmen C. Esteves.
    Fredonia, NY: White Pine Press, 1995. 175 pp.
Narrated by a young girl, the story of a visit by an uncle from New York to a Puerto
Rican family.
Original title: *Felices días, tío Sergio.* Puerto Rico.

N G5
Garro, Elena. *First Love and Look for My Obituary: Two Novellas.* Trans. David
    Unger. Willimantic, CT: Curbstone Press, 1997. 99 pp.
The book includes two novellas. *First Love* details the consequences of two tourists
befriending German prisoners of war in France. *Look for My Obituary* explores a
love affair that takes place in a world of arranged marriages. Winner of the 1996 Sor
Juana Inés de la Cruz Prize.
Original titles: *Primer amor* and *Busca mi esquela.* Mexico.

N G5.1
———. *Recollections of Things to Come.* Trans. Ruth C. Simms. Austin: University
    of Texas Press, 1969. 289 pp.

A tale of the violent era of the Cristero Revolution in Mexico and its impact on the local populations.
Original title: *Los recuerdos del porvenir*. Mexico.

N G6

Glantz, Margo. *The Family Tree: An Illustrated Novel.* Trans. Susan Bassnett. London: Serpent's Tail, 1991. 186 pp.
The author tells of her dual heritage which involves prerevolutionary Russia and subsequently her parents' immigration to Mexico.
Original title: *Las genealogías*. Mexico.

N G6.1

——. *The Wake.* Trans. Andrew Hurley. Willimantic, CT: Curbstone Press, 2005. 123 pp.
A woman returns to Mexico to attend the funeral of her former husband.
Original title: *Rastro*. Mexico.

N G7

Gómez de Avellaneda y Arteaga, Gertrudis. *Cuauhtemoc: The Last Aztec Emperor, an Historical Novel.* Trans. Mrs. Wilson W. Blake. Mexico: F.P. Hoeck, 1898. 389 pp.
Not available for annotation.
Original Title: *Guatimozin, último emperador de México*. Cuba.

N G7.1

——. *Sab, an Autobiography.* Trans. Nina F. Scott. Austin: University of Texas Press, 1993. 157 pp.
First published in Spain in 1841, this is an exploration of patriarchal oppression of minorities and women. A love story between a mulatto slave and the daughter of his white owner.
Original title: *Sab*. Cuba.

N G8

Gómez Rul, Ana María. *Lol-Há: A Maya Tale.* Trans. Margaret Redfield. Mexico: Ed. Cultura, 1935. 44 pp.
Includes a Maya-English glossary.
Original title: *Lol-Há: un cuento maya.* Mexico.

N G9

Gorodischer, Angélica. *Kalpa Imperial: The Greatest Empire That Never Was.* Trans. Ursula K. Le Guin. Northampton: Small Beer Press, 2003. 246 pp.
Numerous storytellers relate the story of an empire with no name which rises and falls a number of times. Political commentary, oral histories, and fairy tales are seamlessly woven into the narrative.

Original title: *Kalpa Imperial*. Argentina.

N G10

Guerra Cunningham, Lucía. *Más allá de la máscaras. (Beyond the Masks).* Pittsburgh, PA: Latin American Literary Review Press, 1986. 88 pp.

A young woman relates the story of her journey which takes her from being a responsible married woman, mother, and journalist, to her new life as a sexual rebel. Original title: *Beyond the Masks.* Chile.

N G10.1

——. *The Street of Night.* Trans. Richard Cunningham. Reading, Berkshire, UK: Garnet Publishers, 1997. 207 pp.

Set in Chile in 1985 when all but the prostitutes are under the absolute control of a dictator. Original title: *Muñeca brava.* Chile.

N G11

Guido, Beatriz. *End of a Day.* Trans. A. D. Towers. New York: Scribner, 1966. 278 pp.

The story of the Praderes, a wealthy Argentine family during the dictatorship of Perón. Hoping to maintain their wealth, members of the family work with a government they oppose. Original title: *El incendio y las vísperas.* Argentina.

N G11.1

——. *The House of the Angel.* Trans. Joan Coyne MacLean. New York: McGraw-Hill, 1957. 174 pp.

The author's first book; the story of Buenos Aires high society in the 1920s. Original title: *La casa del ángel.* Argentina.

N G12

Gutiérrez Richaud, Cristina. Trans. Michael B. Miller. *Woman with Short Hair and Great Legs.* (Forthcoming).

A woman who is possessed by uncontrollable rage questions her obligations and her dreams. Original title: *Mujer de cabellos cortos y buenas piernas.* Mexico.

N H1

Herrera, Andrea O'Reilly. *The Pearl of the Antilles.* Tempe, AZ: Bilingual Review Press, 2001. 353 pp.

Set in Cuba and the United States, this is the story of Margarita and her family, as told through the letters of Margarita's mother, Rosa. Originally written in English. Cuba.

N I1

Iparraguierre, Sylvia. *Tierra del fuego*. Trans. Hardie St. Martin. Willimantic, CT: Curbstone Press, 2000. 199 pp.
Based on the story of Jemmy Button, an Indian from Cabo de Hornos who lived in London in 1830.
Original title: *La tierra del fuego*. Argentina.

N J1

Jacobs, Barbara. *The Dead Leaves*. Trans. David Unger. Willimantic, CT: Curbstone Press, 1993. 126 pp.
A tribute to an idealistic father with details concerning political and historical events.
Original title: *Las hojas muertas*. Mexico.

N J2

Jorge, Lidia. *The Painter of Birds*. Trans. Margaret Jull Costa. New York: Harcourt, 2001. 233 pp.
A young girl struggles with the memory of her absent father.
Original title: *Vale da paixão*. Brazil.

N J2.1

———. *The Murmuring Coast*. Trans. Natalia Costa and Ronald W. Sousa. Minneapolis: University of Minnesota Press, 1995. 274 pp.
The story of the wedding of a Portuguese ensign in Beira, Mozambique, during the final years of Portugal's colonial African wars.
Original title: *Costa dos murmurios*. Brazil

N K1

Kociancich, Vlady. *The Last Days of William Shakespeare*. Trans. Margaret Jull Costa. New York: Morrow, 1991. 297 pp.
The story of Santiago Bonday, a South American writer who returns home after being exiled to Europe. A satire on the bureaucratic workings in South America.
Original title: *Los últimos días de William Shakespeare*. Argentina.

N K2

Kozameh, Alicia. *Steps under Water*. Trans. David E. Davis. Intro. Saúl Sosnowski. Berkeley: University of California Press, 1996. 149 pp.
A mixture of letters, testimony, and memories that tell the story of Alicia Kozameh's experiences as a political prisoner in Argentina during the Dirty War of the 1970s.
Original title: *Los pasos bajo el agua*. Argentina.

N K2.1

———. *Two Hundred Fifty-nine Leaps, the Last Immortal*. Trans. Clare E. Sullivan. San Antonio, TX: Wings Press, 2006. 185 pp.
Unavailable for annotation.

Original title: *259 saltos, uno inmortal*. Argentina.

N L1

Lamazares, Ivonne. *The Sugar Island*. Boston: Houghton, 2000. 205 pp.
A Cuban family escapes to Miami on a raft.
Originally written in English. Cuba.

N L2

Levinson, Luisa Mercedes. *In the Shadow of the Owl*. Trans. Sylvia Ehrlich Lipp.
    Barcelona: Salvat, 1989. 211 pp.
Staged in three parts, 1800s, 1960s, and 1980s, this is the story of the women of one
family through various generations.
Original title: *A la sombra del buho*. Argentina.

N L3

Lispector, Clarice. *The Apple in the Dark*. Trans. Gregory Rabassa. New York: Alfred
    A. Knopf, Inc., 1967; London: Virago, 1985. 361 pp.
Lispector's fourth novel to be published, and the first to be translated into English.
Set in Northeast Brazil, this is the story of Martim, a man searching for a new beginning
who finds work on a farm and enters into a complicated relationship with the two
women living there.
Original title: *Maçã no escuro*. Brazil.

N L3.1

———. *An Apprenticeship, or, The Book of Delights*. Trans. Richard A. Mazzare and
    Lori A. Parris. Austin: University of Texas Press, 1986. 126 pp.
The story of Ulysses, a lecturer in philosophy, and Lori, a school teacher. Ulyssess
helps Lori find herself and lose her inhibitions.
Original title: *Uma aprendizagem; ou, O livro dos prazeres*. Brazil.

N L3.2

———. *The Besieged City*. Trans. Giovanni Pontiero. Manchester, UK: Carcanet, 1999.
    196 pp.
A novel that details women's emotions and explores how they are suffocated by society.
Original title: *Cidade sitiada*. Brasil.

N L3.3

———. *Discovering the World*. Trans. Giovanni Pontiero. Manchester, UK: Carcanet,
    1992. 652 pp.
A variety of genres compiled into one book. Lispector takes the reader through the
various stages of womanhood.
Original title: *A descoberta do mundo*. Brazil.

N L3.4

Lispector, Clarice. *The Hour of the Star.* Trans. Giovanni Pontiero. Manchester, UK: Carcanet, 1986. 96 pp.

The story of Macabea, a young woman from the country who moves to the city and takes up residence in the red light district. She is ultimately killed by a Mercedes. Original title: *A hora da estrela.* Brazil.

N L3.5

———. *Near to the Wild Heart.* Trans. Giovanni Pontiero. Manchester, UK: Carcanet, 1990. 192 pp.

Lispector's first novel, published in 1944. The story of Joana and her unhappy marriage which ultimately fails.
Original title: *Perto do coração sellvagem.* Brazil.

N L3.6

———. *The Passion According to G.H.* Trans. Ronald W. Souza. Minneapolis: University of Minnesota Press, 1988. 173 pp.

An erudite novel that has a single character. The first person narrative plays with the nature of words.
Original title: *A paixão segundo G.H.* Brazil.

N L3.7

———. *The Stream of Life.* Trans. Elizabeth Lowe and Earl Fitz. Minneapolis: University of Minnesota Press, 1989. 79 pp.

Philosophical investigations through interior monologue. A woman writes a letter to someone called "you."
Original title: *Agua viva.* Brazil.

N L4

Lobo, Tatiana. *Assault on Paradise.* Trans. Asa Zatz. Willimantic, CT: Curbstone Press, 1998. 297 pp.

The invasion of Central America by the Spanish conquerors and the church. The story of politicians and struggles between the invaders and the native population. Winner of the 1995 Sor Juana Inés de la Cruz Prize.
Original title: *Asalto al paraíso.* Chile.

N L5

Luft, Lya Fett. *The Island of the Dead.* Trans. Carmen Chaves McClendon and Betty Jean Craige. Atlanta: University of Georgia Press, 1986. 106 pp.

An exploration of human relationships and societal pressures.
Original title: *O quarto fechado.* Brazil.

N L5.1
Luft, Lya Fett. *The Red House*. Trans. Giovanni Pontiero. Manchester, UK: Carcanet, 1994. 182 pp.
This book explores the various roles of women in society.
Original title: *Exilio*. Brazil.

N M1
Mastretta, Ángeles. *Lovesick*. Trans. Margaret Sayers Peden. New York: Riverhead Books, 1997. 292 pp.
Set in Puebla, Mexico, the story spans fifty years of history. Emilia is a young woman who loves two men, one stable, the other a revolutionary.
Original title: *Mal de amores*. Mexico.

N M1.1
———. *Mexican Bolero*. Trans. Ann Wright. New York: Viking, 1989. 267 pp.
A love story and marriage between Catalina and Andrés Ascencio, who turns out to be unfaithful. As Andrés succeeds politically, Catalina discovers her inner strengths.
Original title: *Arráncame la vida*. Mexico.

N M1.2
———. *Tear This Heart Out*. Trans. Margaret Sayers Peden. New York: Riverhead Books, 1997.
A love story and marriage between Catalina and Andrés Ascencio, who turns out to be unfaithful. As Andrés succeeds politically, Catalina discovers her inner strengths.
Original title: *Arráncame la vida*. Mexico.

N M1.3
———. *Women with Big Eyes*. Trans. Amy Schildhouse. New York: Riverhead Books, 2003. 384 pp.
A series of interrelated stories about eccentric women with special powers.
Original title: *Mujeres de ojos grandes*. Mexico.

N M2
Matto de Turner, Clorinda. *Birds without a Nest; A Story of Indian Life and Priestly Oppression in Peru*. Trans. J. C. H. London: C.J. Thynne, 1904. Transemended by Naomi Lindstrom, 1996. Austin: University of Texas Press, 1996. 181 pp.
The relationship between the landed gentry and the indigenous peoples of the Andean mountain communities is explored. First published in Peru in 1889.
Original title: *Aves sin nido*. Peru

N M2.1
———. *Torn from the Nest*. Trans. John H. R. Polt. Oxford: Oxford University Press, 1998. 288 pp.

The relationship between the landed gentry and the indigenous peoples of the Andean mountain communities is explored. First published in Peru in 1889. Edited with a foreword and chronology by Antonio Cornejo Polar.
Original title: *Aves sin nido*. Peru.

N M3
Medina, C. C. *A Little Love*. New York: Warner, 2000. 352 pp.
The story of four wealthy Hispanic Miami women as they share the ups and downs of their romantic relationships.
Originally written in English.

N M4
Melo, Patricia. *Black Waltz*. Trans. Clifford E. Landers. London: Bloomsbury, 2005. 209 pp.
A conductor fears his violinist wife is having an affair, which threatens his sanity.
Original title: *Valsa negra*. Brazil.

N M4.1
———. *The Killer*. Trans. Clifford E. Landers. Hopewell, NJ: Ecco Press, 1997. 217 pp.
A young used car salesman becomes a hit man in exchange for free dental care and soon has more business than he can handle.
Original title: *Matador*. Brazil.

N M5
Menéndez, Ana. *Loving Che*. New York: Atlantic Monthly, 2003. 229 pp.
The narrator's mother had an affair with Che and she is told that she is his daughter. She then travels to Cuba to verify the story.
Originally written in English. Cuba.

N M6
Miranda, Ana. *Bay of All Saints and Every Conceivable Sin*. Trans. Giovanni Pontiero. London: Harvill, 1992; New York: Viking, 1991. 305 pp.
The story of 17th century Brazil under Portuguese rule.
Original title: *Boca do inferno*. Brazil.

N M7
Molina, Silvia. *Gray Skies Tomorrow: A Novel*. Trans. John Mitchell and Ruth Mitchell de Aguilar. Kaneohe, HI: Plover Press, 1993. 104 pp.
The story of first love and the sorrow it leaves behind.
Original title: *La mañana debe seguir gris*. Mexico.

N M7.1
Molina, Silvia. *The Love You Promised Me.* Trans. David Unger. Willimantic, CT: Curbstone Press, 1999. 228 pp.
The story of Marcela, an advertising executive, and her extramarital affair in Mexico in the mid-1990s.
Original title: *El amor que me juraste.* Mexico.

N M8
Molloy, Sylvia. *Certificate of Absence.* Trans. Daniel Balderston. Austin: University of Texas, 1989. 125 pp.
The narrator of the book is a woman writing in a small room, remembering a former relationship and thinking of one in the future. As she writes she reflects on the dual powers of love.
Original title: *En breve cárcel.* Argentina.

N M9
Mondragón Aguirre, Magdalena. *Someday the Dream.* Trans. Samuel Putnam. New York: Dial Press, 1947. 240 pp.
Life in the garbage dumps of Mexico City.
Original title: *Yo como pobre.* Mexico.

N M10
Montero, Mayra. *Captain of the Sleepers.* Trans. Edith Grossman. New York: Farrar, Straus and Giroux, 2005. 181 pp.
A dying man wishes to tell his story about an affair with a former friend's mother.
Original title: *Capitán de los dormidos.* Cuba.

N M10.1
——. *Dancing to Almendra.* Trans. Edith Grossman. New York: Farrar, Straus and Giroux, 2007.
A young reporter is assigned to cover the death of a hippopotamus at the Havana Zoo and finds himself involved in a mobster's death.
Original title: *Son de Almendra.* Cuba.

N M10.2
——. *Deep Purple: A Novel.* Trans. Edith Grossman. New York: HarperCollins Publishers, 2003. 182 pp.
A music critic who has slept with numerous great musicians decides to write his sexual memoirs upon his retirement.
Original title: *Púrpura profundo.* Cuba.

N M10.3
——. *In the Palm of Darkness: A Novel.* Trans. Edith Grossman. New York: HarperFlamingo, 1997. 181 pp.

Set in Haiti, the story of an American herpetologist who must deal with his emotional alienation.
Original title: *Tú, la oscuridad*. Cuba.

N M10.4
Montero, Mayra. *The Last Night I Spent with You*. Trans. Edith Grossman. New York: HarperCollins, 2000. 128 pp.
Marital problems develop between a couple haunted by past infidelities.
Original title: *La última noche que pasé contigo*. Cuba.

N M10.5
——. *The Messenger*. Trans. Edith Grossman. New York: HarperPerennial Library, 2000. 224 pp.
Based on real events, the Italian tenor Caruso disappears for a weekend after a bomb explodes in the Teatro Nacional in Havana.
Original title: *Como un mensajero tuyo*. Cuba.

N M10.6
——. *The Moon Line*. Trans. Kathryn Renée Dussan. MA Thesis, University of Puerto Rico, 1993. 196 pp.
The initiation and training of a voodoo priest in Haiti.
Original title: *La trenza de la hermosa luna*. Cuba.

N M10.7
——. *The Red of His Shadow*. Trans. Edith Grossman. New York: HarperCollins, 2001. 159 pp.
Set in the Dominican Republic, the story of two powerful spiritual leaders, Mistress Zulé, a Voudon priestess, and Similá Bolosse, a rival Voudon priest.
Original title: *Del rojo de su sombra*. Cuba.

N M10.8
——. *You, Darkness*. Trans. Edith Grossman. London: The Harvill Press, 1997. 182 pp.
Set in Haiti, the story of an American herpetologist who must deal with his emotional alienation.
Original title: *Tú, la oscuridad*. Cuba.

N N1
Novas, Himilce. *Don't Look Back*. New York: Steck-Vaughn Company, 1995. 64 pp.
Two friends experience an adventurous weekend. Adolescent literature.
Originally written in English. Cuba.

N N1.1

Novas, Himilce. *Mangos, Bananas and Coconuts: A Cuban Love Story.* Houston,
TX: Arte Público Press, 1997. 168 pp.
The story of a Cuban farm worker with special healing powers.
Originally written in English. Cuba.

N N2

Nunes, Lygia Bojunga. *The Companions.* Trans. Ellen Watson. New York: Farrar,
Straus & Giroux, 1989. 57 pp.
A rabbit, a bear, and a dog meet on a beach where they form a friendship. Their lives
are altered when they return to their homes. Illustrated by Larry Wilkes. Winner of
the 1982 Hans Christian Andersen Award.
Original title: *Os colegas.* Brazil.

N N2.1

——. *My Friend the Painter.* Trans. Giovanni Pontiero. Orlando, FL: Harcourt Brace,
1991. 85 pp.
The story of a young boy named Claudio who forms a friendship with a painter who
teaches him to see as an artist.
Original title: *Meu amigo pinto.* Brazil.

N O1

Obejas, Achy. *Days of Awe.* New York: Ballantine Books, 2001. 371 pp.
An exploration of the issues of exile and return of a Jewish Cuban family.
Originally written in English. Cuba.

N O1.1

——. *Memory Mambo.* San Francisco: Cleis Press, 1996. 249 pp.
Juani, a 24 year-old lesbian, is obsessed with memory as she struggles to deal with
family relationships. Includes a Spanish-English glossary of Cuban terms.
Originally written in English. Cuba.

N O2

Orphée, Elvira. *El Angel's Last Conquest.* Trans. Magda Bogin. New York: Ballantine
Books, 1985. 142 pp.
The story of an Argentine torturer.
Original title: *La última conquista de El Ángel.* Argentina.

N O3

Ortiz Cofer, Judith. *Call Me María: A Novel.* New York: Orchard Books, 2004. 127
pp.
A young girl leaves her home in Puerto Rico to live with her father in a New York
neighborhood. Juvenile fiction.
Originally written in English. Puerto Rico.

N O3.1

Ortiz Cofer, Judith. *The Line of the Sun: A Novel*. Athens: University of Georgia Press, 1988. 291 pp.

The author's first novel, the story of a Puerto Rican family's struggles to adapt to life in the United States.

Originally written in English. Puerto Rico.

N O3.2

——. *The Meaning of Consuelo*. Boston: Beacon Press, 2004. 196 pp.

The story of two very different sisters in a Puerto Rican family.

Originally written in English. Puerto Rico.

N O4

Osorio, Elsa. *My Name Is Light*. Trans. Catherine Jagoe. London: Bloomsbury, 2004. 388 pp.

A fictional account of the children of the *desaparecidos* in Argentina.

Original title: *Mi nombre es Luz*. Argentina.

N P1

Perez, Loida Maritza. *Geographies of Home*. London: Penguin, 2000. 321 pp.

After finishing college, a young woman returns home to Brooklyn to find her family suffering from a number of problems.

Originally written in English. Dominican Republic.

N P2

Peri Rossi, Cristina. *Dostoevsky's Last Night*. Trans. Laura Dail. New York: Picador, USA, 1995. 180 pp.

The story of Jorge, an obsessive gambler, and the role that chance plays in life.

Original title: *La última noche de Dostoievski*. Uruguay.

N P2.1

——. *The Ship of Fools*. Trans. Psiche Hughes. London: Allison and Busby, 1989. 205 pp.

A novel dealing with the themes of sex and power, which are presented in a series of ambiguous events.

Original title: *La nave de los locos*. Uruguay.

N P2.2

——. *Solitaire of Love*. Trans. Robert S. Rubber and Gloria Arjona. Raleigh, NC: Duke University Press, 2000. 120 pp.

Peri Rossi follows the evolution of a love affair and sexual obsession.

Original title: *Solitario de amor*. Uruguay.

N P3

Petit, Magdalena. *La quintrala*. Trans. Lulú Vargas Vila. New York: Macmilan, 1942. 190 pp.

An historical novel which tells the story of Doña Catalina de los Ríos. Half Indian and the daughter of the Corregidor of Santiago, she poisoned her father when she was a teenager.

Original title: *La quintrala*. Chile.

N P4

Piñón, Nélida. *Caetana's Sweet Song*. Trans. Helen Lane. New York: Knopf, 1992. 401 pp.

Caetana returns to Trinidade, a Brazilian town, to make her acting comeback.

Original title: *Doce cancão de Cartana*. Brazil.

N P4.1

——. *The Republic of Dreams: A Novel*. Trans. Helen Lane. New York: Knopf, 1989; Austin: University of Texas Press, 1991. 663 pp.

The story of four generations of one family led by an iron-willed patriarch from Spain who immigrated to Brazil.

Original title: *A republica dos sonhos*. Brazil.

N P5

Poletti, Syria. *The King Who Forbade Balloons*. Trans. Norman Thomas di Giovanni and Susan Ashe. Buenos Aires: Arte Gaglianone,1987. 33 pp.

Children's fiction. Illustrated by Carlos Manso.

Original title: *El rey que prohibió los globos*. Argentina.

N P6

Poniatowska, Elena. *Dear Diego*. Trans. Katherine Silver. New York: Pantheon Books, 1986. 87 pp.

The story of Diego Rivero, the Mexican muralist.

Original title: *Querido Diego, te abraza Quiela*. Mexico.

N P6.1

——. *Here's to You, Jesusa!* Trans. Deanna Heikkinen. New York: Farrar, Straus and Giroux, 2001. 303 pp.

The story of an illiterate Mexican woman, based on conversations with Poniatowska.

Original title: *Hasta no verte, Jesús mío*. Mexico.

N P6.2

——. *Massacre in Mexico*. Trans. Helen R. Lane. New York: Viking Press, 1975. 333 pp.

The 1968 massacre of students in Mexico City.

Original title: *La noche de Tlatelolco: Testimonios de historia oral*. Mexico.

N P6.3

Poniatowska, Elena. *Nothing, Nobody: The Voices of the Mexico City Earthquake.* Trans. Aurora Camacho de Schmidt and Arthur Schmidt. Philadelphia, PA: Temple University Press, 1995. 327 pp.

Documentation of the Mexico City earthquake of September 19, 1985. Weaving together a multitude of voices, Poniatowska uses testimonies to tell the many stories of the survivors.

Original title: *Nada, nadie.* Mexico.

N P6.4

——. *The Skin of the Sky.* Trans. Deanna Heikkinen. New York: Farrar, Straus & Giroux, 2004. 322 pp.

The story of Lorenzo de Tena's life, a Mexican astronomer.

Original title: *Piel del cielo.* Mexico.

N P6.5

——. *Tinísmia: A Novel.* Trans. Kathleen Silver. New York: Farrar, Straus & Giroux, 1996. 357 pp.

The novel is based on the life of the Italian photographer Tina Modotti.

Original title: *Tinísima.* Mexico.

N P6.6

——. *Until We Meet Again.* Trans. Helen Lane. New York: Pantheon, 1987. 300 pp.

Story of an illiterate Mexican woman, based on conversations with Poniatowska.

Original title: *Hasta no verte, Jesús mío.* Mexico.

N P7

Porzecanski, Teresa. *Sun Inventions and Perfumes of Carthage: Two Novellas.* Trans. Johnny Payne and Phyllis Silverstein. Albuquerque: University of New Mexico Press, 2000. 189 pp.

Sun Inventions is the author's first novel and was published in 1982. The story is semi-autobiographical and deals with the life of an immigrant family. *Perfumes of Carthage* was published in 1994 and relates the story of a Sephardic family. Includes an introduction by Ilan Stavans.

Original titles: *Invención de los soles* and *Perfumes de Carthage.* Uruguay.

N P8

Puig Zaldívar, Raquel. *Nothing in Our Hands but Age.* Binghamton, NY: Bilingual Press, 1980. 56 pp.

Offprint *The Bilingual Review/La Revista Bilingüe,* v. 6, no. 2-3 (May/Dec. 1979).

A couple flees Cuba to establish themselves in Miami with the hopes of also freeing their daughter.

Originally written in English. Cuba.

N P8.1

Puig Zaldívar, Raquel. *Women Don't Need to Write.* Houston, TX: Arte Público
 Press, 1998. 352 pp.
A 95 year-old woman looks back on her eventful life.
Originally written in English. Cuba.

N R1

Restrepo, Laura. *The Angel of Galilea.* Trans. Dolores M. Koch. New York:
 Vintage, 1999. 193 pp.
The retelling of the story of a savior who comes from Galilea to save mankind. A
journalist is assigned to investigate the story of an angel forced to perform for
audiences.
Original title: *Dulce compañía.* Colombia.

N R1.1

——. *The Dark Bride.* Trans. Septhen A. Lytle. New York: HarperCollins, 2001.
 358 pp.
The protagonist, a journalist, interviews the inhabitants of a small Colombian oil
town to learn about the local prostitute named Sayonara. Her story evolves through
a series of interviews.
Original title: *La novia oscura.* Colombia.

N R1.2

——. *Delirium.* Trans. Natasha Wimmer. New York: Nan A. Talese/Doubleday,
 2007. 336 pp.
A love story set in Colombia amid the chaos of drug trafficking.
Original title: *Delirio.* Colombia.

N R1.3

——. *Isle of Passion.* Trans. Dolores M. Koch. New York: Ecco, 2005. 298 pp.
Based on a true story, the narrative unfolds as related by a journalist. The story of a
small Pacific island named Clipperton which becomes cut off from the world during
the Mexican Revolution and World War I.
Original title: *Isla de la pasión.* Colombia.

N R1.4

——. *Leopard in the Sun.* Trans. Stephen A. Lytle. New York: Crown Publishers,
 1999. 242 pp.
Two drug families in Colombia commit violence against one another.
Original title: *Leopardo al sol.* Colombia.

N R1.5

——. *A Tale of the Dispossessed.* Trans. Dolores Koch. New York: Ecco, 2003.
 98 pp.

A hotel where refugees can take shelter from violence is the scene of love triangles. Bilingual English/Spanish edition.
Original title: *La multitud errante*. Colombia.

N R2

Rheda, Regina. *First World Third Class and Other Tales of the Global Mix*. Trans. Adria Frizzi, REYoung, David Coles, and Charles A. Perrone. Austin: University of Texas Press, 2005. 304 pp.
This volume contains the novel *First World Third Class* as well as eight tales from *Stories from the Copan Building*. The stories are set in a residential building in São Paulo and reflect modern-day urban Brazil.
Original title: *Pau-de Arara classe turística*. Brazil.

N R3

Ribeiro, Stella Car. *Sambaqui: A Novel of Pre-history*. Trans. Claudia Van der Heuvel. New York: Avon Books, 1987. 132 pp.
A novel set in the last days of prehistoric Sambaquis culture at a time when it confronts extinction by a more advanced tribe.
Original tite: *O homen do Sambqui*. Brazil.

N R4

Riesco, Laura. *Ximena at the Crossroads*. Trans. Mary G. Berg. Fredonia, NY: White Pine Press, 1998. 269 pp.
A coming-of-age story of Ximena, a young Peruvian girl growing up in the 1940s. Selected as the Best Novel of the Year in Peru in 1994.
Original title: *Ximena de dos caminos*. Peru.

N R5

Ríos, Mi-Chelle L. *Chola*. Pittsburgh, PA: Latin American Literary Review Press, 2005. 189 pp.
An 18-year-old Mexican American girl tells her story of a cultural triangle from a jail cell where she waits to stand trial for the murder of the mother's ex-boyfriend. Originally written in English.

N R6

Rivera, Beatriz. *Midnight Sandwiches at the Mariposa Express*. Houston: Arte Público Press, 1997. 118 pp.
Trish Izquierdo, a councilwoman in a small town, does her best to put the town on the map.
Originally written in English. Cuba.

N R6.1

——. *Playing with Light: A Novel*. Houston, TX: Arte Público Press, 2000. 240 pp.
A tale of Cuban-American women in Miami who meet in a reading group to discuss

the novel *Playing with Light* about a family in 19th century Cuba. Originally written in English. Cuba.

N R7

Rivera, Martha. *I've Forgotten Your Name.* Trans. Mary G. Berg. Buffalo, NY: White Pine Press, 2004. 143 pp.

Winner of the International Novel Prize of the Casa de Teatro in 1996. Young Dominicans struggle with their national identity in the wake of a political crisis in the Dominican Republic in 1965.

Original title: *He olvidado tu nombre.* Dominican Republic.

N R8

Robles, Mireya. *Hagiography of Narcisa the Beautiful.* Trans. Anna Diegel with Mireya Robles. Colunbia, LA: Readers International, 1996. 188 pp.

The story of a dysfunctional Cuban family.

Original title: *Hagiografia de Narcisa la bella.* Cuba.

N R9

Rojas, Marta. *Dead Man's Cave.* Trans. Margarita Zimmermann. Havana: José Martí Pub. House, 1988. 146 pp.

An historical novel of Cuba detailing the Moncada Barracks attack.

Original title: *La cueva del muerto.* Cuba.

N R10

Romo-Carmona, Mariana. *Living at Night.* Duluth, MN: Spinsters Ink, 1997. 257 pp.

The story of women orderlies who work at night caring for institutionalized adults while earning a substandard salary.

Originally written in English. Chile.

N S1

Santos-Febres, Mayra. *Any Wednesday I'm Yours.* Trans. James Graham. New York: Riverhead Books, 2005. 288 pp.

San Juan, Puerto Rico, after dark, and the life of four loners in a motel.

Original title: *Cualquier miércoles soy tuya.* Dominican Republic.

N S1.1

———. *Sirena Selena.* Trans. Stephen Lytle. New York: Picador, 2000. 214 pp.

A sensual novel about the gender confusion of the protagonist Selena, a 15 year-old hustler with a beautiful voice.

Original title: *Sirena Selena vestida de pena.* Dominican Republic.

N S2

Schroeder, Agustina. *Mother of Fair Love*. Trans. Veronica Kirtland. Milwaukee, WI: The Bruce Publishing Co., 1957. 182 pp.
Unavailable for annotation. Uruguay.

N S3

Serrano, Marcela. *Antigua and My Life Before*. Trans. Margaret Sayers Peden. New York: Doubleday, 2000. 352 pp.
Original title: *Antigua vida mía*.

N S4

Shua, Ana María. *The Book of Memories*. Trans. Dick Gerdes. Albuquerque: The University of New Mexico Press, 1998. 178 pp.
The story of a Jewish family in Argentina and the trials and tribulations of its various generations.
Original title: *El libro de los recuerdos*. Argentina.

N S4.1

———. *Patient*. Trans. David William Foster. Pittsburgh, PA: Latin American Literary Review Press. 1997. 122 pp.
A patient enters an Argentine hospital and suffers a number of humiliations and frustrations with the system.
Original title: *Soy paciente*. Argentina.

N S5

Silveira de Queiroz, Dinah. *Christ's Memorial*. Trans. Isabel do Prado. London: Sel Books, 1978. 214 pp.
The story of Jesus Christ as He would tell it.
Original title: *Eu venho*. Brazil.

N S5.1

———. *The Women of Brazil*. Trans. Roberta King. New York: Vantage Press, 1980. 289 pp.
The tale of violent events surrounding two men searching for gold in the jungle.
Original title: *A muralha*. Brazil.

N S6

Steimberg, Alicia. *Call Me Magdalena*. Trans. Andrea G. Labinger. Lincoln and London: University of Nebraska Press, 1992. 137 pp.
The story of a young Argentine woman who comes to terms with her childhood memories of growing up in a multicultural and multifaith home.
Original title: *Cuando digo Magdalena*. Argentina.

N S6.1

Steimberg, Alicia. *Musicians and Watchmakers.* Trans. Andrea G. Labinger. Pittsburgh, PA: Latin American Literary Review Press, 1998. 127 pp.

A semi-autobiographical story of a young woman with an eccentric family who comes of age in Buenos Aires in the 1940s.

Original title: *Músicos y relojeros.* Argentina.

N S6.2

———. *The Rainforest.* Trans. Andrea G. Labinger. Lincoln: University of Nebraska Press, 2006. 134 pp.

The story of an Argentine writer who travels to a spa in the Brazilian rain forest in search of healing. There she examines her relationships with three men: her former husband, her son, and her current lover.

Original title: *La selva.* Argentina.

N S7

Strejilevich, Nora. *A Single, Numberless Death.* Trans. Cristina de la Torre and the author. Charlottesville: University of Virginia Press, 2002. 176 pp.

A fictional memoir dealing with the 30,000 disappeared during Argentina's Dirty War.

Original title: *Una sola muerta numerosa.* Argentina.

N S8

Subercaseaux, Elizabeth. *The Song of the Distant Root.* Trans. John J. Hassett. Pittsburgh, PA: Latin American Literary Review Press, 2001. 88 pp.

The story of Satustio who searches for a place he dreamed, called Tapihue, where he can feel a sense of peace and complete a longed-for goal.

Original title: *Canto de la raíz lejana.* Chile.

N T1

Traba, Marta. *Mothers and Shadows.* Trans. Jo Labanji. Columbia, LA: Readers International, 1985. 178 pp.

The story of two women and their experiences during the 1973 coup in Chile and a stint in a Uruguay jail during the time of the "Dirty Wars."

Original title: *Conversación al sur.* Argentina.

N V1

Valdés, Zoe. *Dear First Love.* Trans. Andrew Hurley. New York: HarperCollins Publishers, 2002. 291 pp.

A young girl is sent to the Cuban countryside to work in the fields; there she falls in love.

Original title: *Querido primer novio.* Cuba.

N V1.1

Valdés, Zoe. *I Gave You All I Had*. Trans. Nadia Benabid. London: Arcade Publishing, 1999. 238 pp.

The story of Cuca Martínez, born in prerevolutionary Cuba, and her efforts to survive in Cuba from the 1940s to the present as she waits for her true love.
Original title: *Te di la vida entera*. Cuba.

N V1.2

——. *Yocandra in the Paradise of Nada: A Novel of Cuba*. Trans. Sabina Cienfuegos. London: Arcade Publishing,1999. 192 pp.

The story of Yocandra and her struggles to cope with life in Cuba.
Original title: *La nada cotidiana*. Cuba.

N V2

Valdés-Rodríguez, Alisa. *The Dirty Girls Social Club*. New York: St. Martin's Press, 2003. 316 pp.

A group of Latina friends from Boston College with very different backgrounds continue to meet after graduation to discuss their lives.
Originally written in English. Cuba.

N V3

Valdivieso, Mercedes. *Breakthrough*. Trans. Graciela Daichman. Pittsburgh, PA: Latin American Literary Review Press, 1987. 96 pp.

Originally published in Chile in 1961, this is one of the first feminist novels to be written in Latin America.
Original title: *Brecha*. Chile.

N V4

Valenzuela, Luisa. *Bedside Manners*. Trans. Margaret Jull Costa. London: High Risk Books, 1995. 121 pp.

A political satire where everyday activities are banned for a woman who returns home to supposedly enjoy restored democracy in her country.
Original title: *Realidad nacional desde la cama*. Argentina.

N V4.1

——. *Black Novel (with Argentines)*. Trans. Toby Talbot. New York: Simon & Schuster, 1990. 220 pp.

Set in New York, the story follows the life of an Argentine novelist attempting to write in an unfamiliar and daunting city.
Original title: *Novela negra con argentinos*. Argentina.

N V4.2

——. *Clara*. Trans. Andrea G. Labinger. Pittsburgh, PA: Latin American Literary Review Press, 1999. 159 pp.

The story of Clara, a prostitute in Buenos Aires.
Original title: *Hay que sonreír.* Argentina.

N V4.3

Valenzuela, Luisa. *Clara, Thirteen Short Stories and a Novel.* Trans. Hortense
   Carpentier and J. Jorge Castello. New York: Harcourt, Brace and Javanovich,
   1976. 233 pp.
Includes the novel *Clara* (original title: *Hay que sonreír*) and the following stories:
The Heretics: Nihil obstat; The Door; Trial of the Virgin; City of the Unknown; The
Minstrels; The Son of Kermaria; Forsaken Woman. The Teacher; Irka of the Horses;
The Legend of the Self-sufficient Creature; The Sin of the Apple; The Alphabet; A
Family for Clotilde. Argentina.

N V4.4

——. *He Who Searches.* Trans. Helen Lane. Elmwood Park, IL: The Dalkey Archive
   Press, 1987. 134 pp.
Set in Barcelona, Mexico, and Buenos Aires, the story of a psychologist who frequents
a prostitute in order to analyze her without her knowledge. The themes of love and
violence and erotic pleasure and death are explored in various forms of narrative.
Original Title: *Como en la guerra.* Argentina.

N V4.5

——. *The Lizard's Tail.* Trans. Gregory Rabassa. New York: Farrar, Straus & Giroux,
   1983; London: Serpent's Tail, 1987. 279 pp.
The fictional biography of López Rega, the minister of social well-being during Isabel
Peron's rule in Argentina.
Original title: *Cola de lagartija.* Argentina.

N V4.6

——. *Strange Things Happen Here: Twenty-six Short Stories and a Novel.* Trans.
   Helen Lane. New York: Harcourt, Brace and Javanovich, 1979. 220 pp.
The stories chronicle the paranoia felt in Argentina during the dictatorship. List of
stories can be found in the Anthology Index.
Original title: *Aquí pasan cosas raras.* Argentina.

N V5

Vallejo, Gaby. *Son of the Murdered Maid.* Trans. Alice Weldon. Lewiston, NY: Edwin
   Mellen Press, 2002. 193 pp.
A work of social protest against political repression in Bolivia dating from the 1950s
through the 1970s.
Original title: *Hijo de opa.* Bolivia.

N V6

Van Steen, Edla. *Early Mourning*. Trans. David S. George. Pittsburgh, PA: Latin American Literary Review Press, 1997. 142 pp.

The stories of several people who are at a funeral parlor in São Paulo at the same time. Received the "Coelho Neto" Prize for the Novel in 1993 and the Pen Club of Brazil Best Book Award.

Original title: *Madrugada*. Brazil.

N V6.1

———. *Village of the Ghost Bells*. Trans. David George. Austin: University of Texas Press, 1991. 197 pp.

The story of a fictitious utopian society near São Paulo which is ultimately destroyed by the greed and corruption of the community.

Original title: *Coraçoes mordidos*. Brazil.

N V7

Varsavsky, Paula. *No One Said a Word*. Trans. Anne McLean. Princeton, NJ: Ontario Review Press, 2000. 152 pp.

A coming-of-age novel about Luz, a young Argentine woman who lives in Buenos Aires during the 1970s when Argentina is under a dictatorship.

Original title: *Nadie alzaba la voz*. Argentina.

N V8

Veciana-Suárez, Ana. *The Chin Kiss King*. New York: Farrar, Straus & Giroux, 1997. 311 pp.

The first novel for the Miami Herald columnist. A chronicle of the lives of three generations of Cuban-American women in Miami.

Originally written in English. Cuba.

N V9

Vicens, Josefina. *The Empty Book: A Novel*. Trans. David Lauer. Austin: University of Texas Press, 1992. 123 pp.

The account of José García who wishes to write something significant in one of his journals, the "empty book."

Original title: *El libro vacío*. Mexico.

N V9.1

———. *False Years*. Trans. Peter G. Earle. Pittsburgh, PA: Latin American Literary Review Press, 1989. 94 pp.

An extended dramatic monologue of a 17-year-old boy as he stands near the grave of his father. He wishes to emulate his father and engages in unsavory acts to do so.

Original title: *Los años falsos*. Mexico.

N Y1

Yánez Cossío, Alicia. *Bruna and Her Sisters in the Sleeping City*. Trans. Kenneth J.
A. Wishnia. Evanston, IL: Northwestern University Press, 1999. 228 pp.
Set in Ecuador, the novel traces through magic-realism, the history of one family from
the Conquest to modern times. Includes translator's notes.
Original title: *Bruna, soroche y los tíos*. Ecuador.

N Y1.1

———. *The Potbellied Virgin.* Trans. Amalia Gladhart. Austin: University of Texas Press,
2006. 208 pp.
The second of Yánez Cossío's novels to be translated, this is a portrait of Ecuadorian
life in the twentieth century as told through a rivalry between the Benavides and Pandos
families.
Original title: *La cofradía de mullo del vestido de la Virgen Pipona*. Ecuador.

Novels and Novellas by Authors' Country of Origin

This index is organized by country in alphabetical order. Annotations for these titles can be found in the index titled Novels and Novellas in Alphabetical Order by Author.

ARGENTINA

Borinsky, Alicia. *All Night Movie.* Trans. Cola Franzen and Alicia Borinsky. Evanston, IL: Hydra Books/Northwestern University Press, 2002. 204 pp. Original title: *Cine continuado.*

———. *Dreams of the Abandoned Seducer.* Trans. Cola Franzen and Alicia Borinsky. Lincoln: University of Nebraska Press, 1998. 211 pp. Original title: *Sueños del seductor abandonado.*

———. *Mean Woman.* Trans. Cola Franzen. Lincoln: University of Nebraska Press, 1993. 179 pp. Original title: *Mina cruel.*

Bullrich, Silvina. *Tomorrow I'll Say Enough.* Trans. Julia Shirek Smith. Pittsburgh, PA: Latin American Literary Review Press, 1996. 189 pp. Original Title: *Mañana digo basta.*

Gambaro, Griselda. *The Impenetrable Madam X.* Trans. Evelyn Picon Garfield. Detroit: Wayne State University Press, 1991. 149 pp. Original title: *Lo impenetrable.*

Gorodischer, Angélica. *Kalpa Imperial: The Greatest Empire That Never Was.* Trans. Ursula K. Le Guin. Northampton, MA: Small Beer Press, 2003. 246 pp. Original title: *Kalpa Imperial.*

Guido, Beatriz. *End of a Day.* Trans. A. D. Towers. New York: Scribner, 1966. 278 pp. Original title: *El incendio y las vísperas.*

———. *The House of the Angel.* Trans. Joan Coyne MacLean. New York: McGraw-Hill, 1957. 174 pp. Original title: *La casa del ángel.*

Iparraguierre, Sylvia. *Tierra del fuego.* Trans. Hardie St. Martin. Willimantic, CT: Curbstone Press, 1997. 200 pp.

Original title: *Tierra del fuego*.

Kociancich, Vlady. *The Last Days of William Shakespeare*. Trans. Margaret Jull Costa. New York: Morrow, 1991. 297 pp.
Original title: *Los últimos días de William Shakespeare*.

Kozameh, Alicia. *Steps under Water*. Trans. David E. Davis. Intro. Saúl Sosnowski. Berkeley: University of California Press, 1996. 149 pp.
Original title: *Los pasos bajo el agua*.

———. *Two Hundred Fifty-nine Leaps, the Last Immortal*. Trans. Clare E. Sullivan. San Antonio, TX: Wings Press, 2006.185 pp.
Original title: *259 saltos, uno inmortal*.

Levinson, Luisa Mercedes. *In the Shadow of the Owl*. Trans. Sylvia Ehrlich Lipp. Barcelona: Salvat, 1989. 211 pp.
Original title: *A la sombra del buho*.

Molloy, Silvia. *Certificate of Absence*. Trans. Daniel Balderston. Austin: University of Texas Press, 1989. 125 pp.
Original title: *En breve cárcel*.

Orphée, Elvira. *El Angel's Last Conquest*. Trans. Magda Bogin. New York: Ballantine Books, 1985. 142 pp.
Original title: *La última conquista de El Angel*.

Osorio, Elsa. *My Name Is Light*. Trans. Catherine Jagoe. London: Bloomsbury, 2004. 388 pp.
Original title: *Mi nombre es Luz*.

Poletti, Syria. *The King Who Forbade Balloons*. Trans. Norman Thomas di Giovanni. Buenos Aires: Arte Gaglianone,1987. 33 pp.
Original Title: *El rey que prohibió los globos*.

Shua, Ana María. *The Book of Memories*. Trans. Dick Gerdes. Albuquerque: The University of New Mexico Press, 1998. 178 pp.
Original title: *El Libro de los recuerdos*.

———. *Patient*. Trans. David William Foster. Pittsburgh, PA: Latin American Literary Review Press. 1997. 122 pp.
Original title: *Soy paciente*.

Steimberg, Alicia. *Call Me Magdalena*. Trans. Andrea G. Labinger. Lincoln and London: University of Nebraska Press, 1992. 137 pp.
Original title: *Cuando digo Magdalena*.

———. *Musicians and Watchmakers*. Trans. Andrea G. Labinger. Pittsburgh, PA: Latin American Literary Review Press, 1998. 127 pp.
Original title: *Músicos y relojeros*.

———. *The Rainforest*. Trans. Andrea G. Labinger. Lincoln: University of Nebraska Press, 2006. 134 pp.
Original title: *La selva*.

Strejilevich, Nora. *A Single, Numberless Death*. Trans. Cristina de la Torre and the author. Charlottesville: University of Virginia Press, 2002. 176 pp.
Original title: *Una sola muerta numerosa*.

Traba, Marta. *Mothers and Shadows*. Trans. Jo Labanji. London and New York: Readers International, 1985. 178 pp.

Original title: *Conversación al sur.*

Valenzuela, Luisa. *Bedside Manners*. Trans. Margaret Jull Costa. London: High Risk Books, 1995. 121 pp.

Original title: *Realidad nacional desde la cama.*

——. *Black Novel (with Argentines)*. Trans. Toby Talbot. New York: Simon & Schuster, 1990. 220 pp.

Original title: *Novela negra con argentinos.*

——. *Clara*. Trans. Andrea G. Labinger. Pittsburgh, PA: Latin American Literary Review Press, 1999. 159 pp.

Original title: *Hay que sonreír.*

——. *Clara, Thirteen Short Stories and a Novel*. Trans. Hortense Carpentier and J. Jorge Castello. New York: Harcourt, Brace and Javanovich, 1976. 233 pp.

Original Title: *Clara.*

——. *He Who Searches*. Trans. Helen Lane. Elmwood Park, IL: The Dalkey Archive Press, 1987. 134 pp.

Original title: *Como en la guerra.*

——. *Strange Things Happen Here: Twenty-six Short Stories and a Novel*. Trans. Helen Lane. New York: Harcourt, Brace and Javanovich, 1979. 220 pp.

Original title: *Aquí pasan cosas raras.*

——. *The Lizard's Tail*. Trans. Gregory Rabassa. New York: Farrar, Straus & Giroux, 1983; Londton: Serpent's Tail, 1987. 279 pp.

Original title: *Cola de lagartija.*

Varsavsky, Paula. *No One Said a Word*. Trans. Anne McLean. Princeton, NJ: Ontario Review Press, 2000. 152 pp.

Original title: *Nadie alzaba la voz.*

BOLIVIA

de Quiroga, Giancarla. *Aurora*. Trans. Kathy S. Leonard. Seattle, WA: Women in Translation, 1999. 178 pp.

Original title: *La flor de "La Candelaria."*

Vallejo, Gaby. *The Son of the Murdered Maid*. Trans. Alice Weldon. Lewiston, NY: Edwin Mellen Press, 2002. 193 pp.

Original title: *Hijo de opa.*

BRAZIL

Albues, Tereza. *Pedra Canga* Trans. Clifford Elanders. Los Angeles: Green Integer, 2001. 153 pp.

Original title: *Pedra Canga*. Brazil.

Cunha, Helena Parente. *Woman between Mirrors*. Trans. Fred P. Ellison and Naomi Lindstrom. Austin: University of Texas Press, 1989. 132 pp.

Original Title: *Mulher no espelho.*

de Queiroz, Rachel. *Dora, Doralina*. Trans. Dorothy Scott Loos. New York: Avon, 1984. 281 pp.
Original title: *Dora, Doralina*.
——. *The Three Marías*. Trans. Fred P. Ellison. Austin: University of Texas Press, 1963. 178 pp.
Original Tttle: *Tres Marias*.
Fagundes Telles, Lygia. *The Girl in the Photograph*. Trans. Margaret A. Neves. New York: Avon Books, 1982. 247 pp.
Original title: *As meninas*.
——. *The Marble Dance*. Trans. Margaret A. Neves. New York: Avon Books, 1986. 184 pp.
Original title: *Ciranda de pedra*.
Felinto, Marilene. *The Women of Tijucopapo*. Trans. Irene Matthews. Lincoln and London: University of Nebraska Press, 1994. 132 pp.
Original Title: *Mulheres de Tijucopapo*.
Galvão, Patricia (Pagu). *Industrial Park: A Proletarian Novel*. Trans. Elizabeth and Kenneth David Jackson. Lincoln: University of Nebraska Press, 1993. 153 pp.
Original Title: *Parque Industrial*.
Jorge, Lidia. *The Painter of Birds*. Trans. Margaret Jull Costa. New York: Harcourt, 2001. 233 pp.
Original title: *Vale da paixão*.
——. *The Murmuring Coast*. Trans. Natalia Costa and Ronald W. Sousa. Minneapolis: University of Minnesota Press, 1995. 274 pp.
Original title: *Costa dos murmurios*.
Lispector, Clarice. *The Apple in the Dark*. Trans. Gregory Rabassa. New York: Alfred A. Knopf, Inc., 1967; London: Virago, 1985. 361 pp.
Original title: *Maçã no escuro*.
——. *An Apprenticeship, or, The Book of Delights*. Trans. Richard A. Mazzare and Lori A. Parris. Austin: University of Texas Press, 1986. 126 pp.
Original title: *Uma aprendizagem; ou, O livro dos prazeres*.
——. *The Besieged City*. Trans. Giovanni Pontiero. Manchester, UK: Carcanet, 1999. 196 pp.
Original title: *Cidade sitiada*.
——. *Discovering the World*. Trans. Giovanni Pontiero. Manchester, UK: Carcanet, 1992. 652 pp.
Original title: *A descoberta do mundo*.
——. *The Hour of the Star*. Trans. Giovanni Pontiero. Manchester: Carcanet, 1986. 96 pp.
Original title: *A hora da estrela*.
——. *Near to the Wild Heart*. Trans. Giovanni Pontiero. Manchester, UK: Carcanet, 1990. 192 pp.
Original title: *Perto do coração sellvagem*.
——. *The Passion According to G.H.* Trans. Ronald W. Souza. Minneapolis: University of Minnesota Press, 1988. 173 pp.

Original title: *A paixão segundo G.H.*
Lispector, Clarice. *The Stream of Life.* Trans. Elizabeth Lowe and Earl Fitz. Minneapolis: University of Minnesota Press, 1989. 79 pp.
Original title: *Agua viva.*
Luft, Lya Fett. *The Island of the Dead.* Trans. Carmen Chaves McClendon and Betty Jean Craige. Atlanta: University of Georgia Press, 1986. 106 pp.
Original title: *O quarto fechado.*
———. *The Red House.* Trans. Giovanni Pontiero. Manchester, UK: Carcanet, 1994. 182 pp.
Original title: *Exilio.*
Melo, Patricia. *Black Waltz.* Trans. Clifford E. Landers. London: Bloomsbury, 2005. 209 pp.
Original title: *Valsa negra.*
———. *The Killer.* Trans. Clifford E. Landers. Hopewell, NJ: Ecco Press, 1997. 217 pp.
Original title: *Matador.*
Miranda, Ana. *Bay of All Saints and Every Conceiveable Sin.* Trans. Giovanni Pontiero. London: Harvill, 1992; New York: Viking, 1991. 305 pp.
Original title: *Boca do inferno.*
Nunes, Lygia. *The Companions.* Trans. Ellen Watson. New York: Farrar, Straus & Giroux, 1989. 57 pp.
Original title: *Os colegas.*
———. *My Friend the Painter.* Orlando, FL: Harcourt Brace, 1991. 85 pp.
Original title: *Meu amigo pinto.*
Piñón, Nélida. *Caetana's Sweet Song.* Trans. Helen Lane. New York: Knopf, 1992. 401 pp.
Original title: *Doce cancão de Cartana.*
———. *The Republic of Dreams: A Novel.* Trans. Helen Lane. New York: Knopf, 1989; Austin: University of Texas Press, 1991. 663 pp.
Original title: *A republica dos sonhos.*
Rheda, Regina. *First World Third Class and Other Tales of the Global Mix.* Trans. Adria Frizzi, REYoung, David Coles, and Charles A. Perrone. Austin: University of Texas Press, 2005. 304 pp.
Original title: *Pau-de Arara classe turística.*
Ribeiro, Stella Car. *Sambaqui: A Novel of Pre-history.* Trans. Claudia Van der Heuvel. New York: Avon Books, 1987. 132 pp.
Original tite: *O homen do Sambqui.*
Silveira de Queiroz, Dinah. *Christ's Memorial.* Trans. Isabel do Prado. London: Sel Press, 1978. 214 pp.
Original title: *Eu venho.*
———. *The Women of Brazil.* Trans. Roberta King. New York: Vantage Press, 1980. 289 pp.
Original title: *A muralha.*

Van Steen, Edla. *Early Mourning*. Trans. David S. George. Pittsburgh, PA: Latin American Literary Review Press, 1997. 142 pp.
Original title: *Madrugada*.
——. *Village of the Ghost Bells*. Trans. David George. Austin: University of Texas Press, 1991. 197 pp.
Original title: *Coraçoes mordidos*.

CHILE

Allende, Isabel. *Aphrodite: A Memoir of the Senses*. Trans. Margaret Sayers Peden. New York: HarperCollins, 1998. 315 pp.
Original title: *Afrodita: cuentos, recetas y otros afrodisíacos*.
——. *Aphrodite: The Love of Food and the Food of Love*. Trans. Margaret Sayers Peden. London: Flamingo, 1999. 272 pp.
Original title: *Afrodita: cuentos, recetas y otros afrodisíacos*.
——. *City of the Beasts*. Trans. Margaret Sayers Peden. New York: HarperCollins, 2002. 406 pp.
Original title: *La ciudad de las bestias*.
——. *Daughter of Fortune*. Trans. Margaret Sayers Peden. London: Flamingo, 1999. 352 pp.
Original title: *Hija de la fortuna*.
——. *Eva Luna*. Trans. Margaret Sayers Peden. New York: Knopf, 1988. 392 pp.
Original title: *Eva Luna*.
——.*Forest of the Pygmies*. Trans. Margaret Sayers Peden. New York: HarperCollins, 2005. 296 pp.
Original title: *El bosque de los pigmeos*.
——. *The House of the Sprits*. Trans. Magda Bogin. New York: Knopf, 1985. 368 pp.
Original title: *La casa de los espíritus*.
——. *Inés of My Soul*. Trans. Margaret Sayers Peden. New York: HarperCollins, 2006. 321 pp.
Original title: *Inés del alma mía*.
——. *Infinite Plan: A Novel*. Trans. Margaret Sayers Peden. New York: HarperCollins, 1993. 382 pp.
Original title: *El plan infinito*.
——. *Kingdom of the Golden Dragon*. Trans. Margaret Sayers Peden. New York: Harper Trophy, 2005. 437 pp.
Original title: *El reino del Dragón de Oro*.
——. *Of Love and Shadows*. Trans. Margaret Sayers Peden. New York: Knopf, 1987. 274 pp.
Original Title: *De amor y de sombra*.
——. *Paula*. Trans. Margaret Sayers Peden. New York: HarperCollins, 1995. 330 pp.
Original title: *Paula*.

Allende, Isabel. *Portrait in Sepia.* Trans. Margaret Sayers Peden. New York: HarperCollins, 2001. 304 pp.
Original title: *Retrato en sepia.*
——. *Zorro: A Novel.* Trans. Margaret Sayers Peden. New York: HarperCollins, 2005. 390 pp.
Original title: *Zorro: una novela.*
Bombal, María Luisa. *House of Mist.* Trans. María Luisa Bombal. New York: Farrar-Straus, 1947. 259 pp.
Original title: *La última niebla.*
——. *House of Mist* and *The Shrouded Woman.* Trans. María Luisa Bombal. Austin: University of Texas Press, 1995. 259 pp.
Original titles: *La última niebla* and *La amortajada.*
——. *The Shrouded Woman.* Trans. María Luisa Bombal. New York: Farrar-Straus, 1948. 198 pp.
Original title: *La amortajada.*
Castedo, Elena. *Paradise.* New York: Washington Square Press, 1990. 328 pp.
Originally written in English.
del Río, Ana María. *Carmen's Rust.* Trans. Michael J. Lazzara. Woodstock, NY: Overlook Duckworth, 2003. 128 pp.
Original title: *Oxido de Carmen.*
del Valle, Rosamel. *Eva, the Fugitive.* Trans. Anna Balakian. Berkeley: University of California Press, 1990. 105 pp.
Original title: *Eva y la fuga.*
Eltit, Diamela. *E. Luminata.* Trans. Ronald Christ (with the collaboration of Gene Bell-Villada, Helen Lane, and Catalina Parra). Santa Fe, NM: Lumen, Inc., 1997. 240 pp.
Original title: *Lumpérica.*
——. *The Fourth World.* Trans. Dick Gerdes. Lincoln: University of Nebraska Press, 1995. 113 pp.
Original title: *El cuarto mundo.*
——. *Sacred Cow.* Trans. Amanda Hopkinson. London: Serpent's Tail, 1995. 106 pp.
Original title: *La vaca sagrada.*
Guerra Cunningham, Lucía. *Más allá de la máscaras.* Pittsburgh, PA: Latin American Literary Review Press, 1986. 88 pp.
Original title: *Beyond the Masks.*
——. *The Street of Night.* Trans. Richard Cunningham. Reading, Berkshire, UK: Garnet Publishers, 1997. 207 pp.
Original title: *Muñeca brava.*
Lobo, Tatiana. *Assault on Paradise.* Trans. Asa Zatz. Willimantic, CT: Curbstone Press, 1998. 297 pp.
Original title: *Asalto al paraíso.*
Petit, Magdalena. *La quintrala.* Trans. Lulú Vargas Vila. New York: Macmillan, 1942. 190 pp.

Original title: *La quintrala.*

Romo-Carmona, Mariana. *Living at Night.* Duluth, MN: Spinsters Ink, 1997. 257 pp. Originally written in English.

Serrano, Marcela. *Antigua and My Life Before.* Trans. Margaret Sayers Peden. New York: Doubleday, 2000. 352 pp.
Original title: *Antigua vida mia.*

Subercaseaux, Elizabeth. *The Song of the Distant Root.* Trans. John J. Hassett. Pittsburgh, PA: Latin American Literary Revew Press, 2001. 112 pp.
Original title: *Canto de la raíz lejana.*

Valdivieso, Mercedes. *Breakthrough.* Trans. Graciela Daichman. Pittsburgh, PA: Latin American Literary Review Press, 1987. 96 pp.
Original title: *Brecha.*

COLOMBIA

Buitrago, Fanny. *Señora Honeycomb.* Trans. Margaret Sayers Peden. New York: HarperCollins, 1996. 232 pp.
Original title: *Señora de la miel.*

Chávez-Vásquez, Gloria. *AKUM: La magia de los sueños/The Magic of Dreams. A Bilingual Novel.* Trans. Gloria Chávez-Vásquez. Brooklyn, NY: White Owl Publications, 1996. 116 pp.
Original title: *AKUM: La magia de los sueños.*

Restrepo, Laura. *The Angel of Galilea.* Trans. Dolores M. Koch. New York: Crown Publishers, Inc., 1997. 193 pp.
Original title: *Dulce compañía.*

———. *The Dark Bride.* Trans. Stepthen A. Lytle. New York: HarperCollins, 2001. 358 pp.
Original title: *La novia oscura.*

———. *Delirium.* Trans. Natasha Wimmer. New York: Nan A. Talese/Doubleday, 2007. 336 pp.
Original title: *Delirio.*

———. *Isle of Passion.* Trans. Dolores M. Koch. New York: Ecco, 2005. 298 pp.
Original title: *Isla de la pasión.*

———. *Leopard in the Sun.* Trans. Stephen A. Lytle. New York: Crown Publishers, 1999. 242 pp.
Original title: *Leopardo al sol.*

———. *A Tale of the Dispossessed.* Trans. Dolores Koch. New York: Ecco, 2003. 98 pp.
Original title: *La multitud errante.*

CUBA

Bevin, Teresa. *Havana Split.* Houston, TX: Arte Público Press, 1998. 368 pp. Originally written in English.

Engle, Margarita. *Singing to Cuba.* Houston, TX: Arte Público Press, 1993. 164 pp. Originally written in English.

Engle, Margarita. *Skywriting: A Novel of Cuba*. New York: Bantam Books, 1996. 288 pp.
Originally written in English.

García, Cristina. *The Agüero Sisters*. New York: Alfred A. Knopf, 1997. 300 pp.
Originally written in English.

——. *Dreaming in Cuban*. New York: Ballantine Books, 1992. 146 pp.
Originally written in English.

——. *A Handbook to Luck*. New York: Random House, Inc, 2007. 288 pp.
Originally written in English.

Gómez de Avellaneda y Arteaga, Gertrudis. *Cuauhtemoc: The Last Aztec Emperor, an Historical Novel*. Trans. Mrs. Wilson W. Blake. Mexico: F.P. Hoeck, 1898. 389 pp.
Original title: *Guatimozin, último emperador de México*.

——. *Sab, an Autobiography*. Trans. Nina F. Scott. Austin: University of Texas Press, 1993. 157 pp.
Original Title: *Sab*.

Herrera, Andrea O'Reilly. *The Pearl of the Antilles*. Tempe, AZ: Bilingual Review Press, 2001. 353 pp.
Originally written in English.

Lamazares, Ivonne. *The Sugar Island*. Boston: Houghton, 2000. 205 pp.
Originally written in English.

Medina, C. C. *A Little Love*. New York: Warner, 2000. 352 pp.
Originally written in English.

Menéndez, Ana. *Loving Che*. New York: Atlantic Monthly, 2003. 229 pp.
Originally written in English.

Montero, Mayra. *Captain of the Sleepers*. Trans. Edith Grossman. New York: Farrar, Straus & Giroux, 2005. 181 pp.
Original title: *Capitán de los dormidos*.

——. *Dancing to Almendra*. Trans. Edith Grossman. New York: Farrar, Straus & Giroux, 2007. 283 pp.
Original title: *Son de Almendra*.

——. *Deep Purple: A Novel*. Trans. Edith Grossman. New York: HarperCollins, 2003. 182 pp.
Original title: *Púrpura profundo*.

——. *In the Palm of Darkness: A Novel*. Trans. Edith Grossman. New York: HarperFlamingo, 1997. 181 pp.
Original title: *Tú, la oscuridad*.

——. *The Last Night I Spent with You*. Trans. Edith Grossman. New York: HarperCollins, 2000. 128 pp.
Original title: *La última noche que pasé contigo*.

——. *The Messenger*. Trans. Edith Grossman. New York: HarperPerennial Library, 2000. 224 pp.
Original title: *Como un mensajero tuyo*.

——. "The Moon Line." Trans. Kathryn Renée Dussan. Master's thesis,

University of Puerto Rico, 1993.
Original title: *La trenza de la hermosa luna.*
Montero, Mayra. *The Red of His Shadow.* Trans. Edith Grossman. New York: HarperCollins, 2001. 159 pp.
Original title: *Del rojo de su sombra.*
——. *You, Darkness.* Trans. Edith Grossman. London: The Harvill Press, 1997. 182 pp.
Original title: *Tú, la oscuridad.*
Novas, Himilce. *Don't Look Back.* New York: Steck-Vaughn Company, 1995. 64 pp.
Originally written in English.
——. *Mangos, Bananas and Coconuts: A Cuban Love Story.* Houston, TX: Arte Público Press, 1997. 168 pp.
Originally written in English.
Obejas, Achy. *Days of Awe.* New York: Ballantine Books, 2001. 371 pp.
Originally written in English..
——. *Memory Mambo.* San Francisco: Cleis Press, 1996. 249 pp.
Originally written in English.
——.*We Came All the Way from Cuba So You Could Dress Like This?* San Francisco: Cleis Press, 1994. 133 pp.
Originally written in English.
Puig Zaldívar, Raquel. *Nothing in Our Hands but Age.* Binghamton: Bilingual Press, 1980. 56 pp.
Originally written in English.
——. *Women Don't Need to Write.* Houston, TX: Arte Público Press, 1998. 352 pp.
Originally written in English.
Rivera, Beatriz. *Midnight Sandwiches at the Mariposa Express.* Houston, TX: Arte Público Press, 1997. 118 pp.
Originally written in English.
——. *Playing with Light: A Novel.* Houston, TX: Arte Público Press, 2000. 240 pp.
Originally written in English.
Robles, Mireya. *Hagiography of Narcisa the Beautiful.* Trans. Anna Diegel with Mireya Robles. Readers International, 1996. 188 pp.
Original title: *Hagiografía de Narcisa la bella.*
Rojas, Marta. *Dead Man's Cave.* Trans. Margarita Zimmermann. Havana: José Martí Pub. House, 1988. 146 pp.
Original title: *La cueva del muerto.*
Valdés, Zoe. *Dear First Love.* Trans. Andrew Hurley. New York: HarperCollins Publishers, 2002. 291 pp.
Original title: *Querido primer novio.*
——. *I Gave You All I Had.* Trans. Nadia Benabid. New York: Arcade Publishing, 1999.
Original title: *Te di la vida entera.*
——. *Yocandra in the Paradise of Nada: A Novel of Cuba.* Trans. Sabina

Cienfuegos. London: Arcade Publishing, 1999. 192 pp.
Original title: *La nada cotidiana*.
Valdés-Rodríguez, Alisa. *The Dirty Girls Social Club*. New York, St. Martin's Press, 2003. 316 pp.
Originally written in English.
Veciana-Suárez, Ana. *The Chin Kiss King*. New York: Farrar, Straus & Giroux, 1997. 311 pp.
Originally written in English.

DOMINICAN REPUBLIC

Alvarez, Julia. *Before We Were Free*. New York: Alfred A. Knopf, 2002. 167 pp.
Originally written in English.
——. *A Cafecito Story*. White River Junction, VT: Chelsea Green Publishing Co., 2001. 58 pp.
Originally written in English.
——. *How the Garcia Girls Lost Their Accents*. New York: A Plume Book,1992. 290 pp.
Originally written in English.
——. *How Tia Lola Came to Visit/Stay*. New York: Alfred A. Knopf, 2001. 145 pp.
Originally written in English.
——. *In the Name of Salomé: A Novel*. Chapel Hill, NC: Algonquin Books, 2000. 368 pp.
Originally written in English.
——. *In the Time of the Butterflies*. New York: Plume, 1995. 325 pp.
Originally written in English.
——. *Monkey Hunting*. New York: Ballantine Books, 2004. 269 pp.
Originally written in English.
——. *Saving the World*. Chapel Hill, NC: Algonquin Books of Chapel Hill, 2006. 368 pp.
Originally written in English.
——. *The Secret Footprints*. New York: Alfred Knopf, 2000. 40 pp.
Originally written in English.
——.*Yo!* New York: Plume, 1999. 414 pp.
Originally written in English.
Pérez, Loida Maritza. *Geographies of Home*. London: Penguin, 2000. 321 pp.
Originally written in English.

ECUADOR

Yánez Cossío, Alicia. Trans. Kenneth J. A. Wishnia. *Bruna and Her Sisters in the Sleeping City*. Evanston, IL: Northwestern University Press, 1999. 228 pp.
Original title: *Bruna, soroche y los tíos*.
——. *The Potbellied Virgin*. Trans. Amalia Gladhart. Austin: University of Texas Press, 2006. 208 pp.
Original title: *La cofradia de mullo del vestido de la Virgen Pipona*.

EL SALVADOR

Alegría, Claribel. *Family Album: Three Novellas*. Trans. Amanda Hopkinson. London: Women's Press, 1990. 170 pp.
Original title: *Pueblo de Dios y de Mandinga*.

——. *Luisa in Realityland*. Willimantic, CT: Curbstone Press, 1988. 152 pp.
Original title: *Luisa en el país de la realidad*.

Alegría, Claribel, and Darwin J. Flakoll. *Ashes of Izalco*. Trans. Darwin J. Flakoll Willimantic, CT: Curbstone Press, 1993. 173 pp.
Original Title: *Cenizas de Izalco*.

HONDURAS

Díaz Lozano, Argentina. *And We Have to Live*. Trans. Lillian Sears. Palos Verdes, CA: Morgan Press, 1978. 181 pp.
Original title: *Y tenemos que vivir*.

——. *Henriqueta and I*. Trans. Harriet de Onis. London: D. Dobson, 1945. 152 pp.
Original title: *Peregrinaje*.

——. *Mayapan*. Trans. Lydia Wright. Indian Hills, CO: Falcon's Wing Press, 1955. 185 pp.
Original title: *Mayapan*.

MEXICO

Alcalá, Kathleen. *The Flower in the Skull*. San Diego, CA: Harcourt Brace, 1999. 180 pp.
Originally written in English.

——. *Spirits of the Ordinary: A Tale of Casas Grandes*. Trans. Eduardo Hojman. Buenos Aires: Emecé, 1998. 252 pp.
Original title: *Espíritus de las pequeñas cosas*.

——. *Treasures in Heaven*. San Francisco: Chronicle Books, 2000. 224 pp.
Originally written in English.

Alves Pereira, Teresinha. *While Springtime Sleeps*. Trans. Angela de Hoyos. San Antonio, TX: Ed. Azteca, 1975. 29 pp.
Original title: *Mientras duerme la primavera*.

Benítez, Sandra. *Bitter Grounds*. New York: Hyperion, 1997. 445 pp.
Originally written in English.

——. *Night of the Radishes*. New York: Hyperion Press, 2005. 288 pp.
Originally written in English.

——. *A Place Where the Sea Remembers*. Minneapolis, MN: Coffee House Press, 1993. 163 pp.
Originally written in English.

——. *The Weight of All Things*. New York: Hyperion, 2001. 256 pp.
Originally written in English.

Bermin, Sabina. *Bubbeh*. Trans. Andrea G. Labinger. Pittsburgh, PA: Latin American Literary Review Press, 1998. 90 pp.
Original title: *Bobe*.

Boullosa, Carmen. *Cleopatra Dismounts*. Trans. Geoff Hargreaves. New York: Grove Press, 2005. 240 pp.
Original title: *De un salto descabalga la reina*.
——. *Leaving Tabasco*. Trans. Geoff Hargreaves. New York: Grove Press, 1999. 244 pp.
Original title: *Treinta años*.
——. *The Miracle-worker*. Trans. Amanda Hopkinson. London: Jonathan Cape, 1995. 137 pp.
Original title: *La milagrosa*.
——. *They're Cows, We're Pigs*. Trans. Leland Chambers. New York: Grove Press, 1997. 180 pp.
Original title: *Son vacas, somos puercos*.
Calderón, Sara Levi. *The Two Mujeres*. Trans. Gina Kaufer. San Francisco: Aunt Lute Books, 1991. 211 pp.
Original title: *Las dos mujeres*.
Campos, Julieta. *The Fear of Losing Eurydice: A Novel*. Trans. Leland H. Chambers. Normal, IL: Dalkey Archive Press, 1993. 121 pp.
Original title: *Miedo de perder a Eurídice*.
——. *She Has Reddish Hair and Her Name Is Sabina*. Trans. Leland H. Chambers. Athens: University of Georgia Press, 1993. 135 pp.
Original title: *Tiene los cabellos rojizos y se llama Sabina*.
Castellanos, Rosario. *The Book of Lamentations*. Trans. Esther Allen. New York: Marsilio Publishing, 1996. 400 pp.
Original title: *Oficio de tinieblas*.
——. *The Nine Guardians*. Trans. Irene Nicolson. New York: Vanguard, 1960. Colombia, LA: Readers International, 1992. 272 pp.
Original title: *Balún-Canán*.
Cerda, Marta. *Señora Rodríguez and Other Worlds*. Trans. Sylvia Jiménez-Andersen. Durham and London: Duke University Press, 1997. 133 pp.
Original title: *La señora Rodríguez y otros mundos*.
Durán, Gloria. *María de Estrada: Gypsy conquistadora*. Pittsburgh, PA: Latin American Literary Review Press, 1999. 227 pp.
Originally written in English.
Domecq, Brianda. *The Astonishing Story of the Saint of Cabora*. Trans. Kay García. Tempe, AZ: Bilingual Review Press, 1998. 304 pp.
Original title: *Insólita historia de la Santa de Cabora*.
——. *Eleven Days*. Trans. Kay S. García. Albuquerque: University of New Mexico Press, 1995. 226 pp.
Original title: *Once días*.
Escalante, Beatriz. *Magdalena, A Fable of Immortality*. Trans. Jay Miskowiec. Minneapolis, MN: Aliform Publishing, 2002. 126 pp.
Original title: *Fábula de la inmortalidad*.
Esquivel, Laura. *The Law of Love*. Trans. Margaret Sayers Peden. New York: Crown Publishers, 1996. 266 pp.

Original title: *La ley del amor.*

Esquivel, Laura. *Like Water for Chocolate: A Novel in Monthly Installments, with Recipes, Romances, and Home Remedies.* Trans. Carol Christensen and Thomas Christensen. New York: Doubleday, 1992. 245 pp.
Original title: *Como agua para chocolate.*

——. *Swift as Desire.* New York: Anchor; Knopf Publishing Group, 2002. 208 pp.
Original title: *Tan veloz como el deseo.*

Garro, Elena. *First Love and Look for My Obituary. Two Novellas.* Trans. David Unger. Willimantic, CT: Curbstone Press, 1977. 99 pp.
Original titles: *Primer amor* and *Busca mi esquela.*

——. *Recollections of Things to Come.* Trans. Ruth C. Simms. Austin: University of Texas Press, 1969. 289 pp.
Original title: *Los recuerdos del porvenir.*

Glantz, Margo. *The Family Tree: An Illustrated Novel.* Trans. Susan Bassnett. London: Serpent's Tail, 1991. 186 pp.
Original title: *Genealogías.*

——. *The Wake.* Trans. Andrew Hurley. Willimantic, CT: Curbstone Press, 2005. 123 pp.
Original title: *El rastro.*

Gómez Rul, Ana María. *Lol-Há: A Maya Tale.* Trans. Margaret Redfield. Mexico City: Ed. Cultura, 1935. 44 pp.
Original title: *Lol-Há: un cuento maya.*

Gutiérrez Richaud, Cristina. *Woman with Short Hair and Great Legs.* Trans. Michael B. Miller. (Forthcoming).
Original title: *Mujer de cabellos cortos y buenas piernas.*

Jacobs, Barbara. *The Dead Leaves.* Trans. David Unger. Willimantic, CT: Curbstone Press, 1993. 126 pp.
Original title: *Las hojas muertas.*

Mastretta, Ángeles. *Lovesick.* Trans. Margaret Sayers Peden. New York: Riverhead Books, 1997. 292 pp.
Original title: *Mal de amores.*

——. *Mexican Bolero.* Trans. Ann Wright. New York: Viking, 1989. 267 pp.
Original title: *Arráncame la vida.*

——. *Tear This Heart Out.* Trans. Margaret Sayers Peden. New York: Riverhead Books, 1997.
Original title: *Arráncame la vida.*

Molina, Silvia. *Gray Skies Tomorrow: A Novel.* Trans. John Mitchell and Turh Mitchell de Aguilar. Kaneohe, HI: Plover Press, 1993. 104 pp.
Original title: *La mañana debe seguir gris.*

——. *The Love You Promised Me.* Trans. David Unger. Willimantic, CT: Curbstone Press, 1999. 228 pp.
Original title: *El amor que me juraste.*

Mondragón Aguirre, Magdalena. *Someday the Dream.* Trans. Samuel Putnam. New York: Dial Press, 1947. 240 pp.

Original title: *Yo como pobre.*

Poniatowska, Elena. *Dear Diego.* Trans. Katherine Silver. New York: Pantheon Books, 1986. 87 pp.
Original title: *Querido Diego, te abraza Quiela.*

———. *Here's to You, Jesusa!* Trans. Deanna Heikkinen. New York: Farrar, Straus & Giroux, 2001. 303 pp.
Original title: *Hasta no verte, Jesús mío.*

———. *Massacre in Mexico.* Trans. Helen R. Lane. New York: Viking Press, 1975. 333 pp.
Original title: *La noche de Tlatelolco: Testimonios de historia oral.*

———. *Nothing, Nobody: The Voices of the Mexico City Earthquake.* Trans. Aurora Camacho de Schmidt and Arthur Schmidt. Philadephia: Temple University Press, 1995. 327 pp.
Original title: *Nada, nadie.*

———. *The Skin of the Sky.* Trans. Deanna Heikkinen. New York: Farrar, Straus & Giroux, 2004. 322 pp.
Original title: *Piel del cielo.*

———. *Tinismia: A Novel.* Trans. Kathleen Silver. New York: Farrar, Straus & Giroux, 1996. 357 pp.
Original title: *Tinísima.*

———. *Until We Meet Again.* Trans. Helen Lane. New York: Pantheon, 1987. 300 pp.
Original title: *Hasta no verte, Jesús mío.*

Ríos, Mi-Chelle L. *Chola.* Pittsburgh, PA: Latin American Literary Review Press, 2005. 189 pp.
Originally written in English.

Vicens, Josefina. *The Empty Book: A Novel.* Trans. David Lauer. Austin: University of Texas Press, 1992. 123 pp.
Original title: *El libro vacío.*

———. *The False Years.* Trans. Peter G. Earle. Pittsburgh, PA: Latin American Literary Review Press, 1989. 94 pp.
Original title: *Los años falsos.*

NICARAGUA

Aguilar, Rosario. *The Lost Chronicles of Terra Firma.* Trans. Edward Waters Hood. Fredonia, NY: White Pine Press, 1997. 186 pp.
Original title: *La niña blanca y los pájaros sin pies.*

Belli, Gioconda. *The Inhabited Woman.* Trans. Kathleen March. Willimantic, CT: Curbstone Press, 1993. 412 pp.
Original title: *La mujer habitada.*

PERU

Arana, Marie. *Cellophane.* New York: Dial Books, 2006. 384 pp.
Originally written in English.

Matto de Turner, Clorinda. *Birds without a Nest; A Story of Indian Life and Priestly Oppression in Peru.* Trans. J.C.H. London: C.J. Thynne, 1904. Trans. emended by Naomi Lindstrom, 1996. Austin: University of Texas Press, 1996. 181 pp. New translation by John Polt, 1998. Berkeley: University of California Press, 1998. 224 pp. Edited with a foreword and chronology by Antonio Cornejo Polar.
> Original title: *Aves sin nido.*
——. *Torn from the Nest.* Trans. John H. R. Polt. Oxford: Oxford University Press, 1998. 288 pp.
> Original title: *Aves sin nido.*
Riesco, Laura. *Ximena at the Crossroads.* Trans. Mary G. Berg. Fredonia, NY: White Pine Press, 1998. 269 pp.
> Original title: *Ximena de dos caminos.*

PUERTO RICO

Braschi, Giannina. *Empire of Dreams.* Trans. Tess O'Dwyer. New Haven, CT: Yale University Press, 1994. 219 pp.
> Original title: El *Imperio de los sueños.*
——. *Yo-Yo Boing!* Pittsburgh, PA: Latin American Literary Review Press, 1998. 205 pp.
> Orignal title: *Yo-Yo Boing.*
Delgado, Ana María. *The Room In-Between.* Trans. Sylvia Ehrlich Lipp. Pittsburgh, PA: Latin American Literary Review Press, 1996. 91 pp.
> Original title: *La habitación de por medio.*
Ferré, Rosario. *Eccentric Neighborhoods.* New York: Farrar, Straus & Giroux, 1998; New York: Plume, 1999. 336 pp.; London: Abacus, 2000. 352 pp.
> Original title: *Vecindarios eccéntricos.*
——. *The House on the Lagoon.* Trans. Rosario Ferré. New York: Farrar, Straus & Giroux, 1995. 407 pp.
> Original title: *La casa de la laguna.*
——. *Flight of the Swan.* New York: Plume; Penguin Group, 2002. 272 pp.
> Originally written in English.
——. *Sweet Diamond Dust: A Novel and Three Stories of Life in Puerto Rico.* Trans. Rosario Ferré. New York: Ballantine Books, 1988. 197 pp.
> Original title: *Maldito amor.*
García Ramis, Magali. *Happy Days, Uncle Sergio.* Trans. Carmen C. Esteves. Fredonia, NY: White Pine Press, 1995. 175 pp.
> Original Title: *Felices días, tío Sergio.*
Ortiz Cofer, Judith. *Call Me Maria: A Novel.* New York: Orchard Books, 2004. 127 pp.
> Originally written in English.
——. *The Line of the Sun: A Novel.* Athens: University of Georgia Press, 1988. 291 pp.
> Originally written in English.

Ortiz Cofer, Judith. *The Meaning of Consuelo*. Boston: Beacon Press, 2004. 196 pp.
Originaliy written in English.

URUGUAY
Peri Rossi, Cristina. *Dostoevsky's Last Night*. Trans. Laura Dail. New York: Picador, USA, 1995. 180 pp.
Original title: *La última noche de Dostoievski*.
——. *The Ship of Fools*. Trans. Psiche Hughes. London: Allison and Busby, 1989. 205 pp.
Original title: *La nave de los locos*.
——. *Solitaire of Love*. Trans. Robert S. Rubber and Gloria Arjona. Raleigh, NC: Duke University Press, 2000. 120 pp.
Original title: *Solitario de amor*.
Porzecanski, Teresa. *Sun Inventions and Perfumes of Carthage: Two Novellas*. Trans. Johnny Payne and Phyllis Silverstein. Intro. Ilan Stavans. Albuquerque: University of New Mexico Press, 2000. 204 pp.
Original titles: *Invención de los soles* and *Perfumes de Cartago*.
Schroeder, Agustina. *Mother of Fair Love*. Trans. Veronica Kirtland. Milwaukee, WI: The Bruce Publishing Co., 1957. 182 pp.
Original title: Unavailable.

VENEZUELA
de la Parra, Teresa. *Iphigenia: The Diary of a Young Lady Who Wrote Because She Was Bored*. Trans. Bertie Acker. Austin: University of Texas Press, 1994. 354 pp.
Original title: *Ifigenia*.
——. *Mama Blanca's Memoirs: The Classic Novel of a Venezuelan Girlhood*. Trans. Harriet de Onís. Pittsburgh, PA: University of Pittsburgh Press, 1993; Washington, DC: Pan American Union, 1959. 183 pp.
Original title: *Memorias de Mama Blanca*.
Frielich de Segal, Alicia. *Cláper*. Trans. Joan E. Friedman. Albuquerque: University of New Mexico Press, 1998. 182 pp.
Original title: *Cláper*.

Other Sources Dealing with Latin American Women's Literature

Abbassi, Jennifer, and Sheryl L. Lutjens, eds. *Rereading Women in Latin American and the Caribbean: The Political Economy of Gender.* New York: Rowman & Littlefield, 2002.

Acevedo, Luz del Alba. *Telling to Live: Latina Feminist Testimonios.* Durham, NC: Duke University Press, 2001.

Adams, Clementina R. *Common Threads: Themes in Afro-Hispanic Women's Literature.* Miami, FL: Ediciones Universal, 1998.

Adjarian, M. M. *Allegories of Desire: Body, Nation, and Empire in Modern Caribbean Literature by Women.* Westport, CT: Greenwood Press, 2004.

Adler, Heidrun, and Kati Rottger. *Performance, Pathos, Política de los sexos: teatro postcolonial de autoras latinoamericanas.* Madrid: Iberoamericana, 1999.

Agosín, Marjorie. *A Dream of Light and Shadow: Portraits of Latin American Women Writers.* Albuquerque: University of New Mexico Press, 1995.

——. *Invisible Dreamer: Memory, Judaism, and Human Rights.* Santa Fe, NM: Sherman Asher Publishers, 2002.

——. *Passion, Memory, Identity: Twentieth-Century Latin American Jewish Women Writers.* Albuquerque: University of New Mexico Press, 1999.

Alarcón, Norma, and Sylvia Kossnar. *Bibliography of Hispanic Women Writers.* Bloomington, IL: Chicano-Riqueño Studies, 1980.

Alexander, M. Jacqui, Lisa Albrecht, Sharon Day, and Mab Segrest, eds. *Sing, Whisper, Shout, Pray: Feminist Visions for a Just World.* Berkeley, CA: Edgework Books, 2003.

Álvarez, Myriam. *Presente y precedente de la literatura de mujeres latino-americanas.* Guadalajara, México: La Luciérnaga Editores, 1994.

Álvarez-Borland, Isabel. *Cuban-American Literature of Exile: From Person to Person.* Charlottesville: University Press of Virginia, 1998.

Amador Gómez-Quintero, Elena Raysa, and Mireya Pérez-Bustillo, eds. *Female Body: Perspectives of Latin American Artists.* Westport, CT: Greenwood Press, 2002.

André, María Claudia. *Chicanas and Latin American Women Writers Exploring the Realm of the Kitchen as a Self-Empowering Site*. Lewiston, NY: Edwin Mellen Press, 2001.

Andreo García, Juan, and Roland Forgues. *Ser mujer y tomar la palabra en América Latina: pensar y escribir, obrar y reaccionar*. Murcia, Spain: Universidad de Murcia, 1999.

Anim-Addo, Joan. *Framing the Word; Gender and Genre in Caribbean Women's Writing*. London: Whiting and Birch, 1996.

Arambel-Guiñazú, María Cristina, and Claire Emilie Martin. *Las mujeres toman la palabra: escritura femenina del siglo XIX*. Madrid: Iberoamericana, 2001.

Arancibia, Juana Alcira. *Evaluación de la literatura femenina de Latinoamérica, siglo XX*. Westminster, UK: Instituto Literario y Cultural Hispánico, 1985.

Arancibia, Juana Alcira, and Yolanda Rosas, eds. *La nueva mujer en la escritura de autoras hispánicas: ensayos críticos*. Westminster, UK: Instituto Literario y Cultural Hispánico, 1995.

Arosemena Gallardo, Catalina. *La mujer como valor simbólico: el movimiento feminista y sus implicaciones literarias en Hispanoamérica*. Guayaquil, Ecuador: Universidad Católica de Santiago de Guayaquil, 2004.

Arrillaga, María. *Concierto de voces insurgentes: tres autoras puertorriqueñas— Edelmira Maldonado, Violeta López Suria y Anagilda Garrastegui*. Río Piedras: Universidad de Puerto Rico, 1998.

Ascencio, Esteban. *Me lo dijo Elena Poniatowska. Su vida, obra y pasiones, contadas por ella misma*. México, DF: Milenio, 1997.

Avelar, Idelber. *The Untimely Present: Postdictatorial Latin American Fiction and the Task of Mourning*. Durham, NC: Duke University Press, 1999.

Bacarisse, Pamela, ed. *Carnal Knowledge: Essays on the Flesh, Sex, and Sexuality in Hispanic Letters and Film*. Pittsburgh, PA: Ediciones Tres Ríos, 1991.

Balderston, Daniel, ed. *The Latin American Short Story: An Annotated Guide to Anthologies and Criticism*. New York: Greenwood Press, 1992.

——, ed. *The Noel Jitrik Reader: Selected Essays on Latin American Literature*. Durham, NC: Duke University Press, 2005.

——, ed. *Voice-Overs: Translation and Latin American Literature*. Albany: State University of New York Press, 2002.

Barbas-Rhoden, Laura. *Writing Women in Central America: Gender and Fictionalization of History*. Athens: Ohio University Press, 2003.

Bartow, Joanna R. *Subject to Change: The Lessons of Latin American Women's Testimonio for Truth, Fiction, and Theory*. Chapel Hill: University of North Carolina, 2005.

Bassnett, Susan. *Knives and Angels: Women Writers in Latin America*. London: Zed Books, 1990.

Bazán-Figueras, Patricia. *Latin American Women Writers and Horrific Realism*. Lewiston, NY: Edwin Mellen Press, 2004.

Bejel, Emilio. *Escribir en Cuba: entrevistas con escritoras cubanas, 1979-1989.* Río Piedras: Editorial de la Universidad de Puerto Rico, 1991.

Benson Latin American Collection, ed. *Bibliographic Guide to Latin American Studies.* Boston: G.K. Hall, 1978-1998.

Berger, Silvia. *Cuatro textos autobiográficos latinoamericanos: yo, historia e identidad nacional en A. Gerchunoffo, M. Agosín, A. Bioy Casares y O. Soriano.* New York: Peter Lang, 2004.

Beverly, Hoh, and Marck Zimmerman. *Literature and Politics in the Central American Revolutions.* Austin: University of Texas Press, 1990.

Bhalla, Alok. *Latin American Writers: A Bibliography with Critical and Biographical Introductions.* New York: Envoy, 1987.

Biron, Rebecca E. *Murder and Masculinity: Violent Fictions of Twentieth-Century Latin America.* Nashville, TN: Vanderbilt University Press, 2000.

Bleznik, Donald W., ed. *A Sourcebook for Hispanic Literature and Language.* 3rd ed. Lanham, MD: Scarecrow Press, 1995.

Bloom, Harold. *Isabel Allende.* Philadelphia: Chelsea House Publishers, 2003.

Bohner, Charles H., and Lyman Grant, eds. *Short Fiction: Classic and Contemporary.* Upper Saddle River, NJ: Prentice Hall, 2001.

Bomarito, Jessica, and Jeffrey W. Hunter, eds. *Feminism in Literature: A Gale Critical Companion.* Detroit, MI: Thomson Gale, 2005.

Borinsky, Alicia. *Theoretical Fables: The Pedagogical Dream in Contemporary Latin American Fiction.* Philadelphia: University of Pennsylvania Press, 1993.

Boschetto-Sandoval, Sandra, and Marcia P. McGowan, eds. *Claribel Alegría and Central American Literature: Critical Essays.* Athens: Ohio University Center for International Studies, 1994.

Bost, Suzanne. *Mulattas and Mestizas: Representing Mixed Identities in the Americas, 1850-2000.* Athens: University of Georgia Press, 2003.

Boudon, Lawrence, ed. *Handbook of Latin American Studies, vol. 58: Humanities.* Austin: University of Texas Press, 2002.

Brooksbank Jones, Anny, and Catherine Davies, eds. *Latin American Women's Writing: Feminist Readings in Theory and Crisis.* Oxford: Oxford University Press, 1996.

Browdy de Hernández, Jennifer, ed. *Women Writing Resistance: Essays on Latin America and the Caribbean.* Cambridge, MA: South End Press, 2003.

Bryant, Shasta M. *A Selective Bibliography of Bibliographies of Hispanic American Literature.* Austin: Institute of Latin American Studies, University of Texas Press, 1976.

Campuzano, Luisa. *Mujeres latinoamericanas del siglo XX: historia y cultura.* La Habana, Cuba: Casa de las Américas, 1998.

Cantero Rosales, María. *El "boom femenino" hispanoamericano de los años ochenta: un proyecto narrativo de "ser mujer."* Granada, Spain: Universidad de Granada, 2004.

Carey-Webb, Allen, and Stephen Benz, eds. *Teaching and Testimony: Rigoberta*

Menchú and the North American Classroom. Albany: State University of New York Press, 1996.

Carlito, Delores M., ed. *Cuban-American Fiction in English.* Lanham, MD: Scarecrow Press, 2005.

Carrera, Liduvina. *Literatura de mujer: ¿quiénes escriben?* Mérida, Venezuela: Fondo Editorial SOLAR, Dirección de Cultura del Estado Mérida, 1995.

Castellucci Cox, Karen. *Isabel Allende: A Critical Companion.* Westport, CT: Greenwood Press, 2003.

Castillo, Debra A. *Easy Women: Sex and Gender in Modern Mexican Fiction.* Minneapolis: University of Minnesota Press, 1998.

———. *Talking Back: Toward a Latin American Feminist Literary Criticism.* Ithaca, NY: Cornell University Press, 1992.

Castro, Rafaela G. et al., eds. *What Do I Read Next? Multicultural Literature.* Madrid: Iberoamericana, 2003.

Castro-Klarén, Sara. *Literature, Feminism and the Alpha Male: A Search Beyond the Dominance Metaphor.* Washington, DC: Latin American Program, Wilson Center, 1994.

———. *Narrativa femenina en América Latina: prácticas y perspectivas teóricas/ Latin American Women's Narrative: Practices and Theoretical Perspectives.* Madrid: Iberoamericana; Frankfurt am Main, Germany: Vervuert, 2003.

Castro-Klarén, Sara, Sylvia Molloy, and Beatriz Sarlo, eds. *Women Writing in Latin America.* Detroit, MI: Gale Research, 1997.

Chancy, Myriam J. A. *Searching for Safe Spaces: Afro-Caribbean Women Writers in Exile.* Philadelphia: Temple University Press, 1997.

Charnon-Deutsch, Lou. *An Annotated Bibliography of Hispanic Feminist Criticism.* Stony Brook, NY: Feministas Unidas, 1994.

Chávez-Silverman, Susana, and Librada Hernández, eds. *Reading and Writing the Ambiente: Queer Sexualities in Latino, Latin American, and Spanish Culture.* Madison: University of Wisconsin Press, 2000.

Chevigny, Bell Gale, and Gari Laguardia, eds. *Reinventing the Americas: Comparative Studies of Literature in the United States and Latin America.* Cambridge and New York: Cambridge University Press, 1986.

Cobos, Ana María, and Ana Lya Sater, eds. *Latin American Studies: An Annotated Bibliography of Core Works.* Jefferson, NC: McFarland and Company, Inc., Publishers, 2002.

Colville, Georginana M. *Contemporary Women Writing in the Other Americas.* Lewiston, NY: Edwin Mellen Press, 1996.

Corbatta, Jorgelina. *Feminismo y escritura femenina en Latinoamérica.* Buenos Aires, Argentina: Corregidor, 2002.

Correas Zapata, Cecilia. *Isabel Allende: vida y espíritus.* Barcelona, Spain: Plaza & Janes, 1998.

Cortés, Eladio, ed. *Dictionary of Mexican Literature.* Westport, CT: Greenwood Press, 1992.

Cortina, Guadalupe. *Invenciones multitudinarias: escritoras judiomexicanas contemporáneas.* Newark, NJ: Juan de la Cuesta, 2000.

Cortina, Lynn Ellen Rice. *Spanish-American Women Writers.* New York: Garland Press, 1983.

Cortina, Regina, ed. *Mexico: The Artist Is a Woman.* Providence, RI: The Thomas J. Watson Jr. Institute for International Studies, Brown University, 1995.

Corvalán, Graciela. *Latin American Women in English Translation: A Bibliography.* Los Angeles: Latin American Studies Center, 1980.

Cosse, Rómulo, and Lucía Invernizzi et al., eds. *Cristina Peri Rossi, papeles críticos.* Montevideo, Uruguay: Librería Linardi y Risso, 1995.

Covington, Paula H., ed. *Latin America and the Caribbean: A Critical Guide to Research Sources.* Westport, CT: Greenwood Press, 1992.

Craft, Linda J. *Novels of Testimony and Resistance from Central America.* Gainesville: University Press of Florida, 1997.

Craig-Odders, Renee, Jacky Collins, and Glen S. Close, eds. *Hispanic and Luso-Brazilian Detective Fiction: Essays on the* Género Negro *Tradition.* Jefferson, NC: McFarland & Company, Inc., Publishers, 2006.

Cróquer Pedrón, Eleonora. *El gesto de Antífona o la escritura como responsabilidad: Clarice Lispector, Diamela Eltit y Carmen Boullosa.* Santiago, Chile: Editorial Cuarto Propio, 2000.

Cruz, Anne J. et al., eds. *Disciplines on the Line: Feminist Research on Spanish, Latin American and US Latina Women.* Newark, NJ: Juan de la Cuesta, 2003.

Cuchí Coll, Isabel. *Grandes poetisas de América: Clara Lair, Alfonsina Storni, Julia de Burgos, Gabriela Mistral.* San Juan, Puerto Rico: n.p., 1982.

Cuneo, Ana María. *Para leer a Gabriela Mistral.* Santiago, Chile: Universidad Nacional Andrés Bello: Editorial Cuarto Propio, 1998.

Cypress, Sandra M., David R. Kohut, and Rachelle Moore, eds. *Women Authors of Modern Hispanic South America: A Bibliography of Literary Criticism and Interpretation.* Metuchen, NJ, and London: Scarecrow Press, 1989.

Dale, Corrine H., and J. H. E. Paine, eds. *Women on the Edge: Ethnicity and Gender in Short Stories by American Women.* New York: Routledge, 1998.

Davies, Carol Boyce, and Molara Ogundipe-Leslie, eds. *Moving Beyond Boundaries: International Dimensions of Black Women's Writing.* Washington Square, NY: New York University Press, 1995.

Davies, Catherine. *A Place in the Sun: Women Writers in Twentieth-Century Cuba.* London: Zed Books, 1997.

——. *Women Writers in Twentieth-Century Spain and Spanish America.* Lewiston, NY: Edwin Mellen Press, 1993.

Dávila Gonçalves, Michele C. *El archivo de la memoria: la novela de formación femenina de Rosa Chacel, Rosa Montero, Rosario Castellanos y Elena Poniatowska.* New Orleans: University Press of the South, 1999.

De Beer, Gabriella. *Contemporary Mexican Women Writers: Five Voices.* Austin: University of Texas Press, 1996.

de la Cinta Ramblado-Minero, María. *Isabel Allende's Writing of the Self: Trespassing the Boundaries of Fiction and Autobiography*. Lewiston, NY: Edwin Mellen Press, 2002.

de Valdés, María Elena. *The Shattered Mirror: Representations of Women in Mexican Literature*. Austin: University of Texas Press, 1998.

———. *Women and the Personal Genres (Autobiography, Memoir, Diary, Epistolary) in Latin American Literary History*. Pittsburgh, PA: Latin American Studies Association, 1998.

Dejbord, Parizad Tamara. *Cristina Peri Rossi: escritora del exilio*. Buenos Aires, Argentina: Galerna, 1998.

Di Antonio, Robert E. *Brazilian Fiction: Aspects and Evolution of the Contemporary Narrative*. Fayetteville: University of Arkansas Press, 1989.

Díaz, Gwendolyn Joise, and María Inés Lagos-Pope. *La palabra en vivo: narrativa de Luisa Valenzuela*. Santiago, Chile: Editorial Cuarto Propio, 1996.

Domenella, Ana Rosa, and Luzelena Gutiérrez de Velasco. *Territorio de leonas: cartografía de narradoras mexicanas en los noventa*. México, DF: Universidad Autónoma Metropolitana, Unidad Iztapalapa, 2001.

Domenella, Ana Rosa, and Nora Pasternac, eds. *Las voces olvidadas: antología crítica de narradoras mexicanas nacidas en el siglo XIX*. México, DF: El Colegio de México, 1991.

Dreyfus, Mariela et al., eds. *A imagen y semejanza: reflexiones de escritoras peruanas contemporáneas*. Lima, Peru: Fondo Editorial de Cultura, 1998.

Duncan, J. Ann. *Voices, Visions, and a New Reality: Mexican Fiction Since 1970*. Pittsburgh, PA: University of Pittsburgh Press, 1986.

Edmondson, Belinda. *Making Men: Bender, Literary Authority and Women's Writing in Caribbean Narrative*. Durham, NC: Duke University Press, 1999.

Eldridge Miller, Jane. *Who's Who in Contemporary Women's Writing*. New York: Routledge, 2001.

Ellison, Fred P. *Brazil's New Novel; Four Northeastern Masters; José Lins do Rego, Jorge Amado, Graciliano Ramos and Rachel de Queiroz*. Berkeley: University of California Press, 1954.

Erro-Peralta, Nora, and Caridad Silva. *Beyond the Border: A New Age in Latin American Women's Fiction*. Gainesville: University Press of Florida, 2000.

Escliar, Myriam. *Mujeres en la literatura y la vida judeoargentina*. Buenos Aires, Argentina: Editorial Mila, 1996.

Espinosa Rugarcía, Ampara, Marcela Ruiz de Velasco, and Gloria M. Prado Garduño, eds. *Palabras de mujer*. México, DF: Editorial Diana, 1989.

Fares, Gustavo, and Eliana Cazaubon Hermann, eds. *Contemporary Argentinean Women Writers: A Critical Anthology*. Trans. Linda Britt. Gainesville: University Press of Florida, 1998.

Feracho, Lesley. *Linking the Americas: Race, Hybrid Discourses, and the Reformulation of Feminine Identity*. Albany: State University of New York Press, 2004.

Ferreira-Pinto, Cristina. *Literary Criticism and Collections/Medieval*. Lafayette, IN: Purdue University Press, 2004.

Fiol-Matta, Licia. *A Queer Mother for the Nation: The State and Gabriela Mistral*. Minneapolis: University of Minnesota Press, 2002.

Fisher, Jerilyn, and Ellen S. Silber, eds. *Women in Literature: Reading through the Lens of Gender*. Westport, CT: Greenwood Press, 2003.

Fister, Barbara. *Third World Women's Literatures: A Dictionary and Guide to Materials in English*. Westport, CT: Greenwood Press, 1995.

Flores, Angel. *Spanish American Authors: The Twentieth Century*. New York: Wilson, 1992.

Flores, Juan, ed. *Divided Arrival: Narratives of the Puerto Rican Migration, 1920-1950*. New York: Centro de Estudios Puertorriqueños, Hunter College, City University of New York, 1987.

Flores, Yolanda. *The Drama of Gender: Feminist Theater by Women of the Americas*. New York: Peter Lang, 2000.

Flori, Mónica Roy. *Streams of Silver: Six Contemporary Women Writers from Argentina*. Lewisburg, PA: Bucknell University Press, 1995.

Forgues, Roland. *Mujer, creación y problemas de identidad en América Latina*. Mérida, Venezuela: Universidad de los Andes, Consejo de Publicaciones, 1999.

Fornet, Jorge. *Reescrituras de la memoria: novela femenina y revolución en México*. La Habana, Cuba: Editorial Letras Cubanas, 1994.

Foster, David William. *Cultural Diversity in Latin American Literature*. Albuquerque: University of New Mexico Press, 1994.

Foster, David William, ed. *Mexican Literature: A History*. Austin: University of Texas Press, 1994.

Foster, David William, and Daniel Altamiranda, eds. *Spanish American Literature: A Collection of Essays*. New York: Garland Press, 1997.

Foster, David William, and Cynthia Tompkins, eds. *Notable Twentieth-Century Latin American Women: A Biographical Dictionary*. Westport, CT: Greenwood Press, 2001.

Fox-Lockhert, Lucía. *Mujeres: escritura y subversión*. East Lansing, MI: Editorial La Nueva Crónica, 1995.

France, Peter, ed. *The Oxford Guide to Literature in English Translation*. Oxford: Oxford University Press, 2000.

Frederick, Bonnie, ed. *La pluma y la aguja: las escritoras de la generación del '80: antología*. Buenos Aires, Argentina: Feminari Editora, 1993.

———. *Wily Modesty: Argentine Women Writers, 1860-1910*. Tempe: ASU Center for Latin American Studies Press, Arizona State University, 1998.

Freudenthal, Juan R., and Patricia M. Freudenthal, eds. *Index to Anthologies of Latin American Literature in English Translation*. Boston: G.K. Hall, 1977.

Fuentes, Yvonne, and Margaret R. Parker, eds. *Leading Ladies: Mujeres en la literatura*. Baton Rouge: Louisiana State University, 2006.

338   Other Sources Dealing with Latin American Women's Literature

Fundação Biblioteca Nacional, Ministerio da Cultura. *Brazilian Authors Translated Abroad.* Rio de Janeiro, Brazil: Fundação Biblioteca Nacional, Ministerio da Cultura, 1994.

Gac-Artigas, Priscilla. *Reflexiones: ensayos sobre escritoras hispanoamericanas contemporáneas, volumen 1.* Fair Haven, NJ: Ediciones Nuevo Espacio, 2002.

Galván, Delia V. *Narradoras hispanoamericanas contemporáneas de ficción corta, 1974-1989.* Querétero, México: Universidad Autónoma de Querétero, 1997.

Garcia, Jorge J. E. *Philosophy and Literature in Latin America: A Critical Assessment of the Current Situation.* Albany: State University of New York Press, 1989.

García, Kay S. *Broken Bars: New Perspectives from Mexican Women Writers.* Albuquerque: University of New Mexico Press, 1995.

García Barragán, María Guadalupe. *Narrativa de autoras mexicanas, 1900-1950: breve reseña y bibliografía.* Guadalajara, México: Universidad de Guadalajara, 2002.

García Pinto, Magdalena. *Historias íntimas: conversaciones con diez escritoras latinamericanas.* Hanover, NH: Ediciones del Norte, 1988.

——. *Women Writers of Latin America: Intimate Histories.* Trans. Trudy Balch and Magdalena García Pinto. Austin: University of Texas Press, 1991.

Garfield, Evelyn Picon. *Women's Voices from Latin America: Interviews with Six Contemporary Authors.* Detroit, MI: Wayne State University Press, 1985.

Garner, Jane, ed. *Sampling of Spanish American Novels in English Translation.* Austin: Benson Latin American Collection, University of Texas, 1985.

Gascón Vera, Elena. *Un mito nuevo: la mujer como sujeto/objeto literario.* Madrid: Editorial Pliegos, 1992.

Gazarín-Gautier, Marie-Lise. *Interviews with Latin American Writers.* Elmwood, IL: Dalkey Archive Press, 1989.

Geisdorger Feal, Rosemary, and Yvette E. Miller, eds. *Isabel Allende Today: An Anthology of Essays.* Pittsburgh, PA: Latin American Literary Review Press, 2002.

Ghosh, Bishnupriya, and Brinda Bose, eds. *Interventions: Feminist Dialogues on Third World Women's Literature and Film.* New York: Garland Publishing, 1997.

Giannotti, Janet, and Laura Esquivel. *A Companion Text for* Like Water for Chocolate. Ann Arbor: University of Michigan Press, 1999.

G.K. Hall & Co., ed. *Bibliographic Guide to Latin American Studies.* Boston: G.K. Hall, 2004.

Gliemmo, Graciela. *Las huellas de la memoria: entrevistas a escritores latinoamericanos.* Buenos Aires, Argentina: Beas Ediciones, 1994.

Gold, Janet N. *Volver a imaginarlas: retratos de escritoras centroamericanas.* Tegucigalpa, Honduras: Guaymuras, 1998.

Gonzáles, María. *Contemporary Mexican-American Women Novelists: Toward a Feminist Identity.* New York: Peter Lang, 1996.

Gonzáles Ascorra, Martha Irene. *La evolución de la conciencia femenina a través de las novelas de Gertrudis Gómez de Avellaneda, Soledad Acosta de Samper y Mercedes Cabello de Carbonera.* New York: Peter Lang, 1997.

González-Vergara, Ruth. *Nuestras escritoras chilenas: una historia por descifrar.* Santiago, Chile: Editorial Hispano-Chilena, 1992.

Gotlib, Nadia Battella. *Clarice: uma vida que se conta.* São Paulo, Brazil, SP: Editora Atica, 1995.

Granier, James Albert. *Latin American Belles-Lettres in English Translation: A Selective and Annotated Guide.* Washington, DC: Library of Congress, 1971.

Gray, Elizabeth Dunbar. *All the Other Voices: An Annotated Bibliography of Fiction by African, Asian and Latin American Women.* Waltham, MA: E. Gray, 1987.

Guerra-Cunningham, Lucía. *Splintering Darkness: Latin American Women Writers in Search of Themselves.* Pittsburgh, PA: Latin American Literary Review Press, 1990.

Guibelalde, César Gabriel. *Aportes para la extracción de la piedra locura: vida y obra de Alejandra Pizarnik.* Cordoba, Argentina: Editorial Dimas, 1998.

Gutiérrez de Velasco, Luzelena et al., eds. *De pesares y alegrías: escritoras latino-americanas y caribeñas contemporáneas.* México, DF: Colegio de México, 1999.

Haase, Donald. *Fairy Tales and Feminism: New Approaches.* Detroit, MI: Wayne State University Press, 2004.

Hart, Stephen M. *Isabel Allende, Eva Luna and Cuentos de Eva Luna.* London: Grant and Cutler, 2003.

——, ed. *White Ink: Essays on Twentieth Century Feminine Fiction in Spain and Latin America.* London: Tamesis Books, 1993.

Henao, Eda B. *The Colonial Subject's Search for Nation, Culture, and Identity in the Works of Julia Alvarez, Rosario Ferré, and Ana Lydia Vega.* Lewiston, NY: Edwin Mellen Press, 2003.

Hernández, Carmen Dolores. *Puerto Rican Voices in English: Interviews with Writers.* Westport, CT: Greenwood Press, 1997.

Hernández, Laura. *Escribir a oscuras: el erotismo en la literatura femenina latinoamericana.* Buenos Aires, Argentina: Lumiere, 2003.

Hintz, Suzanne S. *Rosario Ferré: A Search for Identity.* New York: Peter Lang, 1995.

Hong Kingston, Maxine, and Luisa Valenzuela. *Two Foreign Women.* Leichhardt, NSW: Pluto Press, 1990.

Hooks, Margaret. *Guatemalan Women Speak.* Washington, DC: Ecumenical Program on Central America and the Caribbean, 1993.

Hoving, Isabel. *In Praise of New Travelers: Reading Caribbean Migrant Women Writers.* Palo Alto, CA: Stanford University Press, 2001.

Hulet, Claude L., ed. *Latin American Prose in English Translation. A Bibliography.*

Washington, DC: Pan American Union, 1964.

Ibsen, Kristine. *The Other Mirror: Women's Narrative in Mexico, 1980-1995*. Westport, CT: Greenwood Press, 1997.

——. *Women's Spiritual Autobiography in Colonial Spanish America*. Gainesville: University Press of Florida, 1999.

Ippolito, Emilia. *Caribbean Women Writers: Identity and Gender*. Columbia, SC: Camden House, 2000.

Jamieson, Sally Brewster. *English Translation of Latin American Literature: A Bibliography*. Washington, DC: Pan American Union, Division of Intellectual Cooperation, 1947.

Jaramillo, María Mercedes, Betty Osorio de Negret, and Angela Inés Robledo, eds. *Literatura y diferencia: escritoras colombianas del siglo XX*. Medellín, Colombia: Editorial Universidad de Antioquia, 1995.

Jehenson, Myriam Yvonne. *Latin American Women Writers: Class, Race and Gender*. Albany: State University of New York Press, 1995.

Jiménez, Luis A. *La voz de la mujer en la literatura hispanoamericana fin-de-siglo*. San José: Editorial de la Universidad de Costa Rica, 1999.

Jiménez Corretjer, Zoé. *El fantástico femenino en España y América: Martin Gaite, Rodoreda, Garro y Peri Rossi*. San Juan: Editorial de la Universidad de Puerto Rico, 2001.

Jorge, Lidia. *In Other Words: Lidia Jorge: Por outras palavras*. Dartmouth: Center for Portuguese Studies and Cultures, University of Massachusetts, 1999.

Jorgensen, Beth Ellen. The *Writing of Elena Poniatowska: Engaging Dialogues*. Austin: University of Texas Press, 1994.

Joysmith, Claire, ed. Las *formas de nuestras voces: Chicana and Mexicana Writers in Mexico*. México, DF: Universidad Nacional Autónoma de México, Centro de Investigaciones sobre América del Norte, 1995.

Kaminsky, Amy K. *Reading the Body Politic: Feminist Criticism and Latin American Women Writers*. Minneapolis: University of Minnesota Press, 1993.

Kanellos Nicolas, ed. *Biographical Dictionary of Hispanic Literature in the United States: The Literature of Puerto Ricans, Cuban Americans, and Other Hispanic Writers*. Westport, CT: Greenwood Press, 1989.

——, ed. *En otra voz: antología de la literatura hispana en los Estados Unidos*. Tempe, AZ: Arte Público Press, 2002.

——, ed. *Herencia: The Anthology of Hispanic Literature of the United States*. New York and Oxford: Oxford University Press, 2003.

——, ed. *The Hispanic Literary Companion*. Detroit, MI: Visible Ink, 1997.

——, ed. *Hispanic Literature of the United States: A Comprehensive Reference*. Westport, CT: Greenwood Press, 2003.

Keenoy, Ray, David Treece and Paul Hyland et al., eds. *The Babel Guide to the Fiction of Portugal, Brazil, and Africa in English Translation*. London: Boulevard Books, 1995.

Kester-Shelton, Pamela, ed. *Feminist Writers*. Detroit, MI: St. James Press, 1996.

Kevane, Bridget. *Latino Literature in America*. Willimantic, CT: Greenwood Press, 2003.

Kirk, Pamela. *Sor Juana Inés de la Cruz: Religion, Art, and Feminism*. New York: Continuum, 1998.

Klingenberg, Patricia Nisbet. *Fantasies of the Feminine: The Short Stories of Silvina Ocampo*. Lewisburg, PA: Bucknell University Press, 1999.

Kossnar, Sylvia, ed. *Bibliography of Hispanic Women Writers*. Bloomington, IL: Chicano-Riqueño Studies, 1980.

Knaster, Meri. *Women in Spanish America: An Annotated Bibliography from Pre-conquest to Contemporary Times*. Boston: G.K. Hall, 1977.

Kristal, Efraín. *The Cambridge Companion to the Latin American Novel*. Cambridge and New York: Cambridge University Press, 2005.

Lagos, María Inés. *En tono mayor: relatos de formación de protagonista femenina en Hispanoamérica*. Santiago, Chile: Editorial Cuarto Propio, 1996.

Lagos, Ramona. *Metáforas de lo indecible: Gioconda Belli, Lucía Guerra y Angeles Mastretta*. Providencia, Santiago, Chile: Editorial Cuarto Propio, 2003.

Larson, Catherine. *Latin American Women Dramatists: Theater, Texts, and Theories*. Bloomington, IL: Indiana University Press, 1998.

Latin American PEN Foundation, ed. *Conditional Liberty*. Guadalajara, México: La Luciérnaga Editores, 2000.

Leavitt, Sturgis E. *Hispano-American Literature in the United States: A Bibliography of Translations and Criticism*. Cambridge, MA: Harvard University Press, 1932.

Lee, Juan Tomás, ed. *Latin American Literature Pathfinder*. Salt Lake City: Reforma de Utah, 1998.

Leonard, Kathy S., ed. *Bibliographic Guide to Chicana and Latina Narrative*. Westport, CT: Greenwood Press, 2003.

——, ed. *Index to Translated Short Fiction by Latin American Women in English Language Anthologies*. Westport, CT: Greenwood Press, 1997.

——. *Una revelación desde la literatura: entrevistas a narradoras bolivianas*. New York: Peter Lang, 2003.

Lertora, Juan Carlos. *Una poética de literatura menor: la narrativa de Diamela Eltit*. Santiago, Chile: Para Textos/Editorial Cuarto Propio, 1993.

Levine, Suzanne Jill. *Latin American Fiction and Poetry in Translation*. New York: Center for Inter-American Relations, 1970.

Levine, Suzanne Jill. *The Subversive Scribe: Translating Latin American Fiction*. St. Paul, MN: Graywolf Press, 1991.

Lindsay, Claire. *Locating Latin American Women Writers: Christina Peri Rossi, Rosario Ferré, Albalucía Angel, and Isabel Allende*. New York: Peter Lang, 2003.

Lindstrom, Naomi. *Early Spanish American Narrative*. Austin: University of Texas Press, 2005.

———. *The Social Conscience of Latin American Writing.* Austin: University of Texas Press, 1998.

———. *Women's Voice in Latin American Literature.* Washington, DC: Three Continents Press, 1989.

Lockhart, Darrell B. *Jewish Writers of Latin America: A Dictionary.* New York and London: Garland Publishing, Inc., 1997.

López, Irma M. *Historia, escritura e identitdad: la novelísitica de María Luisa Puga.* New York: Peter Lang, 1996.

López-Cabrales, María del Mar. *La pluma y la represión: escritoras contemporáneas argentinas.* New York: Peter Lang, 1999.

López de Martínez, Adelaida. *Discurso femenino actual.* San Juan: Editorial de la Universidad de Puerto Rico, 1995.

López de Martínez, Adelaida. *Special Issue on Dynamics of Change in Latin American Literature: Contemporary Women Writers.* Manhattan: Department of Modern Languages, Kansas State University, 1996.

López González, Aralia. *De la intimidad a la acción: la narrativa de escritoras latinoamericanas y su desarrollo.* México: Universidad Autónoma Metropolitana, Unidad Iztapalapa, 1985.

López González, Aralia, Amelia Malagamba, Elena Urrutia, eds. *Mujer y literatura mexicana y chicana: culturas en contacto 2.* México, DF: Colegio de México, 1988.

———. *Sin imágenes falsas, sin falsos espejos: narradoras mexicanas del siglo XX.* México, DF: Colegio de México, Programa Interdisciplinario de Estudios de la Mujer, 1995.

Loustau, Laura Rosa. *Cuerpos errantes: literatura latina y latinoamericana en Estados Unidos.* Rosario, Argentina: B. Viterbo Editora, 2002.

Ludmer, Josefina. *The Corpus Delicti: A Manual of Argentine Fiction.* Trans. Glen S. Close. Pittsburgh, PA: University of Pittsburgh Press, 2004.

Luis, William, and Ann González, eds. *Modern Latin American Fiction Writers.* Detroit, MI: Gale Research, 1994.

Lutes, Leasa Y. *Allende, Buitrago, Luiselli: aproximaciones teóricas al concepto del "Bildungsroman" femenino.* New York: Peter Lang, 2000.

McCracken, Ellen Marie, ed. *New Latina Narrative: The Feminine Space of Postmodern Ethnicity.* Tucson: University of Arizona Press, 1999.

Magill, Frank Northen. *Great Women Writers: The Lives and Works of 135 of the World's Most Important Women Writers, from Antiquity to the Present.* New York: Holt, 1994.

Maier, Linda S., and Isabel Dulfano, eds. *Woman as Witness: Essays on Testimonial Literature by Latin American Women.* New York: Peter Lang, 2004.

Maíz, Magdalena, and Luis H. Peña. *Modalidades de representación del sujeto auto/bio/gráfico femenino.* San Nicolás de los Garza, Nuevo León, México: Facultad de Filosofía y Letras, 1997.

Maloof, Judy. *Voices of Resistance: Testimonies of Cuban and Chilean Women.* Lexington: University Press of Kentucky, 1999.

Maratos, Danel C., and Marnesba D. Hill, eds. *Escritores de la diáspora cubana: Manual biobibliográfica/Cuban Exile Writers: A Biobibliographic Handbook.* Metuchen, NJ: Scarecrow Press, 1986.

Marchant, Elizabeth Anne. *Critical Acts: Latin American Women and Cultural Criticism.* Gainesville: University Press of Florida, 1999.

Martínez, Elena M. *Lesbian Voices from Latin America: Breaking Ground.* New York: Garland Press, 1996.

Martínez Wood, Jamie. *Latino Writers and Journalists.* New York: Facts on File, 2007.

Marting, Diane E., ed. *Clarice Lispector: A Bio-Bibliography.* Westport, CT: Greenwood Press, 1993.

Marting, Diane E., ed. *Escritoras de Hispanoamérica: una guía bio-bibliográfica.* México, DF: Siglo Veintiuno Editores, 1990.

——. *The Sexual Woman in Latin American Literature: Dangerous Desires.* Gainesville: University Press of Florida, 2001.

——, ed. *Spanish American Women Writers: A Bio-bibliographical Source Book.* New York: Greenwood Press, 1990.

——, ed. *Women Writers of Spanish America: An Annotated Bio-bibliographic Guide.* New York: Greenwood Press, 1987.

Mattalia, Sonia, and Nuria Girona Fibla. *Aun y más allá: mujeres y discursos.* Valencia, Spain: Ediciones eXcultura, 2001.

Medeiros-Lichem, María Teresa. *Reading the Feminine Voice in Latin American Women's Fiction: From Teresa de la Parra to Elena Poniatowska and Luisa Valenzuela.* New York: Peter Lang, 2002.

Mendoza, María Luisa. *Mujeres que cuentan: siete escritoras mexicanas de su puño y letra.* México, DF: Ediciones Ariadna, 2000.

Merithew, Charlene. *Re-presenting the Nation: Contemporary Mexican Women Writers.* New Orleans: University Press of the South, 2001.

Merrim, Stephanie. *Feminist Perspectives on Sor Juana Inés de la Cruz.* Detroit, MI: Wayne State University Press, 1999.

Meyer, Doris, ed. *Reinterpreting the Spanish American Essay: Translations of 19th and 20th Century Women's Essays.* Austin: University of Texas Press, 1995.

Meyer, Doris, and Margarite Fernández Olmos, eds. *Contemporary Women Authors of Latin America.* Brooklyn, NY: Brooklyn College Press, 1983.

Meyers, Kathleen Ann. *Neither Saints nor Sinners: Writing the Lives of Women in Spanish America.* Oxford: Oxford University Press, 2003.

Miller, James Edwin, Robert O'Neal, Helen M. McDonnell, and Angel Flores, eds. *From Spain and the Americas: Literature in Translation.* Glenview, IL: Scott, Foresman, 1970.

Molloy, Sylvia. *Autobiographical Writing in Spanish America*. New York and Cambridge: Cambridge University Press, 1991.

Morales, Mariano, ed. *Por la literatura: mujeres y escritura en México*. Puebla, México: Universidad Autónoma de Puebla, 1992.

Muñoz, Willy O. *El personaje feminino en la narrativa de escritoras hispano-americanas*. Madrid: Editorial Pliegos, 1992.

——. *Polifonía de la marginalidad: la narrativa de escritoras latinoamericanas*. Santiago, Chile: Editorial Cuarto Propio, 1999.

Nauss Millay, Amy. *Voices from the Fuente Viva: The Effect of Orality in Twentieth-Century Spanish American Narrative*. Lewisburg, PA: Bucknell University Press, 2005.

Nesbitt, Anna Sheets. *Short Story Criticism: Excerpts from Criticism of the Works of Short Fiction Writers. Volume 36*. Detroit, MI: Gale Research, Inc., 2000.

Newson, Adele S. and Linda Strong-Leck. *Winds of Change: The Transforming Voices of Caribbean Women Writers and Scholars*. New York: Peter Lang Publishing, 1998.

Niebylski, Dianna C. *Humoring Resistance: Laughter and the Excessive Body in Contemporary Latin American Women's Fiction*. Albany: State University of New York Press, 2004.

Nisbet Klingenberg, Patricia. *Fantasies of the Feminine: The Short Stories of Silvina Ocampo*. Lewisburg, PA: Bucknell University Press, 1999.

Niyi Afolabi, Marcio Barbosa, and Esmeralda Ribeiro, eds. *Black Notebooks: Contemporary Afro-Brazilian Literature / Cadernos negros: literatura afro-brasileira contemporânea*. Trans. Niyi Afolabi. Trenton, NJ: Africa World Press, 2006.

O'Brien, John. *Writers on Writing: The Best of the Review of Contemporary Fiction*. Normal, IL: The Review of Contemporary Fiction, 1999.

Ocasio, Rafael. *Literature of Latin America*. Westport, CT: Greenwood Press, 2004.

O'Connell, Joanna. *Prospero's Daughter: The Prose of Rosario Castellanos*. Austin: University of Texas Press, 1995.

Olea, Raquel. *Lengua víbora: producciones de lo femenino en la escritura de mujeres chilenas*. Santiago, Chile: Editorial Cuarto Propio, 1998.

Olea, Raquel, and Soledad Farina, eds. *Una palabra cómplice: encuentro con Gabriela Mistral*. Santiago, Chile: Editorial Cuarto Propio, Isis Internacional, 1997.

Olmos, Margarita Fernández, and Lizbeth Paravisini-Gebert, eds. *Placer de la palabra-Pleasure in the Word: Erotic Writings by Latin American Women*. Fredonia, NY: White Pine Press, 1993.

Ortega, Julio. *El combate de los ángeles: literatura, género, diferencia*. Lima, Peru: Pontificia Universidad Católica del Perú, 1999.

Ostrov, Andrea. *El género al bies: cuerpo, género y escritura en cinco narradoras latinoamericanas*. Córdoba, Argentina: Alción, 2004.

Owen Steiner, Patricia, ed. and trans. *Victoria Ocampo: Writer, Feminist, Woman of the World.* Albuquerque: University of New Mexico Press, 1999.

Parks, George B., and Ruth Z. Temple. *The Literatures of the World in English Translation: A Bibliography.* New York: Frederick Ungar Publishing Co., 1970.

Payne, Johnny. *Conquest of the New Word: Experimental Fiction and Translation in the Americas.* Austin: University of Texas Press, 1993.

Payne, Judith A., and Earl E. Fitz. *Ambiguity and Gender in the New Novel of Brazil and Spanish America.* Iowa City: University of Iowa Press, 2005.

Paz, Octavio. *Sor Juana, or, the Traps of Faith.* Trans. Margaret Sayers Peden. New York: Cambridge University Press, 1988.

Pérez, Janet, and Genaro Pérez J., eds. *Experimental Fiction by Hispanic Women Writers.* Odessa State, TX: Monographic Review, 1992.

———. *The Nueva Novela Histórica in Hispanic Literature.* Lubbock, TX: Classical and Modern Languages, Texas Tech. University, 2003.

Pérez Sarduy, Pedro, and Jean Stubbs, eds. *Afro-Cuban Voices: On Race and Identity in Contemporary Cuba.* Gainesville: University of Florida Press, 2000.

Pertusa, Imaculada, and Melissa A. Stewart. *The Canon Unplugged: Rethinking the Writer, the Reader, and the Critic in Hispanic Women's Literature.* Greeley: University of Northern Colorado, 2003.

Pfeiffer, Erna. *Exiliadas, emigrantes, viajeras: encuentros con diez escritoras latinoamericanas.* Frankfurt: Vervuert, 1995.

Phelan, Marion. *A Bibliography of Latin American Fiction in English.* Phoenix, AZ: Latin America Area Research, 1956.

Pino-Ojeda, Walescka, and Elena Poniatowska et al., eds. *Sobre castas y puentes: conversaciones con Elena Poniatowska, Rosario Ferré y Diamela Eltit.* Santiago, Chile: Editorial Cuarto Propio, 2000.

Poey, Delia. *Latino American Literature in the Classroom: The Politics of Transformation.* Gainesville: University of Florida Press, 2002.

Porter, Dorothy B. *Afro-Braziliana: A Working Bibliography.* Boston: G.K. Hall, 1978.

Postlewate, Marisa Herrera. *How and Why I Write: Redefining Hispanic Women's Writing and Experience.* New York: Peter Lang, 2003.

Prentice Hall Literature Library, ed. *Biography and Autobiography.* Upper Saddle River: Prentice Hall, Inc., 2000.

Quinlan, Susan Canty. *The Female Voice in Contemporary Brazilian Narrative.* New York: Peter Lang, 1991.

Quintana, Alvina E. *Reading U.S. Latina Writers: Remapping American Literature.* New York: Palgrave, 2003.

Ramos Rosado, Marie. *La mujer negra en la literatura puertorriqueña: cuentística de los setenta: Luis Rafael Sánchez, Carmelo Rodríguez Torres, Rosario Ferré y Ana Lydia Vega.* San Juan: Editorial de la Universidad de Puerto Rico, 1999

Resnick, Margery, and Isabelle de Courtivron, eds. *Women Writers in Translation: An Annotated Bibliography, 1945-1982.* New York and London: Garland Publishing, Inc., 1984.

Rivera, Carmen S. *Kissing the Mango Tree: Puerto Rican Women Rewriting American Literature.* Houston, TX: Arte Público Press, 2002.

Roca, Ana, and Helena Alonso. *American Women Writers: A Critical Reference Guide from Colonial Times to the Present.* Detroit, MI: St. James, 2000.

Rodríguez, Ileana, ed. *House/Garden/Nation: Space, Gender and Ethnicity in Postcolonial Latin American Literature by Women.* Durham, NC: Duke University Press, 1994.

Rosenberg, Roberta, ed. *Women's Studies: An Interdisciplinary Anthology.* New York: Peter Lang, 2001.

Rostagno, Irene. *Searching for Recognition: The Promotion of Latin American Literature in the United States.* Westport, CT: Greenwood Press, 1997.

Ryan, Bryan, ed. *Hispanic Writers: A Selection of Sketches from Contemporary Authors.* Detroit, MI: Gale Research Inc., 1991.

Sadlier, Darlene J., ed. and trans. *Brazilian Women Writing.* Bloomington: Indiana University Press, 1992.

Sáenz de Tejada, Cristina. *La (re)construcción de la identidad femenina en la narrativa autobiográfica latinoamericana, 1975-1985.* New York: Peter Lang, 1998.

Saint-André, Estela Marta, and Adela Rolón, eds. *Cuando escriben las mujeres.* San Juan, Puerto Rico: EFFHA, 1998.

Sánchez-González, Lisa. *Boricua Literature: A Literary History of the Puerto Rican Diaspora.* New York: New York University Press, 2001.

Santos, Cristina. *Bending the Rules in the Quest for an Authentic Female Identity: Clarice Lispector and Carmen Boullosa.* New York: Peter Lang, 2004.

Schaefer, Claudia. *Textured Lives: Women, Art and Representation in Modern Mexico.* Tucson, AZ: University of Arizona Press, 1994.

Schlau, Stacey. *Spanish American Women's Use of the Word: Colonial through Contemporary Narratives.* Tucson: University of Arizona Press, 2001.

Seminar on Feminism and Culture in Latin America, ed. *Women, Culture, and Politics in Latin America.* Berkeley and Los Angeles: University of California Press, 1990.

Shaw, Bradley A., ed. *Latin American Literature in English Translation. An Annotated Bibliography.* New York: New York University Press, 1976.

Shaw, Bradley A. *Latin American Literature in English, 1975-1978.* New York: Center for Inter-American Relations, 1979.

Shea, Maureen E. *Women as Outsiders: Undercurrents of Oppression in Latin American Literature.* San Francisco: Austin and Winfield, 1993.

Silverman, Malcolm. *Diversity in the Prose Fiction of Dinah Silveria de Queiroz.* Lisbon, Portugal: Livraria Bertrnad, 1979.

Simone, Roberta, ed. *The Immigrant Experience in American Fiction: An Annotated Bibliography*. Lanham, MD: Scarecrow Press, 1995.

Sirias, Silvio. *Julia Álvarez: A Critical Companion*. Westport, CT: Greenwood Publishing Group, 2001.

Sosa, José Rafael, and Aída Cartagena Portalatín. *Mujer y literatura*. Santo Domingo, Domincan Republic: Editora Universitaria-UASD, 1986.

Steele, Cynthia. *Politics, Gender, and the Mexican Novel, 1968-1988: Beyond the Pyramid*. Austin: University of Texas Press, 1992.

Steinberg, Sybil. *Writers and Their Craft, vol. 1*. New York: Reed Press, 2003.

Stern, Irwing, ed. *Dictionary of Brazilian Literature*. New York: Greenwood Press, 1988.

Stoner, K. Lynn, Serrano Pérez, and Luís Hipólito, eds. *Cuban and Cuban-American Women: An Annotated Bibliography*. Wilmington, DE: Scholarly Resources, 2000.

Suárez, Lucma M., Lucía M. Suárez, and Kevin A. Yelvington, eds. *Tears of Hispaniola: Haitian and Dominican Diaspora Memory*. Tallahassee: University of Florida Press, 2006.

Swanson, Philip, ed. *The Companion to Latin American Studies*. Oxford: Oxford University Press, 2003.

———. *Latin American Fiction: A Short Introduction*. New York: Blackwell Publishing, 2005.

Taylor, Claire. *Bodies and Texts: Configurations of Identity in the Works of Griselda Gambaro, Albalucía Angel, and Laura Esquivel*. Leeds, UK: Maney Pub. for the Modern Humanities Research Association, 2003.

Taylor, Kathy. *The New Narrative of Mexico: Sub-Versions of History in Mexican Fiction*. Lewisburg, PA: Bucknell University Press, 1994.

Tierney-Tello, Mary Beth. *Allegories of Transgression and Transformation: Experimental Fiction by Women Writing under Dictatorship*. Albany: State University of New York Press, 1996.

Torres, Lourdes, and Inmaculada Pertusa, eds. *Tortilleras: Hispanic and U.S. Latina Lesbian Expression*. Philadelphia: Temple University Press, 2003.

Torres-Pou, Joan. *Aproximaciones a la narrativa femenina del diecinueve en Latinoamérica*. Lewiston, NY: Edwin Mellen Press, 2002.

Treece, David, and Ray Keenoy, eds. *The Babel Guide to Brazilian Fiction in English Translation*. Oxford: Boulevard Books, 2001.

Trevizán, Liliana. *Política/sexualidad: nudo en la escritura de mujeres latinoamericanas*. Lanham, MD: University Press of America, 1997.

Unruh, Vicky. *Performing Women and Modern Literary Culture in Latin America: Intervening Acts*. Austin: University of Texas Press, 2006.

Valis, Noel et al., eds. *In the Feminine Mode: Essays on Hispanic Women Writers*. London: Bucknell University Press, 1990.

Valjalo, David. *Canción de Marcela: mujer y cultura en el mundo hispánico*. Madrid, Spain: Orígenes, 1989.

Van der Plas, Els, and Marlous Willemsen, eds. *Creating Spaces of Freedom: Culture in Defiance.* London: Saqi, 2002.

Vásquez, Ana, Ana Luisa Valdés, and Ana María Araujo. *Las mujeres del Cono Sur escriben.* Stockholm: Nordan Comunidad, 1985.

Vásquez, Carmen. "Bibliographical Resume of English Translations." *Cultural Identity in Latin America.* Ed. Birgitta Leander. Paris: UNESCO, 1986: 201-204.

Virgilio, Carmelo, and Naomi Lindstrom. *Women as Myth and Metaphor in Latin American Literature.* Columbia: University of Missouri Press, 1988.

Watson Miller, Ingrid, ed. *Afro-Hispanic Literature: An Anthology of Hispanic Writers of African Ancestry.* Miami: Ediciones Universal, 1991.

West-Durán, Alan, ed. *Latino and Latina Writers, vol. 2.* New York: Scribner's, 2004.

Wilgus, Kana S., ed. *Latin American Books: An Annotated Bibliography.* New York: Center for Inter-American Relations, 1974.

Wilson, Jason, ed. *An A to Z of Modern Latin American Literature in English Translation.* London: The Institute of Latin American Studies, 1989.

———. "Spanish American Literature in Translation." *SLAS Bulletin* 22 Jan. 1975: 14-18.

Whitson, Kathy J. *Encyclopedia of Feminist Literature.* Westport, CT: Greenwood Press, 2004.

Williams, Raymond Leslie. *The Postmodern Novel in Latin America: Politics, Culture, and the Crisis of Truth.* New York: St. Martin's Press, 1995.

Witalec, Janet, ed. *Short Story Criticism: Criticism of the Works of Short Fiction Writers, vol. 65.* Detroit, MI: Gale Group, 2003.

Yáñez, Mirta, and Marilyn Bobes, eds. *Estatuas de sal: cuentistas cubanas contemporáneas: panorama crítico (1959-1995).* La Habana: Ediciones UNION, Unión de Escritores y Artistas de Cuba, 1996.

About the Author

Kathy S. Leonard received her PhD from the University of California, Davis, and is currently professor of Spanish and Hispanic Linguistics at Iowa State University in Ames. She has published numerous translations of short stories by Latin American women writers as well as a number of books dealing with their work. Professor Leonard has received several prestigious awards and grants for her work with Latin American authors; among them are a Fulbright-Hays grant for research in Bolivia (1998), a National Endowment for the Humanities Fellowship for Translation (2003), and a serial Fulbright grant for research in Bolivia (2006-08).